History of Stevens Institute
of Technology

History of Stevens Institute of Technology

A Record of Broad-Based Curricula and Technogenesis 1870-2000

by Geoffrey W. Clark

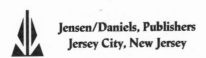

Jensen/Daniels, Publishers
Jersey City, New Jersey

Published in the United States of America by
Jensen/Daniels, Publishers
P.O. Box 3157
Jersey City, New Jersey 07303-3157

Manufactured in the United Sates of America
Printed on acid-free paper

ISBN: 1-893032-24-8

For
Geoffrey F. Clark

Contents

Introduction

During my research for this history of Stevens, I decided to include alumni to document the benefits of the most unusual historical achievement of the institute -- its creation and retention of a broad-based engineering curriculum containing all the major engineering sciences. I took this approach to show the outcomes of the curriculum for graduates, to show how it generated technology in diverse engineering fields, and to tell stories about careers which I found revealing and interesting. Another reason was that I felt, after serving on curriculum committees, that Stevens's broad-based engineering curriculum was not sufficiently appreciated outside the Stevens community. Some academics, on campus and off, portrayed Stevens's early curriculum as narrowly focused on mechanical engineering and that it was devoid of liberal arts content, views which my research found untrue.[i]

Stevens's history shows that Henry Morton, Stevens Institute's first president, created the engineering curriculum and called it a "Liberal Technical" education. It contained civil engineering as well as marine engineering, and metallurgical engineering was an integral part of shop courses and research involving students. Stevens's alumni were pioneers in metallurgical and electrical engineering -- many working with Thomas Edison -- because of funded research and commercial testing performed at Stevens on metal alloys and electrical machinery, and a number of Stevens professors and alumni had early roles in professional societies representing other branches of engineering besides the mechanical branch. Thomas Edison

---

[i] For example, in 1967 Monte A. Calvert in his *The Mechanical Engineer in America, 1830-1910* noted the pioneering role of Stevens Institute of Technology in setting up the first curriculum devoted to mechanical engineering, but he assumed that Robert H. Thurston's well-documented views on mechanical engineering curricula were the predominant ones at Stevens. Calvert correctly determined that Thurston was using advanced science-based French and German models for his ideas. But he wrote that Thurston's "mechanical engineering curriculum . . . could serve as a model for the pure technical school or professional school *with no admixture of general cultural education* (my italics). The establishment of Stevens Institute of Technology, specifically devoted to the training of mechanical engineers, added greatly to the rationale for such programs at other universities . . ."[ii] This assumption that Stevens curriculum was, on the one hand, focused narrowly on mechanical engineering , and, on the other hand, devoid of liberal arts, has been repeated by others. For example, Michael M. Sokal, "Companions in Zealous Research, 1886-1986," *American Scientist*, 74 (1986), no. 5, 486, implied that the Stevens curriculum lacked modern languages, history, and literature.

wrote in 1883 that Stevens was as good as any other college, if not the best place at that time, to study electrical sciences and engineering. In addition, foreign languages and liberal arts courses were included from the beginning.[ii]

The major thesis of the book is benefits of a curriculum which uniquely provided -- and still provides -- every engineering graduate with an overview of all the major engineering specialties through a required set of core courses in all the fundamental engineering sciences: in civil, mechanical, electrical, chemical, and materials engineering. Such a broad-based engineering curriculum was often a struggle to maintain as this history shows.

Success of graduates in various engineering disciplines was appreciated and praised by alumni who fostered the broad-based engineering curriculum and made it a tradition at Stevens. The breadth of the curriculum allowed alumni and Stevens professors to play key roles in the ASME, AIEE, the SPEE and other professional societies in establishing engineering codes and educational standards. During curriculum reviews, faculty and administrations were conscious of the tradition, and consequently, when Stevens updated its engineering curriculum because of technological change, the broad-based curriculum was retained. Later, the institute created other undergraduate curricula in the sciences and management, and they too were broad in scope and aimed to create leaders in the development of technology or in managing technology.

This overview of other engineering disciplines resulted in engineering graduates' successes as entrepreneurs or as top management, because they could manage narrower, more specialized, engineers in technically oriented enterprises and corporations. In addition, new historical data on the father of scientific management, Frederick W. Taylor, ties him to a metallurgical research grant being done at Stevens, and Stevens may have been the first engineering school to introduce the management of technology to its core of required courses in 1884.

Some of the more notable alumni came back to the campus as wealthy professors and trustees and proceeded to close the circle by funding research facilities, promoting funded academic research in partnerships with industry, and investing venture capital in new companies in which professors and the institute had a stake. A striking feature was the extent of graduates'

[ii] Calvert dates the introduction of liberal education at Stevens to the era of its second president, Alexander C. Humphreys, instead of Morton. Calvert, *Op.Cit.*, 83.

connections with each other, a network of research and enterprise which spanned companies run by Stevens graduates or which hired Stevens graduates. Alumni helped in a struggle to overcome the small size of the campus and its modest original endowment. A small private institution with limited resources, Stevens relied on its alumni and other philanthropists, many but not all trustees, to keep the institute afloat and progressing in hard times: in the recession of the late nineteenth century; during the Great Depression of the 1930s; and in the second half of the Cold War. The trustees helped to guide Stevens through controversies over the curriculum, through a faculty strike, and through the Vietnam war which challenged the Stevens honor system. Thus, particularly crucially supportive trustees like Andrew Carnegie, Alexander C. Humphreys, and Walter Kidde are included in the history -- they assured the institute's growth into more expansive times.

Military-related research was conducted on campus throughout the history of Stevens Institute, particularly for the Navy, but also for other branches of the armed forces. Success in this area was dramatized during the buildup of the Navy before the Spanish-American War, in both World Wars, and in the Cold War. Professors and alumni made brilliant contributions to military advances which disclose the less well-known role of engineers in bringing military technologies to fruition, for example, in the Manhattan Project.

Another theme at Stevens was involvement of undergraduates, as well as graduate students, in funded research of professors. The stories show that some of these professors and students were entrepreneurs who generated technology on campus and transferred it to industry. Of course, most of the successful stories of alumni showed links between their own generation of technology after graduation and programs or professors at Stevens. To further this tradition of generation of technology more systematically, the current administration of Harold J. Raveché has consciously created programs for an environment of "technogenesis" on campus, to teach students be aware of the marketability of designs, to generate technologies on campus through research teams of faculty and students, and then to bring these new technologies to commercial realization.

My interest in the history of Stevens Institute of Technology began during my first years at Stevens when I collaborated with Professor Edward H. Foster on a book about Hoboken which included the Stevens family and some history of the institute. I received encouragement from professors Harold

Dorn, Joseph Manogue, Ernest Robb, and former president Kenneth C. Rogers, as well as the secretary of the trustees, David Barus. Later, I was encouraged to write the history of the Stevens curriculum by President Harold J. Raveché, Dean Arthur Shapiro, and indirectly by alumnus and trustee Wesley J. Howe -- the story of the engineering curriculum became a central theme in the book.

I would especially like to thank the following individuals for having read and commented on chapters while they were in some stage of being written: Frank Boesch, Cass Bruton-Ward, Harold Dorn, Ellen Durkin, Ed Friedman, Peter Jurkat, John Kidde, Hugo Kijne, Anita Lang, Tom Lunghard, Leslie Maltz, James McClellan, Joe Moeller, Roger Pinkham, Hal Raveché, Ken Rogers, Dan Savitsky, Pete Schaefer, Art Shapiro and Salvatore Stivala. Nydia Cruz and her predecessor, Jane Hartye, curators of Stevens Special Collections, and Mark Samolewicz, secretary of the board of trustees and keeper of the trustee's minutes, were decidedly helpful, and Richard Widdicombe, director of the Samuel C. Williams Library, has been invaluable for encouragement, for opening the archives to me at unofficial times, and providing a member of his staff as a copy editor. I am most indebted to those who read the whole manuscript and supplied editorial comments and minute corrections: Bernie Gallois, Dick Widdicombe, and especially Scott Smith. In addition, Cass Bruton-Ward, Hal Raveché, Jim Snyder and Ed Foster have each had key roles in guiding the manuscript to publication. In spite of this help, I am solely responsible for errors and omissions. Lastly, I would like to thank my wife, Rogelita, and my son, Geoffrey F. Clark, for bearing with me during the last one-and-a-half years as I put the book together.

CHAPTER 1
The Stevens Family

The story of the Stevens family begins with John Stevens III (1749-1838) who bought the land on which Stevens Institute sits. The buyer was of the third generation of the Stevenses, a family married into landed gentry that came to colonial America in 1699. With income from extensive real estate in New Jersey and from a merchant fleet plying the Atlantic trade routes, the second and third generations of Stevenses had intermarried with other wealthy New Jersey and New York families and immersed themselves in the pursuits typical of their class in the enlightened 18th century: education, natural philosophy, architecture and civic activism. John Stevens III was educated at Kings College (Columbia) and followed the example of his father and most of the landed elite by joining the patriot party during the Revolutionary War. While his father was secretary to Governor Livingston of New York, the son, at twenty-seven years old, was appointed captain in Washington's army. Later, as a colonel, he collected taxes for the American cause as Treasurer of New Jersey. After the war in 1784, John Stevens III or "Colonel John" as he became known, bought at public auction from the state of New Jersey land that had been confiscated from a Tory landowner. The land, described as "William Bayard's farm at Hoebuck," comprised approximately what is now the mile-square city of Hoboken just across the Hudson river from mid-Manhattan.[1]

Almost from the start of his ownership, Colonel John was interested in steamboats. In 1783, the Englishmen Matthew Boulton and James Watt had manufactured their first patented steam engine in their Soho Works in London, thus revolutionizing steam engine technology with a low pressure steam engine coupled with an outside condenser that could move much more rapidly than the earlier Newcomen engine. The Boulton and Watt engine was immediately applied to textile manufacturing which was the key industry during the world's first Industrial Revolution in England. The success of the new steam engine made men dream of applying it to boats. In general, the interest of Americans was whetted by the inventor John Fitch's public demonstration of a primitive model steamboat in 1787 before mem-

---

[1] On John Stevens III and his sons, see the biography by Archibald Douglas Turnbull, *John Stevens; An American Record*(1928); F. DeR. Furman, "Classified Record of the Engineering Work of John, Robert L., and Edwin A. Stevens," in *Morton Memorial*(1904), 106-116; "John Stevens," *Stevens Indicator*, 87 (1930), 216-7, 227; Raymond S. Willets, "Colonel John Stevens," *Stevens Indicator*, (1940), 7-8; and the unpublished notes of Basil M. Stevens, "The Stevens Family of Castle Point," Stevens Special Collections.

bers of the Constitutional Convention in Philadelphia. Stevens witnessed this demonstration and it changed his life. Using a crude steam engine, John Fitch used a jet of water to propel the world's first "steamboat" at a speed too slow to be practicable, but from that point on Stevens had an entrepreneurial vision of inventing his own commercially feasible steamboat. In the late 1780s interest was further stimulated by a pamphlet war among proponents of the application of steam power to boats over feasibility and the issue of monopoly rights in the waters of the several states. Colonel John became an enthusiastic and active supporter of steam navigation and envisioned, as did Fitch before him, the public benefits and personal profits resulting from steamboats linking the geographically separated population centers in the early United States. This combination of civic and private motivation was natural in the eighteenth century when transportation projects required large initial outlays of private capital given the limited functions of government; investments in turnpikes, canals and bridges were repaid by tolls, and the risks of investment were lessened by the award of monopoly rights for a number of years. It was also natural that Stevens quickly entered into steamboating given his wealth and his family's experience in marine transportation. In addition to owning a merchant fleet, his father had been commissioner of turnpikes for the colony of New Jersey before the war, and Colonel John himself was a planner and later president of the Bergen Turnpike Company incorporated in 1802.

By 1790 the colonel had designed improvements in boilers for steamboats, and, to protect his interests, he used his influence to help pass the law for the first United States patent office.[2] One of his early designs was for an internal combustion engine that burned alcohol -- also a pioneering design although he did nothing with it.[3] After obtaining one of the first U.S. patents for an improved vertical steam boiler and a modified Savery-type engine in 1792, he and his partners obtained monopoly rights from the New

---

[2] Even though Dorothy Gregg in her Columbia University Ph.D. dissertation, "The Exploitation of the Steamboat: The Case of John Stevens," footnote 3, page 112, questioned the validity of this claim (which is indeed not footnoted in most books, articles, and encyclopedia accounts), J. Elfreth Watkins, curator of the section of transportation and engineering in the U.S. National Museum in his *Biographical Sketches of John Stevens, Robert L. Stevens, Edwin A. Stevens, John S. Darcy, John P. Jackson, Robert F. Stockton* (Washington, 1892), 3, was correct in citing the *Journal of the House of Representatives*, 1790, page 30, as a source. Page 30 of the House *Journal* corresponds to page 149 in the 1826 edition of the *Journal*, and, even though page 149 only refers to Stevens' petition for a boiler patent, the index for the *Journal* on page 812 lists Stevens' name with a reference to page 149 with the notation "Bill HR no. 41," the number of the bill establishing the patent office -- no other petitioner for a patent has such a reference linking his name with the bill.

[3] Horst O. Hardenberg, *The Middle Ages of the Internal Combustion Engine; 1794-1886*(1999), 27-32, 36, 46.

York legislature to operate steamboats on New York state waters.[4] The exclusive rights were easier to secure since one of his partners in the venture was the chancellor of New York, Robert R. Livingston, who was also Colonel John's brother-in-law. Together, they enlisted the help of the

Colonel John Stevens, was handsome enough to capture one of the "Cox beauties," the five daughters of another revolutionary-era colonel, in marriage in 1782. Living in a villa on his Hoboken estates in the summertime, the family reared nearly a dozen children in New York City at 7 Broadway, near the winter residence of Robert R. Livingston. Livingston had married Colonel John's sister, Mary Stevens, in 1771, and they spent their summers at the Livingston estates on the Hudson at Clermont, New York.

master mechanic Nicholas Roosevelt of Belleville, New Jersey, a noted builder of earlier, slower steam engines for pumping water. With the help of John Hewitt, an English immigrant who had worked in Boulton's Soho Works, the team proceeded to produce the first non-condensing double-acting steam engine modeled on the Watt type in America for the steamboat *Polacca* driven by paddle wheels. However, when Stevens and Hewitt sailed the *Polacca* on the Passaic River in 1798, the boiler and other packing leaked excessively and the wooden hull suffered from excessive vibrations.

Stevens tried other designs to solve the problems. Stevens patented a boiler with multiple fire tubes that produced higher pressures without breaking down.[5] Then in 1803 he and his son, Robert Livingston Stevens (1787-1856) tried an innovative design combining the first use of high pressure steam in the multitubular boiler with screw propulsion on the 20-foot test boat, *Little Juliana*.[6] This boat successfully and repeatedly sailed in New York harbor in 1804. The boat's technology was decades ahead of its

---

[4] Watkins, *Op. Cit.*, 3.

[5] There were multitubular boilers before Stevens's one. David Read, *Nathan Read, His Invention of the Multitubular Boiler and Portable High Pressure Engine, and Discovery of the True Mode of Applying Steam Power to Navigation and Railways*(1870), 47-48; and Dorothy Gregg, "The Exploitation of the Steamboat; The Case of John Stevens," Ph.D. Dissertation, Columbia University, 1951, 12.

[6] Watkins, *Op.Cit.*, 4.

time, was recognized as one of the earliest twin screw steamboats, and now resides in the Smithsonian Museum along with several Stevens boilers and engines.[7]

By 1806 when Colonel John started to build a one hundred-foot steamboat, the *Phoenix*, designed for passengers and freight service, he had fallen out with Livingston who had teamed up with Robert Fulton to build a rival boat, the *Clermont*. Unfortunately for Stevens, Robert Fulton had quickly produced his *Clermont* by importing a Boulton and Watt engine and had stolen the publicity. As history has recorded, Fulton's *Clermont* sailed the length of the Hudson in 1807 as the world's first full-sized serviceable steamboat. Meanwhile, Fulton's backer Livingston had obtained a new New York state law giving the new Fulton-Livingston partnership exclusive rights to service on New York waters including New York harbor. Thus, when John Stevens's wholly American-made *Phoenix* was completed successfully one year after the *Clermont*, the Stevenses had to sail it by sea to set up their own passenger and freight service between Philadelphia and Trenton on the Delaware River. In this way, the Stevens's *Phoenix* has gone down in history as the first steamboat in the world to sail upon the ocean seas.[8]

During these years the Colonel dreamed of developing his wooded estates in Hoboken into a profitable weekend resort for increasingly crowded city dwellers in Manhattan. But in order to attain his goal he needed an efficient and regular steam ferry service to link the city with his estates. Thus, in 1811 the Colonel purchased a commercial ferry license in New York state and operated a horse-powered ferry while building a steam ferry, the *Juliana*. When the *Juliana* was put into service from Hoboken to New York, the Stevenses inaugurated what is reputed to be the first regular commercially operated steam ferry in the world. However, service was interrupted by Colonel John's old nemesis, Livingston, who forced the Colonel to run

---

[7]John Bourne, *A Treatise on the Screw Propeller, Screw Vessels and Screw Engineers*(1867), 14; Carl W. Mitman, *Catalogue of the Watercraft Collection in the United States Museum(1923)*, 50; Frank A. Taylor, *Catalogue of the Mechanical Collections of the Division of Engineering, U.S. National Museum*(1939), 38-9, 105, 107, 109; Carl W. Mitman, "Steven's 'Porcupine' Boiler, 1804," *Transactions of the Newcomen Society,* 19 (1938), 165-71; Francis B. Stevens, "The First Steam Screw Propeller Boats to Navigate the Waters of Any Country," *Stevens Indicator,* 10 (1893), 2-30..

[8] On differences between Fulton and Stevens designs see, James Renwick, *An Account of the Steam Boats Navigating the Hudson River in the State of New York*(1928), 2-3; George H. Preble, *A Chronological History of the Origin and Development of Steam Navigation. 1543-1882*(1883), 41-43; W. A. Shoudy, "The Contributions of the Stevens Family to Steam Navigation," *Stevens Indicator,* 26 (1919), 337-53; and Robert H. Thurston, *A History of the Growth of the Steam Engine*(1939), 264-95.

the *Juliana* outside New York waters on the Connecticut River. Nonetheless, after much dissension and litigation with Livingston, and, finally, after Livingston's death, the Stevenses owned and operated the steam ferry *Hoboken* between Manhattan and Hoboken by 1821. In subsequent years, the Stevens-owned Hoboken Ferry Company became a primary conduit for New Jersey commuters traveling daily to work in New York City. A fleet of ferries, including the Stevens-designed first screw ferry *Bergen* and the fabulous *Netherlands* crossed the Hudson scores of times a day. Again, the Stevenses were recognized internationally, by such premier marine engineers as England's John Scott Russell, as having ushered in original improvements in ferry designs. This ferry company was kept in the Stevens family until 1904 when it was sold to the Erie Lackawanna Railway.

Actually, it was not the Colonel who made most of the innovative breakthroughs in ferries and their accessories. Colonel John was neither a mechanic nor a machinist, and many of his patented diagrams were sketchy. If he had failures and delays in his projects, it was because he had to rely on practical mechanics to implement concepts rarely detailed enough for direct execution.[9] It was his son, Robert Livingston Stevens (1787-1856) who was the practical designer, innovator, and transportation entrepreneur in ferryboats and railroads. Like his father and brothers, Robert had attended Columbia, but, unlike them, he had left before graduation to dedicate himself to work in machine shops in Hoboken in 1804-05. Credited with being

Encouraged by his father to use tools
and learn mechanical drawing as a boy,
Robert Livingston Stevens
had enthusiasm
for practical aspects of engineering.
He remained a bachelor
and dedicated himself to the design,
experimentation,
and improvement of inventions
for the family's transportation businesses.
After reaching adulthood,
he lived in Hoboken all his life,
first in the Stevens villa
and then in the Stevens Castle
that he built three years
before his death.

---

[9] John H. White, Jr., "Col. John; Not Really a Great Inventor? A Reappraisal of the Work and Talent of John Stevens III," *Stevens Indicator*, 99 (1982), 4-9.

a marine engineer of the first rank, his technical improvements in steamboats and ferries were praised in marine engineering circles: The first concave waterlines on a steamboat (1808); the first supporting iron rods for projecting guard beams on steamboats (1815); the first skeleton walking beams for ferries (1822), the spring pile ferry slip (1822); the placement of boilers on guards outside the paddle wheels of ferries (1822); the hog frame or truss for stiffening ferryboats longitudinally (1827); spring steel bearings of paddle wheel shafts (1828); and improved packing for pistons (1840). In addition, he was the first to burn anthracite coal in a cupola furnace (1818).[10]

It was Robert Livingston Stevens, as innovator, and his brother Edwin Augustus Stevens (1795-1868), as business administrator, who realized their father's dream of establishing a commercially successful railroad -- the first -- in the United States.[11] As early as 1810, the Colonel started to promote his scheme in correspondence, several years after the English had used small locomotives to haul coal. Then, in 1812 the father published a widely distributed pamphlet entitled *Documents Tending to Prove the Superior Advantage of Railways and Steam Carriages over Canal Navigation* in which the Colonel considered every phase of railway transportation, including engineering aspects and costs of construction. Dismissed at first as a visionary dreamer, the Colonel doggedly lobbied with the New Jersey state legislature until he had obtained the first American railroad act authorizing his company to erect a railroad from the Delaware in Trenton to the Raritan at New Brunswick in 1815. His idea was to connect the railroad with his ferry service from Trenton to Philadelphia. In 1823, again before any passenger railroad had been created anywhere in the world, he obtained from the Pennsylvania legislature another railroad act for a line running from Columbia, Pennsylvania, to Philadelphia -- an act which historians of the Pennsylvania Railroad consider the forerunner of the act establishing their company. Although the time limits ran out on these acts, both routes were later laid with track. Subsequently, in 1826 at the age of seventy-seven, the Colonel and his sons built a demonstration prototype locomotive on a circular track in Hoboken, the first American-built locomotive to promote his scheme. A model of this locomotive is also in the Smithsonian.[12]

---

[10] Watkins, *Op.Cit.*, 6.

[11] "Edwin Augustus Stevens," *Stevens Indicator*, 67 (1930), 244-5, 253.

[12] Carl W. Mitman, *Catalogue of the Mechanical Engineering Collection in the U.S. National Museum*(1922), 69-71; John H. White, Jr., *The John Bull: 150 Years of Locomotion*(Smithsonian, 1981).

From that point on, his sons vigorously entered the railroading business to supplement their ferry and steamboating lines. Urgency was added to the implementation of the plan for a railroad after 1823 when the Stevenses had established their Union Line Transportation Company that ferried passengers from Manhattan to Perth Amboy in the Lower New York Bay where an overland stage ran to the Trenton terminus for steamboat service to Philadelphia. The New York-Philadelphia through-service took only ten to eleven hours instead of the days it took before the advent of the steamboat. A rival route had been established by ferry to Jersey City and overland by stage to Trenton. The Stevenses wanted to capture the two thousand passengers per week who paid some $400,000 per year on both routes. Robert and Edwin were determined to seize this market by building a fast and comfortable railroad over the shortest possible route, Perth Amboy to Bordentown, to connect with their steamships on the Delaware.

Teaming up with Robert F. Stockton, the Stevens brothers lived in a hotel in Trenton while lobbying and negotiating a new railroad charter. Stockton was a politician, entrepreneur and adventurer whose more flamboyant personality complemented the Stevenses' talents in engineering and business. After two years of effort, a charter was granted in 1830 that gave exclusive rights to two transportation companies in return for taxes on traffic and other emoluments. The Stevenses were granted the Camden and Amboy Transportation Company (C and A) and Stockton was granted the Delaware and Raritan Canal Company that was to run along the same route as the railroad. The state obtained a tax on all passengers and freight as long as no other railroad was given rights to lay track within three miles of the C and A. The act also authorized the C and A to sell capital stock totaling one million dollars which was fully subscribed the day it was offered in April 1830 by the company's officers, President R. L. Stevens and Treasurer E. A. Stevens. This legislation for monopoly was strengthened by 1832 by a new act which prevented the building of any railways across the state between New York and Philadelphia without the consent of the Joint Companies, a holding company in which John Jacob Astor was a partner and which held the stock of the C and A and Stockton's Delaware and Raritan Canal Company. In return, the state received $100,000 worth of stock and was to obtain not less than $30,000 per annum in transit taxes.

Meanwhile, a month after the railroading engineer George Stephenson ran his famous pioneering locomotive, the *Rocket*, on tracks between Manchester and Liverpool, Robert L. Stevens sailed for England to buy a locomotive from the Stephensons and railroad tracks of wrought iron from English mills. While crossing the Atlantic, Stevens pondered designs for the tracks and conceived of a modification of the T-shaped Birkenshaw rail used in England. Robert whittled at a piece of wood in order to design the shape, a T but with a tapering base or the I shape of the modern railroad rail. This new shape had the advantage of doing away with the clamps or "chairs" needed to hold the Birkenshaw rail upright, thus cutting costs. The plan was to affix the I rail to wooden ties with a hook-headed spike, also the design of Robert L. Stevens. In England he bought the locomotive *John Bull* that came to be the first efficient passenger locomotive in the United States. By the spring of 1834, the *John Bull* was pulling a Camden and Amboy Railroad train from Perth Amboy to Camden on the Delaware River, cutting the travel time from New York to Philadelphia to nine hours.

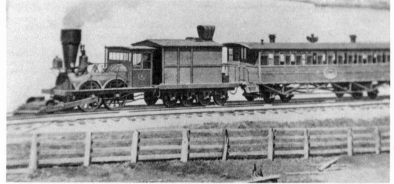

The *John Bull* now resides in the Smithsonian museum in Washington, D. C. Given the open countryside in America as opposed to the enclosed fields of England, Robert also invented the first cowcatcher that doubled as a guiding mechanism when the *John Bull* was rounding curves.

The growth of the C and A was enormous, both in terms of track and rolling stock and in profits. By 1837 the C and A had fifteen locomotives, nine built in the company's machine shops in Hoboken, and had purchased coal fields in Schuykill County, Pennsylvania. The company had merged with another railroad running from Trenton to Philadelphia on the Pennsylvania side of the Delaware and linked up with a new line running from Jersey City to New Brunswick. At that time, through-service from New York to Philadelphia was reduced to five and one-half hours. By 1840 the C and A investments were worth $13 million; it owned eight steamboats, seventeen locomotives, seventy-one passenger and baggage cars and sixty-five freight cars. By 1869, investments totaled $30.5 million and one hundred trains a day carried six million passengers a year. Monopoly rights meant huge profits. Between 1834 and 1860 dividends were never less than six percent and reached as high as thirty percent as a result of high fares that were often protested but to no avail. Since an estimated twenty percent of the State of New Jersey's income came from transit duties, in addition to dividends on one-fifteenth of the outstanding C and A stock, the state legislature was not interested in meddling with this lucrative enterprise. Later in the century, the Camden and Amboy was leased for 999 years to the Pennsylvania Railroad Company on favorable terms for the Stevens family.

The C and A also made a fortune for the Hewitts. In 1848, the Stevens brothers bought new American-made rails from their friend Abram Stevens Hewitt who had been given the Trenton Iron Works by his father-in-law, Peter Cooper. Abram was the son of John Hewitt who had sailed the *Polacca* with Colonel John, and the father had once introduced his son Abram to Colonel John and said, "See the greatest engineer in the world."[13] The younger Hewitt befriended and visited Colonel John's sons both in New York and Hoboken, and Edwin A. Stevens became a major stockholder in the Trenton Iron Works by the 1850s when its success in the age of steel made Hewitt a millionaire. At first Abram ran the iron works with his brother Charles and later with his brother's son, William Hewitt. The latter obtained an M.E. degree from Stevens Institute in 1884 and later became the first president of the Stevens Alumni Association and a trustee. Moreover, Abram's son, Peter Cooper Hewitt, the future inventor of the mercury vapor lamp, attended Stevens Institute of Technology for two years before graduating from Columbia. The purchase of rails at mid-century made a fortune for the firm of Cooper, Hewitt and Company and cemented a lifelong friendship between Abram Stevens Hewitt and Edwin Augustus Stevens, the president of the Camden and Amboy and the future founder of the institute.

Amassing a huge fortune through these engineering and entrepreneurial feats in the field of transportation, the Stevenses spent their money lavishly on, among other things, experimental ironclads and yachts. The Colonel had a vision of an indestructible iron-sided ship defeating the British in the War of 1812. Subsequently, Robert L. Stevens and his brother Edwin spent a considerable amount of energy and some fraction of their wealth on the ironclad called the *Stevens Battery*. Edwin A. Stevens, at nineteen, in 1814 had experimented with armor for warships by using a bronze cannon to fire six-pound shot against iron plate. On the brink of the war with Mexico in 1841 and with no technology available to manufacture armor plate, Edwin devised a method of laying plates over each other and riveting them

---

[13] Allan Nevins, *Abram S. Hewitt, with Some Account of Peter Cooper* (New York, 1935), 498-9.

9

together. From more firing experiments he found that his armor plates could resist the navy's largest sixty-four-pound shot if it was four and one-half inches thick. An ordnance board of army and navy officers appointed by President Tyler then conducted tests on Stevens's armor plate, and it was upon the recommendation of this board that the Tyler administration and Congress passed a bill authorizing expenditures to have Edwin A. Stevens build a "war steamer, shot-and-shell-proof, to be built principally of iron." Thus, twenty years before John Ericsson's *Monitor*, Edwin obtained funding of $500,000 from Congress to design and build an ironclad vessel some 250 feet in length. Subsequently, E. A. Stevens and his brother Robert L. jointly designed and started to build the *Stevens Battery* in a drydock just beneath the family estate in Hoboken. Their ambitious plans called for an expanded vessel 410 feet long with a 45-foot beam. The deck was to be low, two feet above the water line. One innovation in the planned vessel was patented by Edwin A. Stevens in 1842, namely, the air-tight fire room that was sub-sequently used by all the navies of the world by the late nineteenth century. This monstrous vessel, longer than a football field from bow to stern, was built but not finished when Robert L. Stevens died in 1856. By that time it had cost the Stevens brothers $250,000 more than they were paid by the government. Although it was never completed, the *Stevens Battery* was the earliest American ironclad.[14]

Some of the design features of the *Stevens Battery* were subsequently used in Ericsson's smaller *Monitor* that was hastily built during the Civil War, particularly the low waterline, the armor plates, and the central location of the turret. Built in Brooklyn, Ericsson's ironclad was less than half the length of the Stevens warship, only 172 feet, with a deck three feet above the waterline. The armor plates were laid on top of each other and riveted together according to the Stevens method, the revolving protruding turret, also similar in overall appearance and positioning to the Stevens one, was protected by eight layers of one-inch iron.[15] During the Civil War, Edwin tried to rekindle the federal government's interest in the *Stevens Battery*, but to no avail. He then built a smaller ironclad, the *Naugatuck*,

---

[14] R. H. Thurston, "The Stevens Ironclad Battery," *Journal of the Franklin Institute*, 68 (1874), 165-85; R. H. Thurston, "The Earliest Ironclad," *Cassier's Magazine*, 6 (1894), 312-4; R. H. Thurston, "The Messrs. Stevens of Hoboken, as Engineers, Naval Architects, and Philanthropists," reprint from the *Journal of the Franklin Institute*, Oct. 1874; and "Liberty Ships Launched," *Stevens Indicator*, 61 (1944), 4, 7-8.

[15] C. W. MacCord, the first professor of mechanical drawing at Stevens, was Ericsson's draftsman. He left the drawings to F. DeR. Furman, the second professor of mechanical drawing, and Furman left them to Stevens Special Collections in 1944. "Stevens Receives Monitor Drawings," *Ibid.*, 62 (1944), 3, 3-5.

which was captained by the Stevens family associate and future original trustee of the institute, W. W. Shippen. This small one-hundred-foot iron-clad saw action with the *Monitor* in one of its battles against the Confederacy's *Merrimack* before sinking in a storm. When Edwin died in 1868, he remained stubbornly loyal to the *Stevens Battery*. He bequeathed it to the state of New Jersey along with one million dollars so that it could be properly completed. The state commissioned the engineer George B. McClellan to finish the ship and prospects looked bright for a launching a year after work commenced in 1869. McClellan was forced to make design changes due to new technological developments in ironclads, and, when work stopped in 1874 because Edwin's one million dollars had been used up, some $450,000 were still needed to finish the warship. By that time, neither the Stevens family nor the state of New Jersey would contribute more funds for what newspapers of the day called "a notorious old scandal." In 1881, the *Stevens Battery* was sold by the state at public auction and broken up for scrap metal. All told, the Stevens family spent over two million dollars on the ironclads *Stevens Battery* and *Naugatuck*.

Yachting was the interest of the Colonel's youngest son, the sportsman of the family, John Cox Stevens (1785-1857). John Cox was one of the original founders of the New York Yacht Club (NYYC) in 1844. Although there were forerunners, the NYYC was the first yacht club in the United States to have a continuous life until the present time, and it became the premier yacht club in the country if not the world.[16] The founding meeting of the original nine members was held on board Stevens's yacht *Gimcrack*, and John Cox Stevens was made the first commodore of the NYYC, a position he held until 1854.

The first NYYC headquarters were built by John Cox Stevens in the Ely-sian Fields just north of the Stevens residence at Castle Point in Hoboken in 1845, and it is reputed to be the first yachting clubhouse in the country.[17] The first commodore provided the gift of the clubhouse, a low-studded wooden structure in gothic revival style with overhanging eaves and a re-petitive gingerbread trim, large windows, and a verandah. The architect was Alexander Jackson Davis, the designer of the italianate Stevens Castle built in 1853. The spot on Castle Point was an ideal place to observe yacht racing in the Hudson River with New York City in the background.[18] Early races

---

[16]Yachting clubs before the NYYC did not survive, and their existence is often only known by their date of establishment: They were the Knickerbocker Boat Club of New York (1911-1912), the New York Boat Club (1830), the Boston Yacht Club (1835-1837), and the Hoboken Model Yacht Club (1840). W. P. Stephens, *American Yachting*(1904), 26-27.

[17]J.D. Jerold Kelly, *American Yachts; Their Clubs and Races*(1884), 70-71.

[18] "The America's Cup Races," *Stevens Indicator*, 85 (1965), no. 1, 9.

11

of the NYYC started in the Hudson opposite the clubhouse and went north around a stake boat off Fort Washington Point (near the Washington Bridge now) and then south around a stake boat off the Narrows (near the current Verazzano Narrows Bridge) and then back to Castle Point -- a course of about forty miles that could be run in a day. The original Stevens clubhouse remained the sailing headquarters of the NYYC through the terms of the second and third commodores, namely, William Edgar (commodore 1854-1859) and none other than Edwin A. Stevens (commodore 1859-1866). In 1868 the Stevens family sold the property on which the clubhouse sat to the Pennsylvania Railroad which was intent on building a yard at the foot of 10th street and the Hudson River; the NYYC moved out, let the structure be briefly occupied by a younger club, the New Jersey Yacht Club, then removed it on a barge and towed it to NYYC property at Clifton, Staten Island.[19] Too small as a clubhouse for the expanded NYYC, it remained there in disrepair until Commodore J. P. Morgan, the famous banker, removed it to Glen Cove and restored it around the turn of the century. In Glen Cove it became "Station number 10" of the NYYC, a way-station for cruises down the sound. Finally in 1949, members of the NYYC provided funds to send the historic clubhouse to the Mystic Seaport Museum in Mystic, Connecticut, where it now resides as a permanent exhibit.[20]

Commodore John Cox Stevens was also responsible for the establishment of the America's Cup races, the world's most famous yachting competition. Since the NYYC's founding, its wealthy members had been interested in improving the speed of their yachts and in using the talents of builder-designers like the famous George Steers whose specialty was adapting New York pilot boats to racing needs. It was before the days of fully worked out paper designs, and the method involved miniature models and half-models from which full-sized boats would be developed with adaptations during the building process -- a kind of innovative and intuitive adaptation of old rule-of-thumb methods. Steers redesigned the bow of the *Maria,* built by another Stevens brother, Robert Livingston Stevens, the *Maria* being moored off Castle Point in Hoboken. Such boats as the *Una* and *Cornelia* were built along the same lines of pilot boats but with sharper bow angle instead of the blunt "cod's head" bow. These fast New York yachts became well known with English yachtsmen across the Atlantic by 1850 when the NYYC was invited to send a yacht to participate in races organized by the Royal Yacht Squadron -- the reward being an ornate silver cup.

---

[19]Stephens, *Op.Cit.*, 36.

[20]J. Owen Grundy, "Exclusive NYYC Had Its First Home in Hoboken", *Jersey Journal,* July 15, 1969, 8, and Kelly, *Op. Cit.,* 164.

The occasion of this challenge was the first World's Fair to be held in London starting in 1850, the races to be held in 1851. Commodore John Cox Stevens and five other wealthy NYYC members, the first American yachting syndicate, commissioned George Steers to build an ocean-going keel boat along modified pilot boat lines -- the result was the famous *America* after which the famed cup was named. The yacht was speedily built between its commissioning by the syndicate in late 1850 and the spring of 1851; trials were held, the boat outfitted for voyage, and it was sailed across the Atlantic in time for the races in August 1851.

On the day of the race, August 22, 1851, the fleet of Royal Yacht Squadron vessels, mostly of the short-bowed type except for a few experimental ones, was, in retrospect, at a disadvantage. First, they all had sails of hand-woven flax or linen, a canvas loose in texture, cut with fullness according to the theory of the day. The *America* had machine-woven cotton or hard canvas cut to fit as flat as possible; her sails were fewer in number than most of the other yachts, but they were very effective drivers close to the wind. Second, most of the yachts were of the cod's head and mackerel tail variety, only one, the *Titania*, having a fairly fine bow to test the British marine engineer John Scott Russel's wave theory, but that boat had a faulty rig that prevented victory against the *America*.

The course from the yachting center of Cowes on the south coast of England was eastward and then south and westward around the Isle of Wight back into the channel called the Solent between Cowes and the island. The *America* started slowly in light winds from the mooring line, there being fifteen boats in all, but moved near the head of the fleet when the wind stiffened. After the first hour or so as the leaders neared the Noman buoy about seven miles eastward, the *America* was fifth but only two minutes behind the leader, and, as the fleet passed to the South of the Isle of Wight, the *America* already led by a mile. Although the SSW wind became light at the western tip of the island off the Needles, the Yankee yacht held off her leading rival, the *Aurora*, as she made her way slowly up the Solent, finishing in eight hours and thirty-four minutes to the *Aurora's* second place finish of eight hours and fifty-eight minutes.

The victory of the *America* influenced the course of yacht design, of yacht materials and construction as well as sailmaking in both England and the United States. General opinion follows that of the yachting historian W. P. Stephens who wrote, "The whole history of yachting down to 1848-1849 . . . may be considered as merely a formative period; and this race for the Cup marked the beginning of real yacht racing; or perhaps more correctly, the systematic racing of yachts built for that purpose as well as for cruising."[21]

During the race, Queen Victoria, aboard the royal yacht *Victoria and Albert*, asked who was ahead, and she was told the *America*. Then she asked who was second, and her boatswain answered, "Madame, there is no second." The next day the queen, her consort, and retinue were shown around the *America*, at left, by John Cox Stevens. The cup, at right, was originally the World's Fair version of the Royal Yacht Squadron's Queen's Cup for the 1851 race around the Isle of Wight.

After the cup was brought back to the NYYC, it became known as the "America's Cup," becoming a perpetual international challenge prize of renown by the 1870s and 1880s. It was in those years that the America's Cup yachts designed by Edward Burgess for syndicates like the one headed by General Charles J. Paine and J. Malcolm Forbes popularized yachting in the United States by successful defense of the cup. Such was the popularity of yachting that it led to the proliferation of college yacht clubs, supplementing the traditional sculling or rowing as the main college activity on the water.[22]

---

[21] Stephens, *Op. Cit.*, 67.

[22] "The Stevens Family and the America's Cup," *Stevens Indicator,* 29 (1911), 279-298.

CHAPTER 2

Hoboken-New York: The Setting

In the beginning of the nineteenth century, Hoboken simply consisted of Colonel John Stevens's private estates of a little over one square mile in area. These estates were attractive for what became Castle Point -- a promontory overlooking the Hudson atop cliffs of serpentine green-gray rock -- and the wooded Elysian Fields in the northern part of the property. The west was swampy and brackish, and on some maps Hoboken had been drawn as an island with the western lowlands under water at high tide. In 1784, the Colonel built a Georgian-style mansion on top of a cliff, the highest point of his estates with a stunning view of New York City directly across the Hudson River. Since the large family of thirteen children obtained better care at 7 Broadway in Manhattan during the winter, the family only used its "Stevens Villa" during the summers.

After the turn of the century, John Stevens slowly developed his estates: In 1802, the Colonel became president of the Bergen Turnpike that he built to terminate at his Hoboken boat dock. In 1804, he sold lots parallel to the Bergen Turnpike that intersected with surveyed but unpaved streets eighty feet wide. In 1814, the year that the Colonel and his family came to live permanently in Hoboken because of ready access through his steam ferry, Stevens sold the salt marshes in west Hoboken to the brothers Swartout. Failing in their venture to grow vegetables on the land, the Swartouts sold it to John G. Coster who was then plagued by the chronic flooding in his properties.

With the advent of the Stevenses' regular ferry service in 1821, the Colonel rapidly improved the unsold bulk of his Hoboken estates to the east and north above Fourth Street. Intending to sell more land and make his turnpike and ferry more profitable, he advertised Hoboken as a healthy rural resort for New Yorkers. He created a "River Walk" winding from the ferry around the cliffs to the northernmost part of Hoboken. There he built a hotel and pavilion with Greek columns called the Colonnade where visitors and guests could find food and refreshment. He partly cleared woods and fields that stretched westward beyond the hotel and the Villa Stevens. Upon these "Elysian Fields" as he termed them, he built amusements such as primitive Ferris wheels and his locomotive on its circular track. Employing the best gardeners and horticulturists, the Colonel manicured the land around the Villa Stevens according to English theories of landscape gardening. Thus, during holiday weekends during the 1820s and 1830s, approximately twenty thousand New Yorkers crossed the Hudson to view choice real estate or to enjoy themselves. Some, like John Jacob Astor, bought lots to build summer villas of their own, and others like William Cullen Bryant and Robert Sands came to write romantic prose and poetry about the rural beauty of Hoboken.[23]

When the population grew to nearly 7,000 two years before the city was incorporated in 1855, Colonel John's sons, Edwin and Robert, started to replace the Villa Stevens with a new mansion, the Stevens Castle. Built by 1858, this residence was designed by Alexander Jackson Davis, a premier architect of his time, and was based on preliminary sketches by Robert L. Stevens. It was an Italian-style mansion with coach portal, campanile, piazzas and a renowned hanging staircase. Later, the upper and middle class property owners built their own smaller mansions on lots just to the south on Castle Point Terrace.

The Stevens family's personal property consisted of about
twenty-five walled-in acres on which the Stevens Castle sat.
Made of the green serpentine stone of the cliffs below Castle Point, the wall existed
until Stevens Institute of Technology bought a part of the estate in 1905, the
only part standing now is the "green gate," shown at the right.

By the 1860s when the population of Hoboken reached some ten to twenty thousand, the personal property of the Stevenses extended from Washington Street eastward to the river and northward through a still-rural section of the Elysian Fields, and by 1900 it had reduced in size to the area between Seventh and Tenth Streets east of Hudson Street. The Stevenses continued

---

[23] Edward Halsey Foster, "A Note on the Stevens Family and the Arts," in E. H. Foster and G. W. Clark, Eds., *Hoboken; A Collection of Essays*(1876), 27-33.

to indirectly own and improve much of the real estate of Hoboken through a corporation established for the purpose, the Hoboken Land and Improvement Company (HLIC)[24] In 1838 when the HLIC was incorporated, the progeny of the Colonel lived in Hoboken, but the Castle itself and the C and A were the properties of Robert L. and Edwin A. Stevens who developed them, and, since Robert never married, they were left to Edwin A. Stevens.

Established in 1838 a few months before the Colonel died, the Hoboken Land and Improvement Company, located at offices at 1 Newark Street, above, was the way Colonel John Stevens provided for his children. The company's stock certificates were distributed among his four surviving sons --
John Cox, Robert Livingston, James Alexander, and Edwin Augustus -- and among the husbands of his two surviving daughters, Thomas A. Conover and Joshua Sands.

The HLIC was also a holding company for the stock in other companies established by John Stevens, namely the Hoboken Ferry Company and the Bergen Turnpike. The charter of the company empowered it to either purchase stock in other Hoboken companies or establish such companies in order to lay Hoboken's streets and sewers for the purpose of selling the family-owned real estate apart from the personal property around Castle

---

[24] A. J. Volk and R. R. Rieser, "Three Centuries of Progress; The Story of Hoboken," *Stevens Indicator,* 63 (1941), 3-4. See also, W. H. Shaw, *History of Essex and Hudson Counties*(1884), and G. L. Moller, *The Hoboken of Yesteryear*(1964).

Point.[25] The presidents of the HLIC included Edwin A. Stevens, Samuel Bayard Dod, the brother of Edwin's widow, and Edwin A. Stevens II and Edwin A. Stevens III, Edwin's son and grandson. Under "the Company," as it was called locally, the Stevenses ran the Hoboken Ferry Company which they sold in 1896 and the Morris and Essex Railroad Company which they sold in 1864.[26] A spur of the latter connected Newark with the Hoboken ferries for the first time. In addition, the company developed the Stevens-owned shoreline with docks and warehouses that were leased to shipping companies like the Hamburg-America Line and the North German Lloyd Line which first settled in Hoboken in 1863.

The company acted as a sort of chamber of commerce by trying to attract businesses, and, through Stevens-owned local banks, it arranged for loans to new industries that were setting themselves up in the city. After 1880, industries such as paint and varnish works, leather industries and iron works moved into the more undesirable, non-Stevens, lowlands property to the west. The number of manufacturing industries in Hoboken increased from 121 in 1879 to 289 in 1889 and then to a peak of 399 in 1899.[27] With 6,443 employees in the manufacturing sector in 1899, the size of firms in Hoboken was clearly small. Most firms had fewer than twenty employees, a usual size for apparel workshops, food processing companies, and building trades establishments throughout the country in the late nineteenth century. Some of Hoboken's larger employers, besides those along the docks, were the American Lead Pencil Company, Keuffel and Esser instruments, Universal Rubber Works, Meyenberg silk factory, Hotopp varnish factory, and the iron foundries of Mansfield and Fagan. In the west, these companies built multi-story brick factories and developers purchased land to build cheap wooden multi-story dwellings and brick tenements for workers and operatives. The eastern and northern sections continued to be built up with substantial multi-family dwellings and town houses of the middle classes and well-to-do. Banks and a business district arose at the southern end of the city on Newark street adjacent to the HLIC located next to the Hudson River and the ferries.

In the mid-1880s, the Stevenses started to lose political if not economic control of the city they had created. Whereas "the Company" paid one-third of the real estate taxes in Hoboken, it was sued by the city claiming that the

---

[25] Geoffrey Clark, "The Stevens Legacy," *Stevens Indicator*, 99 (1982), 11.

[26] *Hoboken Advertiser*, July 30, 1881, 2.

[27] *Report Upon the Statistics of Manufactures Compiled from Returns Received at the Tenth Census*(1882), 405; *Report on the Manufacturing Industries in the United States at the Eleventh Census; 1890*(1895), 242-9; *Census Reports. Twelfth Census of the United States Taken in the Year 1900. Manufactures*(1902), Part II, 559-61.

development of the docks had "blockaded" the city streets from the waterfront. The Company won the suit but then sold most of the docks to foreign German shipping companies; however, this action caused resentment because the waterfront continued to be blocked to the population. Edwin A. Stevens II, also known as Colonel Stevens, along with his uncle Samuel Bayard Dod and his father's trusted administrator W. W. Shippen, served on the boards of directors of Hoboken's financial and utilities companies which they helped to found: The First National Bank of Hoboken, the Hudson Trust Company, the Hackensack Water Company, the Castle Point Coal Company, and the Hoboken Street Car Company.

Between 1880 and 1910, Hoboken was at the height of its economic and industrial expansion. On the one hand, the wharves and industries were among the most thriving in New York Harbor, and ready access to transportation and relatively new housing made the city attractive to professionals and businessmen who found the area overlooking the river attractive living quarters. In the late nineteenth century, the merchants, hotel owners, and tradesmen were largely skilled and successful German-Americans and Anglo-Saxons. Hoboken was a center for German culture. With the German shipping companies established along the docks, German charitable societies, German language churches and newspapers, a German Seaman's Home, and German social clubs and beer gardens sprouted up. This German identification was known as far away as the Middle West. In their politics, the Germans tended to be independents or Republicans, but at least progressive reformers who wanted an efficiently run city.[28]

The lowlands continued to be inhabited by low-income working classes, many of whom were Irish. The newspapers of the era indicate they were not as well-off as the rest of the population but their cheap labor helped the city thrive. According to a Stevens-funded report on health, the tenements were four- and five-story cold-water walk-ups with six or seven railroad-type apartments per building. Plumbing was nonexistent in most tenements, and privy vaults made back yards smell foul in the summers. Insect pests, mostly flies living off garbage and mosquitoes from the swampy areas, as well as stray dogs, abounded. Many of the working families of the city were part of a floating population whose apartments "changed hands all around" each year.[29] In the 1880s, newspapers indicated that job turnovers were swift when incipient unions went on strike. Scab labor was quickly hired to fill

---

[28] Germans comprised more than 1/2 the population, Irish approximately 1/5 and the "American element" 1/5 in the mid-1880s. *Tenth Census of the United States. Report on the Social Statistics of the Cities*(1886), Part I, 690.
[29] *The Hoboken Advertiser*, May 5, 1883, 2.

the jobs after the city's police had cleared out the strikers and agitators. Wages for skilled labor ranged from twenty cents to forty cents an hour, but unskilled laborers and most women workers earned about a dollar a day, children less. Ten- to twelve-hour days and six-day weeks left little time for pleasure activities except on Sunday.[30]

Meanwhile, the Stevenses were not oblivious to the problems of the city of Hoboken as it matured. Edwin A. Stevens's widow, Martha Bayard Stevens,

Edwin A. Stevens, right,
the founder of Stevens Institute,
died in 1868 at the age of seventy-three,
leaving behind six children
ranging from ten to under a year old
and a young widow
of thirty-five years of age.
She was Martha Bayard Stevens,
born Martha Bayard Dod,
whose ancestor was
the Tory farmer whose Hoboken estates
had been confiscated during
the American Revolution.
When the marriage to Edwin
took place twelve years earlier,
it was celebrated as
a joining and reconciliation
of the two families
which had once owned all of Hoboken.

continued to live in the Stevens Castle after her husband's death. The daughter of a cultured Princeton professor, Martha never remarried, brought up her children in the Castle, and left the management of Edwin A. Stevens's millions and the HLIC to her brother, Samuel. Although a main concern was the education and well-being of her family, she entertained lavishly on Castle Point but was also a woman interested in philanthropy in the city of Hoboken. In 1887, she endowed the Industrial Education Association dedicated to teaching young female Hobokenites the skills of home economics, neatness, and the principles of saving. In 1896, she and other Stevenses contributed funds for the establishment of the Hoboken Public Library at 5th and Park Streets. In the same period she used her influence to have the HLIC create the Church Square Park across from the library and

---

[30] *Ibid.*, June 25, 1881, 3; June 24, 1882, 2; July 14, 1883; *Robert L. Stevens Fund for Municipal Research in Hoboken. Survey on Health, 1913.*

the Hudson Square Park and Elysian Park at either end of her Castle Point estate. She established the Martha Institute for training boys in industrial skills, the Hammond Home for Children, and the Robert L. Stevens Fund for Municipal Research. In her will she prevailed upon her husband's creation, Stevens Institute of Technology, to admit with free tuition a number of students from Hoboken each year. On one of her trips to Europe she visited New Lanark, the village created by Robert Owen, the industrialist who built clean and affordable housing for his workers. This inspired her to contribute money for similar housing in Hoboken within a city block located between Willow and Clinton and 6th and 7th Streets, an interesting three-story, almost-miniature housing project with cobblestoned alleys closed to traffic in the center of Hoboken. When she died in 1898, her will divided the estate on Castle Point among her five main heirs, and she distributed stocks and bonds and other property among them and several grandchildren. She also left two plots of land to the institute, both pieces located east of River Street and south of the estate's gatehouse.[31]

In spite of the Stevens's philanthropy, the lot of the working classes was still poor, and some Hoboken politicians blamed "capitalists" and the Company. This trend was especially true as the population grew by 360 percent to 59,364 by 1900 and another 18.5 percent to 70,325 by 1910 when overcrowding was at its height.[32] This era saw Tammany Hall running New York and political machines dominating other urban areas in New Jersey, and a Democratic machine took over Hoboken reflecting the general political trend. The main Hoboken boss was Patrick R. Griffin, an Irish immigrant who settled first in Brooklyn but soon moved to Hoboken's working-class and predominantly Irish fourth ward in the southwest section where he worked as a bartender. Afterwards, he worked in Mike Coyle's saloon in the first ward and became involved in politics. Politically loyal to the Democrats under Jack Haggerty and Maurice Stack, he became an assistant city clerk in 1904. In 1908, he overthrew Stack and became Democratic boss. During his political career, "Paddy" Griffin was able to amass a fortune estimated at two million dollars including a mansion in Monmouth Beach and a summer home in Spring Lake. Spurned by indignant patricians of Hoboken during the first half of his career, Griffin befriended such powerful men as William H. Todd of Todd Shipyards and

---

[31] Furman, *Morton Memorial, Op.Cit.,* 148, and unpublished notes of Basil Stevens on Martha Bayard Stevens, Stevens Special Collections. One plot was donated on the twenty-fifth anniversary of the institute.

[32] *Twelfth Census of the United States Taken in the Year 1900. Population.*(1901), Part I, 879-9; *Thirteenth Census of the United States Taken in the Year 1910. Population.*(1912), 862.

Al Smith who was Democratic Governor of New York.[33] Griffin's lieu-tenants who shared power with him in city hall all came from the working classes. James H. Londrigan had been a shirt cutter who lived in the machine-controlled third ward. He had worked his way up through the ranks from assistant city clerk, to city clerk, and then city commissioner. Bernard McFeely, starting out as a horse teamster from the fourth ward, had worked his way into politics through the Thomas J. Kehoe Association, Kehoe being a machinist who ran his district through a social-political club named after himself. Enormously popular among his Irish followers, "Barney" McFeely broke away from Kehoe and formed his own Bernard N. McFeely Association in 1910.[34] Using the fourth ward as his political base, McFeely became a city councilman in 1906 and won reelection through 1914. Like Griffin, McFeely was able to amass a considerable fortune and an estate in Closter, New Jersey, where his stables enabled him to indulge his continuing love of horses.[35]

The Democratic machine's politics were hardly progressive. In the early years the bosses consistently blocked the city council's bills for sewage and drainage projects in the west of the city. The rationale was that drainage bills necessitated higher taxes that meant higher rents that were unafford-able to the working class. Later, after the turn of the century when the machine started to dominate the city council, the Independents and Repub-licans unearthed scandals in which the bosses were accused of letting contracts for such work to themselves or their cronies. To cite one example, in 1915 there was a grand jury investigation of possible graft on Hoboken's 2nd Street sewer job in 1912, but the jurors were hopelessly divided and the investigation brought no indictments. Rudolph Schroeder was one of the jurors who told his story to the press: McFeely was chairman of the committee of the city council that supervised the improvements. The committee chose the contractor and the inspector and approved the bills submitted to the city for the project. McFeely himself was found to have profited by being a subcontractor on the project, but some of the jurors had not voted for an indictment because they were "crooks." Subsequently, when McFeely denied that he had made money from the project, Schroeder, who was the secretary of the board of trade, continued his allegations by listing companies from which McFeely was said to have bought the sand, cement, and crushed rock used in the contract. Schroeder then revealed that the

---

[33] Obituary, *Jersey Observer*, Jan. 15, 1931, 1.

[34] *Boyd's Jersey City and Hoboken Directory*(1908-9, 370 and 1909-190, 276; *Hudson Observer*, June 22, 1911, 3.

[35] John P. Field, *Halo Over Hoboken*(1955), 116.

grand jury heard testimony from professor of chemistry Thomas B. Stillman of Stevens Institute that the concrete did not come up to specifications.[36]

At the same time that machines ran a good deal of urban politics in the 1890s to early 1900s, a reaction set in with the start of the Progressive Era in America. In Hoboken, the Progressives were led by C. H. C. Jagels, president of the board of trade that was the forerunner of the chamber of commerce and represented business interests. Another leader from the board of trade was W. L. E. Keuffel, president and owner of the firm that produced surveying and technical instruments, Keuffel and Esser Company. They had the support of the prominent patrician families, the Stevenses, Bessons, and Alexanders.[37] Palmer Campbell, the Stevens family's chosen manager of the HLIC was also active. He was also vice president of both Stevens banks, the First National and the Hudson Trust, president of Campbell Stores, and a director of the Hackensack Water Company that supplied water to Hoboken.[38] Edwin A. Stevens's son, Richard Stevens, one of the few family members who did not move to more rural suburbs during the era, was an active supporter. A lawyer, he was a director of the HLIC and of the First National Bank of Hoboken. As vice president of the Hoboken Commission Government League, he supported the Progressives' main cause in their campaigns of 1911, 1913, and 1915 -- a change in city government to the Commission form that was provided by the Walsh Act of 1911.

Under the mayor-council form of government then in existence in New Jersey, the mayor was elected by a city-wide vote for one year and two councilmen were elected from each ward for two years. The essence of this form of government at the time was control of the city council by the machine, because the machine controlled three of the wards, the first, third and fourth in the south and west. The machine-controlled council wielded so much power that the mayor was often powerless to oversee its committees and activities sufficiently. The Walsh act, promoted by Progressives like New Jersey governor Woodrow Wilson, provided another option for the state's city governments. The Commission form of government would allow city-wide election of only five commissioners every four years, the executive

---

[36] *Hudson Observer*, Feb. 6, 1915, 3, Feb. 8, 1915, 3, and *Jersey Journal*, Feb. 2, 1915, 1, Feb. 4, 1915, 1.

[37] See lists of progressive supporters, *Hudson Observer*, May 17, 1911, 3; April 1, 1913, 3; Jan. 23, 1915, 3; Jan. 29, 1915, 3; and *Jersey Journal*, May 15, 1911, 14; May 13, 1911, 6.

[38] *History of Hoboken Issued by the Hoboken Board of Trade*(1907), 77, 87, 101, 103; Daniel Van Winkel, *History of the Municipalities of Hudson County, New Jersey; 1630-1923*, 3 (1924), 638-9; *Hudson Observer*, May 17, 1911, 3; April 1, 1913, and Jan. 29, 1915, 3.

and legislative functions being combined because the commissioners would name the mayor from among their number.[39]

Keuffel kicked off the Progressive's pro-commission campaigns in 1911 with the establishment of the Commission Government League that had three thousand pledged supporters. He said,

Commission government is characterized by directness and simplicity, publicity and efficiency . . . . Hoboken will be a better place to live in and do business in under this form of government.[40]

In the subsequent campaign in 1911, the league used the slogan "Join the 3,000," and claimed to be a core of enlightened reformers not aligned with any political party although in reality many were Republicans. They organized mass meetings and cajoled Woodrow Wilson to speak on the virtues of commission government. In the two unsuccessful campaigns of 1911 and 1913 as well as in its victory of 1915, the Hoboken Commission Government League spent a considerable amount of money on ads in local newspapers, blue and white posters, and silent films shown free of charge in the offices of the board of trade. During their successful campaign of 1915, the Progressives rented an office at 132 Washington Street and hired a campaign manager, Henry Freeman, who had successfully guided a reform movement in Buffalo, New York. On its side, the machine put an ad in the *Hudson Observer* that ironically turned out to be prophetic:

Self preservation and self advancement are among the strongest instincts of man; unlimited power permits the unlimited gratification of these instincts to the detriment of the people at large. Produce five perfect men (do they exist?), make them your rulers under the oligarchic system, and you will have perfect government. On the other hand, five self-seeking scoundrels would do untold harm in the possession of unlimited governmental power . . . . Think of the enormous political power the commissioners would have. They can appoint whom they please when they please. They can remove at will. They are the sole judge of the cause of removal. Such a body would be self perpetuating.[41]

In the special vote in 1915, the Progressives only carried two wards, the one around Castle Point and the Republican second ward, but the commission form of government finally carried -- by only three votes out of 7,137 votes cast.

---

[39] See E. W. Creeraft, *The Government of Hudson County, NJ*(1915).

[40] *Jersey Journal*, May 5, 1911, 14.

[41] *Hudson Observer*, April 8, 1913, 3.

Two days after adoption of the commission form of government, boss Paddy Griffin surprised the still-elated Progressive forces by announcing his candidacy for commissioner. During the next two weeks, candidates of every political description declared their intention of running for one of the five positions as commissioner.[42] Some apolitical candidates saw an advantage in coupling their business ads with a political ad that declared their candidacy. The election was set for March 16, 1915. On March 3, Progressives were disturbed to learn that the Griffin-controlled Democratic City Committee had unanimously endorsed a slate of five men for the five commissioners to be elected, including Griffin himself, McFeely, and Londrigan. At the same time a number of Democrats who had previously announced their candidacies were pressured to drop out of the race and declare their support for the Griffin ticket. In the opposition camp all was a shambles. The Commission Government League had become the New Government League that put up a slate of five candidates including two ex-reform mayors, but it unwisely also endorsed a number of other reform candidates as alternate choices. Meanwhile the fifth ward's Republican Club put up its own list of reformists without the backing of the regular Republican leadership. What made election day confusing to anti-Griffin voters, besides the fact that there were fifty-one candidates, was that some of the league's candidates were supported by reform or non-reform Republicans, some of the Republicans were supported by the league, and one candidate, the ex-bartender Gustav Bach, was supported both by the league and the Democratic machine.[43]

The election results had a familiar ring except more so. The machine swept every ward except the second, and four of the five machine candidates won. When his fellow commissioners named Griffin as mayor, the *Jersey Journal* wrote that the election results demonstrated the "worthlessness" of the new form of government.[44] The long-term results were that Patrick R. Griffin served as mayor of Hoboken from 1915 to 1926. Barney McFeely was made commissioner in charge of the police and fire departments in 1915. The use of police to stop strikes ended, and McFeely declared in 1919 that "Strikebreakers, as a class are recruited from the army of thieves and thugs of the United States . . . . and are therefore a menace to the peace and order of our city . . ."[45] This stance fared well with the increasing power of the unions, especially among Hoboken dock workers in the 1920s and

---

[42] *Ibid.*, February 11, 1915, 1.
[43] *Ibid.*, Jan. 20, 3, Mar. 3, 3, Mar. 6, 3, and *Jersey Journal*, Mar. 4, 10, Mar. 6, 9, all 1915.
[44] *Jersey Journal*, March 17, 1; *Hudson Observer*, March 17, 1915, 2.
[45] *Ibid.*, March 13, 1919, 3.

1930s. The municipality rarely took action to close the speakeasies during Prohibition when Hoboken had the reputation of being a hospitable environment for imbibing. When Griffin retired in 1926, McFeely became boss and his fellow commissioner Gustav Bach became mayor, but in 1930 McFeely himself became mayor and reigned for seventeen years until 1947.

During World War I, Hoboken's German docks and the ships they contained were confiscated by the federal government, which used them to embark soldiers for the war in Europe. By this act, the federal government cut off the municipal tax revenues from these properties, the considerable sum of $312,775. These tax revenues were not restored in a modest way until 1950, and still the waterfront was blockaded.[46] During Prohibition the

A good look at Hoboken is given in the Oscar-winning Elia Kazan movie starring Marlon Brando, the classic *On the Waterfront* (1954). Many of the scenes were shot on location just south of Castle Point, depicted here in a much older photograph from the pre-World War I era.[47]

municipality had lost another $200,000 from liquor licenses, but this revenue was restored after repeal when legal bars and saloons sprung up

---

[46] The figure is the average for the years 1919-1922. *United States. Claims Committee. Senate, 67th Cong. 2-4 Sess. Hearings Before a Subcommittee of the Committee on Claims. Pursuant to S. Res. 254 to Investigate Claims of the City of Hoboken, NJ for Losses as a Result of the Occupation by the United States of Certain Docks. July 15 and August 8, 1922*(1922), 8; a description of the seizure by the army and marines is in *Hudson Observer*, April 6, 1917, 1, 14.

[47] Carol Strickland, "On the Waterfront, the Filming of Hoboken," in Foster and Clark, *Op.Cit., 85-95.*

along the length of River Street opposite the docks.[48] Another lasting effect of World War I was the destruction of the German community in Hoboken; because of their proximity to an embarkation point for American soldiers, Hoboken's German population was screened by the military and removed from the area adjacent to the docks. After the war, a new immigrant wave of Italians moved in, and the city took on an Italian and Irish orientation.

More importantly, the number of manufacturing establishments declined in the 1920s and did not recover until the 1950s. Established industries in the city decided to close down plants or to move to the suburbs. Causes were structural obsolescence of factories, the need for improved transportation access, and high municipal taxes. Trucking worked against Hoboken by offering manufacturers new freedoms in selecting suburban sites, and Hoboken's former advantage as a railroad terminal and port vanished in the subsequent era of container trucks. The rise in tax levies effected both industry and owners of housing stock. Between 1920 and 1954, the need for city revenues doubled, but the assessed valuation of all land, improvements, and chattels decreased from $107,538,000 in 1919 to $81,567,000 in 1954 because of structural obsolescence and abandonment. A most damaging result of the fiscal squeeze in which the city found itself was the cutback in spending on municipal services and capital improvements; with an already moderate debt load and a reduced taxable income, the city deferred improvement in city streets, municipal buildings, and other facilities including sewers.[49] The population dropped steadily from its high in 1910 of 70,324 to a more manageable 45,380 by 1970 as a result of the decay of housing stock. In 1940, 75 percent of Hoboken's housing was built before 1900.[50] By 1950, 36.3 percent of 15,170 dwelling units were rated substandard by U.S. Census criteria: They were dilapidated, lacked hot water, or lacked private toilet or bath. Twenty-seven percent had only cold water. Given these housing conditions, during the period from 1920 to 1940 there was a movement of second- and third-generation European immigrants to the suburbs, and the age structure of Hoboken from 1930 to 1950 clearly showed a trend towards an older population of aging parents left behind. As in a lot of

---

[48] *United States Claims Committee, Op.Cit.,* 75

[49] Edgar M. Hoover and Raymond Vernon, *Anatomy of a Metropolis; The Changing Distribution of People and Jobs within the New York Metropolitan* Region(1962), 21-26; *Fourteenth Census of the United States Taken in the Year 1920. Manufactures.*(1923), 944; *United States Census of Manufactures. 1954. Area* Statistics(1954), Part III, 129-35.

[50] *Sixteenth Census of the United States. 1940. Housing supplement to the First Series Housing Bulletin for New Jersey. Hoboken Block Statistics.*(1942), 5.

American inner-urban areas, Hoboken reached its nadir in the early 1960s.[51]

It was during the political imbroglio just before and after World War I that the Stevenses and other wealthy families moved to rural estates in the New Jersey hinterlands. Economically, the Stevenses and their relatives continued to own properties in Hoboken through the HLIC. But, during the Great Depression of the 1930s, the Company started to liquidate its Hoboken real estate -- rollbacks in rent and bankruptcies of companies that leased their properties made the Stevens heirs' stock in the Company less profitable. In 1946, the HLIC sold the Hoboken docks to Webb and Knapp of New York for $10 million. The liquidation was completed, the Company's stocks liquidated, and the proceeds divided among the family.[52] Seven years later in 1953, Hoboken's voters decided to revert back to the mayor-council form of government, which, for Hoboken at least, largely ended machine politics as it existed under Griffin and McFeely.[53]

Starting in the 1950s, Hoboken's underlying problem of housing obsolescence was recognized: fifty-four housing units were built between 1940 and 1949, 746 units between 1950 and 1960, and 891 between 1960 and 1970.[54] Most of these were housing projects built with grants in part from federal funds, and they replaced some of the worst and abandoned dwellings in the western part of the city. In the late 1960s grants were obtained to level the tenements and bars along River Street. These were replaced with high-rise, middle-class apartment buildings in the 1970s when conditions started to improve.

By the early 1970s, Hoboken started to turn around dramatically as a new expectation arose, namely, that Hoboken would experience the same kind of renewal that took place in Greenwich Village in Manhattan or in Georgetown in Washington, D.C., i.e., piecemeal reconstruction and remodeling of existing structures. In fact, between 1971 and 1986 an "incredible real estate boom swept the municipality. Developers converted nearly one-fifth of the private rental stock to condominiums, and boutiques, cafes, and frame shops" were built. Around 1976, a renaissance was proclaimed in Hoboken, and newspapers from the *Wall Street Journal* to the *Washington Post* heralded a "Mile Square Miracle" in the once dismal Hoboken that was

---

[51] *United States Census of Housing. 1950. Block Statistics. Hoboken, New Jersey.*(1951), Part 79, 3; Isadore Candeub, *Basic Studies. Hoboken Master Plan. Housing Analysis*(1955), 1-11; *U.S. Census of Population and Housing. 1960. Census Tracts*(1961).

[52] "Purchase of Hoboken Waterfront," *Stevens Indicator*, 63 (1946), no. 6, 18.

[53] Foster and Clark, *Op.Cit.*, 12.

[54] *Ibid.*, 71, and *1970 Census of Population. Characteristics of the Population. New Jersey*(1973), Part 32, 128.

"having the last laugh." In the 1970s, whole brownstones sold for $40,000 to $50,000, but by 1986 condominiums were selling for $100,000 to $200,000.[55] During the 1980s, Hoboken was a focus of gentrification, and invaded by middle-class and upper-class young people, or "yuppies," who bought brownstones and renewed them causing sales prices of dwellings to skyrocket. As a result, the city become less affordable to poorer housing and apartment seekers. Many of the new younger well-to-do residents worked on Wall Street or in the World Trade Center area, the PATH trains providing transportation within ten minutes to Manhattan.

Stevens played a role in this "Hoboken Renaissance" through its Center for Municipal Studies and Services (CMSS). Funded by both the U.S. Department of Housing and Urban Development (HUD), CMSS brought together the city of Hoboken and the Port Authority of New York and New Jersey (PATH), as well as other bodies, to focus on the redevelopment of the Hoboken waterfront. One of the first projects of CMSS under Professor Peter Jurkat was a study for the renovation of the Erie-Lackawanna Terminal and its surrounding neighborhood, the gateway to Hoboken and terminus for the railroads and PATH trains to Manhattan. With the decline in shipping along the Hoboken docks in the 1960s in favor of Port Newark, which could accommodate container ships and trucks to haul the containers to the hinterlands, CMSS recommended that the docks be used for a "commercial, residential and recreational" complex. Stevens students were involved in research by CMSS.[56]

This study as well as many others done by the city, the Port Authority of New York and New Jersey, and citizen groups finally resulted in a plan to develop the docks. Announced by Mayor Anthony Russo in 1995, the plan was for the Port Authority to invest $75 million as part of a $252.4 million total investment to develop the Hoboken waterfront. The plan was for an esplanade along the water, three parks and recreational areas, and a complex of buildings for residential, commercial, and recreational facilities. The buildings were not to exceed either 125' or the tree level on Castle Point, and they were to be separated into three lots so Hobokenites would have access to the river for the first time in over a century. The development would bring in some $8.6 million per year in new municipal taxes.[57] By

---

[55] Joseph Barry and John Derevlany, eds., *Yuppies Invade My House at Dinnertime; A Tale of Brunch, Bombs, and Gentrification in an American City*(1987), ix-xx.

[56] "CMSS: The Center for Municipal Studies and Services," *Stevens Indicator*, 95 (1978), 8-10, and John Schwab and M. Peter Jurkat, "Center for Municipal Studies and Services; Hoboken Urban Observatory, Final Report National League of Cities and U.S. Department of Housing and Urban Development, Contract no. UO-T-R-08," 2 and 25.

[57] *Hoboken Reporter*, Feb. 5, 1995, 1, and Apl. 13, 1997, 1.

1999, the old docks had been cleared and two of the parks had been built, one almost directly below Castle Point. Moreover, Washington Street, Hoboken's main street had become a restaurant row with red-brick side-walks, wrought-iron benches, and Victorian-style street lamps.[58]

---

[58] *Ibid.*, Feb. 2, 1997, 4.

CHAPTER 3

A Science-Based Liberal-Technical M.E. Curriculum

In 1867, one year before he died, Edwin A. Stevens decided to leave part of his estate for the establishment of a college. That year, on a trip to France aboard the *Great Eastern,* his wife Martha remembered that her husband had conversations with their long-time friend Abram Stevens Hewitt about what type of college to endow. During the twenty-fifth anniversary of Stevens Institute, Hewitt gave a speech recalling the conversations. He said that Edwin A. Stevens was anxious to know about Cooper Union, endowed by Abram Stevens Hewitt's father-in-law, Peter Cooper. Hewitt said he told his friend that Cooper Union was founded for the training of mechanics, and he advised that, since the Stevens family were engineers, it would be "natural and fitting" that the future institution be for engineers: "I explained to him that all the resources of the Cooper Union were used in giving the education which the mechanic needed, and that what was wanted in this country was a higher institution which could start where the mechanic ended, and produce the engineers who were to become the leaders of modern enterprise and the captains of industry."[59]

Edwin A. Stevens's last will had been written before his trip to Europe, and it did not bind the executors of his estate to a specific type of school or curriculum. It provided one city block assessed at $112,500, a building fund of $150,000, and an endowment of $500,000 "for the uses of an institution of learning" for the "benefit, tuition and advancement in learning of the youth residing, from time to time, hereafter within the state of New Jersey."[60] The will specified that the executors of his estate be the trustees of the institution of learning, namely his manager of the Hoboken Land and Improvement Company, William W. Shippen, his wife's brother, Samuel Bayard Dod, and Martha herself. According to the family historian, Martha recalled Edwin's intentions after his discussions with Hewitt, and she was influential in convincing the other two trustees to found an engineering college.[61]

However, she left the details to her brother, Samuel Bayard Dod (1837-1906), who became president of the trustees of Stevens Institute of Tech-

---

[59] Speech of Abram Stevens Hewitt included in "The 25th Anniversary of the Founding of Stevens Institute of Technology," *Stevens Indicator,* XIV (1897), 117-8.
[60] *An Act to Incorporate the Stevens Institute of Technology,* Stevens Institute of Technology, Hoboken, n.d.
[61] See page 6 of the chapter called "Descendants of Edwin A. Stevens" in unpublished typescript by Basil M. Stevens "Stevens Family History," n.d., Stevens Special Collections.

nology from 1871 until his death. He and his sister were grandchildren of Daniel Dod (1778-1823), a clockmaker and maker of mathematical instruments, who was offered a chair in mathematics at Rutgers. Daniel became a steamboat pioneer in 1811, holding patents for engines, boilers, and condensers. He was a partner of Aaron Ogden, the rival of John Stevens in ferry service in New York harbor, and he constructed the machinery for the *Savannah*, the first steamboat to cross the Atlantic. Samuel and Martha were the children of Daniel's son, Albert Baldwin Dod (1805-1845) who graduated from Princeton in 1822 and served as a professor of mathematics there from 1830 until his death -- mathematics being a talent which ran in the family. Albert was a friend and colleague of Joseph Henry, the foremost American scientist of the era. Joseph Henry was a Princeton professor of natural philosophy before becoming the founding director of the Smithsonian Institution in Washington. Albert married Caroline Bayard of Princeton, a descendant of the pro-British Bayards who had their Hoboken estates confiscated -- the estates bought by John Stevens. The marriage of Albert's daughter to Edwin A. Stevens thus joined the two families who had owned the whole of Hoboken.[62]

Samuel Bayard Dod graduated from Princeton in 1857 and studied for a year in Germany before entering Princeton Theological Seminary to prepare for a career as a Presbyterian minister. This religious persuasion also ran in the family, Daniel Dod being a Calvinist and his father being a part-time licensed Presbyterian preacher who wrote several commentaries of a religious nature. Samuel Bayard Dod was a minister in several places, the last being Wilkes-Barre, Pennsylvania. Like an archtypical Calvinist, he seemed very willing to become a successful businessman when given the chance. He gave up his ministry when he became an executor of the estates of Edwin A. Stevens in 1868. He became director of the Hoboken Land and Improvement Company, the manager of the Hoboken Ferry Company, and he was president of the First National Bank, which was the Stevens bank in Hoboken. Encouraged by his success in banking, Dod founded another bank, the Hudson Trust Company, located at 52 Newark Steet, across form the First National Bank.[63] He also became president of the Hudson County Gas Light Company, and director of the New Jersey State Fire Insurance

---

[62] "Daniel Dod," *Dictionary of American Biography*, V (1930), 339-40; "Dod, Daniel," *National Cyclopaedia of American Biography*, XXIV (1935), 359-60; "Albert Baldwin Dod," *Dictionary of American Biography*, V (1930), 338-9. The Hudson Trust Commune held the Home Trust Company, Andrew Carnegie's personal bank run by Robert L. Franks after 1902.

[63] "Samuel Bayard Dod," *Universities and Their Sons*(Boston, 1899), II, 335; "Samuel Bayard Dod," *Princeton Theological Seminary Necrological Report*(1908), 533-34.

Company. He reportedly felt the job of creating an engineering school to be a "congenial task which enlisted his hearty interest."[64]

Martha Baryard Stevens and her brother Samuel Bayard Dod
had literary interests. He wrote poetry which he published in a Scottish journal
as well as three novels which had Christian morals as a theme.

Dod carried out a careful examination of engineering programs elsewhere before hiring the first president of the institute and the faculty. He obtained detailed information on the technical schools of Berlin, Zurich, and Mannheim and visited many mining and engineering schools in America.[65] Dod followed Hewitt's advice in rejecting the type of curriculum then taught at Cooper Union and the Worcester Free Institute, both of which focused on shop practice for the training of machinists. He found older institutions specializing in civil engineering which had added mechanical engineering courses to their C.E. programs: Polytechnic College of Pennsylvania added such a course in 1854, Rensselaer in 1862, Yale's Sheffield Scientific School added "dynamical engineering" leading to an M.Phil. degree in 1863, Massachusetts Institute of Technology added a similar course in 1865, the U.S. Naval Academy added a "steam engineering" course in 1866, and Cornell followed suit with a mechanical course in 1868. But he found there was no school dedicated to mechanical engineering. Hence, the first minutes of the trustees of Stevens Institute of Technology state that,

---

[64] F. DeR. Furman, *Morton Memorial, A History of Stevens Institute of Technology*(Hoboken, 1905), 149. This history was written one year before Dod died, and Furman probably based his remarks on conversations with Dod who was active in mind and body until the end. Furman's book contains short biographical sketches of all Stevens graduates up to 1904.

[65] *Ibid.*

After a careful examination of the facilities afforded to students at institutions of learning in this and neighboring states, the trustees determined to make this school a school of technology with special reference to mechanical engineering. In this they were influenced by a two-fold consideration. First, that there was no school of mechanical engineering in actual operation in this country, and therefore such an institution securely established would fill a gap in the educational system in America; and, secondly, that the distinguished ability of the Stevens family for two generations in this direction made it eminently proper that the endowment left by the Stevenses should at once be a public benefit and a fitting memorial of the family's talent.[66]

More importantly, Dod consulted his older "friend of Princeton days," Joseph Henry.[67] Dod's father died when he was six, and, since Joseph Henry was forty-six at the time, the older man was a surrogate father and mentor to the boy. When Henry died, Dod said, "To those who knew Professor Henry personally, there was the charm of a singularly gentle and unaffected sincerity of heart and manner, that made him approachable to all. His attachments were warm and lasting."[68] Dod's 1850's correspondence with Henry contained discussion of scientific matters, including the apparatus Henry used to discover the inductive effect of magnetism and electricity.[69] Thus it was natural that Dod would ask for Henry's advice on setting up the institute in 1870. Joseph Henry wrote back to Dod that he should choose a high-class science-based faculty for "fitness alone" and give them adequate salaries and time for original research. He recommended Alfred M. Mayer (1836-1897), a member of the National Academy of Sciences, of which Henry was the founder, as physics professor. Henry advised that "success in original investigation never fails to ensure enthusiasm on the part of the teacher, and to beget by sympathy a like feeling on the part of the pupils." Henry urged that laboratories be well supplied with equipment, and he later helped in obtaining the Bancker collection of scientific instruments for Stevens.[70] Henry was decidedly in favor of a higher science and mathematics "disciplinary" approach to engineering, and he favored faculty "who discover new principles."[71] Henry's ideas resulted in Mayer being appointed

---

[66] "Stevens Institute of Technology; Trustees Minutes," I (1871), 4. The unpublished manuscripts of the Trustees' minutes are held in the Institute's Samuel C. Williams Library's vault.

[67] Thomas Coulson, *Joseph Henry, His Life and Work* (Princeton U. Press, 1950), 72.

[68] *Ibid.*, 291.

[69] *Ibid.*, 143.

[70] S. Dillon Ripley, Director of the Smithsonian Institution, "Talk for Stevens Institute of Technology," unpublished typescript dated May 26, 1977, Stevens Special Collections.

[71] Coulson, *Op. Cit.*, 100-1.

as the first physics professor, and in the rest of the outstanding appointments.

Dod offered the presidency of Stevens Institute to Henry Morton (1836-1902) of the Franklin Institute in Philadelphia. The Franklin Institute was founded in 1824 to promote advancement and research in the "mechanic arts." Until the creation of the American Society of Mechanical Engineers (ASME) in 1880, the Franklin Institute and its *Journal of the Franklin Institute* were the sole organization and periodical dedicated to promoting and sharing information on the application of scientific methods applied to the field of mechanical engineering. Through the publication of technical papers, book reviews, the results of experiments, and efficiency trials of water wheels and steam engines, the mechanical engineering manufacturers communicated with each other before the establishment of the ASME and before mechanical engineers were educated outside the shops of manufacturing establishments. In addition, the Franklin Institute provided young men with practical instruction in shop work as well as informal lectures by professors on the latest theory which often came from German and French polytechnical schools in Europe. The Franklin Institute never aspired to be an engineering college, but, especially in its *Journal*, it was the one place where both academics and the most advanced manufacturers could exchange the latest scientific methods applied to mechanical engineering.

The Franklin Institute benefited when the foremost American machine tool manufacturer, William Sellers (1824-1905), became its president in 1864. The organization experienced an "infusion of new spirit" and regeneration allowing it to see itself as "the representative institution of the connection of mechanics with science for the whole country."[72] Sellers, particularly through establishment of the Sellers standard screw-thread sizes by lobbying with Congress, brought attention to the Franklin Institute as a prototype professional society for mechanical engineers. He also created new "professorships" in chemistry, natural philosophy, and mechanics, appointed a new committee for scientific investigations, and created a permanent secretary who also edited the *Journal*.

The first permanent secretary at the Franklin Institute was Henry Morton. Morton was a young and ambitious graduate of the University of Pennsylvania, where he had taken the classical liberal arts and sciences curriculum majoring in chemistry before studying law. At the Franklin Institute, Morton had demonstrated administrative ability and energy in building up the *Journal*'s reputation until, by 1870, it was considered the leading Amer-

---

[72] Bruce Sinclair, *Philadelphia's Philosopher Mechanics; A History of the Franklin Institute, 1824-1865*(Johns Hopkins U. Press, 1974), 308-9.

ican engineering journal. As editor, he solicited articles from innovative scientists and engineers who saw the need for more science in engineering. Assisted by William Sellers's cousin, Coleman Sellers (1827-1907), Morton used his oratorical talent to gave a series of lectures at the Philadelphia Academy of Music on light, chemical effects, and acoustical phenomena. Accompanied by startling demonstrations, these immensely popular talks communicated difficult scientific subjects to the general public in a dramatic and simple manner.[73]

Morton's educational ideas were congenial to Dod. Morton desired to have an advanced, science-based engineering curriculum on German and French models leading to the degree of Mechanical Engineer (M.E.). Unlike French and German higher technical schools which omitted liberal arts, Morton insisted that Stevens offer such non-technical content. In 1896, on the occasion of the twenty-fifth anniversary of Stevens Institute, his speech recalled that when he became president in 1870, he knew that the best students in the German technical schools were graduates of gymnasia where liberal arts were a central to the curriculum. Such students were superior to graduates of realschule which gave mainly technical training. His plan, carried out at Stevens, was to combine liberal arts with the kind of science-based technical education given in German higher technical institutions, and he called such a curriculum a "liberal technical" education. He went on to say,

Naturally the study of the classic languages and literature was the first to be introduced, for it was the first subject to which individual scholars devoted their labor and their genius, and consequently it was the first subject reduced to such systematic organization to be a fit exercise for the training of the faculties and developing the judgment. . . . Such courses as combine with an efficient technical training a large amount of 'liberal' culture most deserve the attention of those who are in a position to develop them. . . . What has been accomplished in the direction of liberal technical courses the present writer can, he believes, fully appreciate because it has been his good fortune during the last twenty five years to carry out plans in the organization and operation of an institution where a "Liberal Technical" course has been the object aimed at, and, as he believes, developed with some measure of success. . . To the capitalist who has no object greater than the most rapid augmentation of his capital and who views education only as a means of enlarging the supply of high-grade labor, who engages bright young 'hustlers' to

---

[73] Coleman Sellers' father was also a Coleman Sellers (1781-1834), and Morton's friend had a son, Coleman Sellers Jr. (1852-1922); *Mechanical Engineers in America. A Biographical Dictionary*(ASME, 1980), 273. For the early history of the Sellers family see Anthony F. C. Wallace, *Rockdale; The Growth of an American Village in the Early Industrial Revolution*(1978), 220-22.

rush his business and is always ready to replace them with newer and brighter ones, . . . (an educational plan) of rapid production commends itself as it would in the case of a production machine. To the true educator, however, who works with his eyes turned to the community, of his country and even of the race of men, a very different policy presents itself. *He* will not hasten to meet the demand of the present by turning out the article most desired irrespective of its intrinsic value and enduring qualities, but will labor to produce the best possible product trusting to the future to vindicate and crown his work.[74]

Henry Morton, the first president of Stevens Institute, had an affinity, as did Dod, for literary studies and biblical criticism. Morton wrote poetry -- for example his lengthy poem *Per Aspera ad Astra*, based on the Stevens motto -- and he had joined other scholars in attempting to translate the hieroglyphs of the Rosetta Stone.

---

[74] See unpublished manuscript in Morton's hand entitled "Modern Education" in volume II of his papers in Stevens Special Collections. It is not dated but his reference in the text to twenty-five years of work at Stevens indicates he wrote it in 1896.

Thus, the liberal part of the curriculum at Stevens Institute consisted of the equivalent of four years of literature, philosophy and languages from the school's inception. Morton agreed with Dod's christian bias and appointed the Reverend Edward Wall, a colleague of Dod's at both Princeton and Princeton Theological Seminary, as professor of belles lettres to teach literature and logic. Wall was also the principal of the Stevens School, a preparatory school on the Stevens campus set up by the trustees to prepare students for entry to the institute. Morton hired a colleague from the Franklin Institute, C. F. Kroeh, a linguist with a scientific background, as professor of French and German.

The early curriculum had a heavy emphasis on pure science. The distinguished Alfred M. Mayer, a pioneer researcher in acoustics, was made professor of physics. Before the acoustical measurements with transducers, Mayer along with Koenig, Helmholtz and Rayleigh were the first to devise methods to measure the intensity of sound by nonelectrical means. Mayer used the term "pendulum vibration" for simple harmonic motion, and his experiments with ticking clocks in soundproofed rooms showed that one sound could be "obliterated" with a second lower-frequency sound. He was the first to discover the phenomenon of masking, in which a lower-pitched sound could obliterate a higher-pitched sound even if the latter was intense. It wasn't until the 1920s that further research was conducted in this field.[75] Albert R. Leeds, a Harvard chemistry graduate, a professor at Haverford as well as a lecturer at the Franklin Institute, was made first professor of chemistry.

Another extraordinary scholar and teacher, DeVolson Wood, who later became first president of the Society for the Promotion of Engineering Education, was made professor of mathematics. He was a child prodigy in mathematics who started teaching the subject in his teens; he specialized in the application of higher mathematics to several engineering fields, his first professorship being that of civil engineering at the University of Michigan, and he was so versatile that he became a professor of mechanical engineering at Stevens in 1885. During the early years of the institute each student received two years of chemistry and applied chemistry, three years of physics, and four years of applied mathematics. A little known fact is that in the first ten years of the institute there was also a small program in the sciences

[75] Robert T. Beyer, *Sounds of Our Times*(AIP Press, 1998), 138, 153, 210; and Alfred M. Mayer, "On The Experimental Determination of the Relative Intensities of Sounds and on the Relative Intensities of the Powers of Various Substances to Reflect and to Transmit Sonorous Vibrations," *Philosophical Magazine*, 1873, a copy of the title page being included in Malcolm J. Crocker, "Direct Measurement of Sound Intensity and Practical Applications in Noise Control Engineering," *Inter-Noise*, 81 (1984), 33.

leading to B.S. and Ph.D. degrees. Under "Degrees," catalogs before 1882-83 described the M.E. degree but went on to state,

In certain cases, however, graduates from other institutions, or meritorious students, of at least two years standing, may pursue a special course, from which they may graduate, upon passing the requisite examinations, with the degree of Bachelor of Science; and such graduates, on presenting a thesis embodying the results of original investigation in the subjects of chemistry and physics, may receive a further degree of Doctor of Philosophy.

While most graduates earned an M.E. degree, there were five earned B.S. degrees and four earned Ph.D.s in science between 1876 and 1884.

President Morton chose Robert H. Thurston (1839-1903) as the key professor of mechanical engineering. Thurston was committed to the French and German science-based models of technical education, and, even though he disagreed with Morton on the inclusion of liberal arts, he had demonstrated his breadth and skill in mechanical engineering through publications in the *Journal of the Franklin Institute* while Morton was editor. Thurston was then a professor at the U.S. Naval Academy and a published specialist on iron and steel as well as steam engines. Charles W. MacCord was chosen as professor of mechanical drawing; he was a Princeton graduate who had achieved distinction as Ericsson's draftsman for the *Monitor,* and he had been employed in Hoboken as chief draftsman for the completion of the *Stevens Battery* under the supervision of General George B. McClellan between 1868 and 1870.[76]

Robert H. Thurston deserves to be called a founder of Stevens Institute because of the indelible mark he left there. He became respected internationally for his 574 articles and twenty-one books and for being a founding editor of the journal *Science.* In scores of his articles, he was a veritable propagandist for his view of engineering as applied science, and, consequently, was largely responsible for Stevens Institute's high reputation in spite of failing to mention the curriculum's liberal arts content. He was elected the first President of the ASME in a meeting held at Stevens in 1880 -- another factor which brought Stevens a special identification with mechanical engineering at the time.

In 1872 he wrote the first of many articles of many advertising the excellence of the Stevens curriculum for the *Journal of the Franklin Institute.* He said that the engineer had to "cultivate knowledge of the physical laws" in order to "make use of scientific principles in planning work," and the best

---

[76] Furman, *Morton Memorial,* 219-20.

way to obtain such knowledge was to attend a college similar to the advanced French and German technical schools upon which Stevens was modeled.[77] In a pamphlet in 1875 he wrote that graduates would always find value in the higher mathematics of Cardan, Lagrange, Laplace, and Gauss; in "the science of exact sciences" or thermodynamics, and in the work of chemists and metallurgists like Liebig, Wohler, Calvert, and Bunsen on the materials of engineering. Thurston did not reject shop practice but said it was a complement to theory. Thurston summed up by saying that Stevens's engineering program combined "theory and practice."[78]

If the theory in the curriculum consisted of sciences, higher applied mathematics, engineering science, and scientific laboratory methods, the practice consisted of foundry and shop training. Professor Thurston thought that shop work was an occupation of trade schools, but if it was not taught in high school it had to be included in the Stevens curriculum. Well-known guest lecturers, Morton's friend Coleman Sellers, Alexander Lyman Holley who introduced the Bessemer furnace to America, and J. E. Hilgard of the U.S. Coastal Survey, provided education in practical engineering. For Thurston, such lectures had dual functions, namely, to introduce students to problems of engineering in the context of business and to provide faculty with knowledge of the state of the art in the practice of the profession. Other programs initiated by Thurston which integrated practice into the curriculum were readings of foreign technical journals in French and German, field trips to industrial sites, and a senior thesis consisting of either original research or an investigation into a particular development of mechanical engineering in the field.[79] Actually, the notion of theory and practice was an old idea of the Franklin Institute, but Thurston's popular articles identified the term with Stevens's curriculum.

By 1880, Thurston developed a vision for the United States of a complete "symmetrical" system of government-sponsored technical education as existed in Germany.[80] He stressed the efficiency of the German system, which included technical training at all levels, from mechanics, to technical

---

[77] Robert H. Thurston, "The Improvement of the Steam Engine and the Education of Engineers," *Journal of the Franklin Institute,* XCIV (1872), 17-25, and Geoffrey W. Clark, "Thurston, A Learned Man of Science," *Stevens Indicator,* 1981, no.4, 10-14.

[78] Robert H. Thurston, *The Mechanical Engineer, His Preparation and His Work*(Van Nostrand Press, 1875).

[79] Clark, "Thurston," *Op. Cit.,* 12-13.

[80] Monte Calvert, *The Mechanical Engineer in America, 1830-1910*(Johns Hopkins Press, 1967), 47.

personnel, to engineers, to researchers. His ideal grand plan included "trade schools in every town, technical schools in every city, colleges of science and the arts in every state, and a great technical university as the center of the whole system."[81] Thurston became convinced that the German exclusion of liberal arts from engineering schools was a more focused and efficient way to teach engineering; such "general subjects" ideally being taught in preparatory schools. However, given Morton's liberal-technical program, Thurston was not in a position to establish such a focused program without admixture of general culture at Stevens. When in 1885 he became director of Sibley College at Cornell, a government-sponsored land grant college, he tried to create such a program.[82]

At Stevens, Thurston's crucial role, besides winning support for the institute's science-based engineering curriculum from traditionalists who still favored training in shops, was to create the specifically mechanical engineering part of the curriculum in the junior and senior years, a program which securely anchored the overall curriculum leading to the M.E. degree. As it turned out, his ideas of involving students in funded research led to the remarkable pioneering successes of the early graduates of Stevens.

---

[81] Quoted in *Ibid.,* 65 from Robert H. Thurston, "Our Progress in Mechanical Engineering," *ASME Trans.,* I (1880), 452-3.

[82] Catalogs and Morton's paper cited above make questionable the statement by Calvert, *Op.Cit.,* 49 that "From 1871 to 1885 Thurston devoted his life to creating a mechanical engineering curriculum that could serve as a model for the pure technical school or professional school with no admixture of general cultural education."

CHAPTER 4

Thurston's Pioneering Mechanical Laboratory

Robert H. Thurston is credited with establishing the first mechanical laboratory for conducting funded research at an American academic institution of higher learning.[83] This pioneering effort, combining government-sponsored research with commercial research for companies, was widely promoted by Thurston in leading journals of science and engineering. As a result, several other colleges and universities around the country emulated it by the turn of the century. An integral part of Thurston's plan for the laboratory was an educational function, namely, to train undergraduates in research, a goal which directly led to the remarkable success of early graduates of Stevens Institute.

According to William Kent, who became Thurston's chief assistant in the laboratory, Thurston had conceived of the laboratory as both a teaching and research facility at the time he came to Stevens in 1870.[84] Thurston himself said that the precedents for his laboratory were all European. He pointed out that the first engineering research in mechanics probably began with the foundation of the *Conservatoire des Arts et Metiers* in Paris under the military direction of General Morin during the French Revolution. Testing the strength of materials was even more ancient, dating to Musschenbroek's tensile testing machine in the late seventeenth century. From the 1820s French and German technical colleges had conducted mechanical tests for their governments, but without a specific educational goal. Thurston wrote that it was not until 1870 that European universities, namely King's College in London, the University of Edinburgh, and the Polytechnic of Zurich all "commenced the introduction of such apparatus and the construction of courses including their use both in instruction and research." [85] As a result, Thurston organized this first American laboratory on an informal basis in 1871 by equipping his mechanical engineering department with various

---

[83] For example see "Thurston, Robert Henry," *Dictionary of American Biography*, XVIII, 518; L. Grayson, "A Brief History of Engineering Education in the United States," *Engineering Education*, (1977), 249; J. McGivern, *First Hundred Years of Engineering Education in the United States, 1807-1907,"* (1960), 104; and M. Calvert, *The Mechanical Engineer in America, 1830-1910,"* (1967), 56.

[84] William Kent, "Biographical Notice of Robert H. Thurston," *The Sibley Journal of Mechanical Engineering*, XVIII (1903), 44.

[85] R. H. Thurston, "The Modern Mechanical Laboratory, Especially as in Process of Evolution in America," *Proceedings of the Society for the Promotion of Engineering Education*, VIII (1900), 337.

testing devices. In the first year of Stevens Institute's existence, he performed analyses of condensed steam from boilers for a committee of the American Institute of Mining Engineers.

In 1871 Thurston joined the U.S. Steam-Boiler Explosion Commission to oversee experimentally produced boiler explosions. This commission had been established at the urging of John Cox Stevens's son, Francis Bowes Stevens, who was the superintendent of the Camden and Amboy Railroad's shops in Hoboken, and who had used his influence with friends in Congress to have the commission funded with $100,000. The tests were carried out at a government reservation at Sandy Hook in lower New York harbor, and Thurston described some of the tests in an article in the *Journal of the Franklin Institute*[86].

Stevens Institute's first professor of mechanical engineering, Robert H. Thurston, conducted tests to solve the most notorious engineering problem of the age, the often deadly bursting of steam engine boilers. At right is his autographic torsion testing machine, now on display in the Samuel C. Willliams Library at Stevens Institute.

In 1872, Thurston had his undergraduates construct an autographic torsion testing machine, a device for recording tests of the strength of materials, particularly metals used in boilerplate, tools, and engine parts. This machine was prominently displayed in Thurston's advertisements soliciting work for his laboratory, and the results of such work for commercial enter-

---

[86] Durand, *Op. Cit.*, 77-79.

prises were published by the American Society of Civil Engineers in 1873.[87] During that year, using a loan from the trustees as well as his own money and payments for commercial tests, Thurston had his students build an apparatus for determining the value of different lubricants and machines for conducting steam engine and boiler trials. By late 1873, Thurston's laboratory had a reputation such that "engineers and proprietors" were approaching him with "various problems coming to them in the course of business."[88] This early activity of Thurston's laboratory seems to predate MIT's first commercial research laboratory, a steam engineering laboratory established in 1874.[89]

On January 30, 1874, Thurston petitioned the Stevens board of trustees for recognition of the laboratory on an official footing. In his letter, Thurston claimed that officers of important railroads, iron and steel manufacturers, machine makers, and engineers engaged in general practice were all potential customers for a laboratory "devoted to technical research and to the practical application of science in matters of business." He waxed eloquent in the letter about the ultimate benefits of the laboratory:

It would do most effectively that work which has hitherto been too much neglected, the application of scientific knowledge to familiar work and matters of business. It would do much to close up the space which so widely separates the man of business from the man of science, and would lead to a far more perfect system of mutual aid than has yet existed. An institution like this can do no nobler work than that which, by assisting in the improvement of technical methods, and by the application of science to improvements in practical construction, aids in the development of the natural resources of our country, stimulates the growth, in extent and perfection, of its most important industries, and contributes in a thousand ways to the welfare of the people.

As for the benefits to the institute, Thurston anticipated a "modest income" which he wanted to use in "building up my department" by improving the machinery and hiring full-time research personnel.[90]

The trustees' letter formally establishing the Mechanical Laboratory was published by the *Journal of the Franklin Institute* in 1874: While investing Thurston with the power to direct a laboratory for "technical research . . . especially designed to meet the necessities of the industrial interests of the country" as an "adjunct to your department," the trustees retained an im-

---

[87] R. H. Thurston, "A Note on the Resistance of Materials," *Trans. ASCE*, II (1873), 239-40.

[88] Durand, *Op. Cit.*, 71.

[89] G. Lanza, "Graduate Theses," *Proceedings of the Society for the Promotion of Engineering Education*, I (1893), 312.

[90] *Ibid.*, Appendix III contains a copy of the letter.

portant administrative control -- all contracts had to be submitted to the trustees for approval before they were signed by the director of the Mechanical Laboratory. Moreover, every year Thurston was required to report on the nature of the work done and the condition of the laboratory, and reports on revenues and expenditures were to be made semi-annually. The professor was directed to charge his clients sums large enough not only to cover all expenses but also to provide an income of not less than twenty percent of expenses to support institute operations. He could hire full-time personnel for the laboratory and also faculty on stipends as long as their extra work did not interfere with their duties as educators. Provision was made for use of a two hundred-by-fifty-foot plot of land adjacent to the institute's one building to house the laboratory, and the trustees gave free use of the mechanical engineering department's apparatus to the Mechanical Laboratory.[91]

Scientific American was an enthusiastic supporter of the pioneering laboratory. Its May 1874 issue praised Thurston and the institute for "a really excellent idea" of "great benefit to the entire country" because of the "manifest uses for which such an establishment could be employed by the business community with the greatest benefit."[92] In October *Scientific American* reported that the Mechanical Laboratory was receiving testing equipment "principally from the most successful and intelligent manufacturers."[93] In 1876, *Scientific American* followed up with a description of the laboratory's testing machines displayed in Philadelphia's Centennial Exhibition, machines used during the Mechanical Laboratory's research between 1874 and 1876. The journal stated that the torsion testing machine and a friction testing machine were "finding their way into the largest works of the country."[94]

While still sitting on the U.S. Steam-Boiler Explosion Commission in 1875, Thurston was appointed to a newly federally funded U.S. Board to Test Iron, Steel and Other Metals. This time, another $100,000 grant came at the urging of engineers like Alexander Lyman Holley, president of the American Institute of Mining Engineers (AIME) and also vice president of the American Society of Civil Engineers (ASCE).

Holley and Thurston had a "rare and close friendship" and a common vision, namely, that a scientific type of mechanical engineering could sys-

---

[91] "The Stevens Institute Mechanical Laboratory," *Journal of the Franklin Institute*, XCVIII (1874), 155-157.

[92] "A Proposed Testing Laboratory," *Scientific American*, May 23, 1874, 1.

[93] "Stevens Institute of Technology," *Scientific American*, Oct. 24, 1874, 1.

[94] "International Exhibition of 1876: the Exhibit of the Stevens Institute of Technology," *Scientific American Supplement*, no. 45 (1876), 704-5.

tematically discover the most efficient applications to provide the stimulus for industrial development. This scientific engineering, they thought, could be achieved by government support, as in France and Germany, for technical research and technical education programs. Later, this shared vision was important as part of the underlying reason why Holley and Thurston teamed up as the major founders of the American Society of Mechanical Engineers (ASME).[95]

The Holley-Thurston friendship was based on other shared interests besides their vision. They were both Brown University graduates, and both were prolific technical writers. By 1875, Holley was the foremost steel production engineer in the country, holding ten patents for improving the Bessemer process. Thurston had a similar talent for technical writing for the general reading public in magazines, and he shared Holley's interest in iron and steel -- in 1870, Thurston had written an acclaimed series of articles in the *Journal of the Franklin Institute* on "Iron Manufactures in Great Britain."

Congress funded the new "Iron and Steel Board" through the Ordnance Bureau of the War Department, and the board consisted of three military engineers and three civilians, the most prominent of the latter being Holley and Thurston. Although frustrated with the board for its narrow focus and lack of follow-up funds after initial funding ran out, Thurston, as secretary, took a leading role in its accomplishments. It built a materials testing machine of 800,000 pounds capacity at the Watertown Arsenal in Massachusetts, an act acclaimed as a watershed in engineering testing research in the United States.[96] A second project was to test wrought iron, chain anchor cable, and tool steels for the U.S. Navy.

Most important for Thurston was the third project awarded to his Mechanical Laboratory to test the mechanical properties and physical relations of copper, tin, and zinc alloys as well as engine lubricants. Federal funds for the testing of the strength of materials dated to the 1830s when a grant was made to the Franklin Institute for that purpose. But Thurston's grant may be the first federal military research contract to an academic institution of higher learning. During the years 1875-77 when the research was conducted at Stevens Institute, Thurston devised a new and systematic approach to determine the physical properties and strengths of alloys of copper, zinc and tin with his so-called glyptic experimental system illustra-

[95] Bruce Sinclair, *A Centennial History of the ASME, 1880-1980*(ASME, 1980), 39.

[96] G. Lanza, "A Brief Review of the State of Testing in the U.S.," *Proc. American Section of the International Association for Testing Materials,* IV (1904), 215 and A. L. Holley, "The U.S. Testing Machine at the Watertown Arsenal," *Trans. AIME,* VII (1878), 256-66.

ted with diagrams. These diagrams used three-composition coordinates which exhibited at a glance any specified physical quality of a given alloy. They became standard in presenting results of alloy studies thereafter.[97] Thurston later published the results of this work in a 582-page U.S. Government document with the aid of his laboratory assistant, William Kent of the Stevens class of 1876.[98]

Kent was just one of many Stevens graduates whose successful careers were based on technical-report writing as well as testing research in the Mechanical Laboratory under Thurston. Kent became editor of *American Manufacturer and Iron World,* associate editor of *Engineering News,* and later editor of *Industrial Engineering* and he wrote the popular *Mechanical Engineers Pocket Book* (1895). Kent formed the Pittsburgh Testing Laboratory with another graduate of Thurston's laboratory, William F. Zimmermann, Stevens class of 1876, and the facility was a pioneer private company in commercial physical testing. Kent was also the first of a long line of Stevens graduates who were executives of the boiler manufacturers Babcock and Wilcox Company for whom he served as engineer of tests. Kent went on to be the foremost consulting engineer in combustion design of boilers, an area in which he held patents for a wing-wall furnace and a gas producer. Later, he also specialized in cost-accounting and scientific management, and he was also Dean of Applied Science at Syracuse University.[99] After Kent left the laboratory in 1877, Thurston's main salaried employees were James Denton 1876, William Geyer Ph.D. 1877, Adam Riesenberger 1876, and later David S. Jacobus 1884, all of whom later became professors at Stevens.

According to Kent, Thurston's workload and worries about funding for his programs caused nervous exhaustion in 1876, especially during wrangles with the Ordnance Bureau over continued funding, and the study of alloys were only completed with monetary contributions from the professor himself. After the end of the project in 1879, Thurston was active publishing articles on experiments on boilers and steam engines and had time to write a well-received and lengthy history of the steam engine. In 1879, Thurston's

---

[97] "Robert Henry Thurston," *Dictionary of American Biography,* VIII, 519.

[98] *Report on a Preliminary Investigation of the Properties of Copper-tin-zinc Alloys in the Mechanical Laboratory of Stevens Institute of Technology Made Under the Direction of the Committee on Metal Alloys, U.S. Board to Test Iron and Steel and Other Metals.* Robert H. Thurston, chairman. Washington D.C. U.S. Printing Office, 1879. The award to Stevens to test lubricants was made by the board's Committee on Abrasive Wear, *Scientific American Supplement,* no. 45, Nov. 4, 1876, 704-5.

[99] "William Kent," *Dictionary of American Biography;* "Obituary, William Kent," *Stevens Indicator,* XXXV (1918), 261; "Obituary, William Kent," *Trans. ASME,* XL (1918).

penchant for pushing himself led to a more severe breakdown which necessitated complete rest for several months when he found it hard to concentrate for more than five minutes a day. During this absence, Denton was in charge of the Mechanical Laboratory.[100] Thurston had completely recovered the next year when he was elected first president of the American Society of Mechanical Engineers at a meeting at Stevens Institute. By his own account of the Mechanical Laboratory's historical significance in an annual ASME presidential address in 1881, he said that his methods of inspection of strength and quality of industrial materials developed in 1871-72 were adopted in the Watertown Arsenal testing machine and generally accepted by the government, by industry, and by other engineering schools by the late 1870s. He said that the laboratory was a consultant to the Pennsylvania Railroad and to the Bethlehem Iron Company when those concerns created their own private testing laboratories to evaluate finished products or raw materials offered to them for sale.

In the same address, Thurston alluded to the testing of an Edison "Jumbo" dynamo built in nearby Menlo Park in 1879-80 for Edison's first central station for incandescent light, the historic Pearl Street Station in New York City.[101] During the pioneering years of electrical engineering in the late 1870s and early 1880s, the institute's Mechanical Laboratory became increasingly involved in pioneering testing of electrical equipment. As early as the autumn of 1877, James Denton, assisted by sophomores John W. Lieb and George Meade Bond, both of the class of 1880, were conducting tests of brightness of Brush arc lamps with a photometer designed and constructed at Stevens.[102] During 1877, Kent designed, and undergraduates built and tested, an autographic dynamometer for measuring the efficiency of the mechanical torque power of dynamos. In 1879, the pioneering dynamo makers Brush, Maxim and Weston all commissioned tests of their dynamos by the laboratory.[103] In 1884, Stevens president Henry Morton brought a sizable electrical contract to the Mechanical Laboratory from the Chicago National Exhibition of Railway Appliances for evaluations of the large dynamos of the Weston Company in Newark, New Jersey; the Mechanical Laboratory was refitted for these tests with steam engines, belts and shafting for transmission of power from the engines to the dynamos, and new dynamometers -- the lab had to be extended by one thousand square feet to

---

[100] William Kent, "Dr. Thurston in Literature and Research," *Trans. ASME,* XXXII (1910), 61-7.

[101] R. H. Thurston, "Annual Address as President," *Trans. ASME,* II (1881), 418-9 and 435.

[102] George Orrok, "John William Lieb; An Apostle of Light and Power," *Stevens Indicator,* XLVII (1930), 6-8.

[103] William Kent, "An autographic Transmitting Dynamometer," *Trans. AIME,* VIII (1879), 177-80.

accommodate this equipment and the dynamos, their mountings, and their circuitry. The research team included the newly promoted Professor Denton, Professor of Engineering Practice Coleman Sellers, and Instructor Geyer. Outside consultants for the project included Professor Brackett of Princeton and Professor Thomas of the University of Missouri. Brackett designed the method of testing and a special mounting to hold the dynamos, and Thomas built a galvanometer to test levels of current. Many of the coils, switches, and other electrical equipment were designed and built by Brackett and Geyer, the latter becoming Stevens's first professor of electrical engineering or "Applied Electricity" as it was called, in the same year. This was the first project of the Mechanical Laboratory which involved a multidisciplinary research team from several institutions.[104]

Another spinoff from the Mechanical Laboratory was invention of a measuring machine which had a large impact on increasing production of interchangeable parts during the age of mass production in the period from 1880 through World War I. This machine was the famous Rogers-Bond comparator. Comparators of the time employed micrometer screws and calipers with optical devices for accurate measurement of incredibly short lengths. They were used by the machine tool makers and the manufacturers who used machine tools to accurately reproduce interchangeable parts. For large manufacturers, comparators had replaced the simpler micrometers. The latter had been used by the pioneers in interchangeable parts -- French, English and American musket and pistol manufacturers -- and micrometers were still in use in smaller machine shops on tasks which did not necessitate more precise measurement.[105] However, the comparators in use in 1879 still lacked sufficient accuracy, were too expensive, and were difficult to use without human error. Moreover, the standard lengths of meters and yards from which they were set were also not precise enough for industry. In an 1877 report, J. E. Hilgard, chief of the U.S. Geodetic Survey that oversaw the nineteenth-century forerunner to the Bureau of Standards, the U.S. Bureau of Weights and Measures, found that the federal government's bronze alloy standard imperial yard was shorter than the official standard imperial yard kept in London.[106] In practical terms, this situation resulted in nuts which sometimes failed to fit bolts -- precisely what the Master (railroad) Car Builders' Association was complaining about since the early

[104] News items in *Stevens Indicator*, I, 10-11, and II, 17.

[105] Aubrey F. Burstall, *A History of Mechanical Engineering* (1965), 220.

[106] J. E. Hilgard, *Methods and Results, American Standards of Length* (U.S. Geodetic Survey, 1877), 33-5.

1870s. Its complaint was taken up by Hilgard and by the American Society for the Advancement of Science.

The first step was to obtain new accurate physical standards -- pieces of metal with exact highly polished surfaces -- based on the imperial yard and meter in Europe. For this job, the American Academy of Arts and Sciences chose William A. Rogers (1832-1898), a physicist, mathematician and astronomer who specialized in the optical methods of determining precise minute lengths. With funding from premier machine tool manufacturer Pratt and Whitney, he carefully obtained accurate copies of the meter and the imperial yard in Europe and found them superior to the federal government's copies upon his return. The next step was to design and make an improved comparator, one based on optical observation, using a microscope to measure lines 2,500 to the inch inscribed with a diamond point on hardened steel -- a much more accurate method than the use of calipers in previous comparators.[107] Rogers needed a skilled mechanical engineer to design the "optical calipering" comparator which Pratt and Whitney was going to manufacture. Through consultations with James Denton, Rogers found George Meade Bond 1880 (1852-1935) to do the job even though he had not graduated from Stevens yet.

Denton recommended Bond because he was not only an exceptional student but had been a machinist, taught the old apprenticeship way, for seven years before entering Stevens in 1876 at the age of twenty-four. Bond had been chosen to do responsible research work in the Mechanical Laboratory, and he was respected by A. M. Mayer, Stevens's physics professor, for his dedication to scientific inquiry. The design drawings for the Rogers-Bond Universal Comparator were subsequently made by Bond at Stevens Institute in 1880.[108] Pratt and Whitney then hired Bond to oversee the production of the comparator. Subsequently, he became Pratt and Whitney's engineering executive for gauges and tests, as well as the company's representative to professional societies and its main lecturer on product lines. Because it was immensely popular with manufacturers, this comparator was still in general use when Bond died in 1935, its use continuing in machine shops even though physical standards were replaced by those based on wavelengths of light, the basis of modern comparators by that time.[109]

---

[107] George Meade Bond, *Standards of Length and Their Subdivisions; Standards of Length as Applied to Gauge Dimensions; Two Lectures Delivered Before the Franklin Institute in Philadelphia in 1884*(1887), 42-44.

[108] Charles C. Tyler, "George Meade Bond," *ASCE Memoir*, no. 503; also *ASCE Transactions*, 100 (1935), 1605-8.

[109] "G. M. Bond, Inventor, is Dead at 82," *Hartford Courant*, Jan. 8, 1935.

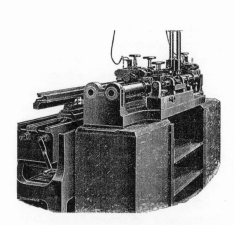

The Rogers-Bond Universal Comparator, left, built by George Meade Bond
when he was an undergraduate at Stevens, has been credited with providing
the means for American manufacturers to mass produce interchangeable parts.
At Stevens, an endowed professorship exists to honor Bond, right.

Another instrument inventor who worked in the Mechanical Laboratory
under Thurston was William H. Bristol, 1884 (1859-1930) who was professor of mathematics at Stevens from 1888 to 1899. He was an inventive
genius in instruments and held over one hundred patents. He is credited
with being one of the pioneering applicators of the bimetallic principle to
the measurement of electrical quantities, the inventor of the helical pressure
element adopted in the manufacture of all pressure-indicating and pressure-
recording instruments, and with inventing the first practical pyrometer for
measuring high temperatures in combustion chambers. He made a fortune
with these and other inventions through the Bristol Manufacturing Co.,
which specialized in recording instruments like the steam engine indicator
which made a graphic chart of steam pressure inside engine cylinders. In
1915, the laboratories of Bristol Manufacturing Co. spent $1,500,000 on
experiments with talking pictures which resulted in the company manufacturing a line of electronics products, amplifiers, and speakers. During
World War I, Bristol Manufacturing Co. had the largest and most complete
line of industrial instruments in the world, including aircraft instruments
developed for the War Department.[110]

---

[110] "Bristol, William Henry," *National Cyclopaedia of American Biography,* XXVI (1939), 26-8.

In 1885 when Robert H. Thurston left Stevens to take over the leadership of the Sibley College of Engineering and Mechanic Arts at Cornell University, President Morton assumed the directorship of the Mechanical Laboratory which was renamed the Department of Tests. Denton was made Professor of Experimental Engineering and Superintendent of Tests and David S. Jacobus 1884 was his full-time assistant for fifteen years before also becoming a Stevens professor. During the period when the laboratory was called the Department of Tests from 1885 to 1908, some noteworthy contracts came from larger corporations: Investigations of boiler scale for Babcock and Wilcox Company, analysis of lubricants for the Standard Oil Company, and tests of lamps and other equipment for General Electric and Westinghouse. Stevens's *bureau veritas,* as faculty called it, also examined the safety of commercial equipment for insurance companies, underwriters, and industry-wide societies interested in standardization and codification.[111]

The modestly larger contracts generated by Thurston's more fundamental research for the government were not forthcoming, and revenues generated by the Department of Tests started to decline around 1892. During the six years from 1887 to 1892, the average income was about ten thousand dollars per year. This yearly average represented approximately twenty percent of faculty salaries and approximately fifteen percent of the overall institute budget for the period. With faculty salaries ranging from $1500 to $3500, with full-time laboratory assistants' wages ranging from $600 to $1200, and with janitorial wages ranging from $350 to $450 per year, one can assume that the revenues generated by the Department of Tests were an important support for faculty salaries and the institute's laboratory facilities and equipment. When revenue started to decline, the institute's catalogs from 1894 to 1908 resorted to lengthy and persuasive advertising in place of Thurston's modest ads, claiming that the demand by industry for testing was being met, that "all the facilities of the institute could be brought to bear upon the solution of any particular problem."[112] With the start of research laboratories by General Electric, Westinghouse, and even modest-sized companies, and with the start of systematic testing by the federal government in its Bureau of Standards by 1902, the income from the Department of Tests declined steadily during the years 1892 to 1908. Finally, in 1908 the Department of Tests was discontinued, thus ending the last vestige of Thurston's brilliant pioneering research facility.[113]

---

[111] *Stevens Indicator,* IV, 6, 24-7, 182-4, VI, 250, 252-3, VII, 286, VIII, 261, and F. DeR.Furman, *Morton Memorial*(1905), 212 and 239.

[112] For example, *Annual Catalogue of the Stevens Institute,* 1894, 45.

[113] *Minutes of the SIT Board of Trustees,* Books II and III, see yearly budgets.

CHAPTER 5

Stevens Leads ASME, Creates Codes

O n the morning of April 7, 1880, some eighty of the most prestigious American engineers arrived in Hoboken by train or ferry and either walked or took a horse and buggy or a horse-drawn streetcar over the cobblestoned streets to the Stevens campus. There, they entered the gas-lit Stevens Institute auditorium to attend the organizational meeting of the American Society of Mechanical Engineers (ASME), the first professional society for mechanical engineers inspired by Alexander Lyman Holley and Robert H. Thurston.

This building was simply called Stevens Institute of Technology when the ASME held its organizational meeting in its auditorium. After the institute built other buildings, it was known as the A-Building before it was renamed the Edwin A. Stevens Building in the 1990s.

Everything went smoothly because there had been a previous planning meeting on February 16, 1880 in the offices of the *American Machinist* in New York City. After the planning meeting, Holley had asked Henry Morton for use of the Stevens auditorium. Morton was an enthusiastic supporter, later becoming an ASME vice president, and he consented to host the organizational meeting.[114] Stevens was an appropriate setting not only because it was at the forefront of education and research in mechanical engineering, but also because of its location just across the river from Manhattan. The metropolitan area of New York City was at the center of engineering establishments on the eastern seaboard and was home to the offices of many engineers at the first meeting. Also, New York was the publishing center for technical journals and magazines whose editors were backers of the new society, for example, the editor of *Iron Age,* James C. Bayles, was secretary of the meeting at Stevens.[115]

Many of these engineers had met before through the Franklin Institute, the American Society of Civil Engineers (ASCE), and the American Institute of Mining Engineers (AIME). For example, Holley had been president of AIME in 1875, and Thurston had been vice president from 1875 to 1879.[116] Moreover, they had read the same journals like the *Journal of the Franklin Institute* or *American Machinist.* They either knew each other or knew of each other and were a sort of club during the early years of the ASME.[117] Besides the educators, the organizational group included many engineer-industrialists like the machine-tool manufacturer Coleman Sellers who at the time was chief engineer for William Sellers and Co., and Francis A. Pratt of Pratt and Whitney. Also participating were Henry R. Worthington, the foremost pump manufacturer, George Babcock of Babcock and Wilcox, the largest American boiler manufacturer, and Charles Porter, a steam engine manufacturer and plant engineer.

None of the prior professional organizations were dedicated to mechanical engineering. By the 1870s, mechanical engineers recognized that their economic success depended on technical knowledge, and a need existed for an organization in their field to discuss, synthesize, and disseminate advanced research work so that it could be applied in industry effectively. At that time, the training of mechanical engineers through apprenticeship in industrial machine shops was common practice, but the science-based education, especially when it combined theory and practice with useful research was increasingly respected. Thus, the new organization served the function of bringing industrialists and supervisory managers together with educators. Another need was to rationalize industrial practices by establishing common standards. The call by William Sellers in 1863 for a com-

---

[114] J. H. Potter, "The American Society of Mechanical Engineers," in unpublished typescript entitled "The Stevens Story," (1977) in Stevens Special Collections, 3-4.

[115] Bruce Sinclair, *A Centennial History of the American Society of Mechanical Engineers, 1880-1980*(ASME, 1980), 23.

[116] *Ibid.,* 27.

[117] *Ibid.,* 24.

mon screw-thread had indicated the need to overcome the chaos of regional differences in sizes of even simple manufactured items. Another compelling stimulus for the formation of the ASME was the desire to attain recognition for mechanical engineering as a profession of equal standing with civil engineering -- at the time the public and the civil engineers tended to regard mechanical engineers as being of lower status.

This meeting adopted rules for the governing structure of the ASME in addition to presenting a slate of names for the first ASME officers -- Thurston was nominated to be the ASME's first president and Coleman Sellers to be one of the six vice presidents. After the election, the highlight of the first annual meeting held in New York City on November 4, 1880, was Thurston's inspiring inaugural speech which set forth a vision of the exalted stature of a professional mechanical engineer and his place in the world of the future. Thurston credited the English philosopher Herbert Spencer (1820-1903) for his ideas by mentioning Spencer by name in several places in the speech.

Spencer had been a civil engineer and a journalist before he was recognized as a philosopher. His *First Principles*(1860-62) was already immensely popular in English and American engineering circles as well as among the middle classes.[118] It is difficult to comprehend the popularity of Spencer since he has been dismissed, ignored, and discredited because of his social Darwinism.[119] However, that popularity was evident at a banquet in New York in 1882 attended by Spencer and many of the New York engineering and financial elite at which the philosopher was toasted as "the greatest philosopher" to address the "problems of science now everywhere recognized as legitimate, immanent, and inevitable."[120] Too often ignored today was Spencer's appeal during the heyday of faith, of belief and conviction, that men of science were going to lead the world into its "inevitable" condition of peace and prosperity for all, that engineers and scientists were the rational "brains" who would correct the incidental ills of modern society while effecting the progressive solutions through ever-increasing provision of goods and the rationalization of society. Spencer was much better known and more quoted than Adam Smith or John Stuart Mill, and, among engineers, superseded some of their other favorites like Jeremy Bentham.

---

[118] James P. Shenton, *History of the United States from 1865 to the Present*(1964), 100; Robert H. Wiebe, *The Search for Order, 1877-1920*(1967), 136-48; and Calvert, *Op. Cit.*, 269.

[119] Henry D. Aiken, *The Age of Ideology*(1956), 161-80.

[120] E. L. Youmans, *Herbert Spencer on the Americans and the Americans on Herbert Spencer; Report on the Farewell Banquet of Nov. 11, 1882*(New York, 1883), 73.

It was Spencer's focus on the progressive role of science and technology and the ethics that derived from such a view that drew engineering leaders like Thurston to him. First, Spencer believed that scientific method was the sole method underlying human knowledge, that knowledge was limited to space and time, and that other than empirical knowledge was unknowable. Second, Spencer believed that mankind was progressing through an evolutionary development for the better; essentially, he thought that mankind had developed from savage societies through militaristic societies characterized by war and myth to an industrial society based on scientific knowledge. He thought industrial society was increasingly differentiated, organized, and individualistic. Using analogies to science, Spencer found that during the process there is increased integration and cooperation, thus decreasing the possibility of social conflict and war. In this evolution, mankind would progress along the line of "least resistance," as "Matter and Motion" were redistributed, and end in "equilibrium," in an integrated, complex, but "cooperative" society. Third, Spencer believed that scientific engineering intelligence would bring forth such integration and cooperation through rational and systematic organization of the increasing division of labor. In this context, each human being would find that intelligence would be a mediator, not "militaristic," and that it would systematize a society characterized by free trade, production, and cooperation. Fourth, Spencer's proposed ethical code followed from his evolutionary view and was geared to industrial societies. One should direct one's efforts towards the general happiness through altruistic furtherance of the inevitable historical trend, promote social peace and prosperity through scientific knowledge and resulting cooperative conduct.

As Thurston put it in his speech, Spencer's "ethics of cooperation," his "principles of morality," his "data on ethics" fostered right conduct or "scientifically correct conduct." Such an ethic "leads to care of self, of family, of friends, of fellow citizens and mankind in such a way as to protect the interests of each individual. This promotion of the mutual welfare is the truest and highest calling."[121] Thurston thought that mechanical engineers should use science to increase productive capacities, supply all groups in society with cheaper goods in greater numbers, and, thus make improvements in the overall wealth of mankind. Scientific engineering research would "hasten the approach of that great day when we shall have acquired a complete and symmetrical system of mechanical and scientific philosophy." The ASME should both generate and disseminate technical knowledge by encouraging research and publishing members' papers. Moreover, the

---

[121] "Inaugural Address of Robert H. Thurston," *ASME Trans.* I (1880), 27-8.

membership should follow those who realized that the highest utilitarian functions, the "greatest good for the greatest number," came from education of the people in scientific methods. He went on to suggest that the ASME take up Spencer's ethics of cooperation as its professional standard.

Thurston's speech earned a resounding and enthusiastic ovation. As the historian of the ASME, Bruce Sinclair, has written, "Thurston's vision, of an association of professional men dedicated to America's technological preeminence and to a standard of material abundance for the country beyond any in the world, was as powerful as it was irresistible. His inaugural address was a marvelous performance, ideally suited to the occasion and full of insight into the needs of mechanical engineers and their employers. He had, as it were, conjured up a whole organization complete with membership, function, style and philosophy."[122] Moreover, Thurston later took his Spencerian vision to popular magazines and journals in scores of articles. These articles must have had considerable influence on promoting the status of engineers, particularly among the middle classes. In the words of Robert H. Wiebe a historian of American culture, in speaking of Spencer and popularized social Darwinism, "Equal opportunity for each man; a test of individual merit; wealth as a reward for virtue; credit for hard work, frugality, and dedication; a premium on efficiency; a government that minded its own business; a belief in society's progressive improvement; these and many more read like a catalogue of mid-nineteenth century values."[123]

If the ASME in the early years was a kind of club of like-minded engineers, it was also a kind of club for Stevens men who formed the major part of the critical mass of early leaders needed by the fledgling enterprise whose offices were in nearby New York City. In the thirty-eight years from 1880 to 1918, there were only two years, 1894-95, when a Stevens professor, graduate, or trustee did not hold a position of leadership in the ASME: In those years, presidents were Thurston (1880-82); a trustee, Henry R. Towne (1889-90); Frederick W. Taylor 1883 (1906-07), Stevens's second president, Alexander C. Humphreys 1881 (1912-13); and D. S. Jacobus (1916-17). Vice presidents were Henry Morton (1882-84), Towne (1884-86), William Kent (1888-90), Professor Wood (1889-91), Jacobus (1903-05), Taylor (1904-05), John W. Lieb 1880 (1907-08), Pratt and Whitney engineer George Meade Bond 1880 (1909-10), Humphreys (1911-12), and H. L. Gantt 1884 (1914-15). Managers were first Stevens Alumni Association president William Hewitt 1874 (1884-87), Bond (1888-91), Professor

---

[122] Sinclair, *Op. Cit.,* 32.
[123] Wiebe, *Op. Cit.,* 136.

Denton (1889-92), Professor Sellers (1890-93), Towne and Yale Lock Company's Gustavus C. Henning 1876 (1896-99), Jacobus (1900-03), Lieb (1903-06), Richard H. Rice 1885 (1904-07), Humphreys (1908-10), Gantt (1909-11), and Harry deB. Parsons 1884 (1916-18).[124] In addition, Anson W. Burchard 1885 was chairman of the finance committee in 1908.

The first major action of the ASME in its first year, its official condemnation of any attempt by the federal government to replace the Anglo-American yard measure with the metric system, came from the influence of big business. Unlike most scientists and electrical engineers who favored metric, the manufacturers in mechanical engineering were vehement in rejecting metric. Long before the ASME was founded, American metal-working businesses had opposed metric from the time it became an issue during the administration of Thomas Jefferson. Later, the machine tool manufacturer who had made Philadelphia the center of American machine building, William Sellers, had led the fight against legal adoption of the metric system in 1864 as president of the Franklin Institute. In rejecting metric, he carefully stressed that standards in measurement must be decided above all on economic considerations. If metric were made mandatory, it would make continental European machine tools in metric sizes competitive in the United States, and it would necessitate redesign of all of American machine tools which had calibrations and dimensions in inches. Not only that, it would cause economic loss to the buyers of the machine tools: the manufacturers of machines and metal goods, who would need new ones. Also, there would be retraining costs for machinists who were used to inches and feet. Other major American machine tool companies, like Pratt and Whitney in Hartford, and Brown and Sharpe in Providence, agreed with Sellers as did most mechanical engineers. As a result, in 1866 the federal government did not replace the English measure with metric, but only made it a legal standard alongside the English measure. By 1880 the issue was not dead, because scientists and academics and the emerging electrical engineering community continued to press for legislation to replace English measures with the metric system.

Thus, in 1880 Coleman Sellers started the ASME on its long anti-metric lobbying which made it the most powerful organizational force to prevent the adoption of metric as the sole U.S. measure. He delivered a paper that concluded metric was no better than the English system and would come at a frightful changeover cost. Subsequently, a resolution was drawn up: "The Society deprecates any legislation tending to make obligatory the introduction of the metric system of measurement into our industrial establish-

---

[124] Compare *Ibid,* 227-245 with *Stevens Alumni Association; Alumni Directory 1995*(1995).

ments." A mail ballot was sent out to the membership and they voted 111 in favor and only 24 against. The resolution was used to lobby Congress to table the issue.[125] When the issue was again revived on a national basis by pro-metric forces in 1896, the ASME council appointed a committee to prepare material in "opposition to legislation seeking to make the Metric System and its use compulsory in the United States." Its members were Professor Coleman Sellers, Bond of Pratt and Whitney, Charles T. Porter, and John E. Sweet.[126] Shortly thereafter, this committee was sent by the ASME to testify in opposition to the metric system before the Congressional Committee on Coinage, Weights and Measures.[127] In spite of the pro-metric forces which included the federal government's U.S. Bureau of Standards after its creation in 1901, the ASME continued to use effective actions to block legislation which would have made the metric system the sole standard of measurement in the Unites States.

Just as important were the reforms of the society's headquarters operations when Frederick W. Taylor 1883 brought his scientific management techniques to bear when he was president of the ASME in 1906-07. Taylor standardized the ASME's office routines by creating standard forms for accounting, and he set forth a code of standards spelling out duties of officers and of standing committees. Taylor's reforms were essentially conservative and did not change the New York orientation of the leadership, but in fact promoted it. He thought that only members who were within close reach of New York would be able to be effective, so he continued to pick them for leadership and committee positions.

Taylor's assistant, Morris L. Cooke, became a thorn in the side of the older club members with his constant agitation for reform of the leadership from 1908-1918. Cooke criticized the ASME's "undemocratic procedures, and the control exercised over it by New York big business."[128] In the early years, the nominating committee was an oligarchy which had no regional representation and which produced only one name for each position. Until 1911, the council had policies which discouraged formation of local sections, but after that date, portions of the dues were returned to support local section activity.

Cooke was also against big business because he believed that service and social responsibility were necessary ideals for engineers in general. Cooke was a Lehigh graduate in mechanical engineering who became the most

---

[125] Calvert, Op. Cit., 178-181.
[126] Ibid., 182.
[127] Tyler, Op. Cit., 2
[128] Sinclair, Op. Cit., 105.

liberal disciple of Taylor. He was influenced by the Progressive Movement in politics, but he went much further than most Progressives in advocating radical reforms. Cooke took on the utilities by supporting a petition for smoke abatement in 1909. By 1915, in an ASME paper called "Some Factors in Municipal Engineering," he implied that executives in public utilities could not be trusted to sit on municipal public service commissions and remain unbiased. During discussion after the reading of the paper, this statement resulted in a row and confrontation with Stevens's second president, who served from 1902 to 1927.

Alexander C. Humphreys (1851-1927) was born in Edinburgh, Scotland. He was educated in his father's school in Boston. A self-made man, he started working in insurance companies at the age of fourteen, and he was so capable that he was made Secretary-Treasurer of the New York Guaranty and Indemnity Company by 1872 at the age of twenty-one. Subsequently he became an executive with the Bayonne Gas Light Company, and, to obtain technical knowledge for this job, he entered Stevens as a part-time student, obtaining an M.E. degree in six years in 1881 at the age of thirty. By 1892 he had set up a company, Humphreys and Glasgow and Co., with Arthur G. Glasgow of the Stevens class of 1885. This company, based in New York City, designed and constructed gas plants in all parts of the world, and, by 1915, Humphreys was a prominent consultant to gas utilities, as well as a member of many of their boards, and president of others. This was in addition to his being president of Stevens Institute. A conscientious and moral man who had donated his extraordinary energy to such activities as being a Presbyterian Church treasurer, sunday-school supervisor, and a member of the volunteer fire department in the 1870s and 1880s, he was infuriated by Cooke's insinuations that men like himself could not serve municipalities impartially. His reaction to Cooke, namely, reporting him to the ASME's ethics committee, unfortunately resulted in him being branded as one of the ASME's arch-conservatives even though he had supported Cooke on the issue of smoke abatement.[129]

Humphreys's side of the story is given in a long letter to Frederick W. Taylor after the incident. Humphreys wrote that although he was president of the Buffalo Gas Co. he had been called as an expert witness by cities to testify in cases against utilities as well as testify for them. He said that Cooke had personally attacked him, that Cooke

. . . places me in a group of educators who are paid by the public service corporations to lecture and write in their interests. I find that I'm in good company,

---

[129] *Ibid.*, 97, 103.

including Dean Cooley of Michigan University, and Prof. Swain of Harvard. It is also intimated that I was made President of Stevens Institute to give me a standing for my part in this propaganda. The lecture is filled with silly charges and insinuations, every one of which could be met successfully before a fair tribunal . . . I have never directly or indirectly been paid for a lecture, address, or talk except once, and that exception was a talk at Harvard for which the authorities insisted ungraciously in sending me $50.00, and which I had to accept or be also ungracious, which check I turned over to the Stevens Athletic Fund.[130]

Even though Cooke was outmaneuvered by Humphreys and others, the creation of regional sections led to reforms in election procedures. By 1918, the New York area membership no longer dominated the leadership. Membership grew in local sections around the country, especially between 1915 and 1920 when it doubled, and more engineers from this regional base showed up in leadership positions. However, big business remained most influential within the ASME, because it employed the bulk of all mechanical engineers. In the early years, big business was represented by the older elite engineering-entrepreneurs who had been trained in apprenticeships in shops, but increasingly it was represented by engineering managers of large corporations.

The first generation of ASME members had an even bigger impact by creating the first ASME codes -- considered the ASME's most important work then and now. The codes established standards where no standards existed before. The need for standards was apparent in everything from the confusion of pipe and pipe-thread sizes to the continuing problem of boilers bursting. The problem for early ASME members was not whether there should be standards, because all agreed there should be, but it was how the process of arriving at standards should be done and by whom. Stevens graduates were at the center of this pioneering work to create the first ASME codes and therefore in establishing the procedures for the way ASME codes were subsequently established. There was disagreement among the members about procedure, but by World War I a procedure was firmly in place, namely, codes were the result of reports of ASME committees of industrial representatives rather than by general ASME endorsement. More importantly for the manufacturers, the standards were being made through their representatives in the ASME rather than by federal legislation or by the federal government's Bureau of Standards. The latter could endorse the codes or use them, but it was important that private

---

[130] Humphreys to Taylor and Fred J. Miller, Mar. 15, 1915, Taylor Papers, Stevens Special Collections.

61

industry should be intimately involved in their creation for economic reasons.

The question of what procedure the ASME should use to establish standards arose in 1882 when George Meade Bond asked the ASME to endorse Pratt and Whitney's machine to measure threads on screws. In spite of the acceptance of the Sellers-thread sizes by Congress in the 1860s, in practice there was still confusion on the shop floor because the manufacturers of taps and dyes, and of gauges did not always use Sellers's standard tools. Pratt and Whitney had produced a gauge intended to solve this problem for the whole industry. Bond was appealing to the ASME to give an "impartial verdict as to its accuracy and practicability."[131] In spite of widespread support for the instrument as a way of establishing the Sellers standard in practice, William Kent and Robert H. Thurston spoke against endorsements which had obvious commercial value to a member of the professional society. Kent made the suggestion which would ultimately result in the ASME procedure for setting standards, namely, to refer the matter to a committee of experts whose findings would be published without endorsement in *ASME Transactions.*[132]

William Kent was also involved in the initial problem of standards for boilers. Here again there were obvious commercial gains to be made by companies which claimed they had a superior product. But these claims were made on the basis of manufacturer's tests, and these tests differed from company to company. Kent's solution as a first step was to head a committee to determine a standard procedure for testing boilers, because there would be no standards in boilers until uniform test procedures existed -- a fact which Kent knew as a specialist in testing boilers for Babcock and Wilcox. Subsequently, Kent's committee report presented a rational set of test procedures which could be agreed upon by all the concerned parties. In part, this acceptance was based on his emphasis on practical utility. For example, his committee recommended the units of boiler power of the 1876 centennial exhibition which were widely used at the time.

Members of the ASME were so enthusiastic about Kent's report that the council decided to seek formal endorsement by a mail ballot as in the case of the metric question. But Thurston used his prestige to overturn this decision on the grounds that, as in the case of a recommended code, "If the report be right, it will be accepted by the profession, whether endorsed by

---

[131] Quoted in Sinclair, *Op. Cit.,* 49.
[132] *Ibid.*

the society or not; if wrong, the Society cannot help it, and will only be injured by its formal endorsement."[133]

Thurston's reasoning was the most clear statement justifying the eventual procedures set up to establish any ASME codes whether they were about testing procedures or standards; they should not be codes endorsed by a vote of the membership, but rather recommended standards from ASME committee reports, which, because of their professional scientific excellence, should be accepted by industry in a spirit of cooperation. But there was still a problem of terminology. By 1895 when Thurston's policy was widely recognized, the membership was referring to these standards based on committee reports as the ASME's "standard codes" or "code of rules," and so arose the linguistic custom of calling them "ASME Codes" in spite of the fact that they were committee recommendations. Nonetheless, Thurston and his protégé Kent were the main creators of the ASME's delicate procedure of arriving at standards by reports of committees instead of general endorsement by the society. They devised the ASME tradition of arriving at standards based on the best previous practices of expert engineers in the particular field. This procedure was in accordance with Thurston's Spencerian vision for the ASME, that industrial practice would inevitably evolve through voluntary cooperation between industrialists and engineers using precise scientific data and rigorous methods.

Another ASME effort was the adoption of international standards for testing the strength of materials. In 1885, the council appointed a committee on strength of materials consisting of Thurston, Gustavus C. Henning 1876, Henning's boss Henry R. Towne (later a Stevens trustee) who ran the Yale and Towne Lock Co., Charles H. Morgan, and Thomas Egleston, another academic who served as chairman. Henning had tested alloys under Thurston in the Mechanical Laboratory, and he was the engineer in charge of testing materials for Towne. This committee gathered samples of metals and sent them to firms and academic institutions willing to test them, but the results were useless because of the variation in test procedures. Then Henning attended international conferences on strength of materials in Germany and translated proceedings from conferences in Munich and Dresden on standard test procedures. In the committee's first report, Henning also included a survey of test practices in France, England, Belgium and Switzerland. Based on Henning's research, the committee subsequently created a standardized form and rigorous procedures for testing materials in America. The committee's final report was a model for all later American routine shop tests. Meanwhile, Henning became the ASME representative to inter-

---

[133] Quoted in *Ibid.*, 53.

national standards conferences and was reimbursed for his travel expenses by the society.[134]

Based on his work on international standards for the ASME, Gustavus C. Henning, one of Stevens Institute's earliest graduates in 1876, took a leading role in the founding of the American Society for Testing Materials (ASTM), and was elected its first president.

Starting around 1887 there was increasing support for organized testing of boilers based on the previous standards of testing established by Kent's committee. Pressure was coming from the newly established electric utilities which were using stationary boilers to generate steam. Concurrently, there was an investigation of standards in the connections between steam engines and dynamos. In 1898, the boiler industry's trade association led by Edward Meier created some specifications for standardizing boilers. The manufacturers of boilers by that time had an interest in standardization, because a bewildering array of state laws had been legislated to deal with the threat of explosions to the general public. These laws differed from state to state and were hampering the process of design as well as disrupting sales across state lines. Nonetheless, when Meier's report came out, boiler manufacturers objected to the specifications as a threat to their individually designed products.

Subsequently, Meier tried again when he was president of the ASME in 1911. He created a Boiler Code Committee which included representatives of boiler manufacturers, boiler users, insurance companies, and iron and steel producers. This kind of wide composition proved successful and was a model for later standards committees. When the report of the committee was sent out in 1913, serious objections from manufacturers forced the

---

[134] *Ibid.*, 57-8.

committee to withdraw it. The main objection was the committee's adoption of the laws of the state of Massachusetts as a baseline for standards. It was felt that standards were always established by the private sector in America, particularly by the manufacturers. The report was revised and sent out again in 1914, but other objections arose from those who again thought it would interfere with their business interests, and the committee was accused of not cooperating with manufacturers sufficiently.

At this point David Schenck Jacobus 1884 (1862-1955) acted as a diplomat and suggested compromises. A contemporary said Jacobus was a man who "knew how to deal with people."[135] Of Dutch Calvinist descent, Jacobus was educated in the Stevens School before entering the Institute. In 1884, he became an instructor of experimental engineering while working in the Department of Tests where his specialty was boilers. He was made a full professor of experimental engineering by 1896. Jacobus obtained his reputation as a foremost authority on testing boilers with his eighty-seven publications while at Stevens. In 1906 he went to work for Babcock and Wilcox, and by 1914 he was a respected member of the ASME, both for having served on numerous committees and having delivered many papers. In 1914 he was appointed to a subcommittee of the Boiler Code Committee by the manufacturers, and he subsequently convinced the full committee to hold open sessions so the manufacturers could participate. He cajoled one manufacturer into withdrawing his objections, and he helped to write the final draft of the committee's report which was finally accepted. He was elected president of the ASME, but, more importantly, he helped establish the stability and permanence of the Boiler Code Committee by serving as its vice chairman from 1915 to 1936 and then chairman until he retired from Babcock and Wilcox at age seventy-nine in 1941.[136]

Part of this stability was created by not changing the membership of the committee, which was like a club, each member holding a seat, as it was called. Jacobus held the Babcock and Wilcox seat for twenty six years. He was a personal friend of William Dixie Hoxie 1889, a nephew of Stephen Wilcox who had married into the Babcock family. Hoxie was made vice president in 1898 and President of this Bayonne, New Jersey company in 1919. Both Jacobus and Hoxie held many patents for improvements and new designs of boilers. In addition, Jacobus and Hoxie hired a raft of Stevens graduates, sat on the board of trustees of the institute together, and eventually had two buildings on campus named for them: a student center

---

[135] Quoted in *Ibid.*, 151.

[136] See obituary in *Stevens Indicator*, 72 (1955), 2, 59. Jacobus was a trustee of Stevens from 1909 until his death in 1955.

and dormitory, Jacobus Hall, and the house of the president of the institute, Hoxie House.

David S. Jacobus, 1884, in straw hat at top center, is seen here taking a break with his experimental engineering class at Stevens in 1900, fourteen years before he joined ASME's boiler-code committee. His teaching assistant in the class was his future fellow trustee of Stevens Institute, Robert C. Stanley, at top rear left (partially hidden).

CHAPTER 6

Genesis of Scientific Management

W ithin months of the first regular meeting of the ASME, twenty-five-year-old Fred Taylor began his two-and-a-half year, especially arranged course of home study to earn an M.E. degree from Stevens Institute of Technology. The starting date was either late in 1880 or early in 1881. Frederick W. Taylor (1856-1915) is today acclaimed (and sometimes disdained) the world over as the Father of Scientific Management. He started experiments in metal cutting in 1881, the same year he started his course of study at Stevens. These experiments of 1881 led to his stopwatch time studies of machinists who cut the metal, and therefore they were a necessary preliminary for the genesis of his system of management which took place close to the date of his graduation from Stevens in 1883.

Taylor's metal-cutting experiments didn't stop for twenty-five years and culminated in his ASME paper "On the Art of Cutting Metals" in 1906. They started after machine tool manufacturers had presented a problem which had been blocking the efficient use of machine tools by their operators. This problem was presented time and again in the *Journal of the Franklin Institute,* in books, and also in want ads and editorials in *American Machinist* in the years immediately prior to Taylor's experiments of 1881. Moreover, the articles and books presented a paradigmatic "scientific" calculation to determine efficiency of human work which was an underlying assumption in Taylor's solution to the problem.[137]

Machine tools were the lathes, planing, and boring machines whose "tools" or "bits" of hardened steel shaved off, or bored into, a spinning piece of metal. They were also machines in which the moving bit drilled into a stationary piece of metal. Historians trace their origins to age-old mill work or turning lathes which spun wood to be cut with chisels, and to clock-makers who cut tiny metal screws on primitive lathes in Europe centuries ago. However, the modern pioneers were usually in the lucrative arms industries funded by governments. In Europe, the Englishman Henry Maudslay constructed large, stable, and accurate machines for boring cannon for the Royal Navy around 1800. His assistant James Nasmyth developed an array of machine tools for the English industrial revolution, and England's Joseph Whitworth became the leading manufacturer of machine tools by

---

[137] Geoffrey W. Clark, "Machine-Shop Engineering Roots of Taylorism; The Efficiency of Machine-Tools and Machinists, 1865-1884" J.-C. Spender and Hugo Kijne, eds., *Scientific Management; Frederick W. Taylor's Gift to the World?*(Kluwer, 1996).

1850. In America, it was the armament manufacturer Eli Whitney who had led the way with machine tools and jigs that produced muskets made from interchangeable parts by the early nineteenth century and then his famous Colt revolver by 1847. Before Whitney, muskets were made individually by one skilled workman, and their parts were all especially fitted and different from those of any other individual musket.[138] By the 1860s, American makers of machine tools eclipsed Wentworth in England and became the world leaders in the accuracy of their metal-cutting machines largely as a result of huge contracts for arms during the Civil War. They were Pratt and Whitney in Hartford, Brown and Sharp in Providence, and, by 1881, the recognized industry leader was William Sellers and Co. of Philadelphia.

William Sellers established his company in 1855, and his cousin Coleman Sellers became its chief engineer from 1856 until 1886 when he became professor of engineering practice at Stevens. These two Americans took the leading role in departing from established designs of machine tools. Instead of adorning their machine tools with decorative embellishments and colors as was the custom, the Sellers's designs were wholly utilitarian and painted with what became known as machine gray. Their machine tools were also heavier and more stable than previous ones, and the company reliably provided repair parts up to fifty years after their original manufacture. Sellers machine tools consistently took top prizes in international competitions and became world renowned for their accuracy and strength. William and Coleman Sellers were the industry's leaders because they continually improved the design of their products to assure they were the most efficient on the market.[139] A machine tool's efficiency in cutting was the starting point of its redesign for improvement, and it was only as efficient as its ability to cut metal as fast as possible. Thus, machine design and efficient use, not to speak of increased sales, were motives for William Sellers's funding of metal-cutting experiments. Sellers needed to know the capacity of his machine tools in terms of work output, i.e. the maximum efficient speeds, feeds, and power needs of his machine tools to cut the most metal in the shortest time.

There was another aspect to the problem of using machine tools, namely, the efficiency of the machinists who operated them. The clearest statement on the problem of machinists was presented by Coleman Sellers in an 1872 article in the *Journal of the Franklin Institute* nearly ten years before Taylor's experiments:

---

[138] Aubrey F. Burstall, *A History of Mechanical Engineering*(MIT, 1965), 212-224.
[139] Lionel Rolt, *A Short History of Machine Tools*(MIT, 1967), 193.

The *problem of the day* (Sellers's emphasis) is not only how to secure more good workmen, but how to enable such workmen as are at our command to do good work and how to enable the really skillful mechanics to accomplish more and better work than heretofore; in other words, the attention of engineers is constantly directed to so perfect machine tools as to utilize unskilled labor. Changes for the better have to be made often in opposition to the prejudices of the workman. Such motions as screwing up the spindle of the popper head, stopping and starting feeds, setting up the slide rests, etc., are motions of habit, and should, if possible, be uniform on all lathes. No complications of motions should embarrass the workman. There should be no hesitation on the part of the workman as to which way he should move the starting gear.[140]

Thus, contrary to twentieth century critics of Taylor who say he was the one responsible for "deskilling" labor by making artisan machinists become mere operators, the deskilling process was already in the air at the time.[141] Taylor started to address the problem in 1880. In that year *American Machinist,* a journal expressing the opinion of the machinist usually, reported in an editorial that

New ways of manipulating metals, and tools for it, have laid him (the skilled machinist) on the shelf. System and contracting have taken his mechanical life. The pistol factories have bred up another class in their stead, and all shops wherein a quantity of machines of one kind are to be made, have instituted a system of machine work which requires no skilled labor and but a limited experience to operate it.[142]

In spite of these precedents, Taylor's metal-cutting experiments of 1881 were indeed literally on the technological and certainly the managerial cutting edge within the machine tool industry.[143]

Taylor was born into a wealthy family in Germantown, an exclusive suburb of Philadelphia, and his parents sent him to Phillips Exeter Academy to study the classics in preparation for law at Harvard. But having passed the entrance exam to Harvard, he decided on a career in engineering, partly because of poor eyesight and partly because engineering had fascinated him

---

[140] Coleman Sellers, "Theory and Construction of the Self-Acting Slide Lathe," *Journal of the Franklin Institute,* LXIV (1872), 106.

[141] See for example Harry Braverman, *Labor and Monopoly Capital; The Degradation of Work in the Twentieth Century*(1974), chapter 4.

[142] *American Machinist,* III (1880), 49: 8.

[143] C. D. Wrege and R. G. Greenwood, "The Early History of Midvale Steel and the Work of Frederick W. Taylor: 1865-1890," *Canal History and Technology Proceedings,* 11 (1992), March 14, 145-176.

from his youth.[144] His wealthy connections in Germantown gave him his opportunity to move up fast in his new choice of work. He was a friend of Clarence Clark, the son of Edward W. Clark whose firm, E. W. Clark and Co., was the most prestigious banking and investment firm in Philadelphia. The Clark family lived in Germantown, and Clarence Clark and Fred Taylor played tennis together, in fact winning the United States men's doubles championship in 1881. Edward W. Clark was a partner in another of William Sellers's companies, Midvale Steel Co., which manufactured cannons for the Navy as well as axles and wheels for railroad companies. By the time Taylor joined Midvale Steel in 1879, Clarence Clark had married Taylor's sister, and so Taylor was one of the owner's sons-in-law. This connection was a road to success in the Sellers-owned company, because the history of the Sellers family showed that the company recruited young men especially if they had some family connection with the owners.[145]

In those days when schooled mechanical engineers were a new phenomenon, the owners and supervising engineers of machine tool companies were of the older generation who had worked up the ranks after starting as apprentices in machine shops. Even if one was wealthy and one's father owned the company, the starting place was an apprenticeship, even though one went up through the ranks at a faster pace than a non-family member. Both William Sellers and Coleman Sellers had served in apprenticeships before attaining their positions as industrial leaders in machine tools. Thus, it was nothing extraordinary that Fred Taylor started out in an apprenticeship as a molder and patternmaker from 1875 to 1879 before entering Midvale and then working as a machinist at the benches for a couple of months before becoming clerk and then a working foreman, or gang boss in 1880.

However, William Sellers was not, as we have seen, simply a conservative member of the shop culture. Rather, he was also the president of the Franklin Institute who had turned it around into a more progressive institution promoting the application of science to mechanical engineering, a president who chose the college-educated Morton as its first permanent secretary and editor of its *Journal*. Thus, when Taylor approached William Sellers in 1880 about conducting metal-cutting tests to determine the efficiencies of machine tools scientifically, Sellers was receptive to supporting and funding them. Taylor's motive was the same as Coleman Sellers's "problem of the day," but from the perspective of the foreman: he lacked scientifically

---

[144] Best explanation of the background underlying this career change is in Robert Kanigal, *The One Best Way; Frederick Winslow Taylor and the Enigma of Efficiency*(Viking, 1997), Part I.
[145] Wallace, *Op.Cit.*, 226.

determined knowledge of how to run the machines at maximum efficiency, knowledge he needed to instruct his men on the most effective way to run machine tools in his shop.

Just prior to the experiments at Midvale Steel Co. in 1881, Taylor started his home-study course at Stevens Institute. Unfortunately, no documents exist about how the special course was set up or its related circumstances. Biographers of Taylor have guessed about his motives, such as the need for improving his status as an engineer by obtaining a degree, and also they have guessed that William Sellers and his friend Henry Morton arranged the exception to the usual four-year, rigorous program. Robert Kanigal, the latest and most comprehensive biographer of Taylor, found that Henry Morton's diaries noted meetings in Philadelphia with William Sellers around this time, that Stevens students were taken on field trips to William Sellers's companies in Philadelphia, but no evidence for a definitive explanation exists in such records as faculty minutes or Taylor's correspondence.[146]

Examination of the activity of the Mechanical Laboratory at Stevens suggests another motivation, that Taylor and perhaps Sellers were also motivated by the need for knowledge which would assure them that Taylor's experiments would be conducted with the correct method and take into consideration all the variables, some of which were beyond Taylor's knowledge at the time. What better place to obtain a degree and learn about the chemical aspects of metallurgy than at Stevens with Thurston, who was an authority on the subject? An important part of Thurston's work for the Iron and Steel Board from 1875 to 1879 involved efficiency of machine tools, and that fact was well known at the time. Thurston had described this work in a report to the American Association for the Advancement of Science printed in its *Proceedings* in 1877, and the document received wide distribution by a separate printing as a pamphlet in 1878. The board had a subcommittee on Abrasion and Wear which, according to Thurston, had "sent out circulars asking assistance and cooperation from manufacturers" to determine the most efficient steels for tools for "turning, planing, boring, and chiseling." The Mechanical Laboratory was experimenting with different cooling lubricants for metal-cutting experiments conducted for the Navy using tools from major machine tool manufacturers, including those from William Sellers and Company. Thus, the Mechanical Laboratory was analyzing the data which included most of the variables Taylor would face at Midvale. According to Thurston,

---

[146] Kanigal, *Op. Cit.*, suggested status after an exhausting search of almost every scrap of paper at Stevens Institute.

The wear of tools, under the various conditions of workshop practice was another subject of investigation. Weighing the tools before and after use, and weighing the amount of metal removed were considered the most accurate method of determining the rate of abrasion. The area of surface finished, and the area of the surface cut by the tool, the rate of feed, etc., were to be accurately ascertained and stated. The description of the tool, its shape, method of operation, the kind of metal used in the tool, the temper adopted, the character of the metal cut by it, the velocity of the tool, and , where peculiarities of behavior were noted, a careful statement of them, were desired. . . . The Committee on Abrasion and Wear is engaged in collating information relating to this subject, and is making experiments at the Stevens Institute of Technology on the abrasion and wear of the metals, and of the effect of lubrication in reducing it.[147]

Taylor's senior thesis completed for Stevens in 1882 described the variables used in the subsequent experiments at Midvale, thus enabling a comparison with Thurston's committee statement above. The list in the thesis suggests an academic completeness, and thus the influence of Thurston in the design of the experiments at Midvale. Taylor's variables relating to the cutting tool were "degree of hardness" and "quality," the "thickness of the shaving," "duration of cut, i.e. the length of time the tool is in the tool post before being reground or replaced by another tool," the "manner of dressing and tempering the tools," "the shape of the cutting edge," the "bulk of metal near the cutting edge," the "clearance or angle of relief," the "lip or angle made by the upper surface of the tool with the horizontal plane," and "the form of the surface from which the metal is to be removed."[148] Also, Taylor's description of the method used in the Midvale experiments suggests advice from Thurston and/or perhaps Sellers. Taylor wrote that four hundred to five hundred tests were conducted using a Sellers-designed vertical boring machine. On this machine, the metal to be cut spun on a table underneath the apparatus which held the cutting tool and which fed it into the metal at controlled speeds. The Midvale experiments cut "tires," or metal railroad wheels, using the method described in these words by Taylor:

Large tires were bored during the experiment so that the form of the surface from which the metal was removed was kept nearly constant during the whole experiment. In this way, the above variable conditions were made as nearly constant as possible, but there still remain the six more important variables, the quality of the steel, the cutting speed, the depth of the cut, the feed, the duration of the cut, and

[147] Robert H. Thurston, *Abstract Statement of the Extent and Character of the Work of the United States Board Appointed to Test Iron, Steel, and Other Metals* (1878), 102 and 108.
[148] Frederick W. Taylor, unpublished senior thesis, (1883) 7-11.

the condition of the tool on its removal from the tool post, and it became the object of the writer to determine the law governing the effect of a change of any one of these variables on any other variable, the four remaining conditions being the true constant.[149]

Frederick W. Taylor, the father of Scientific Management, is shown here around the time that he time that he wrote his Stevens senior thesis on cutting metal, with, at right, a Sellers-designed vertical boring mill.

Because Taylor wrote on the first page of his senior thesis that "This report was presented to the works (Midvale) 3-20-82," one might conclude that Taylor's thesis was really only a report submitted to William Sellers which doubled as a thesis.[150] However, this notation can be explained in another way: Taylor originally thought that he would obtain his Stevens degree in one and a half years which would have meant by June of 1882.[151] Thus, he conducted the first round of experiments so that they would be completed in the spring of 1882. Taylor was required to pass examinations in all subjects, and, although it was easy to pass foundry and shop work because of his apprenticeship, and easy to pass the examinations in belles lettres, foreign languages, and fundamental mathematics because of his schooling at Phillips Exeter, it was much harder to pass the examinations in differential calculus and the sciences in which he had no background. In fact, in 1883, he had to enroll in courses at the University of Pennsylvania

---

[149] *Ibid., 11.*

[150] Taylor, thesis, 1.

[151] Kanigal, *Op. Cit.,* 598 cites a reliable contemporary source, a letter from Taylor to James A. Tufts dated February 23, 1882 in which Taylor predicted that he would graduate in June 1882.

in order to study chemistry.[152] Thus in order to pass the examinations in sciences, his degree was delayed one year longer than anticipated -- this discrepancy explains why he finished the experiments for his thesis one year earlier. Naturally, since William Sellers was funding the experiments on the boring machine at Midvale, Taylor had to turn in a report as soon as these experiments were completed, on March 20, 1882. Thus, the fact that the thesis was one and the same as an industrial report does not mean that Thurston did not have a hand in its original design and its method, and approved of its results a year before it was required to be filed for graduation in 1883. The reason why Thurston would have accepted the thesis was that the Midvale experiments were an extension of his own work for the Iron and Steel Board -- work which for Thurston was a progressive fundamental contribution to science-based engineering knowledge.

Lastly, the thesis also displays academic influence through Taylor's statement that "Before starting the experiments, the writer examined all of the authorities accessible to him on the subject."[153] Perhaps Thurston recommended the authorities on the subject of machine tools. F. W. Hutton, the first historian of the ASME, wrote that one of the reasons for founding the ASME was to disseminate the technical literature more effectively, and that "Joshua Rose, Egbert P. Watson and Coleman Sellers had made contributions with regard to tools and machine shop method."[154] Watson and Rose were two English engineers who were visiting America to write about its leading machine tool industries, and they were also present during the founding of the ASME. Watson was listed by Hutton as in attendance at the ASME's preliminary meeting to which a limited number of engineers were invited. Rose was one of the eighty attendees at the organizational meeting of the ASME at Stevens. Each of their authoritative texts were published in Philadelphia and London simultaneously. Their titles are revealing. Watson wrote *The Modern Practice of American Machinists and Engineers, Including the Construction, Application and Use of Drills, Lathe Tools Cutters for Boring Cylinders and Hollow Work Generally, with the Most Economical Speed for the Same . . . Together with Workshop Management, Economy of Manufacture . . . Belting, etc. etc.* published in 1867. Joshua Rose wrote *The Complete Practical Machinist; Embracing Lathe Work, Vice Work, Drills and Drilling, Taps and Dies, Hardening and Tempering, the Making and Use of Tools, Etc.* published in 1878. The latter book had

---

[152] *Ibid.,* 184.
[153] *Ibid.,* 6.
[154] Frederick W. Hutton, *A History of the American Society of Mechanical Engineers from 1880 to 1915*(ASME, 1915), 2.

previously been published in *Scientific American* and *Scientific American Supplement* in 1874 and 1875.

There can't be any doubt that these works informed not only Taylor but also Thurston before him. Watson stated some thirteen years before Taylor began his experiments that "it is important to know the time required to execute certain portions of the work. This can only be accurately arrived at by a knowledge of the speeds at which cutting tools work." Watson had identified most of the variables Taylor was to use later in his experiments at Midvale: the hardness and diameter of the metal to be cut, the rate of feed of the cutting tool, the speed of the turning metal, the depth of the cut, the thickness of the spiral shaving of metal removed, the shape of the cutting tool, the position of the cutting tool, and the wear rate and the time to re-grind the tool. Watson also identified the labor problem, that some machin-ists were so "shiftless and indifferent" that they used the wrong tool, and that there was a "conservatism among mechanics" resulting in "blind" re-sistance to "more efficient" methods. Taylor repeated this argument in his thesis, writing, "The greatest perhaps of the obstacles to be encountered by one attempting to do anything of this sort, is the blind and almost un-accountable prejudice on the part of most machinists to any improve-ment."[155] Rose reported on the state of the art of cutting metals on the eve of Taylor's tests, including an "actual test" he conducted to determine the depth of cut at various speeds of a machine tool. Rose called for the end to "promiscuous practice" in the shop in favor of "inherent science."[156]

That Taylor was motivated by a need for knowledge and not merely by a desire for status is indicated in a notebook he started to keep in January 1880 entitled "Notes of Importance, Fred W. Taylor, Private, Midvale Steel Works." It is full of technical problems on belting -- the leather belts used to transmit steam engine power to machine tools -- and other related technical formulas, but it also contains two book lists. On page 52 under a heading "Books recommended by Coleman Sellers Sr. as the best of their kind. 9-2-80," there are eight books, including Nystrom, Clark, and Reuleaux on me-chanics, which, according to the catalogs, were textbooks used by Thurston at Stevens. On page 74 another list without a date, labeled, "Good Books of Reference" names ten more academic titles, including Abbot's history of testing machines, James's history of steel, and Gillispie's philosophy of mathematics.[157] In addition, when he obtained entry to Stevens, Taylor later

---

[155] This comparison of texts made in Clark, *Op.Cit.*, 43.
[156] *Ibid.*, 44.
[157] Notebook marked, "Notes of Importance, Fred W. Taylor, Midvale Steel Works, January 28, 1880," in Taylor Papers, Stevens Special Collections.

said that he had sought out suggestions from professors at Stevens "for proper text books," thus exhibiting his initiative and willingness to start studying for his degree.[158]

Unfortunately, although he credited his own assistants, Taylor's classic 1906 paper "On The Art of Cutting Metals" describing his early experiments in metal cutting did not credit any of the above influences. But because of their purpose, technical papers presented to the ASME rarely showed historical depth. Taylor listed all the breakthroughs of the experiments over time, and indicated that the experiments which began in 1881 essentially went on for twenty-five years, with a hiatus here and there, and achieved fabulous results. Discoveries and innovations made by Taylor and his associates included: In 1881, round-nosed cutting tools at slow speeds cut more metal than diamond-shaped tools at high speeds; in 1883, proper belting tension increased power if adjusted regularly; in 1883, dull tools required as much power to feed as to drive the cut; and in 1884, automatic grinding of tools in lots produced greater uniformity. In addition; between 1885 and 1909, practical tables were developed for use by machinists in cutting different types of metal; in 1886, coarse feeds at high speeds with broad-nosed tools were found efficient; between 1894 and 1895, using expensive mushet steel to cut soft metals was found to give ninety percent more efficiency; between 1898 and 1900, the Taylor-White process was discovered for making high-speed cutting tools; between 1899 and 1902, a slide rule to aid machinists' calculations was invented; and in 1906, vanadium was added to the chromium-tungsten tool to prolong its life. By that time, some 500,000 experiments had been completed working out the most effective combination of twelve variables with scientific precision.[159] Taylor's assistants in these experiments were mainly graduates of Stevens, including George M. Sinclair 1884, Henry L. Gantt 1884, Samuel L. B. Knox 1891, and Maunsel White 1879.

Taylor's biggest breakthrough, the Taylor-White high-speed tools, came about by accident. Taylor and White were experimenting with the annealing process of heating and cooling tools to harden them. They tried various methods of attaining very high temperatures in different fires of coke, coal, and gas. They tried different cooling mediums like water, or lime, or powdered charcoal, before settling on a bath of molten lead. Sixteen thousand experiments were made. Some tools were ruined by heating them too high, but Taylor and Maunsel White were amazed that one accidentally over-

---

[158] Quoted in F. DeR. Furman's unpublished paper, "Taylor's Contact with Stevens and Stevens Men," n.d., Taylor Papers, Stevens Special Collections.

[159] Frederick W. Taylor, "On the Art of Cutting Metals," *ASME Proc.* XXVII (1906), 10-12.

heated tool, which should have been ruined, cut metal longer and faster than any before. They found that the widely held assumption that tools heated beyond 1550 degrees fahrenheit would be ruined was simply not true. Their overheated tool cut fabulously. They found from further experimentation that a tool heated beyond 1500 degrees cut less effectively, but, if heating continued beyond 1725 degrees, "the cutting speed turned back the other way, soon equaling that achieved below 1550, and rose, and rose, and rose still further with rising temperature until, past 2200 degrees or so, the steel approached its melting point."[160] This breakthrough Taylor-White process so hardened the tools that speeds of cutting doubled and the cuts were forty percent deeper. The metal chips produced by the tools were so hot that one could light a cigarette by them. Once patented, this process for preparing tools swept the world and made Taylor and White a fortune. Taylor's "On the Art of Cutting Metals" should have been called "The Science of Cutting Metals" because it established Taylor as the authority on modern metal-cutting based on applied science. Taylor subsequently became known as The Father of Cutting Metals in machine tool circles. Even today a standard cut is also known as a Taylor Cut, and modern tables for machinists running machine tools are derivatives of Taylor's tables.

Back in 1881 when Taylor started his experiments in metal cutting at Midvale, the objective was to discover how to cut metal efficiently so that the Midvale foremen like himself could have the scientific knowledge to increase the efficiency of machinists. As Watson had stated in 1867, "it is important to know the time required to execute certain portions of the work," in order to increase efficiency of workmen.[161] Taylor called these portions the "tasks" involved in metal cutting, such as putting the tire on the table, fastening it, and lowering the cutting tool. In 1883, he clocked the time it took to do them correctly, that is, based on procedures derived from his metal cutting experiments. After determining the shortest time to perform the tasks experimentally, in 1884 he introduced "stopwatch time study" into the regular Midvale machine shops in order to clock the men and instruct them how to do the work quickly and efficiently.

This act was the genesis of scientific management. Taylor was applying the same methods to the machinists as he had applied to the boring machine itself. In both sets of experiments he was measuring motions and time to find work output. In the case of the machine, it was pieces of work turned

---

[160] Kanigal, *Op.Cit.*, 326-7.
[161] Watson, *Op.Cit.*, 37-38.

out in the shortest clocked time. In the case of the machinists, it was tasks performed in the shortest clocked time.[162]

It was also the long awaited solution to the "problem of the day" posed by Coleman Sellers, because Taylor used unskilled workmen to run the machines. Resistance of the machinists to stopwatch time study was strong, and Taylor had to fire most of them. He hired green labor, as he called it in his senior thesis, and offered an incentive, a differential piece rate payment scheme instead of the old straight piece rate. Under this scheme, operator-machinists who worked to reach a "first class man" number of pieces per day, determined by Taylor's experiments, received more money per piece for the remainder of the day. Taylor called this "high wages at low cost" because it gave cooperative and able workmen substantially higher wages than before but made more profits for Midvale because far more pieces were turned out. In fact, production rose thirty percent at Midvale by 1884, and Taylor was promoted to chief engineer, a position he held until 1890.

In that position he introduced most of the later innovations contained in his system of management. In an ASME paper of 1903 called "Shop Management," he explained the components of his system:[163] It had to be based on careful scientific stopwatch time study of workmen to determine the most efficient way of doing the tasks of work. He explained his creation of "functional foremen" to plan, to set rates, to efficiently route materials to assure smooth operations. Specialized clerks were put in charge of well-organized tool rooms, in charge of instruction cards for machinists to explain work tasks and the time to complete them, and in charge of standard criteria in personnel selections (the right man for the right job). He also stressed that cooperation between management and labor was achieved as a benefit of his differential piece rate -- those workers who could not achieve the first class man's high wages left the company, and those workers who did earn higher wages kept unions with their lower average wages out.

Taylor was a manager and consultant in management after 1890. He retired after the success of the Taylor-White process and became a full-time promoter of his management system which he called "task management" or the "Taylor system of management" until 1910 when it became known as Scientific Management. In 1911, he published his controversial *Principles of Scientific Management* which established him as the Father of Scientific Management

---

[162] Clark, *Op.Cit.*, 47.
[163] Frederick W. Taylor, "Shop Management," *ASME Trans.*, XXIV (1903).

CHAPTER 7

Edison Pioneers

Eight months after the ASME was founded at Stevens Institute, on December 18, 1880, Charles F. Brush lit the first electric street lights ever used in New York City, namely twenty-two brilliant arc lamps along Broadway from 14th to 34th Streets. This dramatic event inaugurating the Great White Way was followed by the even more dramatic event on September 4, 1882 -- Thomas Alva Edison's lighting up interiors of buildings in a district of lower Manhattan with incandescent electric lights, the first commercially workable incandescent lighting system in the world. It is noteworthy that Stevens Institute of Technology, founded to educate mechanical engineers and identified with the ASME, had so many graduates who had important pioneering roles in these events and in electrical engineering in general.

Experimentation with applications of electricity for lighting and other purposes took off after 1831 when electromagnetic induction was simultaneously discovered by Michael Faraday in England and Joseph Henry in the United States. This fundamental breakthrough allowed mechanical energy to be transmuted into flowing electrical current through generators of electricity. Built in all configurations by numerous inventors after the Faraday-Henry discovery, these machines spun arms of metal, bound with copper wire, through a permanent magnet's field, thus creating electrical current in the armature's copper wire which was commuted to circuits through carbon brushes.

But not until another breakthrough, which dramatically increased the power of generators, did applications of electricity become commercially feasible. The second breakthrough was the replacement of the permanent magnets with electromagnets in 1866. Electromagnets were produced by another result of the discovery of induction, namely, creating a magnet by sending current through copper wires wrapped around a non-magnetic core. Almost simultaneously, Moses G. Farmer of Salem, Massachusetts, Alfred Varley and Charles Wheatstone of England, and Werner von Siemens in Germany each produced the first dynamos by applying electromagnets to generators. These machines used the current they generated from induction to excite electromagnets once the machines were turned over by a steam engine. These dynamos were so powerful and efficient that uses were immediately foreseen for heat, power, and, especially, lighting.

At the time, the world's most common source of artificial light was the oil lamp with its smoking flame, but whale oil had given way to coal oil or kerosene lamps. In big cities, lighting was by gas in open flame or inside a mantel which increased its luminosity. These methods of lighting caused fire hazards, fouling of the air, and depletion of oxygen in closed rooms, especially in winter.

The solution was electric lighting. The first demonstration of illumination by electricity was in 1808 in the laboratory of Sir Humphrey Davy in England. He used a strong galvanic battery of two thousand pairs of plates connected in circuit to two pieces of charcoal which gradually disintegrated as the arc of current between them created a brilliant light. The problem of the costs of the immense battery-power needed to produce the light precluded the use of such arc lights for decades. Even with the invention of electromagnetic generators, the costs were so great that arc lights were only used in government-sponsored lighthouses, the first one being in France in 1863.

In lectures at the Franklin Institute in the mid-1860s, Henry Morton had helped to popularize arc lights before they were commercially feasible. He demonstrated a French self-adjusting arc light, and also Jablochkoff candles which were arc lights whose carbon rods were separated by plaster of paris that made the rods burn evenly.[164] Morton wrote "Electricity," in *Johnson's Cyclopaedia* in 1875, establishing him as an authority on the subject.[165] Later, Morton was a member of the U.S. Light House Board and helped introduce arc lights to American lighthouses. But apart from lighthouses, the arc light's costs relegated it to the realm of novelty used for the professor's demonstration during lectures or for spectacular display in an opera house or theater.

That is, until the invention of the dynamo in 1866. Almost immediately, electric light companies opened up for the business of running arc lights with dynamos of various constructions, the arc lights being set up in streets and large department stores whose huge rooms could be lit with such bright lights. Charles F. Brush, whose arc lamps lit up the Great White Way in Manhattan in 1880, had perfected the first commercially feasible dynamo and self-adjusting arc lights in 1878 in the streets of Cleveland. As mentioned earlier, Brush, Maxim, and Weston dynamos were tested in the Stevens Mechanical Laboratory. As Henry Morton wrote later, "Admirable as is the system of electric-arc lighting for use in streets and open spaces, and in workshops and large halls, it is entirely unfit to take the place of the

---

[164] Henry Morton, "Electricity in Lighting," *Electricity in Everyday Life*(Scribners, 1890), 97.
[165] *Catalogue of the Stevens Institute of Technology, 1879,* 4-5.

numerous lights of moderate intensity employed for general domestic illumination."[166]

In the terminology of the time, the blinding brilliance of the arc light had to be "subdivided" for use in households, and it was here that Edison's incandescent lighting system, the heating of a small filament to brilliance inside a sealed bulb of glass whose air had been removed, filled the need. But, as Henry Morton never tired of testifying when called as a special witness in patent suits brought against Edison's emulators, there were many precedents for Edison's bulb. In 1845, the American Starr and the Englishman King made an electric incandescent lamp with a filament of platinum wire encased in hard carbon to prevent burning up or fusing of the filament. They used an "evacuated" glass globe. In 1848, W. Straite took out a patent for making incandescent lamps from a horseshoe-shaped filament of iridium or iridium alloys. Platinum filaments were widely used by experimenters. Then in the fall of 1878, W. Sawyer and A. Man produced an incandescent bulb with an arch of carbonized paper. It was only after these developments that Edison took up the challenge of the "subdivision of light" in 1878.

Thomas Alva Edison (1847-1931), who had only gone to school for about two months in his entire youth, had invented a vote counting machine in 1868. But, since no one wanted to buy it, Edison dedicated himself only to inventions which would work, saying, "I will never again invent anything which nobody wants." By the age of twenty-three, he earned $40,000 for an improvement in a stock ticker, and in 1876 he decided to spend the money as a full-time inventor with a small staff in a laboratory set up in Menlo Park, New .Jersey. The first completely original invention which made him famous was the phonograph in 1877. His handling of the phonograph showed that Edison was a master of self-promotion, inviting the press and demonstrating his inventions with the intention of obtaining financial backers.

In December 1877, Morton asked to see Edison's laboratory in nearby Menlo Park, and subsequently visited the laboratory with Mayer and Brown Ayres B.S. 1878, one of Stevens's early B.S. recipients. Morton borrowed a phonograph for a lecture and then bought one in 1878. Also in 1878, Morton, representing the Light House Board, requested information about Edison's megaphone device invented that year.[167] In the Summer of 1878, Morton, who was already an authority on eclipses of the sun by virtue of

---

[166] *Ibid.*, 116.
[167] Morton to Edison, December 24, 1877, January 2, 1878, January 21, 1878, February 2, 1878, February 5, 1878, February 11, 1878, April 17, 1878, Edison Papers, Rutgers microfilm.

having organized the photographic division of an 1869 expedition to Iowa to observe an eclipse, took a trip to Wyoming for the same purpose with Edison and their mutual friend George F. Barker of the University of Pennsylvania, among others.[168]

After the Wyoming trip, Edison announced to the press his project for an incandescent lighting system with the obvious intention of obtaining financial backers. The Edison Electric Light Company was formed on October 15, 1878, with Norvin H. Green as president backed up by, among others, the investment banker J. P. Morgan. A capital stock of $300,000 provided the money for development of the incandescent lamp, an efficient dynamo, the underground conductors, and an electrical meter.[169] The plan was to light up a section of lower Manhattan as a showcase, then expand operations to big cities in America and Europe. At this point Morton, an expert in the history of previous attempts to create an incandescent bulb which would not fuse, unfortunately soured Edison for a time by a lecture before the American Gas Light Association in which he reviewed the history of incandescent bulbs and cast doubts on the feasibility of Edison's project given previous failures. Morton's comments were widely reported in the press, and when Edison heard of them he promised to erect a little statue of Morton and eternally illuminate it with one of his lamps -- a promise he did not keep because he forgave Morton later.[170]

Edison had no qualms about hiring Stevens graduates for the development of the system. He increased the number of his research staff dramatically, and, besides hiring established experts like Dr. Herman Claudius to work out the mathematical calculations of power needs for the project, he also hired college graduates for the first time to utilize their mathematical and testing skills, one being John Forrest Kelly, another of the early Stevens B.S. students of the class of 1878, who thus became Stevens's first Edison Pioneer. Kelly was employed as a chemist in Menlo Park in 1878 and 1879 when Edison and his staff were trying every conceivable substance for a filament for an incandescent bulb. Finally, on October 19, 1879, a piece of bamboo from a fan was carbonized and found to work. Edison held the first demonstration of the incandescent lamp at Menlo Park on December 31, 1879, amid much fanfare. In retrospect, this massive trial-and-error process

---

[168] "Morton, Henry," *National Cyclopaedia of American Biography*, XXIV (1935), 374.
[169] Payson Jones, *A Power History of the Consolidated Edison System, 1878-1900*(1940), 25.
[170] Henry Morton, "Lecture Upon Electric Light, *American Gas Light Journal*, January 2, 1879, 4068, and Matthew Josephson, *Edison: A Biography*(1959), 211.

by which Edison found the bamboo filament created the world's first industrial research laboratory.[171]

In 1880, Morton and Mayer tested one of the bamboo lamps in the Mechanical Laboratory at Stevens, the results being published in England's *Telegraph Journal and Electrical Revue.*[172] But the definitive tests of an Edison lamp were done by John W. Howell (1857-1937) of the class of 1881 who wrote his senior thesis on the "Economy of Electric Lighting by Incandescence," a beautiful analysis of one of Edison's bamboo bulbs and dynamos. The dynamometer Howell used was built in the Mechanical Laboratory by the class of 1879. Given the international interest in Edison's light bulb, the thesis was immediately printed as an article in *Van Nostrand's Magazine* and then translated into several foreign languages and printed in Europe.[173] John W. Howell had an inside connection with Edison. His brother, Wilson S. Howell, who had decided to go to work for no pay at Menlo Park, which he called his "little college on the hill at Menlo Park," was one of the original "old boys" of Edison.[174] John W. Howell went to work for Edison in July 1881 and fast became one of his laboratory's brightest men.[175] Soon after joining Edison in 1881, he invented the Howell voltmeter, a standard instrument used by electrical companies until the Weston voltmeter of 1890.[176] In 1882, Howell conducted tests of Edison's Jumbo dynamos as reported by the *New York Tribune:*

The result of tests with Edison's machines by Mr. John Howell, of the Stevens Institute, shows 95.10 percent total and 88.7 percent commercial efficiency; or to put it in popular language, Edison's latest dynamo, while converting into electricity 95.10 percent of the mechanical energy expended, will actually deliver through the conductors to the consumers 88.7 percent of such energy to be used for light or power, or both; Mr. Edison claims to be nearly 50 percent more than the results obtained by any other dynamo."[177]

John W. Howell's specialty, however, was bulbs. In the summer of 1881 he took over the operations of Edison's embryonic company for manufacturing

---

[171] Furman, *Op.Cit.*, 444; *Annual Catalogue of the Stevens Institute of Technology, 1880,* 50.

[172] Henry Morton, A. M. Mayer, and B. F. Thomas, "Some Electrical Measurements of One of Mr. Edison's Horseshoe Lamps," *The Telegraph Journal and Electrical Revue,* London, VIII (1880), 151-2.

[173] *The National Cyclopaedia of American Biography,* XXVII, 22, and "Howell Articles," Edison Papers, reel 95, frame 93.

[174] Francis Jehl, *Menlo Park Reminiscences*(1940), II, 719, 810.

[175] Jehl, *Op.Cit.*, III, 997.

[176] *National Cyclopaedia,* XXVII, 22.

[177] Quoted in Payson, *Op.Cit.,* 205.

the bamboo light bulb, the Edison Lamp Works in Harrison, New Jersey. There, he conducted more photometric tests of bulbs, invented a process to bake the filaments automatically, which was later used throughout the world, and subsequently he obtained over fifty patents for improvements in light bulb manufacture. When Edison's companies were later folded into General Electric in 1893, John W. Howell was made chief engineer of the General Electric Lamp Works in Schenectady, New York and was the foremost developer of the modern incandescent lamp.

In some ways Howell was an exception to other Stevens graduates who were pioneers in the early days of electrical engineering. Most graduates were involved in the generating plants or "central stations" which held the boilers, steam engines, and dynamos. It was mechanical engineers who worked with the Brush, Edison, Stanley, Houston-Thompson, and Westinghouse companies to build the steam engines and dynamos. No fewer than one-third of the class of 1886 and sizable percentages of other classes dating back to 1876 found employment with such pioneering electrical establishments.[178] Thus, the accomplishments of Stevens graduates with degrees in mechanical engineering are not surprising given the stage of electrical technology at the time when electrical power and traction technology were taking off -- electrical engineering technologies were at least half mechanical.

Moreover, Stevens's M.E. and B.S. degree holders had scientific understanding of electricity, a decided advantage over other mechanical engineering programs, which stressed shop over science. Henry Morton assisted Alfred Mayer in teaching the four-year sequence of courses in physics.[179] The second trimester of physics in the sophomore year covered light and the third trimester electricity and magnetism, the third year involved precise measurements and instrumentation, including galvanometers on which Mayer had published an article, "A New Form of Lantern galvanometer," in the *American Journal of Science* in 1872.[180] Two of the five students in the small B.S. program became electrical engineers, namely Kelly,[181] and Durand Woodman B.S. 1880 who worked for Edward Weston between 1884 and the time he earned his Ph.D. from Stevens in 1887.[182]

Stevens undergraduates were able to obtain hands-on experience making electrical equipment in the Stevens machine shop and using it in the

---

[178] From my analysis of alumni biographies in Furman, *Morton Memorial, Op.Cit.*, 287-641.
[179] Coleman Sellers and A. R. Leeds, *Biographical Notice of President Henry Morton*(Engineering Press, 1892), 82.
[180] *Catalogue, 1879, Op.Cit.*, 86.
[181] *Annual Catalogue of the Stevens Institute of Technology, 1880*, 78.
[182] *Ibid.*, 81 and Furman, *Op.Cit.*, 623.

activities of the Mechanical Laboratory. In the autumn trimester of 1877, sophomores John W. Lieb and his best friend George Meade Bond tested the nighttime luminosity of Brush arc lamps installed along the Coney Island pier in Brooklyn. Since there were no bridges or tunnels to cross the Hudson or East River, no Brooklyn Bridge until 1883, Lieb and Bond made the trek by ferry and horsecar, probably staying in Brooklyn for the night. Using a photometer built by Bond and Denton, their tests showed that the supposedly two thousand-candlepower arc lights were only eight hundred candlepower. Next, Lieb and Bond were excited about Alexander Graham Bell's telephone, which had been demonstrated at the Centennial Exposition in Philadelphia in 1876 and which was being installed commercially in New York in 1877. They made replicas in 1878, rosewood phones mounted on cigar boxes and hooked up in Newark to telegraph lines over which they spoke and sang. Lieb and most other Stevens students were especially interested in the latest sensational newspaper accounts of Edison's work at nearby Menlo Park, especially his first successful incandescent lamp announced to the press on October 21, 1879. That spring while the eight members of Lieb's class of 1880 were testing Brush, Maxim, and Weston arc light dynamos using a dynamometer made by William Kent, they were treated to a field trip to the Wizard of Menlo Park's laboratory.

At left, Stevens graduate John W. Howell, was Thomas Edison's light bulb specialist, and, at right, Stevens's John W. Lieb, was Edison's "electrician" at the Pearl Street Station during the historic lighting up of lower Manhattan.

John W. Lieb (1860-1929) turned out to be one of Edison's right hand men. After graduating from the Stevens School and then the Institute in May 1880, Lieb's first job was as a draftsman with the Brush Electric Company in Cleveland, but by November he had been trained as a manager, operator and installer of arc lights. Afraid of the prospect of being stuck in a small town running a local arc light system or "shoe string" operation as they were called, he went to Menlo Park on Christmas vacation and asked Edison for a job. Lieb's enthusiasm for incandescent lighting impressed Edison, and he hired Lieb in January 1881 just at the time the inventor was searching for assistants to help set up the Pearl Street central power station in lower Manhattan.[183]

Lieb's first job for Edison at Menlo Park was to work under Charles L. Clarke as a draftsman, helping to design Edison's "Jumbo" dynamos, the largest dynamos built up to that time.[184] Afterwards, Lieb designed the shaft and couplings for the linkup of the Jumbos to Porter-Allen steam engines.[185] Lieb then shifted to Edison's machine works on Goerck Street in Manhattan where the Jumbos were to be built. First, he used a lathe to make six sets of the shafts and couplings, one for each of the six sets of steam engines and dynamos to be used in the central station. Subsequently, he worked on the dynamos' construction, on simple laboring tasks like winding copper wire around armatures and on complicated assignments like designing and supervising the construction of the dynamos' electrical switches.[186] By this time he was trusted by Edison, who then assigned him the task of devising a voltage, or "tension," indicator on the principle of a telegraph relay for the central station. For this work, Edison assigned John Ott, an instrument maker, to assist Lieb. [187]

Charles L. Clarke and John Lieb then constructed the Pearl Street Station.[188] Lieb was given the assignment of planning the layout and installation of the electrical equipment.[189] In a popular article in *Cassier's Magazine* fourteen years later, Lieb recalled how primitive the Pearl Street Station was in 1882.[190] It consisted of two adjacent brownstones at 255 and 257

[183] George Orrok, "John William Lieb. An Apostle of Light and Power," *Stevens Indicator,* XLVII (1930), 6-9, Orrok being a personal friend of Lieb.

[184] Jehl, *Op.Cit.,* III, 928.

[185] *Ibid.,* 8. and Payson Jones, *A Power History of the Consolidated Edison System, 1878-1900*(1940), 356-357.

[186] T. C. Martin, *Forty Years of Edison Service, 1882-1922*(1922), 8.

[187] Jehl, *Ibid.,* 1059.

[188] Jeyl, *Op.Cit., 1039.*

[189] Payson, *Op.Cit.,* 356.

[190] John W. Lieb, "An Historic Electric Central Station," *Cassier's Magazine,* X (May, 1896), 57-62.

Pearl Street, the former being used for storage and the latter gutted down to the cellar, only the top floor remaining. Iron girders and columns, "not unlike the elevated railway structure," were constructed inside the walls of no. 257 to create space and strength to hold the heavy electrical equipment. The cellar held conveyors to the back yard to bring in coal and remove ash from four Babcock and Wilcox boilers of 240 horsepower each. Pumps, heating chambers, and steam pipes were jammed around them, leading upward to six Porter-Allen steam engines on the heavily reinforced second floor. Each weighed 6,450 pounds and generated two hundred horsepower at 350 revolutions per minute. The boilers and engines were tested on June 29, 1882.

Lieb used his shaft and coupling connectors to directly attach to the engines the six Jumbo dynamos weighing 44,800 pounds apiece, and each having a capacity of 750 amps at 350 revolutions per minute. Lieb's main dynamo switches, "ponderous affairs as big as hay-cutters," connected the current from the dynamos to bus bars, thick half-round copper rods, which were mounted on the wall. They ran the length of the building and connected to the underground system for distribution. Lieb's primitive regulation device controlled the voltage.

Lieb attached the dynamos to the engines and tested them on July 5 to create current for a bank of one thousand bulbs set up inside the station. All seemed to be working well. But when segments of the completed system were tested, unexpected difficulties arose. Distribution from the station was a two-wire instead of the Edison three-wire system introduced later, and consisted of two half-round copper rods in twenty-foot lengths end-to-end. The rods were kept apart only with paraffined cardboard disks, the rods covered by tubes of tar-encased wrappings designed by John W. Howell's brother, Wilson. To go around obstructions underground, the tubes were bent instead of using junction boxes. After testing, whole segments of the eighteen miles of underground cable had to be dug up to find short circuits before the distribution system became operational. Also, the engines were connected in parallel, and under actual working conditions loads showed a tendency to shift from one engine to another, causing "a see-sawing of the governors and great variations in speed, accompanied by brilliant pyrotechnic effects that threatened the destruction of both engines and dynamos." Lieb solved this problem by connecting all the governors which controlled the speed of the steam engines to a common rod so they all moved in unison. There was no central switchboard, not a single ammeter. On the top floor were field regulators for each dynamo; "They were so colossal that the regulators for the six dynamos, together with the connecting shaft and gear for operating the switch quadrants separately or together, took up nearly the entire floor above the dynamo room."

There was even some trouble during the official opening ceremony at 3 p.m. on September 4, 1882. Edison and company members were at the receiving end in the offices of Drexel, Morgan and Co. in lower Manhattan. In attendance were J.P. Morgan and board members of the Edison Electric Illuminating Company, a subsidiary of the Edison Electric Light Company which had raised the original $300,000. With them were some of Edison's old boys, Johnson, Kruesi, Bergmann, and Clarke. At Pearl Street in the power station were Lieb who was given the honor of being "Electrician," his assistant MacQuestion, and two of Kruesi's assistants in charge of the underground system. At the appointed hour of 3 p.m., Lieb, who had designed the main switch, couldn't get it to work:

I remember distinctly that the handle of the breaker could only be reached by standing on tip-toes and, as the breaker was thrown in, the catch which held it in place did not engage properly and it was necessary for me to hang on to the breaker while someone obtained a bench to push the catch into its contact. Once the unit was thrown into service, it started the continuous operation of the station.[191]

Two months later, Edison sent Lieb as Electrician to set up the first Edison central station in Milan, Italy. Edison did not care that Lieb was only twenty-two. Edison himself had become the superintendent of the Gold Indicator Company at twenty-two. Lieb rose to manage the whole Milan Edison enterprise which was the first large central station and lighting system erected in Europe and the second of the real commercial stations in the world.[192] Upon returning to the United States twelve years later, Lieb became vice president and general manager of Consolidated Edison.

Even though Edison was wary of Morton because of his testimony in patent suits which supported the Wizard of Menlo Park's competitors, Edison thought that Stevens Institute was a superior school because of his experience with Howell and Lieb. He also hired George Gibbs 1882 as a chemist in 1882 to work on his "chemical" electrical meter, a device which measured the use of current to Edison's lower Manhattan customers by weighing the loss of metal from zinc and copper plates inside the meter. He wrote a letter in March 25, 1883, in which he stated, "The Stevens Institute

---

[191] Quoted in Frederick W. Collins, *Consolidated Gas Company of New York, A History* (1934), 252.

[192] Jehl, *Op.Cit.*, II, 739.

of Hoboken is probably as good if not the best place at present to study chemical science and engineering."[193]

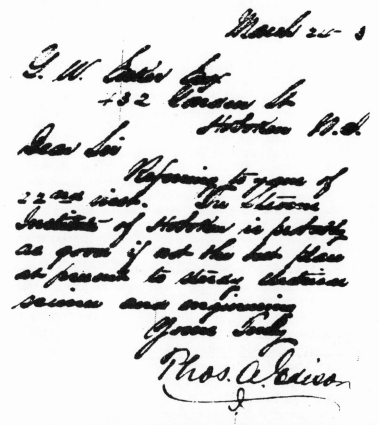

Above is Thomas Edison's letter dated March, 25, 1883, to G. W. Baker, Esq. at 432 Garden Street in Hoboken, stating, "Referring to yours of 22nd inst. The Stevens Institute of Hoboken is probably as good if not the best place at present to study electrical sciences and engineering. Yours truly, Thos. A. Edison."

The success of Edison's work in lower Manhattan had an immediate impact on the curriculum across the Hudson at Stevens. Morton wrote to Edison on July 5, 1883, saying, "The enclosed slip will tell you what we are doing in the line of instructing men with a view to making them useful in the subject which has received so large a development by reason of your

---

[193] Edison to Baker, March 25, 1873, Edison Papers, *Op.Cit.*

work." The slip was a clipping of a newspaper account of June 15 entitled "Stevens Institute Graduates" with a subtitle "A special Department of Applied Electricity to be Established." The article described the graduation ceremonies of the class of 1883 in the German Club in Hoboken and Morton's speech to the graduates:

President Morton said that electricity was an integral constituent of engineering practice and its detailed study an essential part of a course in mechanical engineering. From the first, the subject had held a prominent place in the Stevens Institute course. It had, however, become manifest that, with the rapid growth of mechanical engineering, there should be a special department of applied electricity to keep pace with the requirements of the time. The money necessary to establish such a department had been supplied by a good friend of the Institute, (the good friend is President Morton himself) and the new department had been organized by the Trustees, with Dr. William E. Geyer as the first incumbent of the chair of applied electricity. President Morton did not think the time had come for organizing a special course of electrical engineering in the Institute, but believed that the mechanical engineers of the Stevens Institute of Technology would in the future, as in the past, fulfill the requirements of the profession in this as in other branches.[194]

Thus, in the 1884 catalog there appeared a course in "Applied Electricity," this matching the earliest date in the United States for such a course, the other being at MIT.

The first professor of applied electricity was William E. Geyer (1848-1935) who had graduated with highest honors from CCNY in 1869 with a B.S. degree and then earned the first Stevens Institute Ph.D. in 1877 while working in the Mechanical Laboratory. A brilliant academic internationally known before the turn of the century for his work in chemical dyes, Geyer spanned the disciplines of the era. He was the first member of the Stevens faculty with instructor rank in applied chemistry, the first professor of applied electricity (later electrical engineering) in 1884, and in 1897 he succeeded Mayer as the second Stevens professor of physics.[195]

The year 1884 was also the date when the American Institute of Electrical Engineers (AIEE) organized in preparation for an International Electrical Exhibition in Philadelphia planned by the Franklin Institute. It was thought that electrical engineers should have a professional status and a committee to meet foreign colleagues. Among the seventy-one charter members of the AIEE were three from Stevens Institute: Edward Weston, the Newark-based

---

[194] Clipping of unidentified newspaper attached to letter of Morton to Edison, July 5, 1883, Edison Papers, *Op.Cit.*, reel 64, frame 224.

[195] "Dr. Geyer Rites Held at Tarrytown," *Newark Eagle*, Oct. 10, 1935; "Dr. William E. Geyer," *N.Y. Evening Sun*, Oct. 10, 1935; "Dr. W. E. Geyer Dies," *New York Times*, Oct. 10, 1935.

electrical manufacturer and a Stevens trustee; Edward Pruden Thompson 1878, an inventor of electrical equipment for the Stanley Electric Co. and a patent attorney specializing in electrical engineering; and Joseph Wetzler 1882, an ex-Edward Weston employee who was on the editorial staff of *Scientific American*. In addition, Alfred Mayer was manager of the AIEE's electrical exhibition in New York City in 1887.[196]

At left is William E. Geyer, in 1884 Stevens's first electrical engineering professor.
For the AIEE, he helped to establish American Wire Gauge (AWG) standards.
To the right is Edward Pruden Thompson, 1878, one of the founders of AIEE.

Although Stevens did not have the leading position in the AIEE that it did in the ASME during the early years of both organizations, the institute was nevertheless well represented. In the first twenty years of the AIEE, there were only three years when Stevens men were not officers of the organization. Presidents were Weston (1888-89) and Lieb (1904-05), vice presidents were Weston (1889-91), Wetzler (1890-92), and Lieb (1899-1901 and 1903-04), and managers were Weston (1884-87), Thompson (1887-88), Wetzler (1888-90), Howell (1888-90), Geyer (1888-92), and Lieb (1896-1899 and 1901-03). In addition, William Barstow who later became a Stevens trustee was a vice president in 1903-07, and Dufield Prince 1898 who worked under Barstow at Consolidated Edison was president in 1941-42.

---

[196] *Electrical Engineering, Fiftieth Anniversary AIEE, 1884*-1934(1934), 824, and Stevens *Indicator*, 4 (1887), 213.

More importantly, the first Committee on Standardization created in 1891 contained William E. Geyer. This AIEE committee chaired by A. E. Kennelly made recommendations at the International Electrical Congress of 1893 in Chicago that standard nomenclature be used, namely, the gilbert for magnetomotive force, the weber for flux, the oersted for reluctance, the gauss for flux density, and the henry for the unit of inductive energy. These were adopted for international application by the electrical congress, and legalized by the U.S. Congress for use in America in 1893. Geyer was also on the Standard Wiring and Tube Committee chaired by F. B. Crocker. This committee's report of 1893 assigned the linear resistance of standard conductivity of copper wire at standard temperatures, thus establishing the American Wire Gauge (AWG). Their report included an "AIEE Copper Wire Table" giving diameters, area, and weight of wire, and the resistance in ohms per foot at various temperatures. The table was submitted to the committee by F. B. Crocker, A. E. Kennelly, and William Geyer.[197]

Another early AIEE member was William Henry Peirce (1865-1944) of the class of 1884 who had been a student of Geyer, Thurston, and Leeds in the Mechanical Laboratory. After working briefly for the Edison United Manufacturing Company, in 1890 he was a pioneer in the electrolytic refining of copper for the Baltimore Copper Smelting and Rolling Company. Peirce made this company the foremost copper producer in the United States in the early 1890s at a time when few companies could supply the increasing demand for copper created by the early electric power and light industry. Within six months, Peirce had improved the company's output of electrolytic copper to one ton a day. Later he raised it to thirty-two thousand tons a month by introducing such innovations as the use of water evaporation, instead of water jackets, to cool furnaces, and use of crushed coke instead of charcoal in refining furnaces. Later still, he eradicated hand-ladled furnaces of fifteen tons and substituted tapped three hundred ton charged furnaces which allowed for a copper removal rate of sixty tons an hour. With C. Smith, Peirce invented the Peirce-Smith lined converter into which air was blown into the copper using pipes instead of the earlier "flapping" process, a breakthrough later recognized as fundamental in the advancement of copper production. [198] He became president of the Peirce Smith Converter Company and was vice president of Revere Copper and

---

[197] A. E. Kennelly, "The Work of the Institute in Standardization," *Electrical Engineering. Fiftieth Anniversary AIEE, 1884-1934.*(May 1934), 676-80.
[198] "Peirce, William Henry," *National Cyclopedia of American Biography,* 34, 127-8, "William Peirce '84 Honored," *Stevens Indicator,* 48 (1931), no. 3, 43, and Alfred Bornemann, *Stevens Institute in the Field of Metallurgy During Eight Decades*(1949), 7-8.

Brass Company at the same time that he made Baltimore Copper and Smelting the largest copper producer in the world.

In 1898, the AIEE council appointed another committee on standardization for generators, motors, and transformers chaired by F. B. Crocker. John W. Lieb was on this important committee. It purposefully left sizes and dimensions of electrical machinery to be determined by private industry, but, like Kent's committee in the ASME, it set up standards of testing for the electrical industries in precise understandable language. The report of this committee in 1899 established standard procedures for determining efficiency of engines, dynamos, and motors, and for ascertaining voltages of machines under loads, and determining the efficiencies of insulation -- procedures which were in great demand by industry.

Lastly, Lieb was appointed as one of three AIEE members to ask Andrew Carnegie for a building to house their library and their activities. At the time, the AIEE met in the ASME house at 12 W. 23rd Street in Manhattan. This first attempt to tap the philanthropist for money proved unsuccessful, but, after the AIEE promoted the idea of a "Capitol of Engineering" in New York City and of a joint building in which all engineers could share a library and cooperate, Carnegie donated the funds for the first United Engineering Building to house the AIEE, ASME, AIME, and ASCE at 33 W. 39th Street.[199]

---

[199] Chas. F. Scott, "The Institute's First Half Century." in *Ibid.*, 659-62.

CHAPTER 8
Westinghouse Engineers

In 1885 just after Edison completed building his direct current (DC) lighting system in New York, Lucien Gaulard and John D. Gibbs demonstrated their alternating current (AC) power distribution system at an Inventions Exhibition in London using Gaulard's invention of the transformer. The demonstration proved that AC electrical power could be sent over lines at higher voltage, the transformer stepping up the voltage for transmission and then stepping it down again for use by customers. There were problems with the demonstration because Gaulard and Gibbs had rigged the transformers in series across the transmission lines, and the voltages varied as lamps were turned on and off. Moreover, there were no AC meter and no AC motor at the time. George Westinghouse (1846-1914), the railroad magnate and inventor of the railroad air brake, promptly bought the right to use the AC transformer in the United States.

The main problem with DC illumination and power systems was that they were not commercially practical beyond a range of one-half to three-fourths of a mile from the central station. If sent beyond that range, DC had to run in exceedingly thick copper cables, thus making the extension economically prohibitive. But AC transmission at higher voltages reduced resistive power losses and enabled copper conductors to be thinner and less costly. The new technology held potential for large profits by reducing the number of power plants needed by DC, and by obtaining new customers in less populated areas through long-line transmission. Also, AC could cut costs of transmission of current for the long-distance needs of electric trams, subways and trains -- the railroad man Westinghouse wanted to get the jump on the many companies that were then applying the more costly DC to traction.

In November 1885, William Stanley (1858-1916) redesigned the transformer for Westinghouse. Stanley made it doughnut-shaped, increased the windings, and gave it a heavier iron core as well as lining it up in parallel with the circuit. Stanley made the transformer more efficient and workable which led to the establishment of Westinghouse Electric Company in 1886. During the same year Westinghouse built the first commercial AC distribution system in Buffalo, New York. It was a local system which did not attempt long-line transmission but simply demonstrated that the AC system with transformers was substantially less expensive in copper wiring costs than an equivalent DC system. Orders for Westinghouse AC system equipment began to compete with the Edison DC equipment as local power and light companies spread in the next two years.

Meanwhile, in Europe the Hungarian company of Ganz and Co. of Budapest had pioneered an AC system, and, through John W. Lieb's Edison operation in Italy, the Edison interests obtained Ganz patents for AC transformers in parallel which could have been used by Edison to compete with Westinghouse. The president of the Edison Illuminating Company asked Frank Sprague, another early Edison Pioneer, to make a confidential assessment of AC power in 1886, but, although the report was strongly in favor of AC power, Edison himself chose not to pursue it. He decided to fight AC with arguments like his claim that no AC motor had been developed to utilize AC power for factory work, that there was no AC meter, that DC was useful for battery charging and electroplating, and, most importantly, that AC at higher voltages was dangerous and deadly to use. In fact, in 1887 Edison and his assistant Charles Batchelor conducted "experiments" killing dogs and cats in order to demonstrate for the press the dangers of alternating current. After a polyphase electric motor was invented by Nicola Tesla in 1888 and after Westinghouse developed a meter by 1888, few technical problems regarding AC feasibility remained. Edison was then only left with his safety argument. In that year, Edison was helped by H. P. Brown, previously an assistant of Edison's, who publicly electrocuted cows and horses with "Westinghouse current" to show that it killed quickly and humanely; Brown lobbied with the New York legislature to have a law passed which made electrocution by AC the state's form of capital punishment.[200]

Meanwhile, Edison was trying to have state legislatures pass laws which would ban alternating current. Edison wrote in an 1889 issue of *North American Revue* that, "There is no plea which will justify the use of high tension and alternating current in either a scientific or empirical sense -- My personal desire would be to prohibit entirely the use of alternating currents. They are unnecessary as they are dangerous."[201] When a bill was introduced in the senate of the state of Virginia to prohibit use of electrical potential exceeding eight hundred volts, Edison personally annotated the bill and testified before a committee of senators to obtain its passage. However, Westinghouse sent one of his electrical engineers, Lewis B. Stillwell, and his general counsel, Howard Levis, to Virginia to organize opposition to the bill. They retained a smooth speaking Virginia lawyer to

---

[200] Matthew Josephson, *Edison, A Biography*(1959), 343-8.
[201] C. C. Chesney and Charles F. Scott, "Early History of the A-C System in America," *AIEE Trans.*, 55 (1936), 228-30.

make their argument, and they called in special pro-AC witnesses to testify. Their main witness was Stevens's president, Henry Morton.

According to Stillwell, Edison put on a poor showing as he testified. His deafness made him ask for repetitions of the questions, and his arguments were obscure. His most understandable point was that DC was like the peaceful flow of a river to the sea, but AC was like a torrent of water rushing over a precipice. In contrast, his onetime friend Morton gave a convincing twenty-minute speech in layman's language about the lack of danger of alternating current. He also politely disagreed with Edison's analogy to water: Morton likened DC to water flowing only in one direction in a pipe and AC flowing back and forth in the same pipe. Witnessing the scene, Stillwell later wrote that Morton had a key role in defeating the bill:

It would have been difficult for anyone in 20 minutes in non-technical language to make a statement of the question at issue more reasonable and convincing than Dr. Morton's. While it is highly improbable that any large proportion of the audience, or even of the committee, understood what it was all about, the effect apparently was soothing; and when he finished the alternating current system seemed much less dangerous.[202]

While other attempts to pass prohibitive legislation proved futile, the Virginia decision was a turning point in the battle of the currents, because thereafter the Edison interests decided to abandon Edison and adopt alternating current. Henry Villard, president of Edison General Electric Co., engineered a merger with the AC equipment producer and competitor with Westinghouse, the Thomson-Houston Company, and formed a new entity, General Electric, to compete with Westinghouse. In GE there was no decision-making role for Edison himself, and subsequently the company rapidly developed AC technology which successfully competed with Westinghouse in a few years. As for Edison, by 1908 he told William Stanley's son, "Oh, by the way, tell your father I was wrong."[203]

Meanwhile, William Stanley, now independent of Westinghouse, was carrying out demonstrations at his laboratory at Great Barrington, Massachusetts. He captured the minds of young electrical engineers, one of whom was Stevens's John Forrest Kelly (1859-1922). An immigrant from Carrick-on-Suir, Ireland, Kelly was another electrical prodigy who was working for Edison at Menlo Park in 1879. As a result of his experience and interest in chemistry, he was admitted to a special B.S. program at

---

[202] Lewis B. Stillwell, "Alternating Current Versus Direct Current," *Electrical Engineering Fiftieth Anniversary Number, AIEE 1884-1934*(1934), 709.

[203] Josephson, *Op.Cit.*, 349fn.

Stevens where his brother, James Forrest Kelly 1879, was in the regular engineering program. Both graduated in 1879, one with a B.S. and the other with an M.E. degree. John Forrest Kelly later earned a Ph.D. at Stevens in 1898 after conducting research work.[204] Like Nicola Tesla who briefly worked for Edison, Kelly was more theoretical and mathematical in his research interests than Edison, whose method was painstaking empirical trial and error, a method which Tesla disdained. After graduating, Kelly left Edison and worked first for Western Electric and then for the United States Electric Lighting Company. For the latter he became manager in charge of the company's design and manufacture of a range of electric motors as well as incandescent and arc-light products. When this company was absorbed by the Westinghouse Electric Company, Kelly worked on developing AC systems for Westinghouse. In 1891, he identified the problem of lagging currents on AC motors and lighting systems, and his solution was to supply the lagging component by adding a condenser in parallel with the main motor circuit.[205]

Learning that William Stanley was set on discovering the voltage limits in the transmission of AC, Kelly resigned from Westinghouse and joined the Stanley Laboratory Company in 1892. Working with Stanley who was the overall designer of the system, between 1892 and 1895, Kelly helped to developed what became known as the S-K-C or Stanley-Kelly-Chesney system of AC transmission at Pittsfield, Massachusetts. After joining Stanley and his assistant C. C. Chesney, Kelly pointed out the value of synchronous motors adjusted so the armature current was made to lead or lag behind the AC frequency of the line as desired. Thus, synchronous motors corrected not only the lagging and leading currents of the circuit, but also could be used as a voltage regulator for an AC transmission system -- Kelly's major contribution to the S-K-C system developed by the three. Chesney, who later became a president of the AIEE, designed the overall structure of the transformers and the lines for a circuit for a then-whopping fifteen thousand volt AC transmission on the Pittsfield farm, a one thousand volt potential being stepped up to fifteen thousand volts and stepped down again to one thousand volts.[206] As a result of this successful and well-publicized demonstration of AC controlled voltage transmission, all three

---

[204] *Catalogue of the Stevens Institute of Technology, 1918-19,* 205.

[205] Furman, *Morton Memorial, Op.Cit.,* 444.

[206] C. C. Chesney, "Some Contributions to the Electric Industry," *Electrical Engineering, Fiftieth Anniversary Number, Op.Cit.,* 727-8, and J. W. T. Hammond, *Men and Volts: The Story of General Electric*(1948), 179..

men began to promote the S-K-C system for even higher voltages, which even Westinghouse doubted was possible.

Kelly's stake in the S-K-C patents for the system was considerable since he had thirty-tow patents jointly with Stanley, seven jointly with Chesney, and two others with both Stanley and Chesney. Some of these patents were foreign, including ones granted in numerous European countries. Kelly became a leading project engineer in the design and installation of high voltage AC systems throughout the country.[207] He became known as the "original 60,000 volt man" by designing and installing the Bay Counties hydroelectric power plant at Colgate, California. This project was featured in *Harper's Weekly* and the *New York Herald* in December 1901, and it generated nine thousand horsepower in three dynamos driven by turbines after a seven hundred-foot fall of water, the stepped up pressure of sixty thousand volts being sent to San Francisco 142 miles away. At this time GE's brilliant Charles P. Steinmetz was making guarded statements that sixty thousand volt transmissions could not be guaranteed in practicability. As amazing as it was at the time, voltage again doubled in the next ten years to 120,000 volts and continued to climb.[208]

Another project involving Westinghouse and Stevens was the revolutionary hydroelectric plant at Niagara Falls in the 1890s. In 1889, the New York financier Edward D. Adams consulted Edison on generation of DC electricity by the power of Niagara Falls. The proposed plan was to dig tunnels a mile above the falls into which water would flow through turbines around the falls and debouch at the river edge below them. However, Edison's continued adherence to DC power could not compete with Westinghouse's rival plan to generate AC power which could then be transmitted twenty-two miles to Buffalo.

At that point, the proponents of AC power were consulted: Henry Morton, his friend professor of physics Henry Rowland of Johns Hopkins, and Coleman Sellers.[209] Coleman Sellers wrote their report enthusiastically supported the Westinghouse plan, and, as a result, Sellers was made chief consulting engineer to the Cataract Construction Company. This firm was established by Adams with Westinghouse backing to design and construct the water tunnels, and choose appropriately sized turbines, generators, and transformers for the largest hydroelectric project in the world at the time. In

---

[207] Harold C. Passer, *The Electrical Manufacturers: 1875-1900*(1953), 338, and Furman, *Morton Memorial, Op.Cit.*, 446, and 579-80.

[208] Passer, *Op.Cit.*, 309; Furman, *Morton Memorial, Op.Cit.*, 445; and Harris J. Ryan, "Developments in Electric Power Transmission," *Electrical Engineering Fiftieth Anniversary Number, Op.Cit.*, 712-4.

[209] Passer, *Op.Cit.*, 284-5, 288.

1890, Sellers organized the International Niagara Commission, a consultative body which included Sellers's friend William Thompson (Lord Kelvin) and the Swiss hydroelectric specialist Thomas Turrettini. This commission held a contest offering cash prizes for the best designs for the components of the project, and through this method determined the plans for tunneling, and the types of turbines and generators finally adopted for the Niagara-based, one-hundred-and-fifty-thousand-horsepower hydroelectric plant.[210]

Coleman Sellers (1827-1907) was the friend of Henry Morton, the man who influenced Frederick W. Taylor, the first professor of engineering practice at Stevens (thus perhaps the first in the nation to introduce engineering students to engineering management), as well as as the chief engineer of the Niagara Falls Power Company.

[210] *Stevens Indicator*, 7 (1990), 284.

Subsequently, after the tunnels were completed in 1891, Sellers was made chief engineer or engineering manager of the Cataract Construction Company to coordinate the engineers installing the machinery. The Niagara five-thousand horsepower generating units were in operation by 1895 when Cataract Construction turned over the hydroelectric system to a new Adams-organized firm, the Niagara Power Company whose first president was also Sellers.[211] The turbines were of the Fourneyron type, double-wheeled, turning at 250 RPM at a depth of 140 feet inside a shaft of falling water. Sellers himself designed Westinghouse dynamos as part of the earliest equipment in the first power station.[212] The main generators were designed by Benjamin G. Lamme, the brilliant Westinghouse engineer, and were the first of his "umbrella" type, the rotating field elements being outside the stationary armature to provide two-phase power generated at two thousand volts and twenty-five cycles.[213] The following year, transmission to Buffalo started, voltage being stepped up to eleven thousand volts and stepped down to one thousand volts, the distance being twenty-two miles.[214] The Niagara hydroelectric project was the "largest single step forward" in successful generation and transmission of AC up to that date.[215]

Among Westinghouse engineers was Alexander J. Wurts (1862-1932) of the class of 1884. After two years of post-graduate study in Germany in electrical engineering, Wurts found employment on the research staff of the Westinghouse Electric and Manufacturing Company. From 1897 to 1901, he designed machinery for Westinghouse in the successful development and commercial production of the Nernst Lamp, Westinghouse making Wurts manager of his Nernst Lamp Company to manufacture it. In 1904, Westinghouse introduced Wurts to Andrew Carnegie, and the Stevens graduate who held over one hundred patents was made first professor and head of the electrical engineering department at the Carnegie Technical School which later became the Carnegie Institute of Technology.[216]

Another effort of Stevens graduates was the application of electric current to trains and subways. One Stevens pioneer here was Henry Morton Brinkerhoff (1868-1949) of the class of 1890. Brinkershoff, like Van Vleck and

---

[211] Henry Morton, "Coleman Sellers, A Biographical Sketch," *Cassier's Magazine,* 24 (1903), 362.

[212] "Obituary; Dr. Coleman Sellers," *Stevens Indicator,* 25 (1908), 71-77, "Sellers, Coleman," *Dictionary of American Biography,* 575, and *ASME's Engineers of the 19th Century,* 273.

[213] Biography of Lamme, *Electrical Engineering Fiftieth Anniversary Number, Op.Cit.,* 817.

[214] W. S. Lee, "Water Power Development," *Electrical Engineering Fiftieth Anniversary Number, Op.Cit.,* 714.

[215] P. M. Lincoln, "Some Reminiscences of Niagara," *Ibid.,* 720.

[216] Obituary, *Stevens Indicator,* 49 (1932), 56.

Jacobus, was from Dutch descent, but his mother was a sister of Henry Morton, and so he also had Scottish ancestry -- he was named, of course, after the first president of Stevens Institute of Technology. Brinkerhoff was best known for his development of third-rail technology in electric traction.[217]

 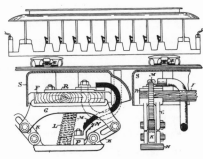

Henry Morton Brinkerhoff, 1890, the son of President Henry Morton's sister, was one of the top 125 civil engineers in the last 125 years according to *ENR: Engineering News-Record.* At right, his patent drawing for the third rail in electric traction.

In 1888, the father of electric traction, Frank Sprague, had set up the first successful DC trolley system in Richmond, Virginia, and electric trolleys, much smaller and slower than steam locomotive trains, had sprung up in major cities in America and Europe in the early nineties. In major cities like Chicago and New York, trolleys powered by overhead supply of electricity had replaced horse-drawn streetcars on tracks in the crowded streets and were competing at ground level with steam-driven trains on elevated tracks or "els."[218]

In 1890-91, Brinkerhoff entered the electric traction field after graduation by working for the Thompson-Houston Electric Company of Boston, a company later bought by Westinghouse. There he gained experience by working on Boston's West End Street Railway on its electric-power-house genera-

---

[217] *ENR: Engineering News-Record 125th Anniversary,* 50.

[218] See R. J. Buckley, *A History of Tramways from Iron Horse to Rapid Transit*(1975): Frank J. Sprague, "The History and Development of Electric Railroads" *Trans. International Elect. Conf.* 1904.

tion, distribution lines, and electric car equipment. He then performed similar duties for the Utica, Brooklyn and Coney Island railways before moving to Chicago to work with General Electric as assistant electrical engineer on the Intramural Railway at the World's Columbian Exposition in 1892-94.

For this railroad in 1894, he co-invented with C. H. Macloskie the first third electrified rail to carry electricity instead of the overhead connectors which street-level trolleys had previously used. The Intramural Railway with its eighteen four-car trains was elevated and made a circuit of the fairgrounds every twenty minutes at a then-rapid speed of twenty-five miles per hour. The project was a showcase of advanced technology for els, the third rail transmitting current to the DC engines in the cars though a shoe which projected from the cars and slid along the third rail -- technology still used by subways today. The 1893 *Street Railway Journal* praised the Intramural Railway's quiet and smooth operation and observed, "(It is) the next advance on the trolley car -- itself a factor in daily life only five or six years -- and the doom of the steam car seems ready to be sealed."[219]

An older Stevens graduate, George Gibbs of the class of 1882, was a world-leading electrical engineer in the field of electric locomotive design and conversion of steam-powered railroad lines to electricity. During his most productive period between 1900 and 1910, Gibbs was personally responsible for the electrification and construction of New York's Pennsylvania Station, the design of subway cars for New York City's first subway, and the electrification of tracks under Grand Central Station. Also, Gibbs designed the world's first all-steel railroad car.

Upon graduation from Stevens Institute, Gibbs immediately went to work for Thomas Edison to test and superintend his chemical meters which measured customers' electrical usage on the original Pearl Street Station project in 1882-83.[220] The meters measured the flow of electricity by the weight of copper deposits on a plate as a result of electrolytic reaction. The Edison papers contain twenty documents of Gibbs's technical notes and

---

[219] Arthur G. Bendelius, "Henry Morton Brinkerhoff," Parsons-Brinkerhoff document sent to Harold J. Raveché from Bendelius, May 8, 2000.

[220] Gibbs's grandfather was a world-renowned mineralogist at Yale University. His grandmother was the daughter of Oliver Wolcott, signer of the Declaration of Independence and a cabinet member in the administrations of Washington and Adams. One of his uncles was Oliver Wolcott Gibbs(1822-1908), Rumford Professor of Science at Harvard whose chemical studies of the complex acids formed by metal alloys and of the electrolytic qualities of copper and nickel were pioneering. Another uncle, George Gibbs (1815-1873) was a well-known American historian, ethnologist and geologist. See *National Cyclopaedia of American Biography*, Vol. E, 120-1. David B. Sloan, *George Gibbs, M.E., D.Eng. (1861-1940), L. Rowland Hill, M.E., E.E. (1872-1948), Pioneers in Railroad Electrification*(Newcomen Society, 1957), 9-10.

drawings during tests of the meter for accuracy and reliability in both laboratory and actual working conditions. Also included are two letters regarding employment. He stayed with Edison until the meters were set up and had proven to be reliable.[221]

His next major job was in the main area of his life's work, railroads. He became chemist and engineer of tests for the Chicago, Milwaukee & St. Paul Railroad. In 1885, Gibbs became mechanical engineer of this railroad and of the Milwaukee and Northern Railroad in charge of design of steam locomotives, railroad cars, and interlocking track signals. He also supervised chemical and mechanical tests of materials. In the next ten years he was credited with the first practical design of steam heating for railroad passenger cars as well as designing systems of electric car-lighting for the first St. Paul railroad. Still working for these companies, in 1895 he established the Gibbs Electric Co. of Milwaukee to manufacture electric motors.

At that point his reputation for inventive brilliance attracted the attention of Samuel Vauclain of the Baldwin Locomotive Works and George Westinghouse who wanted Gibbs to work with them on the cutting edge of electric locomotion technology. In 1897, Westinghouse clearly saw a breakthrough was near in urban mass transit, a breakthrough into heavier, faster electric locomotion, and he invited Gibbs to collaborate in the development of heavy electric rail locomotion.[222]

Gibbs seized the opportunity. He resigned from his railroad positions in the Chicago area, sold Gibbs Electric Co. to Westinghouse, and was made a joint consulting engineer to both the Baldwin Locomotive Works and Westinghouse Electric and Manufacturing Company. Westinghouse's personal connection with Gibbs assured the latter's success. Gibbs's job was to design electric locomotives for both freight and passenger service. From 1897 to 1901, he traveled frequently to Europe where he was chief engineer for electric traction projects of Westinghouse companies in England, France, Germany, Austria and Russia. Gibbs's major projects in Europe were supervision of the electrification of the Mersey railroad near Liverpool and the Metropolitan Inner Circle Line of the London Underground. He was also a consultant on electrification of the Paris Metro.

Gibbs reached the zenith of his career in his forties between 1901 and 1910 when he simultaneously had the leading electrical engineering role in three New York City projects: First, the first New York subway, second, the Pennsylvania Railroad's access to New York City by tunnels and the con-

---

[221] *Edison Papers.* N.Y.U. microfilm, see reels 38, 44, and 60.
[222] Sloan, *Op. Cit.*, 11.

struction of Pennsylvania Station, and third, the electrification of the Grand Central Station by the New York Central Railroad.

The origin of the subway plan went back to 1887 when the Father of Modern Rapid Transit, none other than Abram Stevens Hewitt, who was New York City's mayor at the time, called for a truly rapid subway system to quickly transport people from one end of the city to another to relieve the congestion in lower Manhattan and to develop the unpopulated Bronx. His visionary plan for a public, municipal role in such a subway system resulted in the Rapid Transit Act passed by New York state and ratified by a referendum of New York City citizens in 1894. The plan was to use money raised by a city bond issue to construct a subway using a private company; the overall planning of routes and services was to be determined by a Rapid Transit Commission appointed by the city. The subway would then be leased to the same private company, which would provide rolling stock and management, pledging to pay the city not only the interest on the bonds but one percent per annum for a fund to eventually liquidate the bonds. In the end, the city would inherit a fully equipped subway free of any debt.

The Interborough Rapid Transit Company (IRT) of August Belmont, backed by Rothschild money, emerged with the contract by 1902, and the overall engineering supervision was conducted by William Barclay Parsons, a well-known civil engineer. Henry Morton Brinkerhoff, after traveling to Europe in 1906 to investigate electric railways in England, Belgium, France and Germany, joined Parsons and Eugene Lapp in an engineering consulting firm which became, by the late 19th century, Parson Brinkerhoff Quade and Douglas, Inc., of New York City -- the top-ranked transportation design firm in the United States by that time.

On the IRT project, the older Gibbs was retained as the overall consultant on electrical matters, and other Stevens electrical engineers were retained as well. A key role was given to John Van Vleck 1884, another Edison Pioneer and friend of Lieb who had built central stations for Consolidated Edison. Van Vleck was put in charge of designing the machinery and layout of the subway's central power station located between 58th and 59th Streets and Eleventh and Twelfth Avenues. His innovations included automated coal distribution to boilers and a flexible system of steam pressure distribution to different engine/dynamo units depending on the peak and off-peak hours of the subways.[223] Percy Litchfield 1897 worked on two electrical substations in Manhattan and one in Brooklyn while his brother, Norman Litchfield 1901, worked under Gibbs to test Westinghouse and General Electric mo-

---

[223] Barbara Kimmelman, "Design and Construction of the IRT: Electrical Engineering," *Interborough Rapid Transit Subway. Historic American Engineering Records*(1979), 283-364.

tors on Gibbs-designed rolling stock.[224] Norman Litchfield later became president of Gibbs and Hill, the company founded by Gibbs.

Besides being in charge of the third rail and the signal equipment, George Gibbs designed all the original rolling stock of the IRT.[225] Three problems faced Gibbs: the tunnels, smaller than the later tunnels of the BMT and IND subway lines, put constraints on heights and shapes to allow for clearances especially around curves; the subway was to operate at higher speeds than any existing electric trolley or subway trains, which necessitated great strength and light weight of materials; for safety in tunnels, materials needed to be non-combustible.

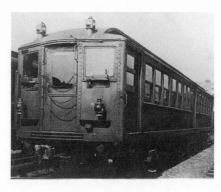

George Gibbs, was the Westinghouse and Penn RR engineer who pioneered the all-steel subway and railroad car. Gibbs-cars, nicknamed "merry widows" and "battleships" by IRT employees, outlasted composite subway cars by decades and were not scrapped until the 1950s.

Gibbs considered all-steel cars from the start, but no car of this type had ever been built, not for trolleys or subways or railroads, and manufacturers who were approached refused to accept the idea. Therefore, Gibbs designed IRT cars made of composites, and he did the best he could to make them safe, using anti-telescoping iron support beams, asbestos under the hard-

---

[224] F. DeR. Furman, *Morton Memorial*(1905), 470-471.
[225] The best description of Gibbs's work on the all-steel car is in David J. Framberger, "Architectural Designs for New York's First Subway," *Interborough Rapid Transit Subway. Historic American Engineering Records*(1979), 18-20.

wood floors, and copper sheathing over the wooden siding. Five hundred of the composite cars were ordered in 1902 in order to meet the 1904 subway opening deadline. Meanwhile, Gibbs continued to work on designs for an all-steel car. Since he was also consultant to the Pennsylvania Railroad (PRR) project, he convinced the PRR that it also needed a similar all-steel car for its tunnels, and it consented to build one in its Altoona, Pennsylvania railroad shops. This first experimental model was too heavy, so Gibbs redesigned it, and the PRR built the first successful all-steel car according to Gibbs's patented design. Gibbs did away with the weight of the first car by eradicating the heavy steel underpinnings which supported the floor and frame. His most novel innovation was to support the floor load by hanging it from the lighter side framing. The general appearance of the all-steel car was the same as the composites, except for rivets on the exterior rolled sheet steel. The interior trim around doors and windows was not mahogany but steel, and sheet aluminum was used on the interior walls to reduce weight. In 1904, the IRT ordered two hundred "Gibbs-cars" and one hundred more soon after. Later versions were modified to expand the size of the doors and to put doors in the center of the car in addition to the ends.[226]

Meanwhile, the Pennsylvania Railroad's plan was to gain access to New York City. Its main line to New York ended at the Jersey City Exchange Place ferry terminal, but the PRR wanted to take a new line from its Jersey City/Harrison terminal, called "Manhattan Transfer," directly into Manhattan under the Hudson River. The plan called for a line running across the Jersey meadowlands, going through a tunnel which started on the west side of Bergen Hill and continuing under the Hudson to mid-Manhattan, thence under Manhattan's 33rd Street, under the East River and terminating in a yard in Long Island. There was to be a monstrous station, Pennsylvania Station, between 31st and 33rd Streets and between Seventh and Eighth Avenues on the west side of Manhattan.[227] The whole line from just south of Newark all the way to Long Island was to be electrified. The PRR created a board of six distinguished engineers led by Charles W. Raymond of the Army Corps of Engineers to carry out the plan; the others were a tunneling engineer, a bridge engineer, a civil engineer, the chief engineer of the PRR, and George Gibbs -- the only electrical traction engineer among them. The work was divided among the engineers on a geographic basis for the most part. Gibbs was responsible for Manhattan, and the rest of the engineers divided up the wetlands, the tunnels and the

---

[226] Gene Sansone, *Evolution of the New York City Subways; An Illustrated History of New York City's Transit Cars, 1867-1997*(MTA, 1997), 25-32.

[227] R. Ziel and G. Foster, *Steel Rails Into the Sunset*(1965), 183-4.

Long Island yard -- except that Gibbs was in charge of the electrification aspects of the whole operation. Since he had Manhattan, it meant that he was responsible for supervision of the work contracts for building the Pennsylvania Station's superstructure as well as for the electrification of its twenty-eight acres of yards underneath.[228]

The PRR had different power needs than the IRT. Instead of cars with motors, the PRR needed an electric locomotive, and Gibbs was made chairman of a design committee to produce one. Two experimental locomotives were built by the PRR using Westinghouse motors by 1905, and they were tested on Long Island Railroad track after the PRR acquired the LIRR around that time. They were found to cause damage to the tracks because of excessive lateral pressure at the rail heads at high speeds. Gibbs had them redesigned with a higher center of gravity, a larger proportion of weight on the springs, greater amplitude of motion, and a new combination of driving and carrying wheels. The redesigned electric locomotives, massive in weight and moving at speeds up to eighty MPH, were not destructive to the roadbed. They were called the DD1 class by the PRR and are considered a classic design today.[229]

Meanwhile, by the end of 1902 the New York Central had decided to electrify its Grand Central Station and the lines into Westchester County. It established an Electric Traction Commission consisting of three experienced electrical engineers led by Frank Sprague, -- the other two were Bion J. Arnold, the AIEE's president in 1903-04, and the relatively younger Gibbs. In the process of the electrification and expansion of gates under the old station, the New York Central brought in architects, Charles Read and Whitney Warren mainly, to redesign the superstructure resulting in the station's current classic appearance.[230]

Gibbs and his assistant E. Roland Hill worked solely on the Pennsylvania Station project in 1909-10 to complete it by the latter year. The architectural plans were by Stanford White, and it was nicknamed "the Temple of Transportation" because he modeled it on the Basilica of Constantinople. It contained 500,000 cubic feet of Milford pink granite supported by 650 steel columns covering eight acres. Beneath the station, twenty-one tracks handled 750 trains a day. Gibbs was entrusted by the Pennsylvania Railroad to spend upwards of a one hundred million dollars on the project. After its

[228] William D. Middleton, *Manhattan Gateway; New York's Pennsylvania Station*(Kalmbach Press, 1996), 20-23.
[229] *Ibid,* 43-49.
[230] William D. Middleton, *Grand Central, The World's Greatest Railroad Terminal*(1982), 57, 71.

completion, Gibbs and E. Roland Hill formed an engineering consulting company specializing in electrification of railroads, and they had their offices inside Pennsylvania Station. During World War I, Gibbs inspected thirty thousand miles of railroads in Russia and Siberia as a member of the United States Government Advisory Committee of Railroad Experts to Russia. In the 1920s Gibbs and Hill became internationally recognized as the world-leading engineers in electric traction, and Gibbs continued actively in the company until he died in 1940[231] -- twenty-four years before the Pennsylvania Station was torn down in what the *New York Times* called a "monumental act of vandalism."

Meanwhile in 1915-16, Henry Morton Brinkerhoff of the Parsons-Brinkerhoff firm served as chief engineer for the Chicago Subway Commission which prepared a comprehensive plan for the consolidation of the windy city's elevated and surface-car lines and construction of a subway system in the Loop district. In 1913-19, he advised the Detroit Board of Street Railway Commissioners on rerouting street railways to alleviate traffic congestion, and in 1919-20 he performed a similar function as engineer for the Cleveland Rapid Transit Commission.

---

[231] Sloan, *Op. Cit., 12-13.*

CHAPTER 9

Tradition of Broad-Based Engineering Curriculum

One of the misconceptions about the early Stevens curriculum has been that it was narrowly focused on mechanical engineering in the early years. Nothing could be further from the actual facts if the catalogs are reviewed. By the end of the nineteenth century, the Stevens curriculum's required core contained all the fundamental courses in the fields of civil, electrical, chemical, and materials engineering, in addition to mechanical engineering and its associated shop courses. Also, Stevens's engineering curriculum was perhaps the first in the United States to include courses in the economic factors of engineering. The success of this uniquely broad-based curriculum was obvious because by 1905 fully one-third of all Stevens graduates were in managerial or entrepreneurial ranks.

Civil engineering content was there from the start as a result of DeVolson Wood's presence as professor of mathematics. DeVolson Wood (1832-1897) was a farmer's son from upstate New York who was a child prodigy in mathematics. Supposedly, he performed mathematical calculations on the rocks of his father's farm because of a lack of paper, and he started teaching mathematics at seventeen years of age while attending the Albany State Normal School from which he graduated in 1853. He then obtained a C.E. degree from Rensselaer Polytechnic Institute (RPI) in 1857 while teaching mathematics in its preparatory school. Thereafter, he was professor of civil engineering at the University of Michigan from 1857 to 1871 and compiled a record of scholarship in applied mathematics by publishing in numerous journals including Morton's *Journal of the Franklin Institute* -- in all, over seventy-five technical articles and six textbooks, which were widely used. Among the titles in civil engineering were *Revision of Mahan's Civil Engineering, Trussed Bridges and Roofs, Momentum and Vis Viva* and *Resistance of Solid Bodies*. Wood applied mathematics to mechanical engineering especially after arriving at Stevens in 1871; some titles were "Dynamics," "Elements of Analytical Mechanics," "Key and Supplement to the Mechanics of Fluids," and a textbook entitled *Thermodynamics*. When Thurston left Stevens in 1885, the versatile Wood became the professor of mechanical engineering. Catalogs show that Stevens students took four years of mathematical instruction under Wood in such topics as differential and integral calculus, analytical mechanics, graphical statics, resistance of materials, theory of bridges and roofs, as well as the use of transit and level.

Catalogs show that Stevens students have always taken statics.[232] An application of his teaching is illustrated with the career of the versatile nephew of Henry Morton, Henry Morton Brinkerhoff, who worked on the design and construction of the Queensborough tunnels under New York's East River during the IRT project.

Electricity and its applications were a subspecialty of physicist Alfred M. Mayer, whose main interest was acoustics. A friend of Joseph Henry, co-discoverer of induction with Faraday, Mayer gave a Harvard lecture on his friend in 1880 entitled "Henry as a Discoverer." Mayer also published articles in the *American Journal of Science* and the *Journal of the Franklin Institute* on a galvanometer he designed in 1872, as well as later articles on instruments to measure inductive capacities and on his experiments giving new proofs of Ohm's law.[233] Mayer participated in electrical research in the Mechanical Laboratory with William Geyer. A CCNY graduate who earned Stevens's first Ph.D. degree at Stevens in physics in 1877,[234] Geyer successfully tested dynamos and electrical equipment while working in the Mechanical Laboratory from 1877 to 1884, and the institute rewarded him with an appointment as professor of applied electricity in 1884 -- the same year as the first electrical engineering course at MIT.[235] Geyer's Laboratory of Applied Electricity was stocked with equipment obtained during the "commercial experimenting" in the spring of 1884, namely, a Weston shunt dynamo capable of four hundred volts and forty amperes and an extensive collection of electrical instruments, voltmeters, dynamometers, galvanometers, and rheostats for testing purposes. By the turn of the century, the institutes' electrical engineering laboratory, one of the first of its kind in existence, was being described in Stevens literature as "second to none," and the electrical engineering offerings were described as comparable to those courses of study at institutions offering a specialized E.E. degree. The inclusion in 1884 of Geyer's electrical engineering courses in the core curriculum leading to the M.E. degree at Stevens was justified in the same way that fundamental engineering science courses in other specialties were later justified, namely, by the claim of ASME leaders at the time, many of them Stevens faculty and alumni, that the expertise and scope of the mechanical

---

[232] Furman, *Op. Cit,* 236-8.

[233] A. M. Mayer, "A New Form of Lantern Galvanometer," *Journal of the Franklin Institute,* 1872; "Experiments with a Pendulum-Electrometer," *American Journal of Science,* May 1890, "On a Large Spring Balance Electrometer," *Ibid.,* June 1890, and "An Experimental Proof of Ohm's Law," *Ibid.,* July 1890.

[234] *Catalogue of the Stevens Institute of Technology,* 1884-5, 67.

[235] David F. Noble, *America By Design* (1977), 136.

engineer was all-inclusive and incorporated all other special branches of engineering.[236]

In the small B.S. degree program, Brown Ayers, who later became president of the University of Tennessee, earned a degree in physics in 1879. Wilbur Brown, who joined the Harvard Observatory, earned a B.S. in mathematics and physics in 1980, William Dougherty, who became a lawyer, earned a B.S. in 1878, and both John F. Kelly and Durand Woodman, who became well-known electrical engineers, earned B.S. degrees in science in 1878 and 1880 respectively. This small program was a model for the larger-scale 1950s Stevens degree program in science leading to the B.S., M.S., and Ph.D. degrees on a much larger scale.[237]

The catalogs show that Albert Ripley Leeds (1843-1902) taught applied chemistry in addition to theoretical chemistry. His seventy-plus publications show his specialty was mineralogy and materials engineering as well as solutions to problems of sanitation and pollution. Some titles were "New Methods for the Estimation of Combined Carbon in Iron and Steel," "A New Test Reaction for Zinc," "Determination of Ferrous Oxides in Silicates," "The Spectra of Certain Metallic Compounds," and "Enlarged and Reduced Photographs of Alloys of Copper and Tin, Broken by Transverse, Longitudinal, and Torsion Strains." This last publication came as a result of Leeds's participation in Thurston's grant from the Navy to study alloys of copper, zinc and tin.[238] His two year course for all students included material common to mining and materials engineering such as "examination of ores, with instruction in the chemistry of metallurgical processes."[239] When Leeds died in 1902, the professorship's name was changed to the more appropriate "Professor of Engineering Chemistry" when it was filled by Thomas B. Stillman, Leeds's assistant since 1876. Stillman held a Master of Science degree from Rutgers earned in 1878. He earned Stevens's second Ph.D., awarded to him in chemistry in 1883.[240]

A goal of the early curriculum design at Stevens was to develop the practical experience of students through shop practice, but shop was not established until 1878 because of financial constraints. The course itself was developed and taught by personnel from the Mechanical Laboratory. Thur-

---

[236] "The Institute's Electrical Facilities," *Stevens Indicator*, IV (1887), 8-13, and "Institute Notes," *Stevens Indicator*, XVI (1899), 51.

[237] See list of graduates and their degrees in *Catalogue of the Stevens Institute of Technology*, 1884-5, 64-75.

[238] Robert H. Thurston, *Abstract of Statement of the Extent and Character of the Work of the United States Board Appointed to Test Iron, Steel, and Other Metals*(1878), 110.

[239] For example, *Annual Catalogue of the Stevens Institute of Technology, 1884-5*, 56.

[240] *Ibid.*, 72.

ston had acknowledged when Stevens opened its doors that the science-based European model for a mechanical engineering curriculum contained no shop work. But he had consulted other engineers in 1870 who favored inclusion of practical methods of apprenticeship training as a concession to the Anglo-American prejudices of employers who might be skeptical of the value of graduates in possession of only theory with no hands-on experience. Thus, although Thurston pointedly wrote in 1884 that shop was usually taught in trade schools and apprenticeships and that it was not central to a curriculum whose core was "higher mathematics and advanced courses in physics and chemistry," it was nevertheless "an essential feature of the school." He wrote that shop acquainted the student of theory with the "practical methods" of the "trades subsidiary to the several branches of engineering" which were ultimately concerned with the design of mechanical apparatus or design of construction:

The engineer is dependent upon the machinist, the founder, the pattern maker, and other workers at the trades for the proper construction of the machinery and structure designed by him. He is himself, insofar as he is an engineer, a designer of construction, not a constructor.[241]

Although Stevens Institute did not have the funds and space to create a fully developed shop course in its first years of operation, a machine shop was established by Thurston in 1871 as an adjunct to the fledgling Mechanical Laboratory. It was in this machine shop that many of the early undergraduates obtained invaluable experience constructing testing devices and other apparatus for the Mechanical Laboratory, where they often also participated in actual funded research. Thurston pushed the trustees for funding of a modest shop course which was in place by 1878. After further appeals for funding, the course was expanded in 1881 but was not fully developed until two years after Thurston left Stevens in 1887. It should be noted that Thurston stressed that shop work in bench tools, mill work, planing, foundry work, machine tooling, and instruction in materials consisted of fewer instructional hours at Stevens compared to other mechanical engineering courses of study developed elsewhere.[242] The relation between the shop and Thurston's research was a close one because the full-time research assis-

---

[241] R. H. Thurston, "Instruction in Mechanical Engineering." *Journal of the Franklin Institute,* CXVIII (1884), 190-191 and R. H. Thurston, "The First Ten Years of Stevens Institute of Technology," *Stevens Indicator,* II (1885), 82.

[242] Thurston, "The First Ten Years," *Op.Cit.,* 81-84, "New Machine Shop at Stevens Institute," *American Machinist,* April 23, 1881, 8, and "The New Shop Schedule," *Stevens Indicator,* IV (1887), 45-6.

tants in the Mechanical Laboratory became the instructors in the undergraduate shop course. For example, James E.Denton, while working in the
Mechanical Laboratory, was made instructor of applied mechanics and shop
practice soon after he successfully taught the first shop course in 1878.[243]

This photo of the faculty of Stevens in 1896 has been cut into two groups:
At top from the left are professors Wood, Ganz, Riesenberger, Furman,
and Graydon, president Morton, and professor Webb. Below are professors
Kroeh, Denton, (unidentified), Bristol (rear), Geyer, and Jacobus.

When Denton was promoted to professor of experimental engineering and
made superintendent of tests in 1886, his assistant in both the laboratory
and the shop, David S. Jacobus, became the instructor in the shop course.
As the student body and tuition revenues grew modestly, Denton developed

---

[243] Interestingly, Denton's father, James W. Denton had been a machinist at the Watertown Arsenal
and then took a job at Stevens as the machine shop's machinist and maintenance man. *Stevens
Indicator,* XVII (1900), 207.

a new "experimental engineering" course which consisted of students performing a series of thirty-three tests on such machinery as a steam boiler, a condensing engine, a compound engine, a rotary engine, a steam pump, safety valves and indicators, steam radiators, hydraulic rams and on metals and lubricants. Students were required to learn methods to calculate the efficiency of an apparatus using statistical and graphic terms and how to relate efficiency to costs. In addition, all experimental engineering laboratory apparatus -- which were housed in the Department of Tests -- had to be dismantled and put back together again unless they were being commercially used.[244] Meanwhile, Jacobus continued to work in the Department of Tests where commercial experiments supplied a good number of his fifty-plus articles to engineering journals. Jacobus also became a professor of experimental engineering at Stevens from 1899 to 1908 after which he did testing and experimental work for the boiler manufacturers, Babcock and Wilcox Company.[245] Jacobus claimed that in 1889, after a trip to Europe to investigate German, French and English technical schools' curricula in the area of experimental engineering, Stevens seemed to be the world leader in the field. The results from his visits to the Polytecnicum of Aix-la-Chapelle, Berlin, Darmstadt, Carlsruhe, Zurich, and Dresden surprised Jacobus. While these institutions had testing laboratories, courses in experimental engineering were not developed as widely as at Stevens -- "the professors not seeming to acknowledge the value, to a student, of being able to apply theory he has learned and thus obtain a confidence and familiarity with it that can be acquired in no other way."[246] In support of Jacobus's observation, an analysis of the 158 members of the Society for the Promotion of Engineering Education in 1894 finds only five professors of experimental Engineering, and they were all from schools which had commercial laboratories by that time, namely, two from Stevens, and one each from Purdue, Syracuse, and Thurston's Sibley College at Cornell.[247]

Perhaps the most important innovative type of professorship at Stevens in the early years was that of "engineering practice," because it introduced the

---

[244] See D. S. Jacobus, *Experimental Mechanics: Tests and Experiments Made by the Class of 1900 of the Stevens Institute of Technology*(Hoboken, 1899); "New Apparatus for Instruction in Engine Testing," *Stevens Indicator*, IV (1887), 24-27: D. S. Jacobus, "Discussion: Original Research by Students," *Proc. Society for the Promotion of Engineering Education*, I (1893), 226-7; and D. S. Jacobus, "Laboratory Courses in Engineering Schools: Discussion," *Trans. ASME*, XXVI (1905), 664-6.

[245] For Jacobus's career see "Stevens Men in the Press: David S. Jacobus '84, Modern Pioneer," *Stevens Indicator*, LVII (1940), 4-5, and Furman, *Morton Memorial, Op. Cit., 257-262.*

[246] D. S. Jacobus, "Experimental Mechanics as Developed in Foreign Technical Schools," *Stevens Indicator*, VI (1889), no. 4, 257-63.

[247] *Proc. Society for the Promotion of Engineering Education*, II (1894), 8-15.

students to the economics of engineering and shop management perhaps before any other engineering school in the country. Thurston's original design for the M.E. course called for guest lectures by practicing engineers, and such lectures commenced in the first year of the institute's operations. One of these lecturers, Morton's friend Coleman Sellers, became Stevens's professor of engineering practice in 1884. As already pointed out, Sellers had been chief engineer at William Sellers and Co. where he had influenced Frederick W. Taylor's early metal-cutting experiments when scientific management had its genesis.[248] The titles of Sellers's lectures included such topics as "The Machine Shop," and "Rules, Tables, and Notes on Engineering Practice." In 1888, Sellers wrote that

The chair of Engineering Practice is founded with the view of bringing the customs and usages of the shop to the knowledge of the student at a time when his previous training in general principles and acquaintance with the actual operations of tools from their use in the Institute workshops, have prepared him to understand and appreciate the instruction given. Rules and regulations governing the methods of work, governing the processes of designing, governing the selection of materials, governing the selection of tools and methods, governing the mercantile relations of the subject, and governing the management of men, will all be naturally developed in the work of this department. The young engineer must know that he may be called upon to manage establishments . . . [249]

Sellers thought that "perfection of the personnel" to improve "their work in quantity and quality" was essential for large earnings in manufacturing establishments. He cited one of his personal mentors, Sir Joseph Whitworth of England whom he had met personally, as being a champion of "shop perfection." He thought that

The highest schooling is needed to make good engineers but such schooling can be made easy if we take the right methods and begin early enough. We must teach the money value of knowledge and how to determine it. We must measure all things by the test, *Will it pay?*[250]

---

[248] Geoffrey W. Clark, "The Machine-Shop Engineering Roots of Taylorism; The Efficiency of Machine-Tools and Machinists, 1865-1884," in J. C. Spender and H. Kijne, eds., *Scientific Management; Frederick Winslow Taylor's Gift to the World?*(Kluwer, 1966), 33-62.

[249] Coleman Sellers, Jr., "The Chair of Engineering Practice," *Stevens Indicator*, V (1888), 260-263.

[250] Coleman Sellers, Jr., "President's Address, 1886," *Trans ASME*, VIII (1887), 667, 685, and 695.

These lectures of Sellers at Stevens, long before the rise of engineering economy and industrial engineering courses elsewhere -- the first being usually attributed to Hugo Diemer or Dexter Kimball, both in 1904[251] -- pioneered the introduction of economic and managerial factors in engineering education.

Sellers continued as professor of engineering practice, delivering lectures at intervals throughout the year, until 1901 when he became professor emeritus of engineering practice.[252] His work formed a link with Alexander C. Humphreys who taught the nation's first course on economics of engineering.[253] Even before he became president of Stevens in 1902, Humphreys created a course on business engineering which he taught with the aid of guest lecturers one hour per week from 1897 to 1902 while he was a trustee.[254] In 1902, he created a department of business engineering and personally taught a mandatory fourth-year course on economics of engineering, again with the participation of expert guest lecturers. This course included topics like accounting, depreciation, planning, contracts and patent law, as well as a text which included material on shop management. Humphreys stated that the aim of his course was to enable the students "to become efficient as managers."[255]

By the end of the Morton administration and the start of the Humphreys administration, the philosophy of the Stevens undergraduate engineering curriculum was firmly in place as a tradition of the institute. In a eulogy for Morton in 1903, Edgar Marburg of the University of Pennsylvania praised Stevens's curriculum in the following words:

With a singleness of aim and steadfastness of purpose, she had adhered consistently to an educational policy which she believed to be based on sound and enduring principles. She has not allowed herself to be beguiled by the educational fads and follies of the time nor to be swerved from her straight course by any popular developments -- more apparent than real -- for short-cut or highly specialized courses. She has wisely held that the increasing necessity of specialization in after-

---

[251] L. Greyson, "A Brief History of Engineering Education in the U.S.," *Engineering Education,* Dec. 1977, 249, and David F. Noble, *America By Design*(MIT, 1977), 276.

[252] *Catalogue of The Stevens Institute of Technology,* 1909-10, under "necrology," 11.

[253] D.S. Jacobus, "Education in Engineering," *ASME Trans.,* XXXVIII (1916), 462.

[254] Humphreys to Taylor, January 28, 1897, Taylor Papers, Stevens Special Collections, *Catalogue,* 1902-3, under "faculty," and Alexander C. Humphreys, "Address Before the Alumni Association," *Stevens Indicator,* XXV (1900), 159-162.

[255] Humphreys to Frederick W. Taylor, Jan. 21, 1914, and June 11, 1914, Taylor Papers, Stevens Special Collections.

life served but to emphasize the need of broad and thorough training in fundamentals.[256]

The "highly specialized" courses were popular at the time. As the number of engineering schools rose from seven in 1862 to eighty-five in 1880, the vast majority of these schools graduated specialized engineers in either civil, mining, or mechanical engineering, but also in a score of subdisciplines. By the 1880s and 1890s electrical engineering and chemical engineering degrees were being given. President Morton had stuck to his "liberal-technical" scheme stressing a unified curriculum based on fundamentals in science, broad engineering, and liberal arts, and Stevens skipped the whole national trend of narrower specialized degrees.

Several other factors guided Stevens to resist diversification of curricula. One was the small size of the campus until 1903 and the relative lack of funds. The total student body in 1902 was 221. Given the relatively small endowment, tuition had largely to pay for faculty, and few students meant few faculty. It was much more efficient to use faculty to teach core courses in a broad-based curriculum than to offer specialized courses in classes which would have been smaller in size. Moreover, during the long recession from 1872 to 1896, the faculty had to take a cut in salary in order to prevent a cut in faculty.[257]

Another factor was the close identification of Stevens with the profession of mechanical engineering. As curricula fragmented into specialized disciplines in the last quarter of the nineteenth century, Thurston and other leaders in mechanical engineering education thought that these subdivisions were branches of mechanical engineering, that mechanical engineers needed to have an all-inclusive knowledge of other engineering fields as well as management to be truly professional. The Stevens catalogues as early as 1883-84 parallel the claims made by mechanical engineers to be all-inclusive in their training:

. . . a large number of our earlier graduates held prominent and responsible positions in electrical companies throughout the country, sufficiently proving that our course was well adapted to prepare those pursuing it for the profession of electrical engineer, who must manifestly be first of all a mechanical engineer.[258]

---

[256] "Address of Prof. Edgar Marburg of the University of Pennsylvania," *Stevens Indicator*, XX (1903), 326.

[257] Henry Morton, "Modern Education," *Op.Cit.*

[258] *Annual Catalogue of Stevens Institute of Technology."* 1883-84, 44..

Such consciousness of professional status among mechanical engineers occurred partly because of their desire to attain respectable professional standing comparable to civil engineers, and many Stevens graduates, after attaining a degree of success, set themselves up as consulting engineers as many of their civil-engineering colleagues had done. [259]

But the main factor which created the Stevens tradition of a broad-based curriculum was the success of its early graduates as managers. For example, President Morton sent a statistical summary of 551 graduates' positions in 1896 to the *New York Sun*: Sixteen were presidents of major companies, 148 were high-level managers, 54 were consulting engineers, 30 were professors or teachers, 6 were editors, 36 were patent lawyers or inspectors, 3 were architects, 4 were chemists, 8 were railroad superintendents, 13 were in foreign corporations, 25 were deceased, 50 were unknown, and only a minority were in lower level positions --103 were drafting and 55 were assistant engineers.[260] Specialized degrees were rejected because of pressure from these successful alumni. According to Franklin DeR. Furman, both an alumnus of the class of 1893 and a professor of mechanical drawing and design,

Their contention was that an understanding of the basic laws covering the whole range of engineering had enabled them to obtain positions immediately on graduation wherever there was an opening in engineering generally, or even in commercial work, without waiting for an opening in a specialized branch. More than this was their insistence that they rose to higher positions, their knowledge of the principles of general engineering came home and more into play and constituted an important factor in promotions and such success as they had achieved.[261]

This theme was repeated by the second president, Alexander C. Humphreys. He said that a college was not a place to store facts in the brain nor was it a place to give a complete training to the engineer -- that could only be done after graduation while on the job. The function of the engineering college, he said, was to give a thorough foundation in the fundamentals.[262] In an address before the alumni association in 1903, he stated:

---

[259] See Calvert, *Op. Cit.*, 111, 197, 200 for a discussion of the concern of mechanical engineers with their status.

[260] "Occupations of Graduates of the Stevens Institute of Technology," *Stevens Indicator*, XIII (1896), 68-9.

[261] F. DeR. Furman, unpublished manuscript dated January 20, 1942, Box 36A, Stevens Special Collections.

[262] A. Humphreys, "The Present Opportunities and Consequent Responsibilities of the Engineer," *ASME Trans.*, XXXIV (1912), 19-23.

I am convinced that our general policy should be to strengthen our course in the fundamentals and that we should not attempt to cover the many specializations in engineering which are today so rapidly developing . . . *that the students must, after they leave the Institute, complete mastery of details in some one line* (Humphreys's italics) we shall try conscientiously to impress on them.[263]

By 1914, Furman presented statistics to show that fully sixty percent of Stevens graduates after twenty years had ceased to be engineers and had become "executives in important corporations."[264]

Lastly, Humphreys carried on Morton's "liberal-technical" notion by re-affirming the need for liberal arts for engineers. In his inaugural speech he called for more content in the areas of the liberal arts, particularly in history, philosophy and English.[265] In his first year in office he created a new Department of English Literature and Logic and added two new faculty.[266] By 1922 the department was named the Department of English and History and the liberal arts content in the curriculum had been expanded to include two semesters of English, four semesters of history and government, four semesters of foreign language, and two semesters of laboratory work in composition, speech, and essay writing.[267] The literacy of graduates was a major concern, and the humanities' stress on writing well was supplemented by a senior thesis in some engineering problem: From 1870 to 1908, Stevens required all its graduates to produce a thesis, a usually well-written lengthy description of a piece of research or of a test on actual machinery or of processes in either chemistry, metallurgy or the business world. Since they were considered part of hands-on practice of the profession, the projects outside Stevens necessitated a considerable amount of time away from the campus. These absences were one of the reasons why the thesis was replaced in 1908 by a shorter senior report. The new senior reports stressed a more scholarly approach, research into the increasing technical literature becoming available by the proliferation of engineering journals and articles.[268]

By 1909, Stevens's tradition of broad-based instruction in engineering had made its curriculum one of the most rigorous in the country. In that year *Engineering Education* published a comparison of the content of

---

[263] "Address of Humphreys at the Annual Meeting of the Alumni Association," *Stevens Indicator*, XX (1903), 326.

[264] F. W. Taylor to Humphreys, Dec. 15, 1914, Taylor Papers, Stevens Special Collections.

[265] "Inaugural Address of Humphreys," *Stevens Indicator*, XX (1903), 170-1.

[266] Catalogue, *Op. Cit.*, 1902-03, 6.

[267] *Ibid*, 1922-03, 112-27.

[268] "Engineering Reports," *Stevens Indicator*, 36 (1919), 104-5. These senior reports were replaced with reports on senior design in the 1950s.

mechanical engineering programs in the United States based on the number of hours of instruction for students over the course of four years.[269] The breakdown of subject matter showed that Stevens had over a hundred hours more in engineering science to cover fundamental material in civil, electrical, chemical and materials engineering besides mechanical. In fact, Stevens had thirty hours less instruction in mechanical engineering core courses than other M.E. programs and also two hundred hours less in shop work. However, Stevens had nearly one hundred hours more in engineering laboratory (experimental engineering) and 150 hours more in subjects like engineering practice and economics of engineering. Stevens had fifty hours less in science but nearly a hundred hours more in liberal arts. The most striking difference seemed to be the fact that the additional engineering science in the Stevens core left no room for technical electives in mechanical engineering -- Stevens had no technical electives at all while the average elsewhere was 90.5 hours of instruction. Finally, the study shows that Stevens gave almost a hundred more hours of instruction than the average elsewhere. Since this instruction was based in the fundamentals of other disciplines instead of shop, the curriculum was demanding, and it became a proud Stevens tradition as graduates referred to their alma mater as "the old stone mill."

---

[269] William T. Magruder, "Mechanical Engineering Curriculums," *Engineering Education*, XVI (1909), 113-120.

CHAPTER 10

Early Trustees: Morton, Carnegie, and the "Czar"

In the years 1870-1906, the president of the institute's corporation was Samuel Bayard Dod, and in the first twenty years the regular attendees at board of trustee meetings were Dod, Martha Bayard Stevens, William W. Shippen, and, after 1885, the first president Henry Morton and various alumni representatives who served shorter terms. The board of trustees decided to double the membership in 1891 to include Andrew Carnegie, Alexander C. Humphreys, Charles MacDonald, Alexander T. McGill, and Edwin A. Stevens II -- Carnegie, MacDonald and McGill being the first prestigious trustees having no previous connection with the Stevenses or the institute.

Until 1906 when Dod died, all the rest of the trustees except George B. M. Harvey and Henry Towne were alumni trustees, the most noteworthy being William Hewitt, William Kent, George Meade Bond, Harry deB. Parsons, Richard Stevens, Lewis H. Nash, Alten S. Miller, and Edward A. Uehling. However, the second president of the institute, Alexander C. Humphreys, an alumnus of the class of 1881, had a decided influence on the board after the death of Morton in 1906. Humphreys, whom the students called "the Czar," was also president of the board of trustees from 1906 until 1927 during the main expansion of the campus to include the Morton Building, the Stevens estate including the Castle, Walker Gymnasium, and the Lieb and Navy buildings. Minutes of the board of trustees show who attended meetings and who contributed to the institute in the crucial early years, which coincided with a general economic depression from 1872 to 1896.

The original endowment in the will of Edwin A. Stevens was modest compared to the millions which endowed comparable colleges. This fact can be explained by the circumstances of the founder in 1868 when he died. He was married twice, the second time to Martha Bayard Dod when she was twenty-three and he was fifty-nine. In the fourteen remaining years of his life, he had six children ranging from ten years old to under a year old when he passed away in Paris, France, on a vacation. Naturally, his will reflected his interest in providing for his yet youthful wife and infant children as well as his gracious bequest to the institute he was founding. Nonetheless, the relatively small initial endowment, coupled with the chronic deficits of the early institute budgets during the depressed years, lowered the endowment by $120,000 by 1888.[270] Thus, the board under Dod had to continually find the means year by year to assure the survival of the institute. In those years, the greatest contributors of funds and property were Henry Morton, Andrew Carnegie, Alexander C. Humphreys and the alumni association, and, in balancing the yearly budget, the Stevens School.

In the Dod years, the most important trustee was undoubtedly Henry Morton, the first president of the institute. Henry Morton's main interest was indeed the institute, but he made additional income through his special interests in chemistry and law. He had graduated from the University of Pennsylvania in chemistry and upon graduation had studied law for two years in the offices of George M. Wharton of Philadelphia. Soon after becoming president of the institute, he became famous in legal circles by being a highly sought-after and therefore highly paid expert witness in court cases involving chemistry and physics. The noted Horsford patent case involving dry phosphate of lime in baking powder gave him notoriety in patent cases because it overthrew the opinions of other noted chemists. Similarly, his testimony obtained noted victories in patent suits over the manufacture of artificial alizarin dyes and celluloid. Not a rich man, he was able to provide for both his family and the institute. In an age when unskilled labor worked for a dollar a day, Morton contributed the following considerable sums to the institute: in 1881, $10,500 to outfit a machine workshop; in 1883, $2,500 for apparatus for the department of applied electricity; in 1889, $10,000 to endow the chair of engineering practice held by Coleman Sellers; in 1892, a $20,000 increase for the same chair; in 1897, stock which sold for $24,000 on the occasion of the twenty-fifth anniversary of the institute; and in 1901 he spent $50,000 for Stevens's professors' pensions as well as an undisclosed sum for a boilerhouse and stack to heat the institute.[271] He not only brought prestige to the institute by his scholarly articles on fluorescent lighting, by being vice president of the American Chemical Society and by becoming a member of the National Academy of Sciences, but he loyally attended every session of the board of trustees as its secretary.

Also, Dod and Morton were responsible for the establishment of the Stevens School in 1871, a subsidiary of the institute which helped to balance the institute's operating budget from 1871 to 1909 and beyond. The "Stevens High School" was a private preparatory school housed in the right wing of the Edwin A. Stevens Building until 1888 when it moved into a new building costing $46,000. The Stevens School building was a three-

---

[270] Minutes of the Board of Trustees, June 9, 1888.

[271] *The National Cyclopedia of American Biography,* 24 (1935), 374-5.

story structure housing eleven classrooms and two big lecture halls, one in the cellar which doubled as a gym for the school and one on the top floor. The architects were Wilson Bros. of Philadelphia, the building being made of red brick with Trenton stone facings and having a slate roof.[272] During the early years of the institute, the Stevens School served several functions. It utilized unused space in the original Edwin A. Stevens building when institute classes had few students in the 1870s and 1880s. It also prepared students to enter Stevens Institute of Technology, and, in 1888 the institute publicly stated that the school's "value as a feeder for the Institute is constantly growing."[273] Besides its regular high school program which included physics, chemistry, Greek, Latin, French, and other high school subjects, it also included a special preparatory class of graduated students from other high schools who needed mechanical drawing and mathematics requirements for entry into the institute.

The Stevens School, later called Recitation Hall after the school moved out, was demolished to make way for the Burchard building in the 1950s. The profits from the Stevens School helped to balance the budget for the institute in the nineteenth century.

---

[272] *Stevens Indicator,* 4 (1887), 187-9.
[273] *Ibid.,* 5 (1888), 155-7.

The importance of the school to the institute in terms of income is demonstrated by comparative enrollment, tuition, and faculty salary figures for 1887-88: There were 182 pupils in the school compared to 186 students in the institute. Tuition revenues were $22,142.14 for the school compared to $25,843.08 for the institute. Faculty salaries were $8,721.38 for the school compared to $39,073.15 for the institute. President Humphreys said in 1904 that "we have been obliged for a number of years to depend on the school to make up yearly deficits of the Institute," a dependence on the "money maker" which the president felt to be "too much."[274] The Stevens School paid some of the salaries of institute faculty, mainly those of professors Wall and Kroeh, the former being institute professor of belles lettres as well as principal of the school. In all, the school had eight faculty in 1888 including Hudson A. Wood, the brother of the institute's professor of mathematics, DeVolson Wood. The Stevens School's net revenues continued to balance the institute's operating budget until 1909 when Humphreys stated that, although the school had three times the number of students than in 1902, "The net income from the School was sufficient until last year to meet the yearly deficit of the Institute" which had risen to a record level.[275] In fact, minutes of the board show that the operational costs of the institute before World War I were chronically larger than revenues and the difference often made up by the Stevens preparatory school.

In 1891, the board of trustees expanded to include Andrew Carnegie. A "special meeting" of the Board was called in that year at the "request of Prof. Morton" at which Carnegie was enthusiastically "unanimously elected" with great expectation of his munificence.[276] Carnegie was the most important trustee of Stevens until World War I in terms of the size of his financial contributions. The Scottish-born immigrant Andrew Carnegie (1837-1919) started life as a bobbin boy and became the leading world producer of steel by the time he came onto the board. In the years 1873 to 1889, Carnegie led the United States past Britain in the production of steel with his daring insistence on using the latest methods and discarding costly equipment when something better appeared. He had already made a fortune by 1886 but continued to expand his company until his retirement in 1901 by investing in new plants during depressed periods, contrary to common practice, and by his judicious choice of men to run his enterprises. In 1886, This self-made millionaire with a humble background stunned the world with his book, *Gospel of Wealth,* in which he stated that "Surplus wealth is

---

[274] Minutes of the Board of Trustees, Jan. 24, 1904.

[275] *Ibid.,* May 27, 1909.

[276] *Ibid.,* Dec. 23, 1891.

a sacred trust which its possessor is bound to administer in his lifetime for the good of the community from which it is derived" and that "The man who dies possessed of millions of available wealth, which was free and his to administer during his lifetime, dies disgraced." By 1889, Carnegie was establishing public libraries and concert halls and was being lauded for his philanthropy in the United States and Great Britain -- Prime Minister Gladstone of England wrote an article praising him, and he was corresponding world-wide with leaders including the President of the United States and international intellectuals like John Morely.

Thus, it was a decided *coup* for Morton to bring in Carnegie when the board was expanded in 1891. On the evidence of his date books, there can be no doubt it was Morton who approached Carnegie about being a trustee. Perhaps another connection was through the fellow Scottish immigrant who entered the board with him, Alexander C. Humphreys. Humphreys was another self-made man, having stopped schooling at the age of fourteen to go to work for a gas light company in Bayonne, New Jersey, and, through diligence, rising to be superintendent of the company before working his way through Stevens to graduate in 1881. By 1891, Humphreys had teamed up with another Scot, Arthur G. Glasgow, a Stevens graduate of 1885, to form Humphreys and Glasgow Co., a New York City-based firm specializing in gas plant construction and equipment world wide -- with offices in Scotland and England.[277]

The leading steel industrialist was a busy man, and, after 1887, Carnegie resided half the year in his estates in his native Scotland. He often went to Pittsburg and had a residence in New York City at No. 2 E. 91st Street. Carnegie did not attend many meetings of the Stevens board, and, when he did, a few members of the board usually met in special session at Carnegie's residence or at the offices of Humphreys and Glasgow Co. at 51 Nassau Street in New York City. In between these infrequent meetings, the board and Carnegie corresponded and the letters were included in the minutes. In the early years of his trustee service, little was asked of the industrialist because he expected the institute to pay for itself. Humphreys later said that, "I have endeavored to explain (to Carnegie) that an institution like ours is not a money making enterprise and that if it were no endowment would be necessary."[278] Two meetings were held with Carnegie in 1892, one at Stevens and one at Carnegie's residence after he had been appointed to the finance committee of the board -- at the latter meeting it was decided to sell some bonds and buy some stocks, but there was no hint of a contribution

---

[277] *Dictionary of American Biography*, 9 (1932), 371.
[278] Minutes of the Board of Trustees, Jan. 24, 1908.

from the multimillionaire.[279] Thereafter, he was evidently left alone and was absent from board meetings until 1897. That year, his attitude to college boards of trustees was revealed by his speech during the ceremonies at the Waldorf Astoria Hotel on the twenty-fifth anniversary of Stevens Institute: "My experience as a trustee in five colleges and universities is this: that if you have the right man in the right place as President, the trustees have nothing whatever to do; but whenever you have a President that don't (sic) know how to manage anything about the college, not even the trustees, then the trustees are sent for in solemn conclave and immediately resolve to set about finding a man who can manage it. So far as I know, I have not yet received a notice to attend any meeting to do anything on behalf of the Trustees of Stevens."[280]

On that occasion he stated that the Stevens family had wisely selected "the best means of perpetuating their name" and that

... the men who have selected a seat of learning -- Harvard, Yale, Cornell, Cooper, Pratt, Stevens -- these are the men who have chosen the means which will keep them in the history of their country and of the world longer and more prominently than any other means which a man can devise. And more than this, they have chosen a living monument with a soul in it -- something that continues to perform useful work, something which shows us that they desired more to benefit succeeding generations than to perpetuate their personal fame. . . . Any celebration of this anniversary of Stevens would certainly be incomplete if a representative of the iron and steel industry were not permitted publicly to acknowledge his obligation to that Institute, to express his gratitude to its founder. You have only to look at your list of graduates and see the number that are now in charge of important enterprises, to know what Stevens has done. It is impossible to enter any of the great establishments without meeting a Stevens graduate.[281]

It was after the above remarks that Morton approached Carnegie about the institute's financial needs for a new campus building to be called the "Carnegie Mechanical Laboratory." Subsequently, a letter to Morton from Scotland dated May 20, 1899, invited Morton to visit Skibo Castle and pledged fifty thousand dollars to build the laboratory because, "We owe much to Stevens from the many valuable men who have come from it."[282] At this time, Carnegie was made vice president of the board of trustees *in absentia.* Soon thereafter, he increased the building fund to $65,000, and, after the

---

[279] *Ibid.,* Jan. 18, 1892 and Feb. 4, 1892.

[280] Speech of Carnegie on the 25th anniversary of the founding of Stevens, *The Stevens Indicator,* 14 (1897), 132.

[281] *Ibid.*

[282] Minutes of the Board of Trustees, Mar. 10, 1899.

formal opening of the laboratory -- the architect being William S. Ackerman of the Stevens class of 1891 -- an event in 1901 which Carnegie attended, he added $100,000 for endowment for its maintenance. In that year, Carnegie sold his steel interests to J. P. Morgan's United States Steel and began his full-time career as a philanthropist giving away an estimated $350 million by the time of his death in 1919. In 1902, after the death of Morton, for whom he expressed his esteem in a touching letter to the board, Carnegie gave Stevens an added $150,000 endowment for the Carnegie Laboratory after Humphreys became the new president of the institute.

As a trustee of Stevens Institute, Andrew Carnegie donated the funds for the Carnegie Mechanical Laboratory, seen here after being built in 1902.

Humphreys brought a new vision of an expanded campus and a new vigor to fundraising when he became president in 1902. At that time, the campus still consisted of one-and-a-half city blocks, and he wanted funding to expand. One of his first acts was to lay before Carnegie, in a letter, the needs of the institute as he saw them -- nothing that one million dollars wouldn't solve. At the end of the letter he seemed to offer to link Carnegie with Stevens in the name of the institute, and unfortunately there doesn't seem to have been a written reply:

Without knowing any of the details, I am aware that Dr. Morton wrote you just before his death. On his deathbed he barely touched upon the object with me, but from what little he said I gathered the idea that he had suggested to you the thought of completely linking your name with that of Stevens, so that while to Stevens might be credited the initiation, to you might be credited the development and perpetuation of our great educational scheme. Believing that such communication was sent to you by our dear friend, I feel I must first take up the subject with you. I will say frankly that I had no thought of broaching this subject to you for the present at least, but as I face my responsibilities in this undertaking, I feel I must speak and you will not blame me for being frank.[283]

This photograph was taken in 1902 in the institute's Carnegie Mechanical Laboratory after the inauguration of Alexander C. Humphreys as the second president of Stevens. In the front row are heads of colleges, Charles F. Thwing, H. M. MacCracken, Henry S. Pritchett of MIT, Humphreys, and then trustees Samuel Bayard Dod, Henry R. Towne, Andrew Carnegie, and Alfred R. Wolff. In the second row, to the right, are Robert H. Thurston and John Fritz. The rest are other faculty and trustees.

In his first year as resident in 1902, Humphreys told the board of trustees that expanding the campus did not come simply because he was a new president, but rather that it was necessitated by increased enrollments. In a long memorandum to the trustees in December, Humphreys wrote that the size of the freshman and sophomore classes mandated dividing them into two groups because "we have not classrooms large enough for them undivided . . . . Therefore it is necessary that we should as promptly as

---

[283] Humphreys to Carnegie, Oct. 18, 1902, Correspondence of A.C. Humphreys, Stevens Special Collections.

possible erect the Morton Laboratory of Chemistry." He went on to say, "I am anxious to make a beginning of dormitory life as soon as possible and I am more convinced that this is necessary *if we are to* secure the best student material from the country at large."[284] He also told the trustees that $700,000 was needed to complete the Morton Memorial Laboratory of Chemistry, to establish a dormitory, to build a "Students House" which would house a gymnasium, to build a library which was "a crying need of the Institute" and which the faculty thought was "the most pressing need," and finally to purchase an athletic field from Stevens family-owned land. He wrote, "It is not safe to allow the neighborhood around the Institute to fill up without providing for the Institute's future." He envisioned purchasing five acres of the Stevens estate for eighty thousand dollars and later the "Stevens Mansion."[285]

In the last years of his life, Morton had asked the alumni to fund a chemistry laboratory which was to be erected on the northwest corner of the original campus consisting of one city block. However, Humphreys organized a fund-raising campaign for the purchase of portions of the Stevens estate and the building of the Morton Memorial Laboratory of Chemistry next to the "Green Gate" which led to the Castle. As Humphreys later admitted publicly, "I was determined, as far as was in my power" to obtain portions of the Stevens estate, including the Stevens Castle, when they became available.[286] With increased numbers of students totaling 349 in the institute and 267 in the Stevens School by 1904, it was impossible to continue instruction for them all, said Humphreys, in three buildings on one city block.[287]

To buy portions of the Stevens estate, Humphreys later admitted, he had to put added pressures on the alumni. The Stevens Alumni Association (SAA) was created in 1876 by William Hewitt 1874, the son of Abram Stevens Hewitt's brother who ran the Trenton Iron Works. Humphreys himself was the SAA's tenth president in 1885-86 before he became a permanent member of the board of trustees. The SAA held its first annual-dinner meeting in 1887 with fifty of over one hundred total graduates of the institute present. At the meeting, "on the suggestion of the Board of Trustees," the SAA began its very first fundraising effort. The trustees suggested a scholarship fund, but a group, including Humphreys, William

---

[284] A. C. Humphreys to the Board of Trustees, letter dated Dec. 10, 1902 inserted loosely in Book II of the Minutes of the Board of Trustees.

[285] Minutes of the Board of Trustees, Mar. 11, 1903.

[286] *The Stute*, June 26, 1911, 3.

[287] Minutes of the Board of Trustees, Mar. 11, 1904.

Kent, and the then-current President George Meade Bond, decided that a Library Fund would be preferable. Thirty-six of the alumni present immediately subscribed with contributions as high as one hundred dollars -- in those days one-third the yearly salary of an unskilled laborer.[288] Thus, Humphreys already had experience with alumni fundraising, and, with his plan to expand the campus, he began to lean on the alumni ever more heavily for contributions, especially when portions of the Stevens estate became available.

As can be seen from this architect's sketch, the Morton Memorial Laboratory of Chemistry was originally slated to be built next to the Carnegie Laboratory, on the institute's original city block, but Humphreys obtained trustee backing to buy, with a mortgage, a portion of the Stevens's estate in 1905, so that the Morton building was built next to the gatehouse.

Martha Bayard Stevens had died in 1899, and her will divided the Castle Point real estate among her five surviving adult offspring. Moreover, she divided her liquid assets between them and their children. Thus, the Castle Point property above the gatehouse was subdivided into five parcels, and the some of the heirs unfortunately wound up falling out over the size of each other's allotments. But two of these heirs were loyal to the institute and were trustees, Edwin A. Stevens II and Richard Stevens. The former had nine children and was thinking about selling his share to the institute at less

---

[288] *Stevens Indicator*, 4 (1887), 169-70.

than market value. The latter was the only one of the five who wished to remain in Hoboken on the most northern portion where he had his own residence. By 1903, Humphreys persuaded the rest of the trustees to obtain a mortgage to make up the rest of the needed money. Subsequently, in 1905 a bank loan of eighty-thousand dollars was obtained to purchase the five acres closest to the gate house on which the athletic field was laid out and the Morton building was erected in 1906. That building, whose architect was again Ackerman, was built with $84,000 donated by alumni and Carnegie and an additional $40,000 mortgage.[289] In short, the institute had to go into debt to purchase the first portion of the Stevens family's Castle Point property and build its first structure on it.

During these years, the relations of Humphreys and Carnegie were not always smooth. At a board meeting of January 31, 1905, in the offices of Humphreys and Glasgow in New York City, Humphreys read from a twenty-nine page, typed report to Carnegie and the rest of the trustees on the needs of the institute. To prevent going into debt for the purchase of the Stevens property, he asked for gifts of some $700,000, the added amount to go to programs and endowment.[290] In a letter to the board written two days later, Humphreys referred to criticism of his plan. Humphreys wrote that if the board did not want to consider his full plan, then "the first thing in order is the election of my successor." He took umbrage at the statement of an unnamed trustee who had intimated that Humphreys should be "cutting my coat according to my cloth."[291] Who could have made this statement other than the ex-bobbin boy? The only other members of the board at the meeting, besides Carnegie, were Dod, Richard Stevens, Henry Towne, and alumni representatives Post, Uehling and Wolff -- Towne being the only other non-graduate of Stevens. Moreover, only Carnegie had not heard the new president's vision for expansion before, and so the best guess is that the criticism was from Carnegie -- especially because the latter then immediately donated fifty thousand dollars. In response, Humphreys also donated fifty thousand dollars and apologetically wrote to Carnegie that, "To assume the beggar role is the greatest sacrifice I have to make for Alma Mater."[292]

In 1907, upon the death of the president of the board, Samuel Bayard Dod, the board created a second vice president because Vice President Carnegie was "frequently absent from the country and there should be some

---

[289] Minutes of the Board of Trustees, May 31, 1906.

[290] *Ibid.*, Jan. 31, 1905.

[291] Letter of Humphreys to the board of trustees, Feb. 2, 1905 inserted into Book III of the Minutes of the Board of Trustees.

[292] Humphreys to Carnegie, Dec. 2, 1905, A. C. Humphreys Correspondence, Stevens Special Collections.

provision for a presiding officer in the absence of the President." Carnegie was then elected first vice president and Humphreys himself was made president of the board of trustees as well as being the president of the institute -- "the Czar," as the students called him, was the only president of the institute to also be president of the board of trustees. Carnegie's absences from the board meetings did not stop Humphreys from making personal appeals for more money, particularly because Carnegie relied on Humphreys's participation in the millionaire's other schemes. For example Humphreys was a trustee of the Carnegie Foundation for the Advancement of Teaching.

At a meeting at Carnegie's residence in 1908, Humphreys met Carnegie alone. Humphreys reported to the trustees that he had told Carnegie, "We are decidedly handicapped in our work by the lack of necessary funding" and that the institute had a deficit of $21,900 the previous year which was only reduced to $6,300 by proceeds from the Stevens School, which was "generally the case." Humphreys told the board that he had pointed out to Carnegie that the maintenance costs of the Carnegie Laboratory were $18,000, but the endowment only provided $3,100. Funds were needed for an extension on the Carnegie Laboratory, which was overcrowded with machinery "to the danger point," and for purchasing another portion of the Stevens family estate containing the Castle. Humphreys reported to the rest of the trustees that he had architectural drawings made by Ludlow and Valentine for the extension and that "I took these drawings to Mr. Carnegie to show to him, but he refused to see them . . . holding to the opinion he had helped us sufficiently and that we depended upon him too much." However, Humphreys's strong appeals resulted in a ten-thousand-dollar pledge from Carnegie as long as it could be matched by another sum of $12,700 from alumni and other sources.[293]

Humphreys was not to be stopped in his vision for expansion. When the Stevens Castle became available from trustee Edwin A. Stevens II in 1910 for $160,000, that, too, was purchased with bank mortgages, similar to the purchase of the portion for the Morton building and the athletic field. Humphreys told the board that the market value was perhaps $250,000 to $260,000 and that the purchase price was a gift from their "benefactor" and fellow board member. Transfer of the keys of the Castle to the institute took place in a ceremony on May 27, 1911, after the building was refurbished to be a dormitory and meeting hall for students and a special room was redecorated for alumni activities. During the ceremony, President Humphreys stated that the alumni had to help to "remove the burden of debt resting

---

[293] Minutes of the Board of Trustees, March 15, 1908.

upon us by reason of the acquisition of the several portions of Castle Point now in our possession."[294] In 1912, Humphreys again obtained mortgages to purchase seven acres from the estate of Robert Livingston Stevens II adjacent to the Castle for $100,000 and another few adjoining portions owned by the Hoboken Land and Improvement Company for $110,000. In all, some 22 acres of Stevens family property had been obtained for a total of $510,000, not including outright gifts of smaller pieces of land worth $71,000 from the Stevens family.[295] By that time, the only Stevens family member left on the point was Richard Stevens at the very northern tip, and his heirs did not sell that property to the institute until 1928.

The Stevens Castle, built in 1858 by Robert Livingston Stevens, remained with the Stevens family until 1910 when Edwin A. Stevens II, a trustee, sold it to the Institute for $160,000. President Alexander C. Humphreys told the trustees taking out a mortgage for the purchase price was necessary, given his estimate that the Castle was worth $250,000. The Stevens Castle remained a beloved part of the Stevens campus, especially by alumni, until it was razed in 1959.

---

[294] *The Stute,* June 26, 1911, 3.

[295] N. H. Memory and F. J. Oliver, "Alexander C. Humphreys" in unpublished manuscripts compiled by J. H. Potter entitled, "The Stevens Story," section 1-b. There is currently a plaque located at the bottom of Wittpenn walk which incorrectly states that the land was donated by the Stevens family to the institute.

Subsequent to the 1912 purchases, the trustees under Humphreys and the SAA, lead by Walter Kidde of the class of 1897, conducted a second fund-raising campaign in 1915 to raise $1,285,000 to clear the institute of its mortgage debt. The sum of $1,385,000 was raised in part due to Humphreys's influence in obtaining Carnegie's outside contribution of $250,000 and an additional Carnegie "make up" figure of $17,727.59. Particularly gratifying to the trustees was a surprise $100,000 bequeathed in Carnegie's will when he died in 1919, thus indicating his very genuine interest in the institute. In all, Andrew Carnegie gave $717,727.59 to the institute, a fabulous sum in those days and nearly equaling the original endowment of Edwin A. Stevens.[296] Carnegie gave more money to Stevens than to any other American college with the exception of the Carnegie Institute of Technology in Pittsburg, an institution which perhaps obtained its considerable endowment of $22 million in 1912 as a result of Carnegie's previous experience with problems with the comparatively small original endowment of Stevens Institute of Technology.[297]

In the fund drive of 1915, Humphreys appealed to wealthy men across the country to donate. He obtained $10,000 from Edward S. Harkness of Standard Oil.[298] He was able to obtain a donation of $100,000 and other gifts and trusts from William Hall Walker after whom the first Stevens gymnasium was named and built in 1916. The architect for the Walker gym with its unique elevated oval-shaped running track was William O. Ludlow of the class of 1892. William Hall Walker was born in 1846 and became a machinist in the Colt armory in Hartford and then for Pratt and Whitney producing machine tools. He next worked at Morgan Iron Works while studying at night at the Cooper Institute before joining the Eastman Dry Plate Company of Rochester, the future Kodak Company, when it was getting off the ground. He developed the first machinery for producing the first roll-holder for film exposures-- the forerunner of the practical hand-held camera. He developed automatic spooling of unexposed film, and the first machines for coating photographic films and papers of continuous lengths. He held many patents and made himself a fortune, later becoming Kodak's managing director of the English Eastman Company.[299] Humphreys, who simply sent his own personal letters soliciting donations from wealthy individuals, obtained a donation from George Eastman for fifty thousand dollars

---

[296] "Obituary: Andrew Carnegie, Trustee," *Stevens Indicator,* 36 (1919), 271-3, and "Vice President Carnegie Dies," *The Stute,* Sept. 19, 1919, 2.

[297] "Andrew Carnegie," *Dictionary of American Biography,* 7 (1929), 499-505.

[298] *Annual Catalog. Stevens Institute of Technology.* (1929-30), 22.

[299] *Stevens Indicator,* Jan. 1916, 1-4.

in the same drive, Eastman perhaps influenced by Walker's gift. During the ceremony which opened the William Hall Walker Gymnasium, Walker said he wanted to "repay the debt" he acknowledged to Peter Cooper who was a surrogate father to him. He continued, "To still another man there was an obligation unfulfilled. He came to me and jogged my memory, and, pointing to the great pile of lapsed promises, said, 'Here is your chance.' That man was Mr. Newcomb Carlton, and to these two men, Peter Cooper and Newcomb Carlton, you owe your splendid gymnasium."[300]

Newcomb Carlton of the Stevens class of 1890 had worked as a mechanical engineer in Buffalo for a number of years until he became vice president of Bell Telephone Company in Buffalo between 1902-04, then vice president of British Westinghouse from 1905-10, then vice president of Western Union Telegraph Company in 1910-14, and finally president of Western Union from 1914 to 1933 -- the longest running president of that company.[301] He also served on the boards of a score of corporations including the Chase National Bank and the Metropolitan Life Insurance Company. His obituary in the *Stevens Indicator* was very short and related that although he was "one of America's most powerful men, he was also one of the least known."[302] He was made a trustee of the institute in 1917 and so he was helping Humphreys raise funds. But the nature of Walker's "obligation" to Carlton remains a mystery. Anyway, it was the alumni's dream for decades to have a gymnasium, and evidently Carlton prevailed upon his friend to provide for it.

Another Humphreys fundraising campaign for endowment to raise faculty salaries among alumni and friends was the "million dollar" campaign which ended successfully in 1924. It took place during the economic upswing of the roaring twenties. The SAA's Walter Kidde played a key role as chairman of the campaign and in organizing the many volunteers.[303] Humphreys asked wealthy men across the country to donate, and again George Eastman and Edward S. Harkness responded with gifts of $50,000 and $100,000 respectively.[304] Under the "Czar," the campus grew from a little over the size of a city block to twenty-three acres, the faculty and student body more than quadrupled, and the endowment grew from $384,800 in 1902 to $2,864,000 in 1927.[305]

---

[300] *Ibid.*, 73.

[301] "Carlton, Newcomb," *Marquis' Who's Who in America,* 23 (1944-5).

[302] *Stevens Indicator,* May 1953, 41.

[303] Potter, *Op.Cit.*, section IX, 1-5.

[304] *Annual Catalog, Op.Cit.*, (1929-30), 22.

[305] Minutes of the Board of Trustees, April 27, 1927.

CHAPTER 11

TIAA-CREF, Engineering Education, and Sports

When Henry Morton died in 1902, other members of the original faculty dating back to 1871 had also died, namely professors Leeds and Wood. All three men were over sixty-five years of age, and they had continued to teach until their deaths. The reason was that before World War I there were no pensions for professors. In the nineteenth and early twentieth century, college professors had to be independently wealthy or had to have outside incomes in order to retire at sixty-five or earlier. It was an age before Social Security, before pension plans, and before health insurance. Most professors' salaries were between $1,500 and $3,500 before World War I, and they had to save for sickness and retirement from these meager earnings and whatever they could make as researchers and consultants. Although in those days unskilled labor earned a traditional a one-dollar-per-day subsistence wage and so professors' salaries were comfortable, they were not anywhere near the salaries of successful managers and businessmen. Trustee Andrew Carnegie supplied the money to change this situation.

In fact, Stevens was one of the places Andrew Carnegie learned of the problem of professors' low salaries, their lack of pensions, and their difficulties if they became ill and their salaries had to stop. For example, several times Carnegie attended board meetings at which the multimillionaire had to approve raises for professors which usually consisted of a hundred dollars here or two hundred dollars there. More importantly for the background of Carnegie's interest in establishing a foundation for pensions was Henry Morton's letter to the board of trustees in 1901. Realizing he was dying of cancer, Morton decided to give fifty thousand dollars worth of securities to the trustees for two purposes, namely for the maintenance costs of the planned chemistry laboratory and for pensions of Stevens professors in case "age or sickness" incapacitated them before death. Carnegie was listed as being in attendance at the board of trustees meeting on December 13, 1901, when Morton's letter of bequest was read and the board passed a resolution thanking him.[306] Carnegie must have been affected by Morton's gesture and the fact that Morton worked almost until the day he died. Carnegie sent a telegram from Scotland saying in part, "We shall not find his likes again.

---

[306] Minutes of the Stevens Board of Trustees, II (June 6, 1901), 115-120 and II (Dec. 13, 1901), 121-123.

President Morton had a place in our hearts all his own."[307] Also, the problem of professors having to take an unpaid leave of absence because of sickness was known to Carnegie through Stevens institute. For example, the minutes record that in May 1903, Carnegie and Humphreys each contributed half of Professor James E. Denton's salary when he had to go on a year's leave to prevent "nervous collapse" brought on by overwork and financial worries.[308]

These portraits of Trustee Andrew Carnegie and President Alexander C. Humphreys date from 1902, Carnegie's appearing in a memorial volume for Morton and Humphreys's appearing in the Stevens catalogue. They were taken one year after the board of trustees thanked Morton for his gift for professors' pensions, and two years before Carnegie announced the formation of the Carnegie Foundation for the Advancement of Teaching.

According to the official history of the Carnegie Foundation for the Advancement of Teaching (CFAT), the man who convinced Carnegie to donate ten million dollars to establish free professors' pensions was Henry S. Pritchett who had been president of MIT since 1900 and who became the first president of the foundation. After meeting Pritchett at a White House luncheon in 1902, the very year Morton died, Carnegie and Pritchett started

---

[307] *Ibid.,* II (June 5,1902), 138.
[308] *Ibid.,* II (May 1, 1903), 150-151.

to discuss the problem. It took two more years for the two men to conceive of the idea for the foundation for professors' pensions at non-sectarian and non-public colleges and universities. The idea and the ten-million-dollar donation was subsequently dramatically announced to the press by Carnegie in April 1905 as he was sailing to Europe on the steamship *Baltic.*[309]

Thereafter, Carnegie asked Pritchett to compile a list of institutions of higher learning which would be eligible to receive pensions and to make up actuarial calculations of costs. Determining eligible colleges was no simple task in an age when private institutions of higher learning lacked standards, and many high schools gave out bachelor's degrees. Pritchett submitted a list of twenty-one colleges, universities, and technical schools in the United States and Canada, and among them were the usual ivy league institutions, Stanford, Johns Hopkins, and others including MIT and Stevens. The only other technical college was the Armour Institute of Technology in Chicago.[310] The task of compiling actuarial data to estimate the permissible a-mounts of the pensions, given the endowment, was daunting, and for this work Pritchett enrolled his friend, the banker Frank A. Vanderlip of the innovative First National City Bank of New York.

Upon receiving Pritchett's reports, Carnegie jotted down in his own hand-writing potential trustees of the new foundation, and these included nine college presidents, mostly from ivy league colleges but two from technical institutes, namely Pritchett himself and Humphreys. An organizational meeting of incorporators was held on November 15, 1905, with Pritchett, Humphreys, Vanderlip, Nicholas Murray Butler of Columbia, and Robert A. Franks of Carnegie's bank, the Home Trust Company of Hoboken, New Jersey, in attendance. The records contain the statement "meeting called to order by Alexander C. Humphreys, and Butler was elected temporary chair-man."[311] Then on May 8, 1905, the Supreme Court of the State of New York approved the certificate of incorporation which listed the five incorp-orators as Butler, Humphreys, Pritchett, Franks and Vanderlip, and this document contained Andrew Carnegie's words in regard to pensions, "re-moving a source of deep and constant anxiety to the poorest paid and yet one of the highest of all professions."[312] Later, when the foundation ob-tained a national charter by act of Congress in December 1905, Humphreys was listed with the rest of the twenty-four Foundation Trustees as incorp-

---

[309] Howard J. Savage, *Fruit of an Impulse; Forty-five Years of the Carnegie Foundation, 1905-1950*(New York, 1953), 3-14.

[310] *Ibid.*, 17-18.

[311] "Organizational Meeting of Incorporators, 10 A.M., Nov. 15, 1905," in *Early Papers of the Foundation for the Advancement of* Teaching(1935).

[312] "Notice of Meeting, 9 April 1906," *Ibid.*

orators. Carnegie had wanted to call the corporation "The Carnegie Foundation for Professors' Pensions," but Pritchett convinced him to call it "The Carnegie Foundation for the Advancement of Teaching" to include the broader activity of establishing national standards on curriculum and on entrance requirements, among other matters of educational policy.

The original incorporators in New York state, Humphreys, Pritchett, Vanderlip, Butler, and Franks, were elected the first executive committee of the foundation by the full board of trustees, but Woodrow Wilson of Princeton University was added at the second meeting. Humphreys was reelected yearly to this administrative body which met several times a year until his death in 1927. Pritchett was made president of the foundation and Carnegie's relative, T. Morris Carnegie of the Home Trust Company of Hoboken, was made treasurer. The Home Trust Company, Andrew Carnegie's personal holding company, was located inside the Hudson Trust Company in Hoboken, the latter bank having been founded by Samuel Bayard Dod. The Hudson Trust Company's vault held Carnegie's securities worth $350 million from which funds were dispensed for Carnegie's philanthropic giving, including the Carnegie Foundation for the Advancement of Teaching. Charles William Eliot of Harvard was the first chairman of the full board of trustees which met yearly, Humphreys being elected chairman for three years between November 17, 1920, to November 21, 1923.[313] Through these connections, Frank A. Vanderlip gave lectures in Humphreys's senior course on economics of engineering at Stevens and became a Stevens trustee in 1908, and Henry S. Pritchett, who had given up his administrative post at MIT in 1906, became a Stevens trustee in 1909.[314] Both Pritchett and Vanderlip served on the board until 1917 when they became overwhelmed with the responsibilities of forming the Teachers Insurance and Annuity Association (TIAA), which, in Pritchett's words, was an "absorbing business."

The need of CFAT to find an alternative to the free pensions based on income from Carnegie's original ten-million-dollar endowment can be seen by the rise in the number of pensionables from 2,042 in 1906 to 6,626 in 1915. The cost of pensions in those years rose from $122,130 to $690,668, obviously a non-sustainable rate of increase. In 1915, Pritchett returned to a plan rejected by Carnegie back in 1905, namely, to have CFAT's pensions based on contributions from working professors and on premiums for life

---

[313] See Minutes of the executive committee, boxes 8a and 8b, CFAT Papers, Rare Books and Manuscripts Collection, Columbia University.

[314] Minutes of the Stevens Board of Trustees, III (May 15, 1908), 165, and III (April 29, 1909), 210.

insurance for professors. Pritchett drew up and disseminated this plan by 1916, and almost immediately the American Association of University Professors (AAUP), formed in 1914, pressured Pritchett for a voice in the arrangements. After consulting with John Dewey, head of the AAUP in 1916, a Committee of the AAUP was established which was initially hostile to elements of CFAT's plan. But negotiations led to an agreement that there be thirteen incorporators, eight from CFAT, three from the AAUP, and one each from the Association of American Colleges and from Canadian institutions. TIAA was to sell termed insurance and deferred annuities of all types on a joint contributing basis. However, the CFAT didn't have the capital to underwrite TIAA's organization and initial fiscal responsibilities, and so Pritchett approached the Carnegie Corporation. This corporation was established in 1911 by Carnegie with a whopping $125 million and with the broadest purposes of any of his philanthropies, that is, "for the advancement and diffusion of knowledge and understanding among the people of the United States." An agreement between the corporation and the foundation in 1917 specified that CFAT would contribute one million dollars outright and the Carnegie Corporation would contribute five million dollars at four percent interest and annual payments of $600,000 for ten years. This agreement was "gratefully" accepted by the executive committee of CFAT. Thereafter, TIAA was incorporated in March 1918 with Pritchett its first president. Among the thirteen incorporators of TIAA who also signed the charter and by-laws, two were from Stevens representing CFAT, Humphreys and Newcomb Carlton 1890 who was then the president of Western Union.[315] By 1937, TIAA became wholly independent of CFAT which spawned it, and a stock fund, College Retirement Equities Fund (CREF), was later added.

CFAT also dealt with educational standards, through white papers, as Pritchett had desired. Its most important work in its first fifteen years was to sponsor a study of engineering education, the Mann Report, the first such comprehensive study in America. This study came as a result of joint efforts of the foundation, the major engineering professional societies, and the Society for the Promotion of Engineering Education (SPEE).

The SPEE had its origins in the World Engineering Congress which met in Chicago in 1893. The engineering educators who made up Section E of this congress decided to form the SPEE the next year, and the first president

---

[315] "Notice of Incorporators," *Journal of Commerce and Commercial Bulletin,* April 23, 1918; *Teachers Insurance and Annuity Association of America; Charter and By-Laws,"* 576 Fifth Avenue, New York, 1918; and *(Confidential) Teachers Insurance and Annuity Association of America; Minutes of Meeting of Incorporators* (April 23, 1918).

was DeVolson Wood who was then professor of mechanical engineering at Stevens Institute of Technology. Wood was elected partly because so many of his students had become professors, partly because of his numerous popular textbooks, and partly because of his reputation for being sincerely dedicated to engineering education as a professor for thirty-nine years. Besides Stevens professors like Denton, Ganz, Geyer, Humphreys, and Jacobus, Wood's students among the SPEE membership included William S. Aldrich 1884, professor of mechanical engineering at the University of West Virginia in 1893 who later became president of Clarkson; Morgan Brooks 1883, professor of electrical engineering at the University of Nebraska; William T. Magruder, professor of mechanical engineering at Ohio State University; Brown Ayers 1878, who later became president of the University of Tennessee; and L. S. Randolph, professor of mechanical engineering at VPI -- just to name a few from Stevens and not counting his fifteen years of teaching at the University of Michigan. In the first years of the SPEE, besides Wood, who was considered "the senior teacher of engineering in the country, if not the world," these professors held leadership positions in the SPEE.[316] Among the SPEE's council members were Wood 1894-95, Kent 1897-99, Ayres 1900-02, Magruder 1900-02, and Randolph 1902-04. Magruder was a vice president in 1905-06 and secretary in 1906-07. Moreover, among Wood's many ex-colleagues was Robert H. Thurston who served as a vice president of the SPEE under Wood in 1894-95 and was a council member continuously from 1894 to 1900.

During his presidential address, DeVolson Wood set forth the vision for the fledgling society. He said "in less than forty years, about one hundred professional engineering schools have come into existence, graduating some twelve hundred annually" and that "engineering education and abstract scientific education have become closely allied," but the process had been "spontaneous in character, without a central head or mutual conference." What was needed was coordination supplied by the SPEE: "If its efforts are properly directed, it may make of all of these schools a kind of university, though widely separated, . . . a kind of unity for accomplishing the best results in this line of education." As another member of the assemblage put it, what was needed was "a uniform system of educating engineers."[317] Consequently, one of the first questions taken up was a review of the bewildering array of different proportions of scientific courses versus shop courses

---

[316] Matthew Elias Zaret, "An Historical Study of the Development of he American Society for Engineering Education," unpublished Ph.D. dissertation, NYU 1967, 94.

[317] Quoted in David Noble, *America By Design*(Oxford, 1977), 44-45, and Harry S. Rogers, "The Threshold of a New Era," *Proc. SPEE*, LIV (1947), 10-11.

in curricula. However, it was several years before the SPEE organized a Joint Committee on Engineering Education made up of representatives from the major professional societies to review engineering education in a systematic manner, this committee being "no doubt the most important SPEE committee in terms of achievement," according to a historian of the organization.[318]

The Joint Committee on Engineering Education was organized by the SPEE's Dugald Jackson in 1907. He was an MIT professor of electrical engineering who was a consultant to the major electrical corporations which had been expressing a need for standardization of electrical engineering curricula. The AIEE had taken a leadership role in pushing the SPEE to establish the committee. Another stimulus was Frederick W. Taylor who was president of the ASME in 1906-07. Taylor not only reorganized the ASME by applying his principles of scientific management to make the organization more efficient, but he also called for application of more scientific methods to engineering education in his article "Comparison of University and Industrial Discipline and Methods." In this article he criticized the haphazard lack of efficiency in teaching and administration of higher education and the lack of standards in curricula.[319] His interest led him to participate in the joint committee personally, and he was among the first members, who included two or three representatives from the SPEE, AIME, ASCE, AIEE, and the American Chemical Society (ACS). The two from the ASME were Frederick W. Taylor and Alexander C. Humphreys.[320]

Humphreys was a key to the joint committee's success because he was responsible for obtaining the necessary funding. After serving as one of the ASME's representatives to the committee in 1907-08, Humphreys then joined Dugald Jackson as one of the three SPEE representatives during the years 1908-14 when Jackson was taking the lead to gather information from engineering schools and generally coordinating the committee's activities. Taylor remained on the committee as a representative of the ASME and corresponded with Humphreys about its lack of progress given disagreements among its members about how to proceed. By 1912, it was apparent to the committee members that they lacked the resources to effectively collect data in a systematic manner. Humphreys, through his role on the executive committee of the Carnegie Foundation for the Advancement of Teaching, appealed to CFAT trustees for funds to help the joint committee.

---

[318] Zaret, *Op. Cit.*, 85.
[319] Frederick W. Taylor, "Comparison of University and Industrial Discipline and Methods." *Stevens Indicator*, XXIV (1907), 37-45.
[320] Zaret, *Op. Cit.*, 95.

Strapped for funds for its pensions at the time, the executive committee of CFAT in turn appealed to Andrew Carnegie, who, on January 31, 1913, wrote a letter providing money for a Carnegie Foundation "Division of Engineering Education . . . to make investigations concerning universities', colleges' . . . problems of education, affecting the improvement of educational methods, the advancement of teaching, or betterment of educational standards."[321]

By late 1913, the funds still had not been dispersed to the joint committee because of Pritchett's concern about them being used effectively. On December 12, 1913, Humphreys wrote to Taylor that he was still "trying to find out what can be done in the Carnegie Foundation. They expect to undertake an investigation, but whether they expect to do it at once, I cannot say, although I am a member of the Executive Committee. I am to have a conference with President Pritchett in the near future on the subject, and will keep you advised."[322] This pressure finally resulted in a meeting of Pritchett with the joint committee on January 2, 1914, in which Pritchett presented his conditions that the CFAT be permanently represented on the joint committee and that Carnegie's money be spent on a study by a "neutral observer" commissioned by CFAT to do the research and write the joint committee's report. Subsequently, Humphreys told Taylor that he had privately "so stated to President Pritchett that the selection of a man for the investigation is all important. If the wrong man is selected, that would be worse probably than if we never had an investigation."[323]

Henry S. Pritchett chose Charles R. Mann, a noted physicist from the University of Chicago, as the neutral observer, and they both joined the Joint Committee on Engineering Education as CFAT's representatives. Four years later, Mann completed his *The Study of Engineering Education* (1918), the first major national study of engineering education. Mann identified as the most serious problem the lack of coordination among engineering schools when it came to standards of admissions, of curricula, and of results for graduates of programs. He called for a set of core courses which would be included in every curriculum, and for more inclusion of sciences, humanities, and economics. The costs of production had to be understood, but engineering colleges could not allow themselves to be only concerned with "the ideals of the market place" and to serve "only the mighty dollar." Humanities courses needed to be increased to create "broad-

---

[321] Minutes of the Executive Committee, CFAT Papers, *Op. Cit.*, Nov. 15, 1911 and Feb. 11, 1913.

[322] Humphreys to Taylor, Dec. 12, 1913, Taylor Papers, Stevens Institute Special Collections.

[323] Humphreys to Taylor, April 2, 1914, *Ibid.*

minded and humanistic men."[324] He emphasized the necessity of fundamentals in the core of the engineering curriculum, a core which should be common to all engineering schools in a particular discipline.

On the issue of multiplicity of specialization, Mann understood Stevens already stressed fundamentals for its one degree of M.E. when he wrote that colleges could "follow the example of Stevens Institute and specialize on one or two groups instead of offering many semi-specialized courses of study."[325] He wrote that Stevens had an integrated curriculum which was approved only after free and complete faculty discussion by the whole Stevens faculty, a coordinated effort among several departments.[326] Thus the main points of this classic study, which was sent to every member of the SPEE and has been widely cited ever since, was to shore up Stevens's resolve to continue its broad-based philosophy of engineering education. Stevens continued to stress its tradition of fundamentals of the major areas of engineering with a large content in liberal arts and to avoid offering an array of specialized engineering degrees as did other engineering colleges.

Alexander C. Humphreys continued to sit on the executive committee of the Carnegie Foundation for the Advancement of Teaching after the death of Andrew Carnegie, because, like Carnegie, Humphreys was antagonistic to commercialized college sports. Humphreys considered them a waste of time and detrimental to the genuine role of physical education for all students. During the 1880s, most colleges in the United States had hired coaches and built stadiums. Gate receipts be-came a focus because of the increasing popularity and lucrative nature of the game of football. By the turn of the century many educators criticized the increasing commercialization of college athletics in general. They thought commercialization caused abuses like reduced admissions standards for athletes and perversion of scholarships by alumni who donated money specifically for the tuition fees of athletes. CFAT was a focus of such opinion. In fact, Pritchett had done away with football at MIT when he was its president in 1905. When Charles W. Eliot of Harvard was chairman of CFAT's trustees in the foundation's first year of existence, 1905-06, he stated,

From the educational point of view, the value of any sport is to be tested chiefly by the number of persons who habitually take part in it for pleasure during the edu-

---

[324] C. R. Mann, "Report of Joint Committee on Engineering Education," *Proc. SPEE,* XXV (1917), 204-6.

[325] Charles Riborg Mann, *A Study of Engineering Education Prepared for the Joint Committee on Engineering Education of the National Engineering Societies*(1918), Bulletin 11 of the Carnegie Foundation for the Advancement of Teaching, 96.

[326] *Ibid,* 30.

cational period and enjoy it in after life. Tried by this test, football is the least valuable of all college sports . . .the exaggeration of such sports in schools and colleges remains a crying evil.[327]

In turn, when Humphreys served as chairman of CFAT's board of trustees in the early 1920s, he also spoke out against the trends in athletics. In an article on "College Athletics" in the *American Physical Education Review* in 1921, he criticized "professionalism or commercialism" in intercollegiate athletics:

Athletics should be subordinated to a wise and comprehensive plan of physical education of all the students and this means that this plan must be kept in balance with the plan for mental education. . . . the farther the students are allowed indulgence as to the curriculum requirements, the more they are allowed to specialize in athletics. We *know* that in not a few colleges and universities in the United States the members of athletic teams are in some measure excused, openly or otherwise, from some of their studies to enable them better to perfect themselves as team performers. That, we, or shall I say, I, do not believe in. As athletes we are, or should be, strictly amateurs. We do not give scholarships because of superior ability in athletics. . . . If such a preparatory student has a reputation for good scholarship also, that is another thing -- but even then I do not think such a prospective student should receive financial help *because* of his ability as an athlete. . . . I am glad to say there is an association of college officials now honestly trying to improve the conditions to which I refer. The man who is conducting its affairs is in earnest and he issues from time to time a bulletin and asks for comments from the members of the association. And these comments are getting to be more and more candid, and they indicate plainly that there has been and there still is need for reform. At Stevens we have always stood and we do stand for clean, absolutely clean, amateur athletics -- and now as part and parcel of our physical education scheme.[328]

In 1922 Humphreys, Eliot and Pritchett and the other members of the executive committee approved of the first CFAT funds to be spent on systematic research into college athletics, the results to be disseminated in another foundation white paper.[329] As in the case of the Mann Report, CFAT published several preliminary reports before the white paper by Howard J. Savage appeared in 1929. Savage's *American College Athletics* documented abuses caused by commercialization and promoted athletics

---

[327] Charles W. Eliot, "Changes in the Game of Football," in W. Carson Ryan, Jr., ed., *The Literature of American School and College Athletics*(CFAT, 1929), 94.

[328] Alexander C. Humphreys, "College Athletics," *American Physical Education Review*, XXVI (1921), 356-8.

[329] Minutes of the Executive Committee, CFAT Papers, Columbia University Rare Books and Manuscripts Collection, Box 8B.

education for the health and recreation of all students to be taught by regular faculty instead of coaches. It stated that at institutions like MIT, Reed College, and Stevens "where intercollegiate games are curtailed or lacking" there was a healthy "competitive tendency and 'instinct' for play." The faculty "responsible for intramural contests need certain qualities of the good teacher," namely "tact, enthusiasm, ingenuity, resourcefulness, and sympathetic understanding of youth." Thus, professionally paid coaches were a "perversion of cultural values." Savage made his point by comparing average scholastic aptitude test scores of athletes recruited for sports like football with the test scores of participants in sports like soccer and lacrosse for which colleges did not recruit. He found the former 150 points below the latter.[330]

Nationally, the Savage Report did not eradicate commercialization in college athletics, but it brought attention to the worst abuses, many of which were eradicated. Meanwhile, the athletics tradition established by Humphreys at Stevens was similar to the kind of physical education promoted by the report.

---

[330] Howard J. Savage, *American College Athletics*(CFAT, 1929), 25, 30, 86, and 126.

CHAPTER 12
Sports Clubs and Stevens Athletics

The most dramatic Stevens sports story is about Stevens's football club, the banning of football at Stevens, and the establishment of the college's unique tradition in athletics. The story begins in the era of amateur football clubs from the 1870s to World War I. Those were the pioneering years when the sport evolved from English football or soccer through Canadian rugby to American football.

In the beginning, Stevens's football club joined what became the Ivy League, which pioneered the American game. In 1873, representatives of Princeton, Yale, Columbia, and Rutgers met in New York City to establish the first American intercollegiate rules for football on the model of the London Football Association. In reality this game was soccer, since the ball was round, and no player could carry or throw it. The ball had to be kicked through the goal posts and dribbled and passed with the foot by players who numbered twenty. In September of that year, the Stevens Football Club of twenty men out of a total student body of seventy-five played its first football game ever, actually soccer, against New York University under the London rules and won six to one but later lost to Columbia two to one.

In those days only a few colleges were playing football, and there were no leagues and schedules, matches being arranged by invitation of one college club to another. Because the Stevens club entered the sport at the outset of intercollegiate club play, Stevens played Yale, Columbia, and Princeton. Stevens's cumulative record playing soccer-style football from 1873 to 1876 was nine wins seven losses and three ties.

Ivy League colleges needed a field on which to play in the New York City area, and they used the Stevens family's playing field in Hoboken, the St. George Cricket Grounds located between 8th and 10th Streets and Clinton and Adams Streets. Its rival was the Polo Grounds in Manhattan --American baseball evolved from rounders on this Stevens-owned field in the 1840s. The field was used by Harvard and Yale to play against Princeton to the south, but, since Stevens trustee Samuel Bayard Dod managed the field, the Stevens Football Club played soccer there "at home."

The start of the evolution from soccer to American football took place at Harvard. The Harvard student-run football club played McGill University in Montreal in 1873 in a Canadian-style rugby match which differed from English rugby. In Canada one could run the egg-shaped rugby ball for a "touchdown," but in England, teams only kicked the egg-shaped ball for a score. Subsequently, Harvard introduced the Canadian rugby rules to Yale in a game in 1875, and then Harvard, Yale, Princeton and Columbia met in 1876 to establish a loose league of clubs called the Intercollegiate Football Association which established new rules based on Britain's Rugby Football Union with one difference -- players could score touchdowns by running the ball, as in Canada. In 1877, the Stevens' club joined the league, and its "eleven" played Harvard, Yale, Princeton, Columbia, Army, and Rutgers. The Stevens record was six wins, five losses, and eight ties from 1877 to 1880.

In 1880, Yale's club captain, the Father of American Football, Walter C. Camp, led the way in the next rule change which substituted the scrimmage for the rugby scrummage. Instead of putting the ball between two inter-locked packs of players, it was possessed by one team which then could put it into play without interference until it was snapped. Other rules established seven forwards on the offensive line, a quarterback, two halfbacks, and a fullback. After the Intercollegiate Football Association adopted the rules, which favored heavier players, Stevens's lighter team had a won-lost record of fourteen wins thirty-four losses and five ties from 1881 to 1888.[331]

During the 1880s most colleges in the nation established football clubs or varsity teams, and many of the more ambitious clubs hired coaches with gate fees paid by supporters. By the early 1890s, colleges themselves started to hire coaches and build stadiums because of the increasing popularity and lucrative nature of the game. In Hoboken, the Stevens family sold the St. George Cricket Grounds and it disappeared under factories by 1906, the Stevens club playing without a grandstand on a portion of the Castle property owned by the Stevens family in 1907.[332]

Less competitive because of a lack of facilities, the Stevens Football Club was also less able to win because of further rule changes. In 1888, tackling under the waist was permitted, and offensive linemen were prevented from blocking with extended arms. These new rules concentrated the offensive line at the center of the field in the close-order alignment of the T and benefited teams from colleges fielding heavy players. Then in 1892, Harvard introduced the flying wedge during kickoffs, a development which led to a rise in the violence and injuries. Stevens's club could no longer compete with its traditional rivals, and in 1887 played lighter teams from Amherst, Trinity, Dartmouth, and MIT. But realignments of the leagues subsequently put Stevens back with the ivy leaguers with disastrous results: In 1890,

---

[331] *Stevens Indicator, Vol. I, 3-4. Morton Memorial*, 70, errs in saying 11 games were played in 1883 and that Stevens had a "banner year."
[332] *Morton Memorial, Op. Cit.*, 72.

there was only one win, over Trinity, out of twelve games played, and scores against the ivy teams were Harvard 28, Stevens 4; Yale 30, Stevens 0; Cornell 35, Stevens 4; Dartmouth 18, Stevens 5; Columbia 12, Stevens 6; and Princeton 49, Stevens 0. The alumni magazine commented, "When the style of the game is so far developed as to require the enormous amount of time and labor which the larger colleges spend, we add too much work to the already difficult (academic) course . . . we can hardly expect to develop football players at Stevens." The article pointed out that all the opponents except one had hired trainers and had extensive athletic facilities by 1890.[333] In 1891, Stevens reached such a low ebb that the club could not attract enough players to field a team and had to withdraw from the Inter-collegiate Football Association to play only intramural games.[334]

In 1892, the club reapplied for admission but was refused. Stevens teams were "remarkably light" and couldn't prevent rushes through the center of the line. By 1893, Stevens's club was playing only Lafayette and Rutgers in intercollegiate play, and most games were with local athletic clubs.[335] Nationally, in spite of some rule changes to curb injuries, the game was so violent that by 1905 there were eighteen deaths and 159 serious injuries in college games. Stevens's club record with other small colleges was twenty-four wins, sixty-five losses, and four ties. The only club which Stevens was able to defeat consistently was City College of New York. Against CCNY, Stevens earned twelve wins, one loss, and one tie, and once won by 162 to 0 -- like Stevens, CCNY dropped football later.

As a result of the deaths and injuries in the 1905 college football season, the president of the United States, Theodore Roosevelt, invited college representatives to the White House and stated that "Brutality and foul play should receive the same summary punishment given to a man who cheats at cards" and made an appeal for a safer game. Around that time, presidents Pritchett of MIT and Nicholas Murray Butler of Columbia did away with their colleges' intercollegiate football programs. At Roosevelt's urging, representatives of sixty colleges convened in New York City late in 1905 to draw up new rules. This group established the Intercollegiate Athletic Association of the United States, whose name was changed to the National Collegiate Athletic Association (NCAA) in 1910. Games were reduced to sixty minutes, the yards of a down were increased from five to ten, and, to promote brains instead of brawn, forward passes were allowed. The subsequent years proved football was still a dangerous game in spite of padded uni-

---

[333] *Stevens Indicator*, Vol. VII, 1890, 77-78.

[334] *Ibid.*, Vol. VIII, 1891, 61-63.

[335] *Ibid.*, Vol. X, 1893, 87-90 and 347.

forms and headgear. These changes resulted in the complicated game of American Football which required full-time coaches and a jump in practice time for the increased precision of play. The Stevens Football Club somehow survived as an amateur student-run club until 1916, one year after the physical education department was established.

As at many other colleges, this department grew out of World War I, the single most important event in the establishment of American physical education programs. Government leaders, especially military leaders, criticized the flabbiness of American soldiers and said that school and college physical education could have prevented it through calisthenics and fitness programs. As a result, Alexander C. Humphreys hired John Davis as athletics director. Serving from 1915 to 1949, Davis organized a physical education program of calisthenics for all students three times a week during the entire four years of undergraduate education not only as part of preparedness for war but also to develop, as he said, "the whole individual." In addition, Davis organized intramural teams in football, baseball, lacrosse and other sports. Some of the student-run clubs which played other schools became varsity teams coached under the direction of Davis, and some remained private clubs.

The football club became a varsity sport and prospered under the new department. For example, in the previous forty-three years as a club, the football team had only six winning seasons, but, in the eight years under Davis's coaches, the varsity had four winning seasons in a new league of similarly ranked colleges. But after a disastrous losing year in 1924, President Humphreys shocked the Stevens alumni and the students by announcing at commencement exercises in 1925 a ban on intercollegiate football. He had more than his own dislike of commercial abuses in the national game to warrant his decision -- there had been a series of injuries and one death in athletics at Stevens during the 1924 football season.

In the Haverford game, Harold "Cally" O'Callaghan 1925, the Stevens team captain and fullback was injured, and then he was reinjured in the University of Delaware game. Most importantly, the team's quarterback Dudly C. "Dud" Allen 1925 suffered a fractured skull and was knocked out cold in the RPI game. In addition, three players on intramural football teams which acted as feeders to the varsity also suffered injuries: another fractured skull, a severely injured knee, and an injured foot. Parents of one footballer brought suit against the institute prompting Humphreys's remark that since he was responsible for injuries he had the final word on the existence of football. Actually, the student fatality occurred after an unauthorized wrestling match between two freshmen, but it coincided with what Humphreys called "near fatal" injuries in football.[336]

Stevens heroes Dudley C. "Dud" Allen and Harold "Cally" O'Callaghan
are seen here in photos taken during Stevens's last football season in 1924.

Humphreys's stated reason for dropping football was the increasing a-mount of time required to field a competitive team. This complaint about football was a favorite theme used against the sport by the Carnegie found-ation in a series of white papers turned out in the 1920's. The dismal 1924 season highlighted the problem: Stevens lost all seven games by scores of CCNY 15, Stevens 0; Haverford 20, Stevens 0; Hamilton 14, Stevens 6; Swarthmore 49, Stevens 0; U. of Delaware 21, Stevens 0; Massachusetts Agricultural 23, Stevens 3; and RPI 27, Stevens 0. At the end of the season, the football coach, George Stallings, announced a stepped-up program of spring training in preparation for the fall season.[337] In January 1925, Stal-lings called meetings of the squad on Tuesdays and Fridays at 4:30 to go over football fundamentals in "skull sessions" in order to "think in a

---

[336] *Ibid.,* Jul. 1925, 77 and 81-83. and *Stute,* June 16,1925, 1.

[337] *Ibid.,* Dec. 3, 1924, 1.

football way." He also asked all footballers to sign up for track and wrestling and to participate in indoor practice to reduce fumbles and increase starting speeds. Once the weather improved in the spring, he envisioned outdoor football practice and attendance by other students to promote the team's "fighting spirit."[338] These developments did not sit well with Humphreys. He said that the course of study was too demanding on the students' time to permit year-round practice for football, and, since the coaching staff determined that either there should be such practice or no football, Humphreys had chosen no football.[339]

Time for academics was also taken away from Stevens students by their activity as fans of the football team. For example, the student newspaper, the *Stute*, reported that the night before the Swarthmore game in 1924 there was the usual mass meeting for pep night, an event which was "the only student enterprise that had the active support of almost the entire student body." All day during Wednesday, classes were disrupted by anticipation of the merriment to come, which, when it arrived, consisted of the entire student body doing a frolicking snake dance down Washington Street to their chosen haven while exhibiting "pompous exhibition of our school spirit." The next day, some 450 Stevens students boarded their flivers, trains, and buses or simply bummed a ride for the trip to Swarthmore. A letter to the editor by an attending student bragged about spending only fifteen minutes on his homework, and it referred to troubles with police and opposing fans during the game as well as fines for traffic violations on the way home.[340] After banning football, Humphreys advised incoming freshmen to avoid the excessive frivolities of upperclassmen and to apply themselves to their studies.[341] Humphreys continued to support physical education strongly by concurring with John Davis that the wartime four years of physical education should continue in the 1920s when many colleges required only two years.[342]

In 1929, the Savage report identified lacrosse as preferable to football as an intercollegiate sport because it did not require recruiting athletes. After the demise of football, lacrosse, along with basketball, became a popular sport at Stevens, where it already had a long history of pioneering club participation. Originally a native-American game which became popular in Canada, Johns Hopkins led the way in founding an Intercollegiate Lacrosse

---

[338] *Ibid.*, Jan. 14, 1925.

[339] *Ibid.*, June 16, 1925, 1.

[340] *Ibid.*,

[341] *Ibid.*, Sept. 30, 1926, 2.

[342] Joseph B. Oxendine, "100 Years of Basic Instruction," *Journal of Physical Education, Recreation and Dance*, Sept. 1985, 32.

Association in 1882, and a Stevens club joined the league two years later. Stevens's club and varsity teams hold the nation's record for continuous uninterrupted competition from 1884 onwards, Johns Hopkins dropping out by 1900 leaving only Stevens and Lehigh playing, the latter having fielded its team one year after Stevens. Twenty-two Stevens lacrosse players have been all-Americans, and some of its players made pioneering contributions to the game.[343]

Rollin Norris entered the class of 1885 as a sophomore in 1882. He was from Baltimore where he had played with the Peinniman brothers who were leading players with the Druid Lacrosse Club, although Norris was not a member of that club. In the spring of 1883, he took his lacrosse stick to the St. George Cricket Grounds and amused himself tossing and catching the ball. His interest caught the attention of other Stevens students, and, in the spring of the following year, they fielded enough players for practice and a game with Johns Hopkins, Norris putting up most of the club members in his house in Baltimore. Subsequently, another Baltimore resident and Druid Club member, Tom Symington, entered Lehigh in 1885, started a club, and then challenged Stevens to a match. He even paid for the expense of Stevens's club traveling to Bethlehem, Pennsylvania. Stevens won, and the club members were hooked on the game. In the same year, Stevens entered the competition for the Oelrichs Cup in Brooklyn, the competition being won by the Druids, the other clubs being the Crescent Athletics Club of Brooklyn, and those from Harvard, Yale, and Princeton. Members of this first lacrosse club included William H. Peirce 1884 and William C. Post 1886.

In the early days of lacrosse the sticks were longer and there was no net between the goal posts. Norris recalled scoring many goals by carrying the ball behind the posts and slamming it through so one of his team could send it back through in the right direction for a score. Another Stevens student from Baltimore, Rossiter S. Scott 1898, while president of the U.S. Intercollegiate Lacrosse Association as a senior, presented a design for a goal net to the association, and it was unanimously approved. Scott then supervised the early manufacture of the nets, which were universally used, only their fastenings changing over time. Scott recalled that his motive for inventing the net was not entirely unbiased. At the time, the goal posts were six feet high and placed six feet apart, and, when fast shots whizzed just inside the posts or high up just beneath their height, it was hard for the goal umpire to call the shots correctly as goals. He recalled that the Stevens team practiced such fast shots. The club painted a replica of the posts and a goalie on a

---

[343] *One Hundred Consecutive Years of Lacrosse, 1885-1985(1985),* 8-9.

wall, the goal's background area being painted black. The team would powder the balls with chalk dust and practice sending them high and just inside the goal posts. During the games in 1898, Scott claimed that the Stevens club lost two games because the umpire, standing to one side, disallowed such fast and closely inside goals because he couldn't see them. Thus, Scott's lacrosse net was designed to solve this problem for all teams once and for all -- but particularly for his own club.[344]

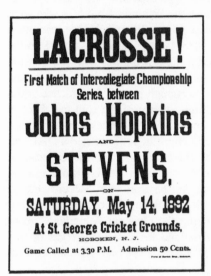 

Stevens's Lacrosse Club and varsity team hold the United States record for continuous uninterrupted competition since 1884.

After the Carnegie foundation published the Savage report in 1929, most members of the Stevens community felt that Humphreys's decision to drop football had been vindicated. Subsequently, in 1936 the Stevens board of trustees, chaired by Robert C. Stanley, officially endorsed an athletics policy in line with the Savage report and the practices at Stevens, an athletics policy which became a tradition on the Stevens campus.[345] The minutes of the board, dated November 25, 1936, stated,

The Board of Trustees reaffirms its conviction that physical education is an integral and important part of the training of every undergraduate and essential to the

---

[344] "60th Anniversary of Lacrosse," *Stevens Indicator,* 61 (1944), 4, 10-13.
[345] *Minutes of the SIT Board of Trustees,* Nov. 26, 1936.

modern concept of education. It heartily approves the Stevens policy of requiring three hours of physical education per week all through the four years for every student who is not incapacitated for such work. It also approves of the Stevens policy of appointing to posts in physical education only men who, by personality, character and training, are appropriate members of the Stevens faculty and notes with pleasure that all who have worked in the Department of Physical Education at Stevens for many years, which includes all who have coached intercollegiate sports teams, have had faculty status. Finally, it approves the Stevens policy of regarding grades by the Department of Physical Education as on a par with grades given by any other department of instruction in determining a student's rank in his class, his eligibility for promotion, graduation and the like, and all other matters affecting his scholastic standing.[346]

By World War II and the start of the Cold War, American colleges were stressing physical fitness to an even greater extent than before, most colleges requiring two or more years of required physical education. In 1944, a survey showed that one-third of American colleges had a four-year requirement like Stevens.[347] By the 1950s, President Jess Davis supported the trustee's 1936 statement by changing the title of Stevens physical education faculty from "Director," "Associate Director," and "Assistant Director" to "Professor," "Associate Professor," and "Assistant Professor." As will be shown later, Davis was liberal in tenuring faculty, and he also extended physical education professors the privileges of tenure similar to the rest of the faculty. He also supported the Stevens tradition in physical education and athletics started by Humphreys, and he said in 1956,

I think the Stevens physical education program accomplishes what many colleges hope for but never attain in as full measure as we do. Based on the principle of the greatest participation by the greatest number rather than by the gifted few, the program really tries to get as many as possible competing for the various Stevens teams. And, where many colleges talk of a big program of intramural sports, Stevens can point to actual accomplishment.[348]

By that year, the freshman and sophomore years were taken up with development of physical strength and basic skills and coordination through progressively more challenging classes in calisthenics, tumbling, and exercise using various apparatus. Special attention was given to the uncoordinated students in a program which was committed to every undergraduate and thought to be essential to the education of the whole person. In the junior

---

[346] Minutes of the SIT Board of Trustees, Nov. 26, 1936.
[347] Oxendine, Op.Cit., 33.
[348] "The 1956 Fund," *Ibid.*, 73 (1956), 3, 7.

and senior years, classes in individual sports such as squash, tennis, and golf were given for the establishment of life-long athletic development and exercise. In addition, intramural competitions were held in football, basketball, softball, squash, badminton and handball to foster such social qualities as leadership, initiative, self-control, loyalty, courtesy and sportsmanship.[349]

The tradition of amateur sporting clubs at Stevens continued. They were supported by student government through a student activities fund and included bowling, karate, skiing, and, perhaps most importantly, yachting. Located on the Hudson River, Stevens Institute has been an ideal location for boating and yachting, part of a tradition inherited from the Stevens family which merits special historical mention. In 1883, the first of Stevens's yacht clubs was organized. Called the Stevens Institute of Technology Yacht Club, it came only two years after the Yale Corinthian Yacht Club, the first collegiate yacht club in the United States -- and one year before the Harvard Yacht Club.[350] Soon defunct, it was replaced by the Stevens Yacht Club in 1891, and this club lasted until 1910.[351] Members were from well-to-do New York families with connections to the New York Yacht Club which hosted trials of Burgess-designed America's Cup yachts in New York harbor before they successfully defended the possession of the cup. Like other collegiate yacht clubs of the late nineteenth century, the Stevens club of 1891-1910 was a cruising club for gentlemen and not a racing club, and its activities were mainly social. For example, on January 14, 1894, members rented a special train to take their party of sixty people to the New York Jockey Club, then located in Morris Park, for a formal dinner followed by cotillion ballroom dancing. That same year the club's prestige rose when General Charles J. Paine consented to be an honorary member, Paine having defended the America's Cup three times by that time. Later in the decade, America's Cup challenger Thomas Lipton, the British tea magnate who owned the huge factory at the northern end of Washington Street in Hoboken, also became an honorary member.[352] The club existed until the waterfront was completely sold to commercial facilities by the Stevens

---

[349] "Physical Education and Athletics at Stevens," *Ibid.*, 73 (1956), 6, 5-7.

[350] Dates obtained from Yale alumni office and from Mike Horn of the yachting program at Harvard. Predating the yacht club at Stevens, in December 1872 members of the Stevens class of 1876 established a Stevens Institute Rowing Club with G. Barry Wall as president and William Hewitt as vice president. The club was reorganized in 1874 to become an institute-wide rowing club by the name of the Stevens Institute Boating Association.

[351] The members of this club erroneously claimed in yearbooks that they were "The 1st college yacht club organized Oct. 1, 1891," but this claim was only made between the years 1894 and 1900 and thereafter they simply gave the date the club was organized.

[352] *Ibid.*, 1893, no.5, 58, and *Links* of the late 1890s.

family, a development which cut off not only the yacht club but also the residents of Hoboken from the Hudson river for decades.

A third Stevens student yacht club was established for racing in 1941. It kept its boats at various locations in the metropolitan area: Patchogue, New York; Newark Bay, New Jersey; City Island, New York; and Perth Amboy, New Jersey. College racing of sailboats as a competitive sport began in the 1930s. A few groups at mostly northeastern colleges and universities started holding races in small sailing craft, mostly dinghies. By the end of the 1930s, the Inter-Collegiate Yacht Racing Association (ICYRA) was formed with its organized rules and standards for regattas. The Stevens club joined the ICYRA soon after its inception. G. Silliman 1942 was the new Stevens Yacht Club's first commodore, but it was E. Dickinson III, C. L. Farrand, W. E. Caldwell, and Charles King, Jr., who built a penguin class dinghy the year before. That year the new club competed in four regattas: two at Annapolis, and one each at Brown and MIT.[353] By 1945, the club entered ten regattas, and the membership had grown to twenty-one students.[354] After World War II, the sport caught on, and the number of participating campuses increased from a few dozen to over two hundred with hundreds of regattas annually. In 1949, in the midst of this expansion, the ICYRA was restructured into a national umbrella organization with regional associations in control of competition. Thus the SYC joined the Middle Atlantic Intercollegiate Sailing Association (MAISA). In the 1940s through the 1960s, the SYC used dinghies of various varieties as well as tempest-class boats.

The most illustrious era for the SYC began around the mid-1960s after the institute had bought a section of waterfront property directly below Castle Point, the Hoboken waterfront piers of the early twentieth century having been cleared because they were no longer competitive with the container ship facilities at Newark Bay and Staten Island. At this point, Richard Eversen, dean of student affairs, became advisor to the club. A boating and sailing enthusiast who had served in the U.S. Coast Guard, Eversen was the institute's "owner's representative" for the *SS Stevens*, a retired passenger ship which served the institute as a dormitory for Stevens students from the late 1960s to the late 1970s. Eversen helped students cobble together the resources and facilities to create the yacht club's facilities on campus. First, Student Council was persuaded by commodore Richard Dell to supply the considerable funding necessary for a small fleet of British-built Kestral sailing dinghies, boats which were used through the

---

[353]*Link,* 1942, 54.
[354]*Link,* 1945, np.

1970s for practice by club members. Second, around 1969 when the club tied for first place in the prestigious Douglas Cup Regatta in California, Eversen persuaded Irving Fishman of Maritime Powers, Inc., to donate a floating dock for the yacht club. Fishman obtained some cut-rate World War II floating steel drums which had held antisubmarine nets across the Narrows in New York harbor, and, as a contribution to the club, Fishman welded them together and shipped them to the campus as supports for the floating docks. Third, Eversen coordinated an effort by the campus machine shop and students to make a crane and hoist to lift the dinghies in and out of the water. Fourth, Eversen and Leonard Frisco of purchasing were able to obtain two trailers at low cost for storing equipment and for use as a clubhouse. After the on-campus facilities were in place by 1970, the number of students in the club doubled and tripled to reach yearly totals of seventy in some years, but the main benefit of facilities on campus was the ability to practice more often. Eversen knew that success in competition was dependent on constant practice.

Among the brilliant successes of the club of that era were first place in the New Jersey Holland Trophy Regatta in 1968 and 1969, fourth in the American Trophy and a tie for first in the Douglas Cup in 1969, seconds in the American and Wood Trophies in 1970, first in the Timme Angsten Trophy in 1971, first in the Danmark Trophy in 1972, and first in the War Memorial Trophy in 1973. The magnitude of the achievement was heightened because most of the colleges and universities beaten by the SYC had regular well-funded sports programs in dinghy sailing while Stevens had only a club, a mere student activity. Also, the opposition included many prestigious and large institutions; for example, the student newspaper, the *Stute*, reported the first in the Angsten Trophy in 1971 under the headline "Sailors Triumphant in Chicago. Sweep Intersectional Regatta," the participants being U.S.C., Ohio State, Notre Dame, Purdue, Harvard, and Navy, among others. In the Danmark win in 1972, the SYC beat Harvard, Tufts, M.I.T., and ten other colleges. In 1972, Graham Hall in his "College Racing" ratings in *Yachting* magazine rated the Stevens Yacht Club fourth in the nation behind Tufts, Yale, and University of Rhode Island.[355] Jonathan G. Ford, Henry M. Krafft, and Mark M. Wheeler were named to the All-American Intercollegiate Sailing Team.[356] Henry M. Krafft had the distinction of being chosen to represent the United States on the American International Intercollegiate Sailing Team which competed with British

---

[355]*Yachting*, Jan. 1972, 392.
[356]Letter of G.Griswold to R. Eversen, Mar. 7, 1976.

college sailors in 1973. According to *Yacht Racing* magazine, this team was "drawn from the best colleges in the ICYRA of North America."[357]

In the late 1960s and early 1970s, student protests and activism against traditional curricula during the Vietnam war resulted in dropping of required physical education by many colleges and universities. By 1972, only 72 percent of four-year institutions retained the requirement, and by 1978 the number had fallen to 57 percent.[358] However, Stevens continued to adhere to the Humphreys-era philosophy and the policy of the trustees statement of 1936. Even though the four-year physical education re-quirement was lowered to three years in the 1980s, the Stevens physical education requirement remained greater than the majority of schools in the nation -- perhaps more than other engineering schools and perhaps more than most liberal arts schools according to Stevens surveys. Stevens conducted three polls, in 1982, 1994 and 1998 among eighteen, thirty-one, and sixteen colleges respectively, including major engineering schools in all three surveys. In these polls, Stevens led all other colleges in the number of required semesters of physical education for credit -- six. The typical number of semesters for colleges polled in 1982 was one year and in 1994 the average was 2.25 semesters. Out of the colleges polled in 1982, one engineering college was most dissimilar to Stevens, because at that institution there was no physical education requirement but a heavy emphasis on intercollegiate competition to win championship berths in NCAA playoffs or conference championships consistently. In the 1982 poll, only a bare majority of the responding colleges granted tenure to physical education faculty, while in the 1994 poll only two colleges out of thirteen reported that promotion and tenure policies were similar to policies governing other faculty.[359] In the late 1990s, Stevens physical education faculty included those of professorial rank who held tenure.

Scholarships based on athletic ability alone have never been permitted at Stevens. In the 1990s "scholar-athletes" were sought at the urging of the sixth president of Stevens, Harold J. Raveché, but, since these students receive no athletic-related scholarship money, they are not easy to recruit. The six-semester physical education requirement for credit for all students in a variety of sports has continued to the end of the twentieth century in all undergraduate curricula. In addition, faculty have supervised intramural

---

[357]Nina Shively, 'Campus Courses' *Yacht Racing*, July 1973, 4.

[358] Oxendine, Op. Cit., 33.

[359] See John S. Lyon, "1981-82 Survey of Physical Education and Athletics at Eighteen Selected Colleges," John S. Lyon, "Physical Education Survey: Selected Engineering-Science Schools (National) and Liberal Arts Schools (Northeast), October 1994," and Roger Cole, "Survey of March 1998." Stevens Special Collections.

sports in interdormitory and interfraternity leagues as well as intercollegiate teams. Thus, Stevens has tried to adhere to the principles laid down by Humphreys and John Davis, namely that "the work of the PE department belonged to every student who came to the college and that the aim was not to make outstanding athletes or train championship teams but to give all students the best opportunities for participation." The goals have been "leadership, initiative, self-control, loyalty, courtesy and sportsmanship."[360]

Under this policy, the records compiled in intercollegiate varsity sports have been successful at times. In the 1920s and 1930s, the basketball team had twenty-five winning or tying seasons and only nine losing seasons, and it went to the ECAC tournament as late as 1996. Baseball had a period when it had a winning percentage in twenty-three of thirty-five years and lacrosse in twenty-seven of thirty-five years. Men's fencing has had winning seasons in thirty-three of the last forty-one seasons, and women's fencing had a record of 83-41 between 1979 and 1985; in 1982 and 1984, the women fencers advanced to the NCAA finals which put them in the top one percent the nation. Such records have been compiled in spite of the policy that intercollegiate competition is important "only to the extent that it usefully supplements the general educational program of the college."[361]

---

[360] "Physical Education and Athletics at Stevens," *Stevens Indicator,* 73 (1956), no. 6, 5-6.
[361] *Ibid.*

CHAPTER 13

Honor Societies, Honor System, Student Government

Whereas some older alumni best remember the "Cremation of Calculus," a ceremony of the old days when students yearly burned a calculus book, student life's serious side involved participation in honor societies, engineering societies and particularly the honor system that has touched every student since 1908. Moreover, student government inculcated responsibility and accountability through its management of a student activities fund.

National honor societies were pioneered with the help of Stevens graduates and students. The national honorary society of Phi Beta Kappa was organized in 1776 to honor scholarship and research covering all subjects in the liberal arts. By the 1880s it was felt that it did not give sufficient recognition to science, and another honorary society, Sigma Xi, was founded by Stevens alumnus Frank Van Vleck in 1886. Both Frank Van Vleck and his brother, the Edison Pioneer John Van Vleck, were descendants of Tielman Van Vleck, an early Dutch settler in New Amsterdam, and their father was the Reverend John Van Vleck. Upon graduation in 1884, Frank Van Vleck went to Johns Hopkins University to take a postgraduate course in physics.[362] Subsequently, in 1885 he joined his mentor Robert H. Thurston at Cornell where the professor had become director of the Sibley College of Mechanical Engineering in 1885.

While teaching as an instructor at Cornell, Van Vleck talked about forming a "scientific Phi Beta Kappa" with a senior, William Day, just before graduation ceremonies in 1886. The two young men then went to Day's room and at one sitting formulated a plan of organization. They adopted Greek letters and a motto, *Spoudon xynones* or "Companions in zealous research." After Day left Cornell, Van Vleck and six Cornell graduate and undergraduate students drew up a constitution and by-laws, elected new members, and started to make contacts with other colleges.

Part of Van Vleck's motivation may have been to promote schooled, science-oriented engineers along the lines established in the shops of William Sellers and at the Franklin Institute and Stevens by Henry Morton -- a tradition which was being carried on at Cornell by Thurston. Van Vleck emphasized that Sigma Xi's aims were to honor those in all scientific fields, and he made no distinction between pure science and engineering. The

---

[362] Furman, *Morton Memorial, Op.Cit.,* 591.

fledgling society attracted a distinguished Cornell geologist as its leader, Professor Henry Shaler Williams, who had been interested in an honorary society for scientists for years before he joined Van Vleck's group in 1887. Williams was elected president of Sigma Xi, and his idea that excellence in research in scientific fields should be the society's distinguishing character-istic led to Sigma Xi's national success as an honor society in the sciences and not in engineering fields.[363]

Through the encouragement of Van Vleck, Stevens Institute of Tech-nology was issued the second charter in the U.S. for the Beta chapter of Sigma Xi on May 19, 1887. The chapter was started by mathematics instructor William H. Bristol, and alumni William O. Barnes, Charles W. Thomas and Benjamin J. Tucker, all of Van Vleck's class of 1884. The fifth charter member was a senior, Benjamin F. Hart, who was graduating that June. Perhaps because all the members were alumni and were scattered to various jobs except for Bristol, who remained on campus as a faculty mem-ber, the chapter was not active thereafter.[364] One possible reason for the inactivity was that Van Vleck himself became a successful engineer instead of staying within academe as a scientist: He left Cornell for the West Coast in 1888, and, after being chief engineer of the Los Angeles Cable Road Company which built the original Los Angeles street car system, he super-vised the electrification of the area's interurban transportation systems. In 1903, he started a long career as a military engineer with a specialty in naval architecture. First he worked for the Navy's Bureau of Steam En-gineering and did research for the U.S. Navy's Liquid Fuel Board which led the Navy to switch from coal to oil. During World War I, he was a major in the office of the Army's Quartermaster Corps's Transport Service where he served as a naval architect. He designed and supervised the construction of early ferrocement transports -- ships whose hulls were made of cement reinforced with steel rods and chicken wire -- for the Army during the war, and subsequently he held the position of supervisory engineer and naval architect for the Quartermaster Corps Transport Service designing ferro-cement and steel ferries and transports for the Army until he retired in 1935 as a lieutenant colonel. He died in Walter Reed Hospital and was buried in Arlington Cemetery.[365] Meanwhile, Sigma Xi had phenomenal expansion:

---

[363] Michael M. Sokal, "Companions in Zealous Research, 1886-1986," *American Scientist,* 74 (1986), no. 5, 486-488.

[364] Henry Baldwin Ward, *Sigma Xi; Quarter Century Record and History, 1886-1911*(1911), 108, lists a sixth member of the Stevens Beta Chapter, a "Burton Morss Tremper," as an elected undergraduate student but also as a "merchant" of Kingston, N.Y. However, both faculty minutes and lists of students in catalogues of the era show no such person ever attending Stevens.

[365] "Col. Van Vleck, 76, Engineer, is Dead," *New York Times,* Feb. 26, 1939, 38.

In this photo of part of the graduating class of 1884, Frank Van Vleck, founder of
Sigma Xi, is seen at top center looking into the camera; to the left, sitting with
head outlined against the door is David S. Jacobus of ASME boiler code fame,
and directly left and below him is William H. Bristol, who helped form the Beta chapter
of Sigma Xi. Sitting on the step at center bottom is John Van Vleck, an Edison
pioneer, and directly above him is John A. Bensel, ASCE's president in 1910.

By Sigma Xi's fiftieth anniversary in 1936, three years before Van Vleck's death, the honor society had 36,000 members in fifty-six countries.[366] On the Stevens campus, the Beta Chapter of Sigma Xi did not reactivate until 1954.[367]

Another possible reason why Sigma Xi became inactive on the Stevens campus in 1888 was that one day after it was founded, another society of even greater importance to Stevens was established on May 20, 1887: the Stevens Engineering Society (SES). Started by members of the class of 1888, Charles V. Kerr, William Whigham, E. M. Drummond, Arthur L. Shreve, Huburt S. Wynkoop, H. Russel Smith, and Thomas A. Vander Willigen, SES's goal was "to aid and encourage its members in the study of engineering practice, in original research, and in the cultivation of their powers of thought and expression." Its constitution specified that membership was open to all Stevens students who wished to join and participate, and from the start it was supported strongly by the faculty. Established in the same year that Coleman Sellers started to teach engineering practice, the SES was an instant success. It held weekly meetings for reading of technical papers by students, by faculty, and by guest lecturers -- some to standing-room-only crowds.[368]

The SES continued to grow and acquire prestige in the New York metropolitan area. After the turn of the century, Alexander C. Humphreys was made the SES's honorary president because of his unstinting support of the society. Its activities included field trips to places of engineering interest, gatherings at which original papers were presented and critiqued by outside authorities, and lectures by eminent engineers. They were brought to Stevens in part by the reputation of Humphreys as well as the dominant representation of Stevens in the ASME and AIEE. In its heyday, when the SES used to pack the Stevens auditorium not only with students but with New York City-area engineers, speakers included Frederick W. Taylor, Calvin W. Rice, Frederick R. Hutton, Charles F. Scott, Dugald Jackson, and Charles W. Baker in 1909-10, James Hartness, William T. Magruder, Charles Kirchhoff, W. R. Warner, and Charles P. Steinmetz in 1911-12, and Harrington Emerson and George F. Swain in 1912-13 -- a who's who of ASME, AIEE, and AIME engineers as well as foremost members of the

---

[366] "In Memoriam, Frank Van Vleck," *Stevens Indicator*, 56 (1939), no 3, 12.

[367] James H. Potter, "The Honorary Fraternity of Sigma Xi," *Stevens Indicator*, 74 (1957), no. 5, 15-16.

[368] "The Work of the Stevens Engineering Society," *Ibid.*, V (1888), no. 1, 8-12, "The Stevens Engineering Society," *Ibid.*, 89-91, and "The Stevens Engineering Society," *Ibid.*, 264-5.

Scientific Management movement.[369] Since the SES had up to ten prominent speakers per year, this list includes only the better known names.

The SES was closely tied with the ASME from its beginning, and by 1908 when the ASME formally recognized student chapters, the SES was the first student branch recognized by the ASME.[370] Run by students with the help of faculty, as well as Humphreys, who usually gave introductory remarks at meetings, these popular lectures widened students' horizons better than any other society on campus during the whole era of the Humphreys presidency. Humphreys kept a scrapbook of New York metropolitan-area newspaper clippings collected for him by the firm of Henry Romeike, Inc., 106-7 Seventh Avenue in New York City, "a newspaper cutting bureau," on the SES lecture series. Newspapers included the *New York Times*, the *Hudson Observer*, the *Evening News*, and many others.[371] The SES lasted until 1956 when its utility ceased due to the rise of student-faculty branches of the specialized societies, ASME proper, AIEE, and ASCE.[372]

One further possible reason for the temporary demise of Sigma Xi on campus was the formation of a national honor society for engineering in 1885 at Lehigh University. In that year, Professor Edward H. Williams, Jr., of the mining engineering department founded Tau Beta Pi to "mark in a fitting manner those who have conferred honor upon their alma mater by distinguished scholarship and exemplary character as undergraduates in engineering, or by their attainments as alumni in the field of engineering, and to foster a spirit of liberal culture in engineering colleges." Membership was restricted to the top quarter and later to the top one-eighth of the senior class, but also to alumni who were elected because of attainment in their fields. Tau Beta Pi's chapters eventually grew to 219 in number, but Stevens Institute's Alpha Chapter of New Jersey founded in 1896, was one of the first, the fifth chapter founded in the United States after Pennsylvania in 1885, Michigan State in 1892, and Purdue in 1893.[373] At Stevens, the charter members of Tau Beta Pi were the top academic quarter of the senior class of 1896: Charles B. Peck, Baylies C. Clark, William C. Maul, Edward M. Toby, John Schimmel, Jr., Douglas S. Bushnell, Charles F. Collyer, Waldo E. Denton, Celestino Garcia, Samuel Hollingsworth, John P. Kennedy, and Merrill V. G. Smith. Tau Beta Pi has existed continuously on

---

[369] See fancy printed brochures, some with photographs of speakers, of the SES advertising their yearly lecture series in Stevens Special Collections.

[370] "Stevens Engineering Society," *Mechanical Engineering*, 52 (1930), no. 4, 269.

[371] Scrapbook is in box on SES in Stevens Special Collections.

[372] R. J. Kellman, "Technical Societies," in Potter, ed., Op.Cit., II-11, 40-42.

[373] *The Bent of Tau Beta Pi*, 6 (1911), no. 2, 3.

campus, and its members have been involved with tutoring other students, as well as with evaluation of faculty and courses.[374]

President Alexander C. Humphreys was also the main creator of the Stevens Honor System which necessarily has touched every Stevens undergraduate continuously since 1908 when it was required of all students. In 1842, the University of Virginia had pioneered the first honor system in which students were not proctored during examinations. Instructors left the examination room after passing out examinations and returned only at the end of the examination period, and a pledge was required, namely, "I pledge my honor as a gentleman that during this examination I have neither given nor received assistance." Students in examinations had to report violators, who could be expelled from the university.[375] At Stevens, the first mention of an honor system appeared in the *Stevens Life,* the weekly student news pamphlet which predated the student newspaper, the *Stute.* The editor-in-chief, Frederic J. Angell of the class of 1884, wrote an editorial in the January 24, 1884, issue which called for an honor system of examinations in order to abolish the "wholesale cheating which now so universally exists in our college."[376]

Angell, a descendent of old Rhode Island families dating to 1630 and to the founding of Providence with Roger Williams, said in his editorial that "cribbing" was so widespread it was hard to understand how professors had not noticed it, and, if they had not, it was because they were "remarkably careless as to the reputation Stevens is rapidly acquiring."[377] Angell claimed that more than half of Stevens's students were entering into examinations with the intention to pass "dishonestly," and that "they do it, and easily do it." He went on to write that, "And it is this fact which prompts *Life* to take the initial step in a movement which shall abolish fraud in examinations, that shall tend to raise the standard of honor among our students, and which shall create sentiment that shall condemn dishonest methods of escaping conditions as unworthy of students who have the slightest claim to be men of honor." The editorial went on to support an honor system similar to the ones "in vogue in a number of our colleges and universities" and that it "is the *only* system which can raise the standards of honor here."

In the next issue there was a letter from Professor Charles Kroeh, teacher of French and German, that chided the editorial for "exaggerated state-

---

[374] P. P. Crowley, "Tau Beta Pi," in Potter, ed., Op. Cit., II-3-6.

[375] *Encyclopedia Americana,* 1991, H, 355.

[376] Editorial, *The Stevens Life,* Vol. V, no. 9, Jan. 24, 1894, 120 of bound volume.

[377] F. DeR. Furman, ed., *Morton Memorial, A History of Stevens Institute of Technology* (SIT, 1905), 295.

ments" and asserted that since "your journal circulates outside the Institute," the paper was "hardly entitled to accuse anyone of carelessness about the reputation of the Institute."[378] Angell's editorial reply stated that evidently the faculty were ignorant of the extent of cheating, and that, contrary to the professor's comments, "If we were careless of Stevens's reputation we would simply have kept silent."[379] Later that year, Angell quoted Lehigh's student publication, *Brown and White*, which criticized lack of action on instituting an honor system there. Angell commented that "We believe that the Honor System, pure and simple, is elevating, and we should like to inaugurate such a system."[380]

Nine years later, the *Stevens Life* again took up promotion of an honor system under the editorial leadership of Howard H. Maxfield of the class of 1895. This time *Life* reported on an article in RPI's *Forum* by a Professor W. LeC. Stevens entitled "Student Honor and College Examinations" which reported on a survey of forty-three colleges. The results of the survey showed that fourteen colleges required a statement from students pledging that their work was independently done, that a majority of colleges were in favor of some honor system, that particularly Southern colleges had developed such a system, and that in a majority of such cases "liberty of the student during examinations" was allowed. This time, the *Stevens Life* editorial was more circumspect, only citing the RPI article as a valuable contribution to the literature and stating that "The progress of the solution is slow but sure."[381]

After Humphreys became president in 1902, there was again a promotion of an honor system which this time met with success. One connection which is little known is that Frederic J. Angell went to work for Alexander C. Humphreys in the offices of Humphreys and Glasgow in 1897 and stayed there at least until 1905. Angell must have known Humphreys well, because he was a high-level manager in charge of constructing gas plants and negotiating new business for the firm.[382] At the very first dinner given by the alumni for the new president in 1902, Humphreys stated that one of his ambitions was to establish an honor system at Stevens to cover academic work.[383] Humphreys's first typewritten report to the board of trustees dated

---

[378] *Stevens Life*, Vol. V, no. 10, Feb. 7, 1894, 135.

[379] Ibid., 134.

[380] Ibid, Vol V., no. 19, June 27, 1894.

[381] Ibid., Vol. VI, no. 10, Feb. 27, 1895, 124-126.

[382] *Morton Memorial*, 295.

[383] A. Bornemann, "The Honor System at Stevens," in the unpublished J. H. Potter, ed., "The Stevens Story; the First Hundred Years at Castle Point" presented to President K. Rogers on July 31, 1997, II-23 which cites a report in the *Indicator* for 1911.

December 10, 1902, reported that at the very first meeting with the students on September 23, "I laid particular stress upon the conduct of examinations and tried to impress upon the students that while I should always be found in favor of fair and reasonable examinations, I should also be severe to the limit upon those students who tried by cheating to pass their examinations on the plea that these examinations were unfairly severe. I urged the students to consider among themselves the advisability of introducing the honor system for the control of examinations." It was not to be an honor system which covered general behavior and dress as in military schools, but one promoted honor and integrity in examinations and academic work. Humphreys subsequently reported that each class had appointed a committee to confer with the president on an honor system, and that he had contacted heads of other colleges and universities to gather information on honor systems. Humphreys concluded that "there is a very definite evil here to be met and conquered."[384] Humphreys did not force an honor system on the students and preferred the initiative to come from them when the time came to obtain faculty approval.

In June 1905, a new student newspaper, the *Stute,* was established, and on the first page of the first issue was a letter from "a junior" who recommended an honor system similar to that in place at a nearby liberal arts college. The student reported that no instructor was present during examinations and a pledge was required: "I pledge my word of honor, as a gentleman, that I neither gave nor received assistance during this examination."[385] The next year the *Stute* reported that the senior class of 1906 had taken its examinations successfully under an honor system as a trial run. Humphreys reported to the trustees that the examinations went well although the students felt that they were the hardest tests they had ever taken.[386] Years later, a graduate of the class of 1906, Henry B. Cross, recalled the motivation of the class of 1906, in petitioning the president to take exams under an honor system, was to abolish "evidence of cheating" which "wasn't general nor pernicious, but it did exist, and some few of us were more or less dependent on it." The petition of the seniors and juniors to be allowed the privilege of taking examinations under an honor system took the form of names signed on the radii of a circle so that no name was first or last, and thus no one appeared "holier than thou" in their aim to be

---

[384] Alexander C. Humphreys, "Report to Trustees," December 10, 1902, attachment to Minutes of the Board of Trustees, Book II, 1888-1903.

[385] *The Stute,* Vol. I, no. 1, Jun. 2, 1905, 1-2.

[386] Stevens Institute of Technology, Faculty Minutes, vol. 3, Nov. 14, 1906, 122; Minutes of the Board of Trustees, Book III, 1904-1909, 107; *The Stute,* Vol. III, no. 3, Oct. 26, 1906, 12.

gentlemen.[387] The class of 1906 had adopted trial rules previously approved by Humphreys, who then obtained faculty approval for the experiment. Later the president read the rules of the class of 1906 before a student forum on January 24, 1907, and similar ones were adopted by all the other classes. These preliminary rules called for five members of each class to form a committee and to be responsible for examinations when the instructor left the examination room. Students could leave the room and building without permission but they were to avoid the "appearance of evil" by refraining from talk. Humphreys reported to the trustees that the students are not expected to "act as spies on each other," but if any student believed that the "honor feature of the examination had been violated," he had to report it to the class committee. The class committee investigated and judged whether there was a violation, and then it reported its findings to the president for action.[388] By March 1907, Humphreys announced at an alumni dinner that the honor system was being successfully and generally adopted, and that Stevens was interested in "uplifting of character" as well as teaching the fundamentals of engineering.[389]

At the September 23, 1907, meeting of the faculty, the Faculty Committee on Discipline recommended a complete set of uniform rules for all classes which were acceptable to the students and the president. These rules were approved by a faculty vote in 1907 and applied in examinations in 1908, thus establishing 1908 as the historical beginning of a uniform honor system at Stevens. The name of the honor system established formally in that year was "Student Self-Government," a designation which existed until 1911 when it was changed to "Honor Board" so it would not be confused with the student council. The comprehensive rules of 1908 established a "Student Self-Government Board" consisting of three men from each class to be elected annually. This board investigated cases, brought charges, allowed accused students to cross-examine witnesses, judged the cases by a vote, and made recommendations to the faculty for punishment.[390] Later, Humphreys suggested to the faculty that a pledge be required on the outside of all examinations and signed by the students.[391] At a subsequent meeting the language of the pledge was determined: "I pledge my honor as a gentleman that I have not applied for help, and that I have neither given nor received help during this examination."[392] After some slight amendments by

---

[387] Henry B. Cross, "The Establishment of the Honor System," *Stevens Indicator*, Oct. 1952, 5-6.

[388] Faculty Minutes, III, 1904-1909, 131.

[389] *The Stute*, Vol. III, no. 9, March 15, 1907, 1.

[390] Faculty Minutes, III, 1904-1909, 148.

[391] Ibid., 150.

[392] Ibid., 155.

the students, the faculty approved the first constitution of the Student Self-Government Board on Sept. 24, 1908, a constitution containing the rules and also by-laws for the internal work of the board.[393] In 1909, Humphreys reported to the trustees that the honor system had been extended to include laboratory and shop work as well as examinations, and, although there were a few cases of violations, the intended result had been attained -- cheating had declined. He stated, ". . . there is very little cheating, much less than before, and under our present system I do not believe any student could cheat his way through the four years to graduation."[394]

Although there were some minor changes, the Stevens honor system did not have any major reforms until 1923, when a controversy occurred. The ruckus was reported in the *Stute* after winter examinations when an editorial spoke of a "storm of criticism" because members of the honor board had "overstepped the bonds (sic) of reason in their administration of the Honor System." The editorial went on to claim that the honor board was making itself "obnoxious" by "continually overstepping the bounds of authority" and appealed for it to be "tempered with common sense and charity."[395] Letters to the editor went back and forth from the honor board and various students. [396] The honor board chairman, P. R. Everett 1923, claimed the paper was hurting the honor system, and that "no man was spied upon without ample grounds for so doing," that he could appoint "any man as a proctor in the examination room," and that "the chairman of the Honor Board will continue to conduct the honor system at all times as he sees fit."[397] In a reply, Frank J. Coyle called the chairman a "dictator" who thought he could "conduct" honor, and that appointing student proctors for examinations was the constitutional right of student government and not the honor board. Coyle claimed the chairman distracted students from taking exams by telling his proctors to watch certain students and interrogate them during an exam. Such "suspicion" without "trust" was making the honor board "remote from the student body," because students had to be trusted to act honorably.[398] With the intervention of President Humphreys, the controversy was quieted by a student-faculty Committee on Student Activities which included professors Halliday and Hazeltine besides Everitt and William Gleason 1923. This committee drew up a new constitution which assured more due process and was "modeled on procedures used in courts of

---

[393] Ibid., 217.

[394] Board of Trustees Minutes, III, 1904-1909, 215.

[395] *The Stute*, Feb. 14, 1923, 2.

[396] Ibid., Feb. 21, 1923, 4.

[397] Ibid., Feb. 28, 1923, 4.

[398] Ibid., Mar. 7, 1923, 4.

law."[399] The constitution of 1923 took the power of judging cases out of the hands of the honor board by creating juries of twelve men from the student body chosen by a committee consisting of the dean of student activities, the defendant, and the judge and prosecutor from the honor board. The jury had to find the defendant guilty by unanimity, and, if they did, they also determined the punishment instead of the honor board.[400]

Thereafter, the Stevens honor system worked well until the late 1960s when it was nearly suspended for upper classes during one semester in the spring of 1969. According to a report written by Dean of Student Affairs William L. Bingham who chaired a committee which consisted of students, faculty and administrators to investigate cheating incidents, a main cause of the crisis was the atmosphere created by the Vietnam War.[401] Partly it was "the rebellious attitude of students elsewhere towards established value systems" which was "changing moral standards" of society and endangering the honor system at Stevens. In particular, "students serving as a trial jury were unwilling to convict, no matter how convincing the testimony, since convictions would lead to expulsion, expulsion to draft, draft to Vietnam and death." The committee had been charged by President Jess Davis with investigating the "present problems," and "strengthening the Honor System and insuring its continuance as an important tradition" of Stevens. Davis knew that alumni strongly supported the tradition, and it had become an important identifying asset of Stevens.

The findings of the committee, which met twenty times, were, first, to investigate the "problems" from 1967 to 1969. These included several groups of students who were caught procuring, selling, and purchasing examinations which were taken from professors' offices. The worst incident involved eighty to one hundred students who had copies of a test before the examination. More information was obtained from a student who had confessed and been expelled but who returned to testify. The committee also conducted a survey answered by 850 students, in which thirty-three percent admitted they had cheated at Stevens but which also showed that "an overwhelming majority of students wish to retain the Honor System." The Bingham-led committee dealt with infractions in several of the cases, meting out F's and other penalties short of expulsion, instead of leaving sanctions up to the honor board.

---

[399] Faculty Minutes, Mar. 18 and May 19, 1923.

[400] *The Stute*, Jun. 6, 1923, 2.

[401] William L. Bingham, "A Report on the Honor System," Jan. 7, 1969 in Stevens Special Collections, Samuel C. Williams Library. The report was sent to all faculty by President Jess Davis on Jan. 8, 1969.

Meanwhile in early February 1969, another committee consisting of professors Alfred Bornemann, James Lawlor, R. Nickerson, and George Schmidt, called for suspension of the honor system for juniors and seniors for the coming spring semester if no reforms were forthcoming. Their report said, "Such action would serve notice to the Student Body that working under the Honor System is a privilege that can be revoked by the Faculty in case it fails to function properly. It would also make it clear that a class is collectively responsible for its toleration of massive infringements of the Honor Code."[402] Instead of suspension the faculty accepted an appeal for speedy reforms by a committee of twenty students headed by Lou Brunetti 1970, a new honor board chairman. Brunetti pledged immediate reforms before the end of the semester and defended the honor system by saying that the "last two years indicate a rebellion against the school, and this rebellion has been taken out on the honor system."[403]

Brunetti's student committee organized a "Student Review Week for Honor Board Evaluation," and reforms were made before the end of the semester, namely a rule that students and faculty remain in the building during examinations. A Student Faculty Committee to Rebuild the Honor System was created by the next semester. In November 1969, soon after an antiwar demonstration outside Palmer Hall, Brunetti participated in a roundtable discussion moderated by Charles V. Schaefer 1936 which included Bingham, Professor Richardson of the humanities department and Richard J. Dell 1964. There were sixty-five alumni representatives present, and, after the discussion, the alumni showed strong support for the Honor System and its further revision. The Schaefer roundtable kept its sense of humor in the crisis, its only recommendation being a "Faculty Pledge" which stated, "I, Prof. _____, firmly resolve that the test here given is based upon information which I honestly believe I imparted to you to the best of my ability and with true dedication to my profession, and that in no way is this test my perverted technique of screwing you!"[404]

In December, Brunetti's honor board made a video of a mock trial and revamped freshman orientation to improve communication with the students. The constitution of the honor board was revised to have section representatives elected at the start of each term, and the section representatives were supplemented by honor board proctors who were appointed for all examination rooms -- the latter being a tough measure for the times which

---

[402] Report to the faculty of A. Bornemann, J. Lawlor, R. Nickerson, and G. Schmidt in Honor Board box in Stevens Special Collections.

[403] "Student Members Selected to Evaluate Honor System," *The Stute*, Mar. 7, 1969, 1.

[404] "Alumni Council Responds to Honor System Problem," Ibid., Nov. 14, 1969.

was dropped later. By January 1970, when he left the position of chairman of the honor board, Brunetti, whose policy was to be "on the level with the students and have fair penalties," could state that "The Honor System has now become acclimated as part of campus life as compared to an alienated state which it previously possessed."[405]

After the end of the Vietnam war in 1975, the new president of Stevens, Kenneth C. Rogers, decided to appoint a blue ribbon "Ad Hoc Committee on the Honor Board" in February 1975, to make the honor system "a viable working moral force for the entire Stevens Community." The committee was chaired by professor of physics Edward A. Friedman, the dean of the college, and included George Habach 1929 who had been president of the ASME and a vice president of Studebaker. It included two ex-department heads, professors Winston Bostick and Alfred Bornemann, as well as other faculty and administrators. Students included P. J. O'Connor 1976, president of the student council, D. Tjon, chairman of the honor board and Anna Lynch 1978. Rogers wanted reforms to assure the honor system was "part of the basic fabric of the Institute" and "belongs to the entire Stevens Community: faculty, staff, alumni, trustees" and which would make it "a viable working moral force for the entire Stevens Community."[406]

The committee's recommendations of April 9, 1975, resulted in a new honor board constitution which was ratified in October 1975, and contained five major improvements. First, faculty involvement in the honor system was improved by abolishing the "section representatives," or elected students to represent the Honor Board during examinations. Faculty were made more responsible for administering examinations and seeing that pledges were used, and all the students in an examination were made responsible for reporting violations instead of relying on "section reps." Second, the number of students in juries was changed from twelve to six in order to speed up the selection process. Third, the defendant was provided with an advisor who understood the workings of the honor board. Fourth, procedures for communication between the honor board and the Stevens community were established including a newsletter and improved orientation of freshmen. Perhaps most importantly, the fifth reform was the establishment of an Honor Board Advisory Council made up of students, faculty, administration, alumni, and trustees to assure the honor board permanent contact with the entire Stevens community as recommended by President Rogers.[407]

---

[405] Ibid., Dec. 19, 1969, 1 and Jan. 9, 1970, 1.
[406] Report of the Ad. Hoc Committee on the Honor Board, April 9, 1975, 1.
[407] *The Stute*, Sept. 12, 1975, 5.

These major reforms of 1975 were still in place at the end of the century. Other constitutional changes over the years have fine tuning of the honor system, but these have been relatively minor compared to the major changes of 1923 and 1975. For example, after the admission of women, a more up-to-date pledge for all work submitted was devised, "I pledge my honor that I have abided by the Stevens Honor System." The main features of the Stevens honor system remain its application only to academic work, assurance of due process for those accused, including right to a jury trial; involvement of the whole Stevens community including faculty, alumni, and trustees, and upholding the ideal of an honorable man or woman who can be trusted to do his or her own work and report violations of that trust.

Two other student organizations which are peculiar to Stevens are the quasi-secret Khoda and the contrastingly democratic Gear and Triangle. On the one hand, the sometimes controversial Khoda was established in 1909 by twelve seniors, and the membership over the years has been limited to some number of seniors. The name "Khoda" means "lion" and "leader" in Sanskrit, and was evidently chosen to characterize the bravery needed for bringing issues for the furtherance of Stevens to the attention of the administration. Khoda has a tradition of shunning publicity by working behind the scenes with its honorary members chosen from the faculty and administration. Thus, Khoda leaves few documented tracks of its activity, and it continues to choose its twelve successors from the junior class each year. Although it has very strong support from alumni who have been members, the self-perpetuating and secretive nature of the organization cause it to be attacked in the student press every few years as elitist, exclusivistic, and undemocratic.[408] On the other hand, Gear and Triangle is a specifically "non-secret," honorary society of students who have demonstrated leadership in extracurricular activities. The aim of the society is to promote loyalty to Stevens, its honor system, and its school spirit in sports activity. It promotes "democratic" good fellowship, and members are elected by a secret ballot of the whole membership. Among its liberal goals are to "broaden the education and views of its members." Founded in 1919 by seven members of the class of 1921, original members included Alexander C. Humphreys's grandson, Henry Sherman Loud, the future tugboat magnate Anthony J. McAllister, and Joseph M. Schoenberg.[409]

---

[408] On the founding of Khoda, see "Seniors Form the Khoda Club," *The Stute*, 5 (1909), no. 22, 1.

[409] *The Stute*, June 14, 1919, 3, George W. Kelsey, "The Founding of Gear and Triangle," *Stevens Indicator*, 69 (1952), no. 5, 7-8, and Gear and Triangle Constitution and By-laws and other materials in Box 23A, Stevens Special Collections.

Outside of the above areas, student life at Stevens followed trends elsewhere: Fraternities were strong at Stevens given the lack of sufficient dormitory facilities before the 1950s. Again, it was the Humphreys administration which started to supply housing for fraternities along Castle Point Terrace, a choice street of late nineteenth century, upper-class Hoboken mansions vacated when the upper classes left for the suburbs after the turn of the century. Occupying these mansions and nearby brownstones are Theta Xi, Delta Tau Delta, Beta Theta Pi, Chi Psi, Chi Phi, Phi Sigma Kappa, Sigma Nu, Sigma Phi Epsilon, Pi Lamda Phi, and the Alpha Sigma Phi fraternities. Today, this fraternity row is supplemented with sororities, Delta Phi Epsilon and Phi Sigma Sigma, and they and the fraternities are organized in an interfraternity council.

Student government has been strong after the establishment of a student council in 1911. The main feature of student government at Stevens has been approving disbursement of a student activities fee to various student organizations. Actually, the first time the students performed this function was in an elected athletic association when early sports clubs were supported by student funding. The student government, currently an executive president and cabinet and a legislative senate, took fiscal responsibility for assessing the needs of the myriad of student clubs and student organizations through the eras. Accountability of student organizations was and is required with submission of budgets and expenditure accounts.

CHAPTER 14

H. L. Gantt: Pioneer of More Humane Management

The dean of the engineering school at Cornell and a past president of the ASME, Dexter S. Kimball, wrote in the 1920s that "To my mind much of Taylor's philosophy would have disappeared had it not been for Gantt. He was the first, I think, to combine Halsey's conciliatory idea of a basic day's wage with Taylor's idea of a large reward for a large task. And to make these ideas workable he introduced sound methods of instruction and encouragement."[410]

Kimball knew that Taylor's system (combining many elements including scientific study of the tasks of work, stopwatch time study of workmen, planning, routing of materials, functional foremen, instruction cards, personnel selection, and incentive piece rates.) had met with resistance by workers and labor unions because of its flawed method of payment of workmen, namely the "differential piece rate scheme." The problem with the scheme was that it penalized workers if they failed to turn out a certain number of pieces by paying low rates and only rewarded them with high piece rates if they exceeded the level considered "first class." Taylor's "differential piece rate" resulted in resentment, and resistance to the whole of Taylor's system.[411]

Thus, Henry L. Gantt (1861-1919), who started his career as Taylor's assistant, rescued his boss with his "task bonus" system of payment in 1901 while helping Taylor implement his system at Bethlehem Steel. Task bonus was a breakthrough which led to the acceptance of Taylorism by workmen at the time when Taylor's reputation was taking off. Taylor himself credited Gantt with creating the task bonus innovation and was enthusiastic about it. Simply put, Gantt set the tasks and the standard as before, but assured the workman of a day's wage even if the workman did not reach the first class cut-off level. However, if he did, he obtained bonuses of increasing value for increasing production as in Taylor's differential piece rate.[412]

A crucial element which also made Gantt's system acceptable to workmen at Bethlehem was his stress on the teaching role of foremen to help the workmen exceed the standard and earn bonuses. Gantt encouraged the foremen to be efficient and helpful instructors by rewarding them with bonuses for bringing their workmen up to standard.

---

[410] Quoted in L. P. Alford, *Laurence Henry Gantt; Leader in Industry*(ASME, 1934), 86.

[411] Milton J. Nadworny, *Scientific Management and the Unions*(Harvard U. Press, 1955), 4-5.

[412] *Ibid.*, 14.

Gantt's appreciation of the instructional role in management -- and his later appreciation of management instruction in engineering curricula -- came from his experience as a teacher. Born in 1861 the son of a modest Maryland plantation owner, Gantt entered the McDonogh School in Baltimore where he paid for tuition through teaching while in the upper level. As a teacher using the blackboard, he developed a lifelong love of graphic presentation. Subsequently, he entered Johns Hopkins on scholarship to earn an A.B. in two years by 1880. After graduation, Gantt returned to McDonogh as a full-time faculty member in natural sciences, a position he kept for three years.

With the help of the president of Johns Hopkins who introduced Gantt to Henry Morton, Gantt obtained entry to Stevens Institute in 1883 under special conditions, as did Taylor before him. Gantt graduated after one summer and one year at Stevens in 1884, having passed special examinations in the sciences, mathematics, and humanities without having to attend class. His class work was in analytical mechanics, the mathematics of the resistance of materials, applied electricity, mechanical drawing, mechanical engineering, and shop, besides senior thesis.[413] Upon graduating, he returned to McDonogh for three more years of teaching applied science and mechanics, teaching altogether some eight years there. If it wasn't for the low salary, one suspects he would have stayed in the teaching profession because he was a talented instructor who loved such work. However, Gantt subsequently obtained a job under Frederick W. Taylor at Midvale Steel Works in 1887, being recommended by George M. Sinclair, an 1884 classmate, already an assistant of Taylor at Midvale.

At Midvale, part of Gantt's work with Taylor was forging metal cutting tools which resulted in Gantt's first important patents. Gantt, Taylor and Taylor's assistant Carl Barth patented a graph to instruct machinists on efficient use of lathes and boring machines. At the same time, Gantt assisted Taylor on time studies of machinists, which were used to set piece rates. According to Gantt, this work led to his own task bonus piece rate system. After Taylor left Midvale in 1890, Gantt remained for three more years before following Taylor into consulting work in management. Gantt remained a loyal disciple of Taylor, rejoining him at Bethlehem Steel and collaborating on other projects which promoted Taylor's until the end of the latter's life.

After he had obtained a degree of wealth from his consulting work in management, Gantt played an active role in promoting the teaching of management in higher education, this instruction being in its infancy. In

---

[413] Stevens Institute of Technology Faculty Minutes, I (1884), 195.

1912, he participated in a symposium on teaching scientific management sponsored by the SPEE. Entitled "The Engineer as a Manager," Gantt's presentation was surprisingly critical of the then-current management. Taylor was also critical of the "military" or "driving" methods of industrialists, but he did not criticize the profit motive to the extent Gantt did here:

. . . wealthy traders and bankers have been able to add to their methods those of the outlaw, and to become . . . the boldest set of buccaneers the world has ever saw. . . . the great trusts are in many cases able to fix both the buying and selling price of the commodities in which they deal. . . . Further, the enormous wealth thus accumulated has enabled the possessors in many cases to become absolute owners of the sources of wealth and the means of transportation, and their training to get as much as possible and to give as little as possible in return is doing much to increase the present industrial unrest in the world. . . . The workmen, on their part, recognize these facts, and realize that the only effort to get a greater reward is by force. Hence under those methods of doing business, the growth of trusts on the one side, and hostile labor unions on the other, is a natural development.[414]

Henry L. Gantt, 1884,
a colleague of
of Frederick W. Taylor,
is recognized as a
forerunner of industrial psychology
and was the inventor
of the Gantt Chart.
He also delivered
lectures to Stevens students
in Alexander C. Humphreys's
economics of engineering
class.

His paper went on to advocate engineers as managers because "the commercial man is opposed to improved methods." He laid out the "management engineering" methods which would result in cooperation between capital and labor, and these were essentially Taylor's system with task bonus,

---

[414] "Symposium on Scientific Management," *Proc. SPEE,* X (1912), vol. 2, 566-68.

but with an emphasis on instruction of the workmen. He concluded, "This preparation it is the duty of the engineering schools to give."[415]

Gantt lived up to this duty himself. He took time to lecture two years running in Humphreys's Economics of Engineering course at Stevens, presenting two different versions of management engineering and task bonus. His last lecture appeared in Humphreys's textbook, *Lecture Notes of Some of the Business Features of Engineering Practice* in 1912. The 565-page volume also had three articles by Frank Vanderlip on banking, three articles on legal aspects including patent law, five on accounting, three on depreciation, and, among others, one on liability and workmen's compensation. In fact, Humphreys himself had attitudes similar to Gantt's; in an address before the alumni association in 1908, Humphreys said that it was important for his course to obtain lecturers "apart from the field of engineering" who will stress upon the student that "money-getting" is not the end of business and engineering, that the students have "their obligations as servants of the community, state, and nation."[416]

Gantt gave his Stevens lectures free of charge, and, in contrast to Taylor, did not criticize Humphreys's course. In 1914, Taylor gave a speech in which he said that no school in the country was teaching a suitable course on management. There was a subsequent exchange of letters in which Humphreys cited his own course, provided an outline, an examination, and noted that Gantt's article was a required reading. Taylor belittled this effort as not teaching correct "management of workers" and being skewed to the "business side." Humphreys replied, "I emphatically do not agree with you," and that he took "strong exception" to Taylor's conclusions.[417] Humphreys was particularly galled about this episode, because he had consulted with Taylor about the course when he established it in 1897.[418] Cemented on the Joint Committee for Engineering Education, the Taylor-Humphreys friendship was never the same after this incident, especially after Taylor absolutely refused to contribute money to the alumni fund drive in spite of two personal letters from Humphreys. The second letter only asked for a token twenty-five dollars to show one hundred percent contributions from Taylor's class. Taylor's reason for refusing to give even that amount was on prin-

---

[415] *Ibid.*, 562.

[416] Alexander C. Humphreys, Address Before the Annual Alumni Dinner," *Stevens Indicator*, XXV (1908), 161.

[417] See Humphreys to Taylor, January 21, 1914 and June 11,1914; Taylor to Humphreys, June 4, 1914, Taylor Papers, Stevens Special Collections.

[418] Humphreys to Taylor, January 28, 1897, *Ibid.*

ciple, that all his money had to go to "the cause of scientific management."[419]

In 1913, Gantt published a book, *Work, Wages and Profits*, which went through several editions as a textbook based on his lectures given at the Amos Tuck business school at Dartmouth. In addition, in 1915, he delivered five lectures at the Sheffield Scientific School at Yale University as part of the Page Lecture Series to the senior class. These lectures were published in America as *Industrial Leadership* by Yale University Press and in England by Oxford University Press. He also published articles in *American Machinist*, the *Revue of Revues, Engineering News, System, Industrial Engineering,* and *Machines* which indicated his more flexible application of management engineering and understanding of the worker's point of view.

Back in 1908, Taylor had already objected to Gantt's more flexible approach in applying his principles. According to Taylor, the elements of his management system had to be applied *in toto* rather than in a piecemeal manner, with the exception of Gantt's task bonus payment schedule. This disagreement arose after Brigadier General William Crozier, who oversaw ordnance production for the War Department, decided to introduce Taylor's methods into arsenals, the first one being the Watertown arsenal. Gantt did a preliminary study of the situation at Watertown and reported to Taylor that, given the attitudes of the skilled workmen there, it was "out of the question" to introduce the whole system except task bonus. By that time, Taylor had retired to promote his system on a full time basis. He was particularly sensitive about other "efficiency engineers," like Harrington Emerson, whom Taylor considered opportunistic newcomers using insufficient methods without a thorough grounding in scientific study of tasks and workmen. Therefore, he had become rigidly attached to all the elements of his system. He insisted to Gantt that without implementation of the whole system at Watertown, "the workmen will surely oppose all work which tends to increase output."[420] Later, in January 1909 after General Crozier decided to proceed with Taylor's system at Watertown, Taylor recommended Barth over Gantt for the job of implementation.

Also, in 1908, Gantt and Taylor disagreed over the former's publication of "Training Workmen in the Habits of Industry," a paper Gantt wanted to present to the ASME. Gantt had sent his mentor an advance manuscript copy of the paper, but Taylor so disagreed with it that he advised that it ought not to be published. After some months of hesitation, Gantt submitted

---

[419] Taylor to Humphreys, January 14,1915, *Ibid.*
[420] Quoted in Nadworny, *Op.Cit.*, 31.

180

it to the ASME for a reading anyway.[421] Gantt's paper contained revolutionary ideas, subsequently generally accepted during and after World War I in training programs by large corporations. Gantt wrote that it was the responsibility of management to teach and help *all* their personnel and to lead them to higher productivity. Gantt had a greater faith and optimism about the ability of workers to learn skills than Taylor. In addition, Gantt's paper recommended taking into consideration psychological factors, the prejudices and habits of workmen, and allowing time for these traits to be overcome by demonstration. Undue and punitive wage pressures would result in confrontation and failure. Galling to Taylor was the statement that there were certain situations in which stopwatch time study was inapplicable, and Gantt condemned its promiscuous and unintelligent use.[422] Many ASME members praised the paper for its "human appreciation." Alexander C. Humphreys showed he was in line with Gantt's way of thinking by commenting, "It is encouraging to see the stress laid by the author upon the ethical influence of the methods he describes, and I venture to believe that, if this system were generally introduced throughout the United States, the resulting moral uplift would attract more attention than the increase in dividend-earning capacity."[423]

However, the attitude of conservative Taylorites to Gantt's flexible management technique is exhibited in H. S. Person's biographical sketch of Gantt in the *Encyclopedia of the Social Sciences* in 1931. Person, the managing director of the Taylor Society, which raised the level of Taylor's status to that of a saint, wrote, "Being inclined towards opportunism and more interested in practical improvement than in engineering perfection, Gantt gradually minimized the methods of precise measurement and predetermination characteristic of Taylor and Gilbreth, relying on voluntary improvement of operating conditions by management and workers jointly through the educating disclosures of his charts."[424]

Even though these disagreements of 1908 took place, Gantt continued to support Taylor's causes. One such cause was the famous "Eastern Rate Case" of 1910. The case arose after all the railroads in the Northeast gave a wage increase and then applied to the Interstate Control Commission for shipping rate increases to pay for it. The eastern shippers of freight organized against the increased rates by hiring Louis D. Brandeis, the famous

[421] George Filipetti, *Industrial Management in Transition*(1953), 89, and Alford, *Op.Cit.*, 129.
[422] Filipetti, *Op.Cit.*, 83-85.
[423] Henry L. Gantt, "Training Workmen in the Habits of Industry," *ASME Trans*, XXX (1908), 1061.
[424] H. S. Person, "Gantt, Henry Laurence," *Encyclopedia of the Social Sciences*, VI (1931), 563.

"Peoples' Lawyer," to present their case at the ICC hearings. After his team investigated the situation, Brandeis decided upon the strategy of proving that the railroads were managed inefficiently, and they did not have to increase rates to consumers if they improved their management.

According to his own recollection, at this point Brandeis remembered what he had read about Taylor and such "efficiency engineers" as Harrington Emerson. However, at that time there was a lot of confusion over the name of the movement in management. Up to 1910, the movement had been called the "Taylor System," "Task Bonus," "Management Engineering," "Efficiency Engineering" or the names Taylor himself favored, namely "Shop Management" or "Task Management." Brandeis wanted a new name to use in court to dramatize his case, a name which would capture the mind of his audience.[425]

Consequently, on October 10, 1910, Brandeis met with H. L. Gantt and others at Gantt's apartment in New York City. The only other attendee who was later to obtain the stature of Gantt in management was the relative newcomer to the movement, Frank B. Gilbreth, the bricklaying contractor who had applied Taylor's principles and was not to give up his business to become a full-time management consultant until 1912. Other attendees were two younger Stevens graduates possessed of writing talent who had attached themselves to Gantt as a sort of mentor, namely, Robert Thurston Kent 1902, editor of *Industrial Engineering* magazine, who was named after Robert H. Thurston by his father, William Kent, and Henry V. Scheel 1905, the founding editor of Stevens student newspaper, the *Stute,* and a manager at the Brighton Mills where Gantt had applied task bonus.

It was this group who helped Brandeis coin the term "Scientific Management." Brandeis then popularized the new name during the *Eastern Rate* case.[426] Brandeis's presentation, closely watched in the press, resulted in the rejection of the railroads' rate increases by the ICC. Incidentally, Gantt and Scheel, but not Taylor himself, were among the expert witnesses called by Brandeis. As a result of Brandeis's theatrical talents -- he talked of the railroad industry saving "a million dollars a day" which caught the public's imagination -- the case was so well covered in the press that the term "scientific management" became instantly recognizable throughout the United States and Europe. Subsequently, Taylor incorporated the term in his major work, *Principles of Scientific Management,* which was published in 1911 and established Taylor as the Father of Scientific Management throughout the world.

---

[425] Nadworny, *Op.Cit.,* 35-43.
[426] *Ibid.,* 35.

But while the *Eastern Rate* case made scientific management popular among managers and consumers, it also made the movement infamous among the leaders of organized labor. The case had pitted the railroad companies in a temporary alliance with their laborers' unions against consumers and scientific management. In this ironic way the Eastern Rate Case sowed the seeds of scientific management's future troubles with organized labor.

These troubles surfaced in 1911 at the Watertown Arsenal where Barth had been carefully studying the processes of ordnance production and making preparations to institute the "whole system" of Taylor. On the very day in August 1911 when Barth finally started stopwatch time study of his first Watertown worker, a molder, the laborer resisted and all molders walked off the job. The famous spontaneous strike, the beginning of the end for not only a rigid application of Taylor's principles but also for Taylor himself, was justified according to the molders' union because time study was "humiliating" and "un-American." The strike was supported by national labor leaders who petitioned Congress for an investigation of scientific management for "sweating" and endangering workers by "speed-up."[427]

Subsequently, a resolution of the House of Representatives established a committee of three congressmen to receive testimony from management and labor, especially in the ordnance industry, and their findings unearthed a depth of labor hostility. Gantt, as well as Harrington Emerson, Barth, and others, testified for the movement, but the most grueling testimony was Taylor's six days before the committee. Taylor stressed that efficiency of labor did not mean "strenuousness" of labor, but, unfortunately, his testimony opened him up to even more criticism by organized labor. Taylor observed that although workers were indeed made to be more disciplined, the workers in turn could discipline management by quitting. He also said that collective bargaining could not compromise the scientifically derived standards set by management, and that scientific management provided for collective bargaining already since individual workers had rights to register their complaints with management. Taylor was pushed into a weak position where he had to say that scientific management could not exist in a confrontational setting, that it needed a thorough "mental revolution" on the part of both management and labor, who had to "cooperate."

The congressional committee's report on March 9, 1912, made concessions to both sides: On the one hand it approved of standardizing tools, routing work, and determining the efficient methods of running machines,

---

[427] *Ibid.*, 57-59.

but, on the other hand, it doubted the efficacy of the stop watch and a "mere" mental attitude on the part of ownership in protecting the interests of workmen. It did not recommend legislation to curb scientific management, but it suggested that time study, piece rates, and bonus schemes should be approved by workmen. In short, the result was a standoff for the time being.

But in 1914, the United States Commission on Industrial Relations was created to conduct a second round of hearings on, among other things, "efficiency systems and labor." Organized labor led by Samuel Gompers testified against scientific management. On the other side, Taylor, Gantt, Emerson, and others conceded in questioning that there might be a role for collective bargaining in certain elements of their systems, but Taylor again insisted that time-study was a scientific matter which could not be subject to collective bargaining. Professor Robert F. Hoxie, heading an investigative committee for Congress, tried to mediate between Gompers and Taylor personally by suggesting that labor would accept scientific management if it would give unions recognition. Taylor replied that would be like cooperating to cut his own throat. Hoxie then submitted his report in April 1915, a report that saw scientific management as a threat to traditional craft skills and unionism. Scientific management, the report said, broke down the workers' craft knowledge into tasks and individualized workmen, and, as such, posed a threat to craft unionism and solidarity. The Hoxie report was a deciding factor in subsequent legislation.

Congress finally gave in to union pressure and passed a law in March 1915 which banned time study and bonus work but only in federal employment, including employment in the arsenals, a law which was not overturned for over thirty years. Another factor was the war in Europe, because congressmen felt that the United States needed industrial peace in its arsenals to remain strong. Less than three weeks after the legislation, a tired Frederick Taylor died on March 21, 1915. If Taylor had accepted Gantt's advice not to implant the complete Taylor system at Watertown but only a minimalist application of task bonus, that is, if Taylor could have been more flexible as Gantt had suggested in 1908, the Watertown strike which brought on the congressional hearings might not have happened.

The legislation had widespread effects during and after World War I. It meant that the classical scientific management of Taylor could not be used during the war in the military or in the war-related industries which were coordinated by the federal government. It also meant increased opposition to these elements in private industry during the war because of the growing strength of organized labor in a period of full employment. However, it was during the War to End All Wars that the industrial psychology movement swept the nation.

The recognized father of industrial psychology, the German-born Harvard professor Hugo Munsterberg, published *Psychology and Industrial Efficiency* in 1913, in which he described industrial psychology as a new science to be systematically placed at the service of industry. He recognized scientific management as a forerunner but criticized Taylor for "helpless psychological dilettantism."[428] After American entry into World War I, the National Research Council funded the use of psychology in the selection process of personnel for the armed services. Tests were administered to over 1.7 million men by eight hundred government-trained psychologists. Industrial management immediately and enthusiastically saw the utility of such tests for industry and used them after the war. Industrial psychology was called the government's "war gift to industry." Later still, the "human factor" or "human element" was studied by corporations and industrial psychologists. This development led to the work of Elton Mayo at the Hawthorne plant of General Electric, which discovered that increased production could result from motivating workers by involving them in management's decision making processes..

Industrial psychologists recognize Gantt and his neighbor in Montclair, New.Jersey, Lillian Gilbreth, instead of Taylor himself, as the points of contact between scientific management and industrial psychology. Gantt had already demonstrated his effort to "create conditions that had favorable psychological effects upon the workers" through task bonus and through his painstaking helpful instruction of workers. Furthermore, his biographer writes that "Gantt had been the first of the pioneers in management to attempt to humanize the science, that is, to fit methods to the average workman or shop foreman, and to take into consideration their states of mind. He always insisted that the worker was the variable, and that all else must be adapted to him."[429] Thus, Gantt was a forerunner of the industrial psychologists in his practices, although he never claimed to be one professionally.

World War I was also a turning point for the engineer in society, because the Spencerian vision that engineering would bring abundance, and therefore peaceful cooperation, had not come to pass. In fact, there was criticism of engineers for developing the weapons of war. Gantt and other

---

[428] Loren Baritz, *The Servants of Power; A History of the Use of Social Science in American Industry*(Wesleyan, 1960), 36.

[429] Quoted in L. Urwick, "Management's Debt to Engineers," *Advanced Management*, Dec. 1952, 8.

progressive engineers reacted by promoting a more humanistic goal for the engineer. Gantt subscribed to Thorstein Veblen's idea that a technocracy should control industry for the provision of goods and services for mankind instead of for the mere profits of stockholders. In accordance with the progressive member of the scientific management movement, Morris L. Cooke, Gantt believed that service and social responsibility were necessary ideals for engineers and industrial managers. In 1914 Gantt wrote that the "truest definition of democracy is *equal opportunity*," by which he meant application of scientific methods in economic organization to give everyone a chance at success. He said, "Each man or woman is rewarded and promoted to positions of responsibility on the basis of his or her record. This is industrial democracy."[430]

In 1916, he started a movement called the "New Machine" at the annual meeting of the ASME. Gantt had delivered a paper in which he had criticized the practice of including in the prices of a product the costs of idle machinery, the point being that it was inefficient management which condoned the idle machinery and not the consumer. In this, paper he stated, "The only men organized for the promotion of productive efficiency are the engineers."[431] Gantt went on to criticize management which failed to plan, failed to build efficient plants, failed to have adequate sales policies, and failed to instruct its labor; also, he criticized inefficient plants, inadequate sales policies, hostility to labor, shoddy materials, improper maintenance of factories, and saddling the consumer with costs of such mismanagement. After other papers and discussion, engineers in attendance formed the New Machine with Gantt as chairman of its executive committee.

The New Machine's main accomplishment was a manifesto sent to President Woodrow Wilson, which obtained wide press coverage. The letter dated February 17, 1917, was signed by Gantt as chairman of the New Machine along with Charles R. Mann, author of the Mann Report on Engineering Education, H. V. R. Scheel, Walter Rautensrauch, a professor of mechanical engineering at Columbia University, Fred R. Low, editor of *Power,* and Fred E. Rogers, editor of *Machinery,* among others. The letter stated that the war was a result of the general failure to grasp the social implications of the productive processes, that what was needed was a progressive elimination of the power of plutocracy, that government had to "free the shoulders of enterprise from the yoke of incomes that are unearned," and that a way had to be found to "take the control of the huge and

---

[430] Alford, *Op.Cit.,* 253.
[431] *Ibid.,* 266.

delicate apparatus of industry out of the hands of idlers and wastrels and deliver it over to those who understood its operations."[432]

Meanwhile, H. L. Gantt played a crucial role in World War I. When the United States entered the European conflict in April 1917, Gantt volunteered his services to the government at no expense. He moved to Washington where he worked first with the Ordnance Bureau of the United States Army to manage the production of rifles, guns, ammunition and other war material. He performed the same function with the War Industries Board when it was set up to coordinate this effort with industry. Later, when submarine warfare decimated merchant shipping, he speeded up the building of ships for the Emergency Fleet Corporation and then improved the efficiency of the operation of ships for the Shipping Board. In all these activities, he introduced his chart as a managerial tool.

The Gantt chart, with a horizontal axis for future time and a vertical axis for work to be done, was developed for the American Locomotive Company as far back as 1903. Subsequently, he had graphed which workers earned bonuses over time at the Brighton Mills and used similar graphs at Remington Typewriter. In all these instances, as Gantt said, *"The essential element in any performance is time, not quantity."*[433] That is, he believed that performance was controlled directly through *rates* of expenditure of labor, materials, and capital, and that full-time utilization of productive machinery was necessary. His charts were used for planning and progress of work. Gantt's symbols -- for example, a thick line for planned work, a thin line for work accomplished, "opening" and "closing" angles for planned start and finish of an operation, a V for current date -- are still standard symbols used today on Gantt charts.[434]

Gantt was given the job of coordinating the production not only in government arsenals but also of coordinating the orders of war material from private industry. Gantt kept track of the progress of the various orders with time charts showing ordering dates, production dates, and delivery dates, to equip units for deployment overseas. He was remembered for his "power of concentration," and as a "driving force" on the various boards he sat on, his aim being to ascertain the facts, fix responsibility, eradicate idleness and forward production. During his war work in Washington, Gantt introduced his unpatented graphical methods in all situations, giving out explanations and specimens to anyone asking about them. The ubiquitous use of his

---

[432] *Ibid.*, 273.

[433] *Ibid.*, 207.

[434] Carl Heyel, "Gantt Chart," *Encyclopedia of Management*(1982), 353-7.

charts by the federal government during World War I popularized the Gantt chart, which justifiably made Gantt famous.

After the war, Gantt died suddenly in 1919, but Wallace Clark, a long-time younger associate of Gantt's in his management consulting work, published a book called *The Gantt Chart* in 1922. This volume was translated into French, German, Japanese as well as Czech, Spanish, and Russian, and popularized the utilization of the Gantt Chart worldwide. It was used in communist countries as well as capitalist ones -- in the Soviet Union alone there were nineteen editions of Clark's book, and the five year-plans as well as factory production were graphically presented on Gantt charts. Today, Gantt charts are used in Performance Evaluation Review Techniques (PERT) and as scheduling devices in Critical Path Methods (CPM), such modern adaptations of the Gantt Chart being made possible by developments in probability and computing technology. Gantt charts are explained in detail in handbooks for industrial engineering, a discipline which burgeoned during and after World War II and which also credits Taylor and Gantt among its main forerunners.

CHAPTER 15

Marine Engineers and the Navy in World War I

Before coming to Stevens Institute, Robert H. Thurston had been an officer in the U.S. Navy for nearly ten years. He obtained a commission in 1861 as a naval engineer and served on various warships during the Civil War. After the defeat of the Confederacy, he taught at the U.S. Naval Academy from 1865 to 1870. During the period from 1868 to 1874, he was consulting engineer for the completion of the *Stevens Battery*, a project on which he was assisted by his colleague Professor C. W. MacCord, Ericsson's chief draftsman for the *Monitor*. Thus, both Thurston and MacCord were naval engineers, the former belonging to the Institution of Engineers and Shipbuilders of Scotland, the British Institution of Naval Architects, the United States Naval Institute, and the Naval Order of the United States, while the latter was a draftsman for the New York City Department of Docks. Between 1866 and 1874, Thurston published four articles on such subjects marine signals, ironclads, and efficiency of paddle wheels, and MacCord published four articles on Ericsson and his accomplishments in marine engineering. At the time, marine engineering was intimately tied to mechanical engineering in all aspects involving propulsion by paddle wheels and screws, steam engines, boilers to raise steam, and iron and steel tests for boilers, armor plate, and ordnance. Thurston's Mechanical Laboratory work with the U.S. Iron and Steel Board in testing strengths of metal alloys was directly intertwined with the production of guns in arsenals for the War Department.[435]

One of Thurston's and MacCord's earliest students became a premier marine architect and marine engineer. Frank M. Leavitt (1856-1928) graduated in the first full graduating class of 1875. Leavitt's first job was with F. E. Sickels, a prominent marine engineer of that day, for whom the young Stevens graduate designed a steam steering gear for the U.S.S. *Trenton,* one of the larger Navy warships of 3,900 tons. Leavitt's career as a brilliant machine and marine engineer took off when he joined the E. W. Bliss Company of Brooklyn in 1884. From that time until 1921, Leavitt turned out a constant stream of patents demonstrating his mechanical skill and inventive genius. Among the patents was the world's first automatic tin-can-body making machine, an invention which, along with Leavitt's machine to stamp out pots and pans, made Bliss machines salable world wide. After the

---

[435] Furman, *Morton Memorial, Op. Cit.,* 133, 210-15, and 219-22.

federal government decided in 1883 to build the "New Navy," Leavitt made E. W. Bliss a manufacturer of the Navy's armor plates, armor piercing projectiles, guns, and most importantly of "automobile torpedoes"-- The "Bliss-Leavitt Torpedo" which made Leavitt famous in Navy circles.

By 1890, the world's navies had developed short-range torpedoes and torpedo boats and soon afterwards faster and bigger torpedo-boat destroyers to combat them with their own torpedoes and guns. On the recommendation of Leavitt, Bliss bought the patent rights for the American production of the Whitehead torpedo which Leavitt dramatically improved. The British Whitehead torpedo was universally used by 1891 when Bliss obtained the American patent rights. Compressed air drove a three-cylinder reciprocating engine attached to a single propeller at twenty-eight to twenty-nine knots over a range of eight hundred yards, a gyroscope controlling the vertical rudders. Leavitt's improvements on the Whitehead torpedo included using steel armor plate for the compressed air chamber to achieve higher pressures, substituting a Curtiss turbine for the reciprocating engine which increased the revolutions from some 1,000 to 10,000 RPM, and, in his most revolutionary innovation, adding an alcohol-burner to heat the compressed air before it entered the turbine. This-hot gas propulsion system dramatically increased torpedo's performance and was copied in torpedoes around the world. In conjunction with the Naval Torpedo Station at Newport, Rhode Island, Leavitt developed a series of Bliss-Leavitt torpedoes including those designated Mark 1 through Mark 10 by the Navy. In Mark 2, Leavitt made another improvement with the addition of two contra-rotating turbines driving two contra-rotating propellers which eradicated instabilities in the first single-propeller Bliss-Leavitt torpedo. His Mark 7 introduced water into the alcohol combustion chamber to lower temperatures by flashing the water into steam. This model was the first of the efficient so-called steam torpedoes which were used until World War II. Leavitt also combined a newer gyro and depth mechanism into a unit which could be checked easily when the torpedo was being readied for firing. These patented improvements and others which came later made the Bliss-Leavitt torpedo run at forty-five knots over a maximum effective range of 13,500 yards by the end of World War I.[436] The Navy only bought 300 Bliss-Leavitt torpedoes in 1903, but by the start of the war, all the U.S. Navy's torpedoes were Bliss-Leavitt models, and all the subsequent Navy torpedoes up to the

---

[436] William Hovgaard, *Modern History of Warships, Comprising a Discussion of Present Standpoint and Recent War Experiences for the Use of Students of Naval Construction, Naval Constructors, Naval Officers, and Others Interested in Naval Matters*(1920), 452-3.

Mark 48 in the post-World War II era were based on Leavitt's fundamental designs.[437]

Another Thurston and MacCord student was Albert W. Stahl of the class of 1876 who subsequently took the full course at the U.S. Naval Academy and graduated there in 1880. Stahl went on to have a career in design and construction of naval vessels as an engineering officer in the U.S. Navy. His main invention was an oval balanced turret with an armored protrusion in the rear, opposite the gun, a design which was adopted by all navies in place of round unbalanced turrets. His turret appeared for the first time on battleships like the 1892 *Iowa* and 1894 *Kentucky* among others, and Stahl rose in position to assistant to the chief constructor at the Washington Navy Department in 1894, and then to chief of the Department of Construction and Repair at the Navy Yard in Norfolk, Virginia, by 1895. In this position, he supervised modernization of over thirty naval vessels at a time, including design and installation of electric shell hoists, and supervised the construction of new warships including the *Oregon*, the Navy's most advanced battleship in the Spanish-American War. During the Spanish-American War in 1898, he superintended the completion of work on the *Illinois*, *Arkansas*, and *Missouri* at the Newport News Shipbuilding and Dry Dock Company, supervised construction of torpedo boats and battleships in private yards, and supervised the expansion of the yards themselves.[438] During World War I, he was a member of the Compensation Board, the Navy's financial control over the building of some five hundred wartime naval vessels constructed at private yards. He retired with the rank of commodore.[439]

Stevens actually taught marine engineering in the 1880s. Lieutenant Clarence A. Carr, U.S.N., became a professor of marine engineering and an instructor of mathematics in 1883. The institute and the Navy had an arrangement so that Carr, who worked as an inspector at the Brooklyn Navy Yard, could teach at the institute while on active duty. As part of the core curriculum required of all students, Carr taught resistances of hull designs, calculations of horsepower needed to overcome resistance at a given speed, types and uses of different marine engines and boilers and their pressures and rates of expansion, and the principles of design of screw propellers. He also taught the ways in which heavy marine machinery was managed, repaired, and overhauled in practice, lectures which were supplemented by

---

[437] Edwyn Gray, *The Devil's Device; Robert Whitehead and the History of the Torpedo*(1975), 156, and Naval Undersea Warfare Center, *A History of Torpedo System Development; A Century of Progress*(1998), 47 and 52-3..

[438] *Stevens Indicator*, 28 (1921), 218-9.

[439] Furman, *Morton Memorial, Op.Cit.*, 569-70.

actual visits to shipyards including those of Roache and Midvale Steel in Philadelphia. Among Carr's students were William S. Aldrich, John A. Bensel, Adolph Faber Du Faur, Henry L. Gantt, David S. Jacobus, Dabny H. Maury, Harry DeB. Parsons, George M. Sinclair, and Frank Van Vleck of the class of 1884, Anson W. Burchard and Richard H. Rice of the class of 1885, and George A. Aldrich, Cornelius James Field, and John A McCulloch of the class of 1886 -- all of whom during their careers were involved directly or indirectly with marine or metallurgical engineering applied to shipping.[440]

At left is Stevens's first professor of mechanical drawing, C. W. MacCord, a marine engineer who had been a draftsman for Ericsson's *Monitor*, and at right is Edwin A. Stevens II, a marine engineer specializing in ferries and a founder of the Society of Naval Architects and Marine Engineers.

Another marine architect and engineer who gave occasional lectures to Stevens students while serving as a trustee from the 1880s through the turn of the century was Edwin A. Stevens II (1858-1918), a son of the founder. The son had graduated from Princeton in 1879, and then become a world-renowned inventive designer of ferries for the Stevens family's Hoboken Ferry Company of which he was president. He continued the work of his

---

[440] *Annual Catalogue of Stevens Institute of Technology* (1884-5), 52 and 58, (1885-6), 36.

grandfather and father in trying to have screw propellers accepted by ferry designers, who favored side paddles until his *Bergen* of 1889. The *Bergen* was the world's first successful screw-driven ferry and a model for ferries for decades, including the Staten Island ferries. It had a symmetrical design with the stack in the center of the boat, each end being the same, with an overhang to protect the boat from pilings in the slips, which could be entered from either direction. The main invention in design was the steam engine's attachment to one long shaft which ran the length of the boat with a screw at each end. Contrary to criticism that the "forward" pulling screw would be damaged by ice and debris, Stevens's design protected both screws and proved to be superior for ferry maneuverability and stopping character-istics as well as speed. This ferry was the first of his designs of classic ferryboats, which included the *Hamburg* and *Netherlands*.[441]

In 1893, E. A. Stevens II was a founding member of the Society of Naval Architects and Marine Engineers (SNAME) and one of its six honorary life members by 1914. Among the founding members were Stevens professors Jacobus, Denton, and Sellers and Stevens alumni including Gantt, Stahl, Aldrich, Field, and Parsons, all of whom were either marine architects or consultants working for companies involved in building the Navy's war-ships or their components. These included George Babcock and Stephen Wilcox in marine boilers, J. Sellers Bancroft of Midvale Steel, and Frank M. Leavitt of the Bliss company. By 1914, the membership list included practically all the names mentioned in this chapter, and the society acted as a sort of club in which the Navy's top marine engineers, like Admiral Melville and Commodore Stahl, and the engineers of private steel, ord-nance, and propulsion systems could exchange information and get to know each other. Albert Stahl was an active participant in the society, publishing articles on "Hydraulic Power for Warships" and "Experimental Test of Tar-get Representing Armored Side of U.S.S. *Iowa*" in its *Transactions*.[442] Stahl and other Stevens engineers in the Navy were also active in the American Society of Naval Engineers (ASNE) which was formed by engineering officers in the Navy in 1888. Although it was run by naval officers, its "civil members" included Leavitt and many other Stevens grad-uates.[443]

---

[441] *National Cyclopedia of American Biography*, 44 (1962), 464-5, and Edwin A. Stevens II, "Thoughts on the Design of New York Ferryboats," *Transactions of the Society of Naval Architects and Marine Engineers*, I (1893).

[442] *Society of the Naval Architects and Marine Engineers. Directory of Members*, 1914, and *Transactions of the Society of Naval Architects and Marine Engineers*, I (1893), ix.

[443] See membership lists in the *Journal of the American Society of Naval Engineers*.

During the Spanish-American War, over fifty alumni entered the United States Navy, including B. Franklin Hart, Jr., 1887 who had studied under Carr. Hart had formed the engineering division of the New Jersey Naval Reserve in 1896 along with two dozen other Stevens graduates. In the 1898 war, Hart was the engineering officer aboard the *Badger,* a cruiser outfitted by Carr at the beginning of the war, and supervised thirteen other Stevens naval reservists in its engine room during the blockade of Cuba. During this blockade, naval engineer Lieutenant William S. Aldrich 1884 was one of three officers on the *Vulcan,* a novel floating repair shop -- also in the blockading American fleet -- designed by the Navy's chief engineer, Admiral Melville.[444]

Another key member of SNAME was William Dixie Hoxie (1866-1925) of the Stevens class of 1889. Hoxie's father was a sea captain and a shipbuilder with the Rhode Island firm of Hoxie, Starbuck and Schmidt, and the son was related to a branch of the Babcocks through marriage. Hoxie was put in charge of the marine boiler division of the Babcock and Wilcox Company soon after graduation. He installed boilers on naval vessels before the Spanish-American War, including the *Chicago, Marietta,* and *Annapolis* in 1896. As a result of this experience and resulting tests, he designed and patented in 1897 his innovative cross-drum water tube boiler, which was more compact than the usual on-shore longitudinal-drum design of previous Babcock and Wilcox boilers used by the electrical generating industry. In 1902, the chief engineer of the U.S. Navy, Rear Admiral George W. Melville, was aware of the increased pressures demanded of reciprocating engines to propel ever larger battleships, and he stated, "The present problem of the modern battleship is not that of the gun and its mount, but the boiler and its installation."[445] Hoxie's boiler solved the problem. Built of steel rather than cast iron, the drum and all pressure parts of the boiler withstood pressures called for by the Navy, and the Babcock and Wilcox cross-drum marine boiler, often improved upon by Hoxie, was superior to all other marine boilers, especially in its ability to raise steam quickly.[446] By the First World War, all large naval vessels in both the U.S. and British fleets, as well as merchant vessels of most nations, were equipped with this boiler, and Hoxie also designed a smaller version for all torpedo boats and smaller vessels. The boilers were remarkable for their ease of repair and

---

[444] F. DeR. Furman, unpublished paper "Stevens in Wartime," Stevens Special Collections, box. on Military, shelf 23.

[445] *Report of the U.S. Navy Liquid Fuel Board*(1904), 55.

[446] George W. Melville, "The War's Teaching in Naval Engineering," *Stevens Indicator,* XVI (1899), 1-13, and *Stevens Indicator,* 61 (1944), 4, 8.

many lasted well over thirty years. Hoxie became vice president of Babcock and Wilcox in 1898 and president in 1919 until his death in 1925, a period during which the Bayonne, New Jersey-based company's capital increased twentyfold.[447]

Another development took place after 1904, namely a switch from coal to oil in U.S. naval ships. The origins of burning oil to create steam dated to the 1870s in Russian ships on the Caspian Sea adjacent to the oil resources of Azerbaijan. By 1902-04, European navies were adopting oil, and the U.S. Navy created a special U.S. Naval Liquid Fuel Board to investigate using oil as a fuel. For this board whose report was crucial in the subsequent acceptance of oil as a fuel by the Navy, Frank Van Vleck was secretary and also conducted a series of tests of European marine fuel oil burners. By 1904, Van Vleck had worked for the Navy's Bureau of Yards and Docks and as a naval architect at the Navy's Hull Department in the Newport News Ship Yard.[448] The Liquid Fuel Board stated in 1904, "The striking and valuable manner in which the burners have been classified, is, in great part, the personal work of Mr. Van Vleck . . . . This practical, concise, and scientific classification should do much in simplifying the construction of burners, thereby reducing the cost while adding to their reliability and ease of operation."[449] During World War I, Van Vleck was one of the first to use an all-weld construction in steel vessels.[450]

Another Stevens graduate specialized in marine-based and land-based oil fuel burners. Ernest Henry Peabody (1869-1965), Stevens 1890, the engineer of tests with Babcock and Wilcox since 1893 and their specialist in classifying efficiency of fuels, invented and patented the first American oil atomizer for marine fuel use. Peabody invented a steam atomizing burner which he installed in the low end of the Hoxie marine boiler furnace. He designed the burner to use a long flame for efficient and complete combustion. This Babcock and Wilcox oil burner became standard in all U.S. Navy vessels, and, during World War I, Peabody closed a contract with the Emergency Fleet Corporation for six-million-dollars worth of Babcock and Wilcox boilers and attached oil burners -- the largest boiler contract the company had ever been awarded. After the war, Peabody started his own company, the Peabody Engineering Corp., and his oil burners became standard on all naval and merchant marine vessels by the 1920s. His firm

[447] *National Cyclopedia of American Biography,* 24 (1935), 250, Babcock and Wilcox Company, *Steam; Its Generation and Use*(1927), 28-9, and Hovgaard, *Op.Cit.,* 370.
[448] Furman, *Morton Memorial, Op.Cit.,* 591.
[449] *Report of the U.S. Navy Liquid Fuel Board, Op.Cit.,* 426.
[450] "In Memoriam, Frank Van Vleck," *Stevens Indicator,* 56 (1939), no. 3, 12.

became the premier twentieth-century company in oil-heating design and manufacturing.[451]

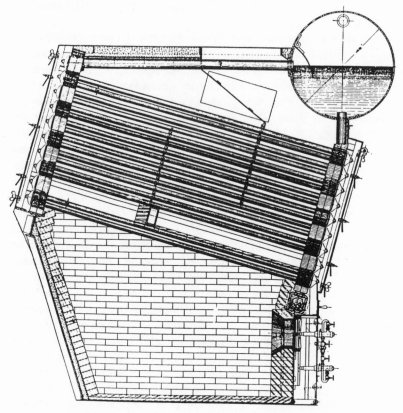

This diagram shows a Babcock and Wilcox, Hoxie-designed, cross-drum marine boiler equipped with a Peabody-designed fuel-oil injection unit. This boiler was used almost exclusively on U.S. Navy ships and merchantmen during World War I.

As a result of the popularity of the Navy's victories in the Spanish-American War, the Theodore Roosevelt administration stepped up construction of battleships and cruisers. Spanning the years 1883 through 1918, the U.S. Navy gradually modernized by adopting the latest technologies not only in warship design but also in metallurgical developments in ordnance and armor plate. From modest beginnings, this buildup became a big business

---

[451] *National Cyclopedia of American Biography,* G (1943-46), 294-5, *Stevens Indicator,* 65 (1948), no 4, 6, and "Ernest H. Peabody '90," *Ibid.,* 82 (1965), no. 2, 16-17.

and a main technological focus of attention in the nation. Huge battleships of 31,400 tons with armor up to fourteen inches thick and with guns of twelve-inch to fourteen-inch bore necessitated cutting-edge engineering skills in design of weapons systems, dockage facilities, steam power, and, particularly, metallurgy. Huge profits were made by the three companies which monopolized the manufacture of nickel-steel armor plate: Bethlehem, Carnegie and Midvale. In 1904, among the nineteen founders of the Navy League, an organization to promote a bigger American navy, were Charles M. Schwab of Bethlehem Steel, J. P. Morgan, who had bought the Carnegie companies, and J. Sellers Bancroft of Midvale Steel. In 1912, a congressional investigation determined that the bids of the three companies were similar and that their contracts with the Navy as far back as 1899 were $616.14 a ton for armor plate sold to the U.S. Navy while they charged were only $249 a ton to the Russian navy.[452]

These companies were not only well represented in SNAME and ASNE but also in the American Institute of Mining Engineers (AIME), which also had many members from Stevens, although in the AIME they did not predominate as in the ASME or hold as many positions as they did in the AIEE. However, Thurston was vice president in 1878, Charles MacDonald, the Stevens trustee and bridge builder was vice president in 1882 and 1889, and William Kent was manager in 1900. Alexander C. Humphreys was a member beginning in 1885 and on the AIME's council in 1909. Jacobus was a member starting in 1888, and, with the rise of the utility of nickel for armor plate, Robert C. Stanley of the class of 1899 was a member starting in 1902.[453]

In America before 1889, nickel was used mostly for coinage and electroplating tableware, but in that year the U.S. Navy along with Canadian producers controlled by the armor-plate pioneer, Bethlehem Steel's Joseph Wharton, visited ordnance manufacturers in France and Germany which had been using nickel-iron alloys since 1886. Nickel-steel was corrosion resistant and stronger than regular steels, and therefore it was ideal for naval guns and armor plate. Its superiority as armor plate compared to regular steel was proved by U.S. Navy tests in 1891. Happily, although there was very little nickel ore in most parts of the world, in the ensuing frantic search for nickel ore that was economically feasible to exploit, it was found in principally two places: French Caledonia and Canada's Ontario province.

---

[452] Donald W. Mitchell, *History of the Modern Navy*(1946), 136 and 164-5.
[453] *Directory of the AIME*(1920), sections on past officers and members, and *Transactions of the AIME*, VIII (1880), v-xxiii.

The latter turned out to have an estimated 80 percent or more of the world's nickel ore.

The son of a miner,
Robert C. Stanley, 1899,
rose to be
president of
International Nickel,
the main supplier of nickel for
nickel-steel armor plate and guns
for the Navy in both World Wars.
Stanley later became
chairman of the
Stevens Board of Trustees.

The takeoff of nickel immensely benefited Robert C. Stanley (1876-1951), who obtained an E.M. degree from Columbia School of Mines in 1901 after graduating from Stevens. In that year he tested Canadian ore samples in the Bayonne-based Orford Copper Company's laboratory. In 1902, this company was combined with Wharton's American Nickel Company to form International Nickel, a company which came to control the Canadian source of nickel which eventually was almost a world monopoly on the metal. Stanley's major metallurgical breakthrough for International Nickel was his improvements in the processes of smelting and refining. The ore from which nickel came contained mostly copper, and Stanley improved the process of copper-nickel separation by designing mechanical furnaces and substituting converters for the older reverberatory process in copper recovery. In effect, he modernized International Nickel's plants just at the time that a huge demand for nickel came from manufacturers of armor plate for the world's navies. As a spin-off of his work, in 1905-06 he developed a process of direct reduction of ores without separation of copper and nickel which resulted in the alloy monel, a white alloy of nickel and copper used for ship propellers. Stanley, who became ice president of International Nickel by World War I and president thereafter, wrote "From 1890 until the end of the World War, the building of great navies, with requisite ordnance, created a demand for nickel in ever-increasing quantities. From 1914 to 1918, this increasing demand reached its peak."[454]

Stevens's main engineer in the field of armor plate was John Lyman Cox (1866-1955) of the class of 1887. He joined Midvale Steel as assistant fore-man of the forge department when Frederick W. Taylor was still chief en-gineer and the company was turning out steel guns for the Navy. Cox help-ed to make the company a leading manufacturer of both armor plate and armor-piercing shells by conducting firing tests. When nickel-steel alloys were being developed for the Navy's armor plate after 1891, he tested and patented an improved nickel-steel alloy made with an innovative heating process which strengthened the steel's protective characteristics. When the company became the Midvale Steel and Ordnance Co. in 1915, Cox was made superintendent of the ordnance department and eventually rose to Taylor's old position of chief engineer.[455] William Whigham (1865-1925), of the class of 1888, performed the same function for Carnegie Steel that Cox did for Midvale. At Carnegie's Homestead Steel Works in 1892, Whig-ham joined the armor plate department where he patented a spraying device and methods of controlling the curvature of armor plate while hardening. After negotiating a large contract to supply the armor plate for the *Rossia* in 1915, he rose to be a vice president of United States Steel's subsidiary, the Carnegie Steel Company, and, during World War I, he was a member of the United States Steel Corporation's Committee on Construction for armor plate.[456] Among many Stevens graduates who worked for Carnegie steel companies was Alfred R. Whitney, Jr., 1890, who negotiated the Carnegie Steel Company's sales of armor plate to the Japanese in 1894-96 during the Sino-Japanese war. In the late 1890s, his construction company, A. R. Whitney Jr. and Co. of New York City, was the local agent for Carnegie Steel in the sale of steel for tall-building framing.[457]

When the First World War started in 1914, the United States sat it out but supplied the allies with loans, food and war material, like nickel, until the sinking of three unarmed American merchantmen in early 1917. War was declared against Germany on April 6, 1917, and the immediate problem facing the allies was the ominous success of German U-Boats. The sinking of neutral and allied shipping used for the supply "bridge" to Europe had risen to an average of 570,000 tons per month in February and March and

---

[454] Robert C. Stanley, *Nickel Past and Present*(1934), 59, and *National Cyclopedia of American Biography*, 55 (1974), 479.

[455] *National Cyclopedia of American Biography*, 46 (1963), 286-7.

[456] "William Whigham," *Stevens Indicator*, 42 (1925), 36.

[457] *Ibid.*, 28 (1921), 223-4.

to 875,000 tons in April. The emergency of the shipping situation can be emphasized by indicating that average freighters were only some 5,500 tons. What was needed was the rapid production of both naval destroyers to protect convoys, and merchant vessels to replace those being sunk, and, more importantly, immediate construction of new docks and facilities in order to do the job.

Rear Admiral Frederic R. Harris (1875-1949), Stevens class of 1898, was crucially involved in all these onshore activities for the U.S. Navy during the war. Harris started his career of over fifty-five years as a marine and civil engineer by drafting and participating in the design and building of wharves, piers and drydocks in New York City in the firm of Henry Steers in 1889-90. Thereafter, he helped to build New York ferry slips with the marine engineering company of Degnan and McLean and was a consultant on containment of water in subway tunnels in the early stages of the IRT. During those years he was assisted by and became a close colleague of John A. Bensel (1863-1922), Stevens 1884 and a student of Carr's. Bensel was a civil and marine engineer who had designed and constructed Manhattan's Hudson River docks and served as engineer in chief, in the Department of Docks, City of New York, from 1898 to 1906. He subsequently became president of the New York City Board of Water Supply, constructing the Catskill reservoir and supply system between 1908 and 1911.[458] Although the American Society of Civil Engineers had many Stevens graduates as members, Bensel became in 1910 the only Stevens graduate to serve as president of the ASCE.[459]

By the age of twenty-seven, Harris had acquired a reputation for brilliant creativeness in design and construction of docks. In 1902, he was chosen by the Navy to supervise the construction of the navy yard in Charleston, South Carolina, including the design of its drydocks, quays, and railroad connections. Recruited by the Navy during this effort, he received a commission in 1903 and immediately caught the attention of the highest levels of the Navy Department and President Theodore Roosevelt by refusing to accept shoddy materials from a subcontractor. His integrity and engineering brilliance thereafter led to rapid promotion which skipped the ranks of captain and commodore, the Navy realizing they had an extraordinarily talented engineer who could have easily been at the top in private industry. Such promotion was unusual for an engineering officer who had not attended the United States Naval Academy. After the Charleston project, he was sent to solve the on-going problem of building the navy's largest drydock, the 563-

---

[458] "John A. Bensel," *Stevens Indicator,* 39 (1922), 82.
[459] *ASCE Transactions,* 75 (1910).

foot "Voodoo" to service battleships in the Brooklyn Navy Yard. Before Harris, its construction had defied its contractor for four years because of the shifting base of mud on which it was built. Twenty-two had died and 350 had been wounded by collapsing walls. Harris designed his own patented pneumatic caissons to remove the mud in sections, and then he designed a steel-reinforced concrete base, eight feet thick, on top of the caissons, which were driven deep into the mud. This method of construction for graving docks, steel-reinforced concrete dry docks, became standard for such conditions afterwards. By designing and building new drydocks and facilities at Guantanamo Bay and Pearl Harbor, among others, he attained rear admiral rank by 1916 when he became chief of the Navy's Bureau of Yards and Docks -- in charge of all onshore construction of U.S. Navy facilities.[460]

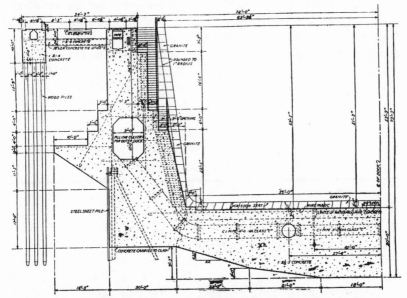

Rear-Admiral Frederick R. Harris, a Stevens graduate of 1897, designed and constructed the main drydocks for the Navy in Brooklyn, Guantanamo, and Pearl Harbor. Above is his design for a drydock at the Philadelphia yard during World War I.

When the United States entered the war in 1917, Harris went before the House Appropriations Committee, and, citing one deficiency after another,

---

[460] "Harris, Frederic Robert," *National Cyclopedia of American Biography,* v. 38, 603, and *Admiral Frederic R. Harris and His Legacy*(Frederic R. Harris, Inc., 1988), 5-6..

obtained $100,000,000 for the Navy's onshore building program, a sum equal to one-third the total defense budget for the previous year. The building program included an enormous new facility around Camden, New Jersey; three 1000-foot drydocks, the largest in the nation's history; floating drydocks, oil-fuel storage plants, from coast to coast. [461] The Camden yards would make the Philadelphia Navy Yard the biggest at the time for construction of battleships, cruisers, and destroyers. Included in the budget were funds to build whole villages for housing the officers, engineers, and contractors and their workers in twenty-three locations around the country.

The largest of these villages, composed of 907 houses on the outlying area of Camden, was built under Navy contract for the New York Shipbuilding Corporation adjacent to the new Navy docks the company was constructing for Harris. The architect for both the houses and their layout in York Ship Village and the connecting Fairview Extension of 770 houses was Electus Darwin Litchfield (1872-1952), Stevens 1892, the brother of Norman Litchfield who worked on the IRT. Electus Litchfield had done civil-engineering construction work for Standard Oil on graduation, but in 1898 had studied architectural design while drafting in the offices of Carrere and Hastings in New York City. He then worked for the architectural firm of Lord and Hewlett, participating in their designs for the huge, marble, Department of Agriculture building in Washington. By 1913, he was working independently under his own name. In the York Ship Village and Fairview Extension, Litchfield used the best materials, such as brick and slate, given the wartime tendency of government to be lavish in its building contracts, and, in addition, he created winding roads and a central "village square," all the architecture designed to resemble that of an English village. The area was sold by the federal government after the war to the Fairlawn Realty Company, and it became known as Fairlawn, still a choice place to live in Camden some eighty years later. Electus Litchfield went on to be a designer of New York City's low-cost Red Hook public housing during the Depression, also becoming a leading New York architect who designed luxury apartment buildings off Park Avenue and worked on Bellevue Hospital and Riverside Hospital projects. William Ludlow, who was the architect of the William Hall Walker Gymnasium, was also an architect for one of the Navy's villages. [462]

---

[461] C. H. Claudy, "Preparing the Navy Ashore; War Work of the Bureau of Docks and Yards," *Scientific American*, vol. 117 (1917), 416-7.

[462] "Litchfield, Electus Darwin," *National Cyclopedia of American Biography*, vol. 50, 192-3 and *Stevens Indicator*, XXXVI (1919), 54, Furman, *Morton Memorial, Op.Cit.*, 469, and Letter of Hobart B. Upjohn to W. A. Shoudy, *Stevens Indicator*, 36 (1919), 54.

Later in 1917, Harris was assigned to the civilian Emergency Fleet Corporation (EFC) as its general manager. The EFC was given almost unlimited funds and nearly absolute power to seize enemy ships in American ports, to purchase neutral ships, and, more importantly, to subsidize thousands of merchantmen built by private industry. The EFC's early leadership ended up squabbling about whether to build wooden freighters or steel freighters and was replaced by Edward N. Hurley. Under the new regime, Harris was made the EFC's general manager in November 1917 in charge of all construction, but only briefly, because of a conflict over authority with the board, which wasn't moving fast enough to approve his directives. However, he laid down the organization and policy of the EFC, which involved dozens of Stevens graduates in varying capacities. Henry Morton Brinkerhoff worked on design and construction of drydocks for the EFC at the Norfolk, Virginia, Naval Yard, where Harris was in charge. Assisted by H. L. Gantt in meeting production schedules and by Anson W. Burchard 1885, Hurley's EFC became immensely successful: The goal of the EFC was to increase construction of American merchant shipping from 500,000 tons a year to 10,000,000 tons. Anson W. Burchard, a vice chairman of General Electric, which supplied marine turbine engines and generators for the merchant ships, was so energetic and readily available that Hurley wrote that he came to "lean heavily" on the General Electric Company."[463]

Around the time of Harris's tenure in the EFC, Hoboken was chosen as the principal port of embarkation for troops going to Europe. Since the opening of hostilities in 1914, sixteen German ships, including the world's largest liner, the 54,000-ton *Vaterland,* had been interned along the Hoboken docks, Hoboken being the principal port for German liners in the United States before the war. In 1917, these docks from 1st to 4th Streets, as well as the ships owned by the North German Lloyd Line and the Hamburg America Line were seized by the EFC. Lower Hoboken was taken over by the Army and Navy, and all German immigrants were ordered to vacate the area.[464] The ships having been damaged by their crews, the EFC and the Navy repaired them. Edwin A. Stevens III (1882-1954), Stevens class of 1905 and a trustee after his father died, designed new propellers, propeller hubs, and bearings for the *Vaterland,* which was renamed the *Leviathan.* Ernest Peabody supervised the conversion of the *Leviathan*'s power system

---

[463] Edward N. Hurley, "Bridging the Atlantic With Ships," *Scientific American,* vol. 118 (1918), 304-5, and his *Bridge to Europe*(1927), 180.
[464] Geoffrey W. Clark, "An Interpretation of Hoboken's Population Trends: 1856-1970," in Foster and Clark, *Op.Cit.,* 50-51.

from coal to oil. This ship subsequently made twenty round trips from Hoboken to France carrying over 100,000 troops to the Western Front.

A larger embarkation port was needed, and Admiral Harris was put in charge of developing such a port at Hampton Roads, Virginia, with a budget of $500,000,000. This facility became the U.S. Navy's largest port for troop and war material movement, and it was 40 percent completed when the armistice came a year later in November 1918. Harris also served as president of the Board of Control of War Construction with a budget of over one billion dollars, the members of the board coming from the departments of War, Navy, and Labor, and the Shipping Board, and so forth. Harris called in Bensel, a reserve major in the Army Corps of Engineers, and made him assistant secretary of the board to chair its meetings given the admiral's busy schedule. Bensel's 1884 classmate, Lieutenant Colonel Dabney H. Maury, was the Army's representative on this board.[465] Harris went on to found his own company after retiring from the Navy in the 1920s, and he was still active during and after World War II, when he was a consultant for the Port Authority of New York on the construction of what became the John F. Kennedy International Airport.[466]

For Stevens, the benefit of the Emergency Fleet Corporation's naval connection was the United States Navy Steam Engineering School, the only one of its kind in the United States during World War I. Once the Navy decided to take control of merchant convoys across the Atlantic with its own officers, there was a need to train engineering naval officers in a crash program. As the undersecretary of the Navy, Franklin Delano Roosevelt, wrote to President Humphreys after the war,

One of the most serious problems which confronted the Navy almost from the entrance of the United States into the World War, and which increased in gravity as the war went on and the Navy's mission became more and more clearly defined, was the one of supplying engineer officers for the very large number of merchant-type vessels which the Navy was called upon to operate. . . . (and) . . . to man the great number of new vessels which the Shipping Board was building for the Navy to operate in the war zone. When it became apparent that we must take advantage of existing educational facilities not under government control we naturally turned to Stevens for help. Your response was immediate and most generous. There were no preliminary negotiations -- nothing but an expression of sincere desire to help in

---

[465] "'Tis Always Fair Weather When Good Fellows Get Together," *Stevens Indicator,* 43 (1926), 36.

[466] *Stevens Indicator,* 65 (1948), no. 1, 22.

every way in which you could be helpful; and the Steam Engineering School was a going concern almost as the matter was broached.[467]

In fact, the arrangements for Stevens' steam engineering school were such that it appeared with very little fanfare in the student newspaper and other press on March 25, 1918. Mechanical engineering professor Frederic L. Pryor was a naval reservist, and he was activated to be director of the school in uniform as a lieutenant commander. Instruction was provided by professors Furman, Anderson, Charabay, Stockwell and Belding.[468] Admission to the program was limited to graduates of an engineering college or the "equivalent," and the program lasted five months divided between the institute, the Pelham Bay Naval Station in the Bronx, and sea duty aboard ship. The theoretical and mechanical laboratory instruction at Stevens lasted a few weeks, and so as one batch of cadets moved on, another batch took its place. In all, 1,779 cadets were admitted and 1,465 actually received commissions in the fifteen months of the program, some sixty-two being Stevens graduates. The Navy expanded this type of short graduate program to include training of officers in other specialties, and the overall direction of the Stevens steam engineering program and programs at eleven other technical schools or universities with engineering faculty was put under the nominal direction of Professor E. F. Miller at MIT. Overall, 3,858 naval engineering officers were produced, some 38 percent at Stevens.[469] For example, Johns Hopkins had 75 students in courses in wireless, gas engines, and ignition systems.[470]

The United States Navy Steam Engineering School enabled Stevens Institute of Technology to acquire two buildings on campus built by the Navy in record time for the program. Initially, the cadets had to commute to Stevens for their few weeks instruction, but the Navy rapidly built a barracks to house the cadets on Stevens's original city block at the corner of Hudson and Sixth Street. However, this barracks proved unable to house all the cadets, so cots were set up in Walker Gymnasium to hold the rest until a second, much larger, barracks could be built on institute property just south of the Gate-house. The latter barracks was never used by the cadets because it was finished after the war ended and the program was terminated. Both these barracks were sold to the institute at nominal cost after the war, one later becoming the Lieb Building on which there is a plaque commem-

---

[467] Roosevelt to Humphreys, June 5, 1919, shelf 6, Stevens Special Collections.
[468] "Professor Pryor Now Made a Lieutenant Commander," *The Stute*, Sept. 20, 1918.
[469] Hurley, *Op.Cit.*, 212.
[470] *Johns Hopkins Alumni Magazine*, 1917-18, 275-6.

orating the wartime casualties who attended the steam engineering school, and the other the Navy Building which housed classrooms.[471]

Even though most Stevens students were in Navy uniforms during World War I, there was also an Army unit, shown above marching through the Green Gate.

In addition to the United States Navy Steam Engineering School, the War Department established military training programs for undergraduates at colleges throughout the country. At the start of the war, the top third of technical school students had been exempt from the draft, but, under a new ruling in 1918, all college students passing the national requirements for fitness and ability had to either go on a condensed two-year course of study without vacations and serve in a Student Army Training Corps, which also had a U.S. Navy section, or be eligible for the draft. Consequently, even though students in these programs were initially assigned to Stevens, most Stevens students joined the Navy unit, making it larger than the Army unit on campus. Even though this program did not last long before it was

---

[471] "Address by President Alexander C. Humphreys," *Stevens Indicator*, 36 (1919), 167-8.

terminated by the armistice in November 1918, it caused some chaos on the Stevens campus. All undergraduate courses were condensed to accommodate the two-year specification, and, after the armistice, lengthened again. Moreover, the Army insisted that its "student-soldiers" live on the campus, which was not a requirement of the Navy. As President Humphreys said later, "We had no trouble whatever with the Navy Unit -- with the Army Section, yes." Humphreys referred to Army "encroachment" on the newly acquired Stevens Castle. It had to be stripped from the first to the third floors to house the Army section, and its basement was altered to comply with the Army's mess requirements. Considerable damage was done to the Castle by the student-soldiers, and squabbles between the Army and Stevens occurred over payments. In addition, most student-soldiers assigned to Stevens by the Army left after peace arrived which was not the case with the Navy students, many of whom were Stevens students before the program was created.[472]

Even though Stevens's Navy connections ran deep during World War I, there were contributions to the Army as well: Samuel Prescott Bush 1885, a manufacturer of steel castings and ordnance, became the War Department's chief of ordnance, Small Arms and Ammunition Section.[473] Professor of mathematics Charles O. Gunther 1900 took leave in 1918 to do research at the Army's Small Arms Ballistic Station in Miami where he worked on elevation tables for newly designed machine guns. These guns had ranges far exceeding previous small arms, and, to make the tables for the Army, Gunther carried out experiments firing them. This work launched Gunther's consulting career as an expert witness in firearms, particularly microscopic identification of markings on bullets, a field in which he became a leading authority.[474] Humphreys's partner in Humphreys and Miller, Inc., consulting engineers in the gas industry, was Alten S. Miller 1888 and a trustee. He became a lieutenant colonel in the U.S. Army Ordnance division in Washington and was in charge of designing all cannon ammunition during the war.[475] John Davis, director of athletics, was chosen to take charge and organize the athletic activities of the Army behind the lines in France. Davis carried out General Pershing's orders that, for able-bodied personnel in rest and recuperation status, half the day be devoted to drill and the other half to recreational athletics and physical conditioning.[476]

---

[472] "Address by President Alexander C. Humphreys," *Op. Cit.*, 167-9.
[473] "Bush, Samuel Prescott," *National Cyclopedia of American Biography*, 40 (1955), 333-4.
[474] *Stevens Indicator*, 36 (1919), 148.
[475] "Miller, Alten Sidney," *National Cyclopedia of American Biography*, 53 (1971), 229.
[476] *Ibid.*, 152.

Moreover, most of the twenty-three Stevens dead in the war were with the Army on the Western Front.[477]

In spite of this contribution to the Army, Stevens seemed most pleased with its contribution to the Navy. At commencement exercises in 1919, there was appreciative applause when President Humphreys finished reading FDR's letter which concluded,

It would be extremely pleasing to the Department if you were to see fit to communicate the contents of this letter to all who have helped in this splendidly successful endeavor, and perhaps to the alumni. The latter have a right to take great pride in their Alma Mater's contribution to the Navy's share in winning the war.[478]

---

[477] "The Great Victory and Peace Dinner Dance," *Stevens Indicator*, 36 (1919), 26-34.
[478] "Commencement," *Stevens Indicator*, 36 (1919), 172.

CHAPTER 16
Automobiles, Radio, and Telecommunications

In 1876 the first Beau de Rochas production of the Otto four-cycle gasoline engine began in Europe, and two years later the first Otto engine was produced in the United States. There, George B. Selden had taken out a patent on a gas-engine automobile in 1879 which challenged Daimler-Benz's patent rights in 1895. This patent conflict was pending for sixteen years in America which meant that it was an open field for automobile manufacturers when the industry was taking off.[479] The Duryea brothers are credited with manufacture of the first feasible American gas automobile in 1892, and by 1898 there were over fifty American companies manufacturing automobiles. It was perhaps natural that the Stevens mechanical engineering curriculum, which included courses on machine design and tested all sorts of engines in the mechanical laboratory, would turn out an automobile pioneer, E. B. Gallaher 1894.

His first jobs involved in the design and manufacture of gas-engines and air compressors, but four years after graduation he organized and was president and general manager of the fledgling Keystone Motor Company in Philadelphia. It was an era in which gasoline engines were vying with steam engines and electric batteries as the motive power of automobiles, and so it is not surprising that Gallaher designed a steam-driven car, the "Keystone," which he manufactured unsuccessfully in 1899-1900. It was thoroughly unconventional, having a three-cylinder steam engine in each wheel hub fed by steam from a multitubular boiler mounted in the body. However, his "Keystone Wagonette," a light car with tiller steering driven by a rear ten horsepower gasoline engine was successful, and Gallaher sold the rights to manufacture the car to the Searchmont Motor Car Company in Philadelphia in 1900, the Keystone company becoming a subsidiary. From 1898 to 1903, Gallaher designed the entire product of these companies -- in all, eleven types of automobiles -- including engines, designs of bodies, and other equipment. By 1903, Keystone was turning out one Keystone Wagonette per day.[480]

Competition was fierce as 241 other automobile manufacturers started businesses between 1904 and 1908. Oldsmobile was particularly successful, selling 425 in 1901 and five thousand by 1904. To be more competitive, in 1903 Searchmont and Keystone were folded into a new company, the

---

[479] Interestingly, the automobiles from this case were given to Stevens Institute.
[480] Furman, *Morton Memorial, Op.Cit.*, 395.

Fournier-Searchmont Automobile Co., led by the French racing car driver Charles Fournier as president and Gallaher as first vice president and general manager. This company brought in L. S. Chadwick to design a thirty-two horsepower front engine, four-cylinder "Fournier-Searchmont," the first American car which had forced lubrication. It proved uncompetitive because of its high cost of $2,500 per car.[481] By 1908, after producing eight more expensive models, Henry Ford grabbed the mass market with the Model T based on the notion of a cheap car for the masses. Thereafter, Gallaher left the automobile business and became a successful manufacturer of gas and diesel engines for central stations and electric traction.[482]

Another Stevens graduate, Daniel K. Wright (1883-1965) 1908, who worked in the Department of Tests, started his career at the Edison Lamp Works in Harrison, New Jersey, but by 1926 was employed in GE's automobile Lamp Development Laboratory in Cleveland, Ohio. There, he took out twenty-six patents including the pioneering bi-post automobile headlight as well as its famous successor, the seal beam headlight. Moreover, he invented machinery and a production process for headlights which GE touted in 1932 as the most important way of making lamps "since Edison invented the incandescent."[483]

The most successful Stevens alumnus in the automobile industry was Charles Stewart Mott (1875-1973). He came from a well-to-do family who manufactured Mott apple juice and vinegar in New York City. His father enrolled Charles in the Stevens School on the Stevens campus when he was thirteen, and, after graduation four years later, young Charles was admitted to the institute. Mott did not graduate in four years because his father sent him to study yeast fermentation in the Technische Hochschule in Munich, Germany, after his sophomore year. Thus, after an education at Stevens which spanned nine years, Mott graduated in 1897. Preferring machine design and manufacturing to the apple juice business, his family helped him start C. S. Mott and Company, a firm which existed briefly to manufacture machines to make soda water. After a stint in the Navy during the Spanish-American War, Mott took over the management of the family owned Utica, New York, Weston-Mott Company, which was formed to manufacture wire bicycle wheels but which had some contracts, mainly with Oldsmobile, to supply wire wheels for automobiles.

---

[481] G. N. Georgano, *The Complete Encyclopedia of Motor Cars, 1885 to the Present*(1973), 402 and 617, and Automotive Quarterly, *The American Car Since 1775*(1971), see Keystone Wagonette, Keystone, and Searchmont after page 231.

[482] *Stevens Indicator*, 64 (1947), 3, 17.

[483] Obituary, *Stevens Indicator*, 82 (1965), no 1., 54.

Just when Mott took over Weston-Mott in 1900, most automobile manufacturers switched from tubular frame construction, in which the axles were part of the frame, to designs in which axles supported springs and the springs supported the frame. At the same time, automobile manufacturers were switching to wooden wheels. As a result, Weston-Mott showed a loss for the year 1900-1901, and in 1902 even Oldsmobile canceled its orders. To stay in business, Mott decided to take the biggest entrepreneurial risk of his life. In his own words,

It was up to me to do something and I went on the road to meet for the first time the automobile manufacturers and to try to sell them artillery wood wheels with which we had neither experience nor production. Sales were impossible. They wanted to buy front and rear chain drive axles with their wheels. Previously they had built their own tubular frames of different construction from what they now wanted. In fact, there was only one other source producing something of the type of what was desired. So, we had to design axles of our own make, drawings and blueprints of what we had never produced, and solicit business for a line of goods with which we had no experience. But before I went home, I had secured orders for a volume of business greater than we had ever done in one year, and still we had never built an axle.[484]

He had rounded up $250,000-worth of orders for the company. Successfully converting the factory's metal cutting tools to axle work, from 1903 to 1905 Mott earned over $600,000 with a profit of nearly $200,000. In 1906, at the urging of William Durant of Buick, Mott largely spent his profits relocating his factory to Flint, Michigan, in order to be in close contact with his customers. However, the move disrupted orders in 1907:

All of our customers except Buick held up their orders and we could make no collections. I can't remember how we scraped together enough money to meet payrolls. I visited all of our customers and prevailed upon them to settle their accounts with us, with bunches of notes of $1,000 or so each, and then I undertook to settle my accounts payable with these notes endorsed.[485]

Passing this crisis, by 1908 the company's sales were over two million dollars for the first time and $500,000 of the proceeds was profit. Mott reinvested the profits to expand operations, given the increased demand for axles and wheels when American automobile production jumped from some 100,000 cars in 1908 to over 450,000 cars in 1910. By 1909 company sales

---

[484] Quoted in C. Young, *In Memorium, Charles Stewart Mott* (1973), 22.
[485] *Ibid.*, 30-1.

of axles reached $5.5 million, and the profits made Mott, the sole owner of the company, a millionaire.

In 1912, Mott traded his shares of Weston-Mott for General Motors stock and ran for mayor of Flint on a reform independent ticket, and this started him on his road to being the city's primary philanthropist. Thereafter, he always had the idea that his giving had to be concentrated on one objective to be effective. Even his Mott Foundation, created in 1926, was dedicated to Flint. In the midst of three terms as mayor of Flint, World War I broke out. As a major stockholder and vice president of General Motors, he was put in charge of production of its military vehicles during the war, and his management skills guided the giant through the post-war depression of 1919-20. He was a vice president of General Motors from 1916 to 1937, and served on its board of directors through its executive, finance and auditing committees for most of his life. His fortune by the 1950s was said to be in the neighborhood of a half billion dollars, making him one of the ten most wealthy men in the United States.[486]

Among other notable automobile-industry graduates was James L. Myers 1911. After war service as a captain of ordnance, he was one of four men who organized the Cleveland Graphite Bronze Company in 1919. He was the original chief engineer of this company which specialized in the manufacture of lined bearings and bushings for tractors and turbine engines. By 1948, he was the president of this twenty-million-dollar company which produced about half of all the lined bearings for the auto industry after World War II.[487] Also, Harry T. Woolson 1897 started out as a marine engineer serving the Navy during the Spanish-American War, and, upon discharge, worked on marine gas engines with the Gas Engine and Power Company. During World War I, he became an expert in the production of PT boats, and after the war, in 1921, he joined Chrysler Corporation. There he became its executive engineer in 1935, then vice president of its marine division, and later the director of the Chrysler Institute. Included in his thirty-year career in the automotive industry, Woolson helped to design and develop Chrysler automobile chassis, Chrysler medium tanks, and Chrysler marine engines. He was president of the Society of Automotive Engineers in 1937 and was made a life member. During World War II, he was responsible for the design and development of Chrysler tank engines.[488]

---

[486] *Encyclopedia of Business Leaders*(1979), 991-3 and "Creator of the Charles Stewart Mott Foundation," *Stevens Indicator*, 74 (1957), 9-12.

[487] *Stevens Indicator*, 65 (1948), no. 4, 15.

[488] *Ibid.*, 64, (1947), 2, 21 and 4, 8.

The boom in automobiles resulting from assembly-line mass production spurred the rise of the petrochemical industry. Before the era of the auto-mobile, the refining of oil was by the simple batch method of heating crude oil until it vaporized, then separating its fractions into various stills. Dis-tilling produced lubricants and illuminating oil, and supplemented mineral oil and kerosene made from coal. Whale oil was phased out as a result. Oil was obtained from wells in America as early as 1859 in Pennsylvania, but there was a scurry for new sources as chemical engineering developed new methods to make distilling processes more efficient. A breakthrough occur-red in 1913 with the introduction of thermal cracking. This technology took the lower, usually waste, fractions of the distilling process and subjected them to high heat under pressure, thus "cracking" the larger molecules into smaller ones and increasing the yield of valuable petrol or gasoline.

Stevens's foremost graduate in this field was Morris W. Kellogg (1873-1946) 1894. He started his company, M. W. Kellogg and Co., as a small pipe-manufacturing shop in Jersey City. He built it up specializing in high-pressure steam piping, and by 1915, Kellogg had seized the new technology and created a reputation for his company in supplying materials and the engineering know-how to build oil-refining cracking plants. During World War I, he was assistant director of production for the Aircraft Board to organize the production of high-octane gasoline for aircraft. By 1937, when catalysts were added to cracking plants, M. W. Kellogg had become a specialist in that petrochemical technology as well as the processes of continuous, instead of batch, production. By mid-century, Kellogg was still president of the chemical engineering company which became a world leader in design and construction of petrochemical plants that used all the remaining residues of crude oil refining including those for making plas-tics.[489]

Another result of the start of the automobile era was a boom in road construction in the 1920s. Governments at all levels became involved in ambitious construction projects, many of them novel: A concept pioneered by William Niles White in the early 1920s resulted in the Bronx River Parkway, the first fifteen miles of divided four-lane highway which pre-served the trees on each side as it wound through an urban area. Close to Stevens Institute, Clifford Holland started tunneling under the Hudson River from Jersey City to lower Manhattan to create the Holland Tunnel by 1927-- the first vehicular tunnel in the world. In New Jersey, the traffic problem was how to channel automobiles and trucks from the west through

---

[489] *Stevens Indicator*, 62 (1945), 4, 5.

the maze of cities and towns, over the Passaic and Hackensack rivers, around Newark Bay into the Holland Tunnel.

This New Jersey highway-engineering problem was taken up by Walter Kidde (1877-1943), who was appointed to the New Jersey Highway Commission by Governor George Silzer in 1923 just when the Holland Tunnel project was underway. Born in Hoboken of German parents, Walter Kidde had attended the full courses in both the Stevens School and the institute with Mott and graduated in the same class of 1897. He entered the construction business specializing in new factories which were switching from steam engine/shaft and belt power to electrical power.[490] By 1905, he had his own construction firm, Walter Kidde and Company, which continued to specialize in constructing huge factory complexes but also built residences, churches, public buildings and housing projects. He started another division of the company with Walter Freygang 1912 which produced fire-detecting systems and fire extinguishers which were used the world over later in the century. His civil engineering company also did road construction, including drives on the estate of John D. Rockefeller, Jr., Kidde's squash partner. Thus Kidde was a well-known contractor and politically connected. He had a reputation for the utmost integrity by virtue of his voluntarism and contributions to civic organizations, including the New Jersey Sanitarium for Tuburculous Diseases, the New Jersey Conference of Social Work, and the Boy Scouts. For the latter, he had in 1919 contributed heavily to the purchase of land for a Bergen County camp where he designed, and had his construction firm build, a dam to create a lake.[491]

Chaired by Major General Hugh L. Scott (U.S. Army, ret.), the four-man New Jersey Highway Commission included two lawyers, as well as Kidde, who was one of the two construction engineers. Its work included a master plan which was the blueprint for New Jersey's highway development to the mid-century mark. It also had managerial oversight of implementing the most immediate parts of the plan. The plan laid out the route from Elizabeth to the Holland Tunnel ramp approaches. Instead of weaving through the major obstacles, the commission decided on one huge elevated expressway over the towns, rivers, and bay, namely the then-revolutionary solution of a huge elevated expressway bridge. This was the thirty-million-dollar Pulaski Skyway, the brainchild of Kidde and the lawyer Percy H. Steward, which, until the building of the Lincoln Tunnel and the George

---

[490] *Morton Memorial, Op.Cit.,* 455.
[491] Judge Harry V. Osborne, "Social Service," in William Collins, ed., *We Give You Walter Kidde*(1940), 39-42.

Washington Bridge in the 1930s, was the sole traffic expressway into New York City from the west.[492]

Comprehensive and covering the whole of New Jersey, the commission dispersed $75 million in expanding the highway system from 728 miles to 1,871 miles to include over half of the state's twentieth-century rural highway routes. The projects included many bridges, including the Victory Bridge spanning the Raritan River and the Delaware River Bridge. Kidde was also innovative, designing the world's first traffic circle in Camden and the world's first cloverleaf design at the junction of routes 4 and 25 near Woodbridge. After he left the commission in 1928, he joined the New Jersey State Chamber of Commerce but kept working on roadways by obtaining a gift of six-million-dollars worth of land along the Palisades from his friend John D. Rockefeller, Jr. Kidde then consented to serve as chairman of a Chamber-of-Commerce sponsored New York-New Jersey committee to keep the Palisades non-commercial as another parkway.[493] Later in the 1930s, Walter Kidde Construction Company designed and built the Manhattan approaches to the George Washington Bridge from the West Side Highway and the Cross Bronx Expressway.[494]

As the love affair with the automobile spawned thousands of miles of long-distance highways, Henry Morton Brinkerhoff moved into the field of highway planning. Thus, for the Pennsylvania Turnpike Commission in 1938, he did a traffic study to predict volume and earnings for the first of the modern long-distance tollways. Then in 1941, Governor Thomas E. Dewey named Brinkerhoff to the New York Thruway Commission to do the same study for the 480-mile road joining New York City with Buffalo.[495]

Another major new technology of the early twentieth century was radio. Radio revolutionized communications, first as wireless radiotelegraphy developed largely for the Navy from 1901 to 1906, then as primitive crystal sets of amateurs giving voice transmissions from 1904 though 1906, then weak vacuum-tube transmissions from 1906 to 1913, and finally as full-fledged commercial radio for the masses starting around 1920. Ever since the mathematician James Clerk Maxwell had worked out the theoretical basis for the existence of radio waves in 1865, the potential of engineering a

---

[492] Percy H. Stewart, "Commissioner Kidde, 1923-1927," *Ibid.*, 46.

[493] George W. Merck, "The New Jersey State Chamber of Commerce," *Ibid.*, 66.

[494] *Stevens Indicator*, 61 (1944), 5, 15. Later, another notable Stevens construction engineer, John W. Kinny of the class of 1925, was in charge of the 1964 construction of the Verrazano Narrows bridge whose span of 4,260 feet joined Brooklyn and Staten Island, the longest suspension bridge in the world at the time. *Ibid.*, 81 (1964), no 1, 15.

[495] Arthur G. Bendelius to Harold J. Raveché, May 8, 2000, and Benson Bobrick, *Parsons Brinkerhoff: The First Hundred Years*(1985), 89-90.

communications device without wires had fascinated students of electricity and mathematics.

Stevens's Frederick K. Vreeland (1874-1964) was one such student. A child prodigy in mathematics and electrical gadgets, Vreeland studied under the electrical engineers Geyer and Ganz, and also William Bristol.[496] After graduation in 1895, he took a postgraduate course in electrical engineering at Columbia University. In 1896, he was hired by the Crocker-Wheeler Electric Company in Ampere, New Jersey, where he worked in its experimental laboratory before being put in charge of the design of new electrical instruments as well as perfecting the company's stock dynamos and electrical motors. When Guglielmo Marconi broke into the news with the first transatlantic transmission of a radio-telegraph message in 1901, Vreeland formed his own company, the Vreeland Corporation, to invent, patent, and sell the patents of his electronic devices and instruments. At the same time, he showed himself to be an advanced student of radio by publishing through McGraw-Hill the book *Maxwell's Theory and the Wireless Telegraph* (1904) which was also published as articles in *Electrical World and Engineer*. This book had wide distribution in America and Europe during the takeoff of radiotelegraphy and was praised by Georges Clemenceau, the French scientist who later became president of France.

Vreeland then worked for the Navy as a consultant on radiotelegraphy in 1902-03, performing advanced top secret work, which, during the later patent wars over radio devices, induced the Navy to suggest that Vreeland should have been given patents which were claimed by others.[497] Then he worked with Reginald Fessenden in 1903 before Fessenden transmitted the world's first long-distance voice transmission via radio in 1906. Lee De Forest, inventor of the first triode vacuum tube, stated in his autobiography that he visited Fessenden's laboratory in 1903 and Vreeland was there working with Fessenden on an early form of electrolytic detector for wireless signals. Although Fessenden obtained the patent for the device, De Forest said that Vreeland had confidently stated that he, and not Fessenden, had designed it.[498] Vreeland went on to patent a host of his own inventions, including high-frequency oscillating instruments manufactured by another of his companies, the Vreeland Apparatus Company, established in 1905 in New York City. One of his oscillators became a standard electronic testing apparatus, and was used for advanced research on telephone diaphragms, on

---

[496] He graduated near the top of his class, Stevens Institute Faculty Minutes, Vol. II (1885-1904).

[497] See sections on U.S. Navy in Lawrence Lessing, *Man of High Fidelity, Edwin Henry Armstrong* (1985).

[498] Lee De Forest, *Father of Radio; The Autobiography* (1950), 161-2.

electrical impedance tests, oscillograph tests, and for testing vibration galvanometers. The AIEE president A. E. Kennelly praised the Vreeland oscillator as "steady in frequency and capable of frequency adjustment over very small measured steps."[499] Vreeland also invented and manufactured a carrier-wave multiplex, a sinewave oscillator, and a beats receiver or heterodyne. In 1925, Vreeland sold licenses for manufacture of his patented beats receiver to AT&T, Western Electric, the War Department, and RCA. He later invented and manufactured one of the earliest and most widely used spectroscopes, the Vreeland Spectroscope, for analyzing the color line spectrum of a sample mineral excited by an electric arc.[500]

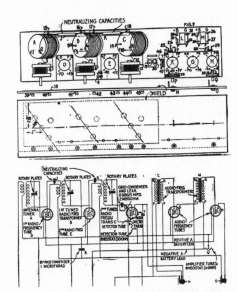

Louis Alan Hazeltine was a professor of electrical engineering and later of physics who made a fortune from his Neutrodyne radio receiver, shown right in a panel layout and schematic diagram. He involved both undergraduates and graduates in his research.

Louis Alan Hazeltine (1876-1964) was another prodigy in mathematics. He graduated from high school at sixteen and from Stevens Institute in 1906 at twenty with honors in mathematics with a special interest in the emerging field of electronics. He said later that he chose the field of electronics because it was at the time more demonstrably connected to mathe-

---

[499] A. E. Kennelly, *Electrical Vibration Instruments*(1923), 22,26,62,243, and 280.
[500] See 1947 biographical form filled out by Vreeland in Stevens Alumni Association records.

matics than other engineering fields. He once said, "there was a blissful realm in mathematics which was beyond figures."[501] Hazeltine was one of the last students of William E. Geyer, Stevens's first electrical engineering professor. Hazeltine followed in Geyer's footsteps, starting his teaching career in electrical engineering and finishing in physics.

Hazeltine became an instructor in electrical engineering in 1906, the year that Irving Langmuir (1881-1957) arrived at Stevens as an instructor of engineering chemistry. Hazeltine and Langmuir were close colleagues working on electrical projects for three years before the latter decided to give up teaching for full-time research at the General Electric Research Laboratories. At Stevens where he did his only teaching, Langmuir worked with two Stevens seniors, J. R. and H. R. Jarvis of the class of 1907, on research into corrosion of underground pipes caused by stray electrolytic currents in the earth.[502] At General Electric Langmuir's research into hot filaments in gases led to improvements in incandescent lighting, and his research into thin molecular films won him a Nobel Prize in 1932.

During World War I, Hazeltine worked for the Navy Department and designed the SE-1420 radio receiver used on destroyers and other naval vessels until the mid-1940s. Hazeltine's biographer claims that the SE-1420 was the "first radio design to be completed on paper," thus making Hazeltine a pioneer in the mathematical derivation of circuit design for radios.

In 1913, the "regenerative" receiver was invented by Columbia University's Edwin Armstrong. This breakthrough used amplified feedback to increase the volume of radio reception so that it could be heard across a room for the first time. The problem from 1920 to 1923 was the squeals, whistles and howls which kept interfering with reception. The solution to this problem led to Hazeltine's most famous invention, the "Neutrodyne" radio receiver which eradicated the noise by use of an amplifier which neutralized the grid-to-plate capacitive coupling. The patented Neutrodyne was the first commercially feasible radio receiver, and it was universally used from 1923 to 1927 in ten million radio sets. The Neutrodyne made a fortune for Hazeltine. He started the Hazeltine Corporation to manufacture electronic components but continued as a professor and conducted his primary research on the Stevens campus in the Navy Building. He said he loved to teach and conduct research with students, something he had learned from Geyer. In a *Scientific American* article in 1927, he was described as an inventor who used mathematical "pen and notebook" as the

---

[501] Obituary, *Stevens Indicator*, 81 (1964), no. 3, 76.
[502] Irving Langmuir, "The Relation Between Polarization and Corrosion and the Corrosion of Iron Pipes by Stray Currents," *Stevens Indicator*, 24 (1907), 348-363.

basis of new electronic devices instead of trial and error. In the same article, he was quoted as saying that the secret of inventing was a "thorough knowledge of fundamental principles," and in his own 1958 autobiographical sketch he stated, "It speaks well for the breadth of the Stevens course that I later headed both the electrical engineering and physics departments, although I never had a degree in either subject." He taught at Stevens from 1906 to 1944 and was one of the most popular professors on campus by involving his students in his research. He often told his students, "The main requisite for success is not so much natural ability as it is fondness for a subject. The only way to solve problems is to solve problems."[503]

Stevens had four presidents of the Institute of Radio Engineers (IRA), namely, Irving Langmuir, Hazeltine, Laurence C. F. Horle 1914, and Frederick B. Llewellyn 1922. Horle was another mathematical genius and student of Hazeltine's who taught physics at Stevens before working with Hazeltine on Navy radio systems. During World War I, Horle was first expert radio aide and then directing head of the Navy's top-secret radio work at the Naval Research Laboratory at Anacosta, Maryland.[504] After the war he was chief engineer for De Forest's Radio Telephone and Telegraph Company, and after 1921 formed his own consulting company. He was an early consultant on radio for the Bureau of Standards, his specialty being design of mobile radio broadcast and receiving equipment which was used in early aircraft and radio direction finders.[505]

Another of Hazeltine's students, Frederick B. Llewellyn 1922, joined the research laboratory of Western Electric under Frank B. Jewett. When the parent company of Western Electric, AT&T, created Bell Telephone Laboratories with Jewett as its head in 1925, Llewellyn was one of its original members. Bell Labs became the twentieth century's world-leading research and development facility in electronic devices, and, in the age of the vacuum tube which lasted until the 1950s, Llewellyn was one of its main research physicists who rose to the position of assistant to the president by 1956. An international authority on vacuum tubes, his theoretical studies led to his invention of the ultra-high frequency (UHF) oscillator tube which

---

[503] Harold A. Wheeler, *Hazeltine the Professor*(1978), vii and 89. See also B. O. Davis, *Electrical and Electronic Technologies*(1983), 91. One of Hazeltine's students, Willis H. Taylor 1916, became his patent lawyer and coined the term "Neutrodyne." Taylor's law firm also included Frederick L. Bissinger 1933. Both these lawyers specializing in patent law later became chairmen of the Stevens board of trustees in the 1960s and 1970s. Another student was Arnold B. Arons 1937 who became a professor of physics at Amherst and was cited by the American Association of Physics Teachers as the best physics teacher in the country in 1965.

[504] "Receives Medal of Honor," *Ibid.*, (1948), no. 3, 13.

[505] "Horle, Laurence C. F.," *Who's Who in Engineering*(1931), 630.

was fundamental in the development of radar during World War II. He was also known for work on stabilized oscillating circuits used in radio and telephones, and his work helped shape the design of land telephone repeaters across America as well as on the bottom of the oceans. He was a special consultant to the secretary of war in 1944 and served on the Weapons Evaluation Group of the Joint Chiefs of Staff during the early 1950s.[506] Another of Hazeltine's students, Gordon N. Thayer of the class of 1930, joined Bell Labs after graduation and specialized in mobile radio communications equipment and systems. In 1940, he working on radar and later on microwave communications relay systems. In 1949, he set up the first AT&T microwave transmission of telephone communications between Boston and New York and subsequently managed the construction of the first transcontinental microwave relay system. In 1952, he was named vice president of Bell Labs in charge of its military development program.[507]

A fabulously successful Stevens graduate whose career was made by early inventiveness in electronics for oil exploration was Brooklyn-born Eugene McDermott (1899-1973) of the class of 1919. He had studied instrumentation and electronics under Hazeltine and had subsequently furthered his knowledge in the field by obtaining a masters degree from Columbia University. He gained experience in electronic instrumentation while working for Western Electric, but in 1925, when there was a need to use more sophisticated scientific methods in the search for underground oil, he joined the Geophysical Research Corporation, a subsidiary of Amerada Petroleum. Placed in charge of its instrument laboratory, he then conceived and designed electronic seismology instruments for the discovery of oil deposits. The equipment was a type of recording ground sonar, a refraction seismograph, that sent electronic signals through the earth to bounce off various underground geological structures, thus identifying likely drilling sites for oil.[508] In 1926, the company began to contract its oil exploration service to oil companies, and McDermott, as the first chief of a crew to test his equipment for the Gulf Oil Company in the field, rapidly discovered ten salt domes in Louisiana and another in New Mexico, thus proving the value of his equipment, which was key to the company's success.

In 1930, McDermott and the head of the subsidiary, the physicist J. C. Karcher, went into business for themselves by forming Geophysical Services Inc. as a privately held partnership. Those were the days of wildcat oil

[506] Who's Who in America(1967), 1280; Stevens Indicator, 63 (1946), 1, 10, and "Fred Llewellyn '22 Moves," Stevens Indicator, 82 (1965), no. 3, 13.
[507] Stevens Indicator, 74 (1957), no. 5, 21.
[508] "Eugene McDermott, 1919," Stevens Indicator, 82 (1965), no. 1, 20.

companies, and Geophysical Services's twelve exploration crews lived a nomadic life in the midst of the Great Depression of the 1930s. The company conducted oil exploration around the world, including Mexico in 1931, Canada in 1932, Venezuela in 1934, Colombia in 1936, Saudi Arabia and Indonesia in 1937, and the Persian Gulf in 1939. However, the company's Texas-based laboratories continued to design and its factory to manufacture and sell state-of-the-art electronic seismic instruments for oil exploration, including those used by aircraft. By 1939, McDermott was president of this company and his management led to expanded operations in actual oil production as well as continuing exploration services for the major oil producers. A private company at the time, its profits soared and made a fortune for McDermott and his partners. During World War II when oil exploration was curtailed, the company made unprecedented profits by producing submarine-detecting sonar for the Navy and compact mobile radar systems for aircraft. After the war, McDermott led the company during a further period of rapid growth and became chairman of the board in 1949. By 1950, the firm was selling $7.5 million worth of products and services a year. In 1951, the management of McDermott and president John Jonsson decided that the future of the company lay in advanced electronics technology, and they went public with a stock offering to raise money for expansion of research and development as well as manufacturing operations. The company was renamed Texas Instruments Incorporated.

Eugene McDermott,
during his valedictory address
in 1919, said, "Success,
when she comes to perch on
our banners,
will see us in partnership
with our Alma Mater."
True to his word,
After he made a fortune
by being one of the founders
of Texas Instruments,
he contributed nearly
$1.5 million to a new
administrative and student
center building.

Equipped with new funds, the management team of Texas Instruments, led by McDermott, Jonsson, and executive vice president Patrick Haggerty, decided in 1952 to buy the patented transistor technology just developed by the Bell Telephone Laboratories team of Bardeen, Brittain and Shockley. This decision was part of their strategy for growth, namely to capitalize on all new electronic technologies and become the premier supplier of military systems. As it turned out, Texas Instruments promptly pioneered the engineering, development and manufacture of semiconductors and subsequently became the world's largest producer of silicon transistors and integrated circuits and their applications. The quick decision by management to manufacture the new technology led to the company's development of the first commercially successful hand-held calculator and the first successful mass-produced pocket radio. The pocket radio was an instant hit with the public. Moreover, the company sold its first commercially available silicon transistors to the military during the Cold War buildup and to all major computer and telecommunications manufacturers, as solid-state electronic circuits replaced those using vacuum tubes in the 1950s. McDermott remained a director after his retirement in 1964, and by the time of his death in 1973, Texas Instruments had world-wide operations, sales of $1.3 billion per year, and forty thousand employees in its laboratories and factories.[509]

---

[509] "McDermott, Eugene," *National Cyclopedia of American Biography,* 58, 493-4; "Haggerty, Patrick Eugene," *Encyclopedia of Business Leaders*(1979), 255; "Haggerty, Patrick Eugene." *Ibid.,* 524-5; and John D. Ryder and Donald G. Fink, *Engineers and Electrons*(1984), 122, 124, 127.

CHAPTER 17
Trustees Lead Stevens Through Great Depression

Nobody was as active in saving the Institute during the Depression than Walter Kidde, the chairman of the board of trustees from 1928 to 1935. Kidde had extraordinary dedication in serving the Institute under three Stevens presidents. He was an undergraduate when chosen by Henry Morton to be the secretary of the 25th anniversary committee in 1897, Morton being chairman. As an alumnus, he ran the alumni part of the fundraising in Humphreys's 1915 campaign to success-fully liquidate the mortgage debt incurred while buying the Stevens family's estate and the Castle. He also ran the 1924 fundraising campaign devised by Humphreys to expand the endowment for the purpose of raising faculty salaries. During the eleven-month period between presidents from 1927 to 1928, Kidde, as the new chairman of the board of trustees, helped choose the new president and also concluded negotiations with the heirs of Richard Stevens to buy the last few acres of Castle Point property to the north of Colonial House.[510]

Walter Kidde of the class
of 1897 formed a
construction company
and became a world-leading
manufacturer of fire extinguishers
and safety equipment.
He contributed to the Boy Scouts,
and particularly to Stevens Institute.
When Humphreys was too sick
to read his final address
at commencement in 1927,
Kidde stepped forward
from the row of trustees
and finished it for him,
and when Humphreys died in 1928,
Kidde was a pallbearer.

---

[510] Franklin B. Kirkbridge, "Trustee-Plus at Stevens," in Collins, ed., *We Give You Walter Kidde, Op.Cit.*, 55-62, and Obituary of Walter Kidde, *Stevens Indicator*, 60 (1943), 2, 9.

In 1929, as an offshoot of his interest in the benefits of the out-of-doors for Boy Scouts, Walter Kidde and the trustees bought four hundred acres of land near Johnsonburg in Warren County, New Jersey, adjacent to the Kittatinny Mountains for a summer camp for Stevens students. Kidde contributed some funds for a down payment for a mortgage, and later he persuaded his aunt, Florence Osgood Rand Lang, the heir to the founder of Ingersoll-Rand, to donate $25,000 to liquidate the mortgage.[511] In 1930, gifts for cabins and a mess hall came from retired professor William H. Bristol and for an athletic field from retired professor William E. Geyer. Thus, from 1930 to 1955 all freshmen took a six-week course in civil engineering at the Stevens-owned Johnsonburg Camp.[512]

Moreover, Kidde did everything possible to make sure that the institute survived during the depths of the Great Depression: He initiated reforms in the way the Stevens Alumni Association (SAA) supported the institute, namely, to enlarge membership and therefore enlarge active giving. Like other college alumni associations, the SAA had incorporated as an independent entity in 1906, and it had its own trustees and alumni journal, the *Stevens Indicator*. Under this arrangement, the SAA and the institute jointly coordinated occasional fund drives such as those in 1915 and 1924, President Humphreys seeking money from non-degree holders and the SAA conducting the drive among alumni. From its inception, the SAA's constitution had specified that membership was limited to those who paid dues. But the reforms of 1929-1930 changed the rules by including as active members any Stevens alumnus. Also, instead of occasional contributions to the institute, the alumni were asked to contribute on a yearly basis, the president of the SAA and class captains doing the solicitations for the "Stevens Fund." Money from the yearly drives was given to the institute after deductions for modest upkeep of the independently incorporated SAA and its magazine. Of course, this type of reform was not unique and was taking place on other campuses during the onset of the Depression when colleges became more reliant on alumni giving.[513]

Also, Walter Kidde was a key member of the finance committee of the board of trustees. In 1932, in the midst of bank failures and 40 percent unemployment rates, the finance committee made a candid assessment of the institute's alarming budgetary deficits. The prolonged and deep downturn in

---

[511] "Mrs. Henry Lang, Friend of Stevens," *Ibid.*, 54 (1937), no. 4, 8.

[512] John Spano, "The Johnsonburg Camp," *Ibid.*, 115 (1998), no. 2, 24-6, and for the closing see "Johnsonburg Camp No Longer To Be Used," *Stevens Indicator*, 72 (1955), 2, 9.

[513] R. Morton Adams, "Our Association -- Its Organization and How It Works," *Ibid.*, 63 (1946) 4, 3.

the economy caused reduced enrollments and reduced giving by alumni. Stevens's small endowment was less than four million dollars throughout the 1930s and was significantly smaller than the endowments of other leading technical institutes at the time. For example, around 1937-38, the approximate endowments of MIT, Carnegie Institute of Technology and California Institute of Technology were $33 million, $16 million, and $10.5 million respectively. Since Stevens had little endowment to draw on, it was forced to try to balance the yearly budget with gifts from trustees and alumni in a hand-to-mouth fashion.[514] The 1932 report made a frank admission of the problem of low initial endowment by the Stevens family: It said that Stevens was "battle scarred" in its efforts to "overcome the handicap of reduced income, decrease in gifts, and a shrunken investment portfolio, which, at best, has never been sufficient to support properly the educational needs of the college." [515]

The deficit in 1930-31 was $29,000, and in 1931-32 it was $60,000, the latter being over ten percent of the yearly budget. The committee concluded that the three thousand alumni had to be a "bulwark" against the strain of these deficits, that "the friends of Stevens can and will rally with new assurance and satisfaction to the support of the college." However, there were so many alumni who were among the unemployed in 1932 that the SAA published a pamphlet, *Experience Records of Stevens Men Available for Employment,* listing 176 job seekers.[516] At the same time, total enrollments dropped below 450 in 1929 and hovered around 500 or below for the duration of the Depression. In 1933, an appeal was made to alumni to "adopt" a needy freshman by buying tuition "coupon books."[517] As chairman of the board of trustees, Kidde was also instrumental in organizing an effort to bring onto the board successful and wealthy alumni and philanthropic outsiders who made crucial contributions during the Depression. Among these were Robert C. Post in 1929 and William S. Barstow in 1934.

Robert Cox Post (1877-1945) was Kidde's friend and a fellow construction engineer with a fabulous reputation based on his having put up the structural steel in the Empire State Building in record time. He was one of five members of his family who graduated from Stevens.[518] A member of the class of 1898, Post was the grandson of Simon Post, one of the founders

---

[514] F. Lundberg, *America's 60 Families*(1937), 376-82.

[515] "Report of the Finance Committee of the Board of Trustees of Stevens Institute of Technology for the Year 1931-2," *Ibid.,* 49 (1932), 118.

[516] *Supplement to the Stevens Indicator,* 49 (1932).

[517] "Adopt a Freshman Plan," *Stevens Indicator,* 50 (1933), 68.

[518] *Ibid.,* 55 (1938), no. 4, 4.

of the ASCE, and his family ran Post and McCord Construction Company, New York City's foremost erector of structural steel during the 1920s and 1930s. He and his brother, Andrew Jackson Post of the class of 1892, obtained a reputation for excellence with their erection of the structural steel for the 1,046-foot Chrysler Building in 1930. This was the first structure higher than the Eiffel Tower, built in Paris in 1889.

Post and McCord's most famous project was the 1,250-foot Empire State Building. In 1929, demolition of the old Waldorf Astoria Hotel started at Fifth Avenue and 34th Street to make way for the tallest building in the world. It was being built there because of its proximity to the Pennsylvania Station, Macy's at Herald Square, and major hotels like the Pennsylvania, Governor Clinton, and New Yorker. While the Chrysler Building was being completed early in 1930, Post and McCord started excavation of the new site. Four major problems confronted Post in erecting the structural steel of the Empire State Building: supply of steel, layout of the plant, steel-handling methods at the site, and actual erection procedure.

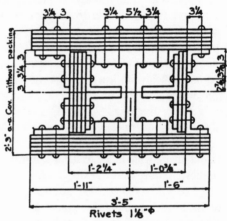

Robert C. Post led the mandolin club while at Stevens. At right, the cross section of the lowest steel columns in the Empire State Building. A 26' 8" length weighed 87,310 lbs.

In order to obtain record time, the Post brothers had the lower structural steel columns put together at the plant of the steel manufacturer, Carnegie Steel Company, a subsidiary of the United States Steel Corporation. The lower steel columns, 210 in number and seated thirty-seven feet below street level on the underlying stratum of granite which makes the New York City

226

skyline of tall buildings possible, had no fewer than twenty-eight parts riveted together. These steel parts included a central I column with five steel plates riveted on the top and bottom, two lateral T columns on either side of the I column attached through elbows riveted to the five plates, and three plates riveted to each of the flat portions of the T's. These lowest columns were twenty-six feet eight inches long and each weighed 87,310 pounds. As the skeleton structure rose, the size and weight of the columns decreased, but they were all riveted together before they arrived at Manhattan so the men working above had only to connect them together.

The columns and beams were shipped from Pennsylvania to the railroad yard in Jersey City, thence around the Battery to an East River dock by barge, and finally to the site by trucks. The trucking was highly coordinated by Post so as not to obstruct traffic in Manhattan. It was sent down 33rd Street, a one-way street, to a setback in the southern side of the building where a derrick on the second floor took the steel directly from the trucks. After the sixth floor was built, the bottom derrick transferred the steel to relay derricks. The upper portion of the building was supplied by relay platforms on the twenty-fifth floor and the fifty-second floor, the steel passing through holes left in the concrete flooring for twenty-five stories in one lift. Once the steel was on a relay platform, nine erection derricks hoisted it to the workers who riveted it into place. Derricks were powered by electric hoisting engines designed by Post and McCord which had drums with a capacity of 3,500 feet of three-quarter-inch wire rope. They had an improved automatic safety mechanism, brakes set by springs and released by a hydraulic ram, to supplement the operator's pedal brakes. This improvement came after a Post and McCord operator dropped a load of steel as a result of being knocked unconscious by a falling brick during construction of the Chrysler Building. At the beginning, the heaviest columns and beams were erected at a rate of four floors a week. [519] At higher altitudes, the rate was a floor a day. Until the twentieth floor, three hundred men were employed above, and thereafter only 150; the maximum number of riveting gangs used at one time on the lower floors was thirty-eight, each gang being made up of two riveters, a heater of rivets, a "bucker-up" for tossing the rivet, and two helpers. At every stage of the shipment, movement of steel on derricks and organization of the men were rigidly scheduled to maximize erection time and minimize any disruption of traffic on 33rd and 34th Streets and Fifth Avenue. Also, with a view to providing safety, every

---

[519] F. T. Llewellyn, "CB Rolled Steel Sections in the Empire State Building," *Stevens Indicator*, 48 (1931), no. 1, 6 and 14, and "Fifty-Seven Thousand Tons of Steel and a Building a Fifth of a Mile High," *Ibid.*, 7 and 14.

second story was planked so that tools could not drop more than twenty-five feet.

Fifty-seven thousand tons of steel were erected in demonic speed by Post and McCord, nearly three times as much as the 21,000 tons Post had erected for the Chrysler Building.[520] The photographer Lewis W. Hines immortalized Post and McCord riveting gangs with his pictorial history of the building's ascent. The *New York Post* called it "a saga of the men who, outlined against the sky on dizzy heights, fuse the iron of their nerves with the steel of the girders."[521] According to the *New York Times,* Post and McCord finished the topping out of the steel construction two months ahead of schedule, with a crowd of five thousand spectators waiting from below. The whole operation took six months and three days. On September 27, 1930, Post and McCord were honored at the Hotel McAlpin by other contractors and ex-governor Al Smith for the record which was touted as "A noble monument to the spirit of cooperation and teamwork attained in the construction field."[522] Robert C. Post was credited with the master plan to erect thousands of tons of structural steel in record time into the midst of the world's most congested area of Manhattan without disrupting traffic.[523]

In 1932, Post and McCord were given the contract for the structural steel in all the buildings of the Rockefeller Center, including the tallest building of the group, the RCA building. One hundred and twenty-five thousand tons of steel were used in the group. Another alumnus worked on the Rockefeller Center project, namely, John C. Hegeman 1905 who was president of the international building company, Hegeman and Harris of New York City. He built the arched, soundproofed walls of the Radio City Music Hall and Roxy Theater for John D. Rockefeller, Jr.'s, agent, John Reynard Todd.[524] Among other buildings, in 1938 Hegeman built the U.S. Embassy building at 2 Grosvenor Square and Earl's Court, a huge exhibition center, both in London. Earl's Court was described in the *London Illustrated* as the "biggest building in the world" with its 47,000,000 cubic feet of space and

---

[520] "Steel Contract Let," *New York Times,* Jan. 12, 1930, II, 19.

[521] Theodore James Jr., *The Empire State Building*(1975), 72.

[522] "Workers Raise Flag 1,048' Above 5th Avenue as Steel Frame of Smith Building is Finished," *New York Times,* Sept. 20, 1, and "Laud Building Unity: Empire State Contractors Honor Post and McCord at Luncheon," *Ibid.,* Sept. 27, 1930, 32.

[523] *Stevens Indicator,* 62 (1945), 4, 6.

[524] "The Theaters at Radio City," *Stevens Indicator,* 50 (1933), no. 2, 4-6, and "RCA Building Topped Out," *New York Times,* Sept. 27, 1932, 39, and "Hegeman-Harris Begins Work on 66 Story Central Office Building," *Ibid.,* Nov. 3, 46.

1,400,000 square feet of floor area. It had a sports and spectacle arena which seated 23,000 people.[525]

John Reynard Todd was manager of Rockefeller Center and a trustee of Stevens Institute. At right, a steel worker wearing a Post and McCord button in his cap works on the RCA building across from St. Patrick's Cathedral on Fifth Avenue.

William S. Barstow (1866-1942) was an Edison Pioneer who served on Stevens's board of Trustees from 1933 until his death. Like Kidde, he was a supporter of the Boy Scouts of America, having contributed Camp Barstow to the organization. He was an early and lasting friend of John W. Lieb and

[525] *Stevens Indicator*, 55 (1938), no. 2, 5. If the Post brothers were the most well known civil engineers from Stevens, there was one other who notably helped "build New York." John M. Kyle of the class of 1925 had directed part of the construction of the foundations of Rockefeller Center as well as parts of the Henry Hudson Parkway and the approaches to the Lincoln and Midtown tunnels, work done in the 1930s for the George J. Atwell Foundation Company of New York. Then, he joined the Port Authority of New York as its chief engineer in 1947. In this capacity he directed the design and construction of the third tube of the Lincoln Tunnel and the second deck of the George Washington Bridge. He designed the terminal areas of La Guardia, Newark and John F. Kennedy airports as well as the Hoboken, Brooklyn, and Port Newark marine terminals and the mid-Manhattan 42nd Street Port Authority Bus terminal. Years later, he designed the foundations of the World Trade Center as well as the layout of the PATH train tunnels and tracks underneath it. Remembered for being the "brains" of the class of 1925, Kyle was class salutatorian and later published 40 papers on soil consolidation, prestressed concrete foundation design, and co-authored the *Port Design and Construction Manual* of the American Association of Port Authorities. See John M. Kyle, "New Arterial Facilities for the Metropolitan Area," *Stevens Indicator*, 72 (1955), 1, 5-8, and obituary, *Stevens Indicator*, 88 (1971), 1, 41.

John Van Vleck, with whom, in 1918, he founded the Edison Pioneers, a society of colleagues of Edison dedicated to honoring the inventor. A Columbia graduate, Barstow had helped move Edison's laboratory from Menlo Park to West Orange, New Jersey, and had been a friend of Edison until Edison's death. He and Lieb and Van Vleck had constructed the first AC power plants for Consolidated Edison in the 1890s, and all three had managed to be loyal to Edison in spite of his early antagonism to alternating current. As vice-chairman of the Stevens board of trustees, Barstow provided funds for the refurbishing of the Navy barracks on the corner of Hudson and 6th streets as the Stevens Library and for a special Lieb Memorial Collection of Vinciana collected by Lieb when he was in Italy. Until 1934, the library of Stevens Institute was inside the original institute building in cramped, inadequate quarters.

Some of the trustees and administrators on hand for the dedication of Jacobus Hall were: from left, William S. Barstow, David S. Jacobus, Charles S. Mott, architect Howland Jones, administrator C. M Chapin, August G. Pratt, J. C. Traphagan, George Gibbs, F. A. Lydecker, Walter Kidde, and vice president George Creese.

In addition, Barstow and the Edison Pioneer Samuel Insull provided special rooms for the Lieb Collection of Vinciana, a collection of rare facsimile editions of notebooks of Leonardo da Vinci collected by Lieb while he was in Italy. This collection has been strengthened and is one of the largest collections of Leonardo materials in the country, along with the collections of Brandeis, UCLA, and the Burndy Library in Norwalk, Connecticut. Barstow also provided funds for the construction and upkeep of a dormitory in 1937: Although the Castle had been used as a dormitory for a few students since its purchase from Edwin A. Stevens II in 1911, the Barstow-funded dormitory, named in honor of his longtime friend and fellow trustee Daniel S. Jacobus, was the first campus structure built for the purpose of being a dormitory. In addition, he had Walter Kidde Construction build the Edison Tower in Menlo Park and gave the monument, along with an endowment fund for its upkeep, to Stevens Institute. Lastly, in his will, Barstow left money for scholarships for Stevens students.[526]

Before his death from cancer, Alexander C. Humphreys personally chose Walter Kidde to be the new chairman of the board and entrusted him with the job of choosing an appropriate president as his successor. After a search, the board chose Harvey N. Davis to be the third president in 1928. Davis led Stevens through the next stage in its curricula history, namely the creation of master's degree programs and several laboratories for funded research. At the same time, Davis reaffirmed the traditional broad-based undergraduate engineering curriculum which was, of course, sacred to the trustees. Adherence to it was a condition of employment as president.

Harvey N. Davis (1881-1952) obtained his Ph.D. in physics from Harvard; he taught mathematics at Brown as an instructor, and then he returned to Harvard as a professor of physics and later as a professor of mechanical engineering, the field of his research being properties of dry steam. He was a manager of the ASME from 1929 to 1930, a vice president from 1931 to 1932, and president in 1938 and 1939, and in 1930, under his auspices, the ASME celebrated its fiftieth anniversary in the Stevens auditorium where the ASME was founded.[527] His speeches and memoranda confirm his reputation of having high intellectual ability. From the very beginning in 1928, Harvey Davis strongly supported the Stevens tradition of a four-year undergraduate engineering education based on fundamentals in a "small but good" college. He stated that engineering was less and less based on experience and increasingly founded on applied science and techniques developed by research, and therefore undergraduate curricula should stress "fundamental science," "humanities," and "fundamental engineering principles."[528] He sought to retain the excellent reputation of the

---

[526] *Ibid.*, 63 (1946), 2, 16, and "Barstow, William Slocum," *National Cyclopedia of American Biography*, 32 (1945), 480-1.

[527] Bruce Sinclair, *A Centennial History, Op.Cit.*, 1-21 and 230.

[528] H. N. Davis, "Seventy-five Years of Engineering Education," *Stevens Indicator*, 58 (1940), no. 3, 1-3, and H. N. Davis, *New Measure, New Man*(1938), 31.

institute for teaching, but, in addition, to build its reputation and com-petitiveness in the area of research.[529]

The broad-based Stevens engineering education had a boost from another SPEE white paper on engineering education, the Wickenden Report of 1929. This report, which was funded by the Carnegie Corporation, the Carnegie Foundation, General Electric, Westinghouse, AT&T, and James H. McGraw of McGraw-Hill, among others, called for a retreat from specialized engineering curricula which had spread in the period from the 1880s to the 1920s. Based on massive surveys among engineers and businessmen, the report stressed a return to fundamentals. It also stressed preparation for management which included increases in the time allotted to the social sciences, particularly economics. Lastly, it called for more cooperation between the business world and academia in research and mutual support.[530] Ironically, because of the success of its broad-based M.E. degree and perhaps because of its small size and limited resources, Stevens had skipped the whole movement towards specialized degrees and had little to change in its curriculum except to foster more industrial-academic research and add some social sciences, the changes carried out by Davis just after his arrival.

Although Harvey N. Davis supported the broad-based undergraduate curriculum, in private memoranda to the board of trustees he neither sup-ported its bias towards mechanical engineering nor the designation of the degree as an M.E. In fact, he quietly changed the name of the Stevens catalogue's subtitle from "A College of Mechanical Engineering" to "A College of Engineering," and by the 1930s the catalogue descriptions of the undergraduate program were stressing "one unspecialized curriculum" con-sisting of the "basic disciplines that underlie all engineering careers." In 1933, Davis wrote to the board of trustees that the mechanical engineer could no longer claim to represent and include all the other engineering specialties; he said that

In the past the degree of M.E. was a far better description of an all-around engineer than it is now . . . A mechanical engineer was, in fact, a general practitioner . . . . And it is what has happened to mechanical engineering now that the electricals and chemicals and management men have gone on to. They too have taken with them the frontiers beyond which presumably lie still newer branches of engineering, and they have left behind them a rather sharply limited specialty. If we are to carry on

---

[529] W. Atkins, "Harvey N. Davis; Twenty Years of Achievement," *Stevens Indicator,* 1948 reprint, 2-3.

[530] Noble, *Op.Cit.,* 241-2.

the spirit of Morton and his trustees, we must not limit ourselves, even formally, to what the broad field he chose has now shrunk to. The degree Mechanical Engineer has become unfair to the best traditions of Stevens.[531]

In spite of this argument, Harvey Davis's recommendation to change the name of the degree from M.E. to a general degree designation like Bachelor of Science, Bachelor of Applied Science, or Bachelor of Engineering was not accepted by the trustees during his administration.

The role of the Humanities Department, which received this name in Davis's first year, was placed more prominently in the catalogue and was said to provide "a liberal education for Stevens graduates" without attempting to make the liberal arts sound useful to engineers as previous Stevens literature had done. Harvey Davis followed the recommendations of the Wickenden Report by adding a social science (psychology), to the Department's offerings in English, history, and foreign languages.

Another recommendation of Wickenden was to introduce economics to engineers, but Stevens had pioneered in this field under Humphreys. Davis's replacement for Humphreys was William D. Ennis 1897, an early adherent of Frederick W. Taylor. Before World War I, Ennis had been a professor of mechanical engineering at Brooklyn Polytechnic and had written a textbook on economics of engineering. He had wide experience in engineering practice, being chief engineering officer at Watervliet Arsenal during World War I, and founder, with Campell Scott, E. P. Goodrich, and George B. Ford, of the Technical Advisory Corporation of New York, consulting engineers. He filled the first Alexander C. Humphreys Professor of Engineering Economics chair, which was funded by Arthur Glasgow 1884, who was Humphreys's partner in the firm of Humphreys and Glasgow. Ennis authored six college texts and was treasurer of the ASME from 1935 to his retirement in 1944. He held economic conferences for engineers at the Johnsonburg Camp in the summers during the Great Depression, including the SPEE's first conference on teaching economics of engineering.[532] Ennis was followed in the Alexander C. Humphreys chair by Arthur Lesser 1931 who carried on Ennis's work in the 1940s by holding symposia at Stevens on engineering economy and founding and editing the journal *Engineering Economy* sponsored by the SPEE.[533]

---

[531] H. N. Davis, unpublished notes to the board of trustees dated 1933, Stevens Special Collections.

[532] *Ibid.*, 61 (1944), 1, 10.

[533] Newell O. Mason, "Harvey N. Davis," in Potter, ed., Op.Cit., I-C, errs when he writes on page 52 that Davis created a "separate department of Economics of Engineering." Humphreys created that department in 1902.

If he followed the recommendations of the Wickenden Report in fostering humanities and economics of engineering, Harvey Davis rejected the co-operative program which the report had suggested. Instead, Davis stressed the need for graduate-level research, and a graduate school to meet the needs of working engineers to understand the increasing sophistication of their fields. He asserted that "research and research spirit" could be achieved in still more advanced instruction leading to a Ph.D. degree, but it was premature to create one. One had to proceed slowly, given the limited faculty and resources. In 1930, Harvey Davis's second year as president, the first graduate courses leading to an M.S. degree began in the fields of industrial engineering, electrical engineering, civil engineering, organic chemistry, and physical chemistry. Twenty-seven courses were offered to only thirty-three graduate students the first year. This program necessitated rearrangement of departmental names and an increase in faculty to sixty-two. The program grew slowly given the onset of the Great Depression, and by 1934 there were still only about thirty graduate students, the total rising to around fifty during the recovery of the late 1930s. However, during the 1937-08 academic year, evening graduate courses were offered on an experimental basis, and this program was so successful that it was expanded and grew rapidly thereafter.[534]

Davis put the new program in historical context for the trustees in a 1933 memorandum:

... the trend in engineering education is definitely towards putting the professional part of the engineer's training on the graduate level .... What the trend of the times does demand of us is . . . our scheme of a professional specialized fifth year (graduate) curricula, together with the inauguration of a strong and carefully planned scheme of part-time adult education for our graduates and for other young engineers in our community . . . examples are those now available in economics of engineering, in industrial chemistry, in communication engineering, and in applied mathematics.[535]

At the same time, Harvey Davis brought in new faculty who would be dedicated to teaching in the generalized undergraduate curriculum, who would teach more specialized graduate courses, and who would perform fundamental research within laboratories funded by industry. Although such activity had been going on from the inception of the institute in mechanical engineering and its associated fields of metallurgy and applied chemistry as

[534] Ralph A. Morgan, "Graduate Studies Program at Stevens," *Stevens Indicator*, 81 (1963), no. 2, 14.

[535] H. N. Davis, unpublished notes, *Op.Cit.*, I-6.

well as electrical engineering, Davis encouraged funded research in other areas such as psychology, acoustics, and marine engineering, such research supported by industry being a recommendation of the Wickenden Report. Davis wrote later,

A very considerable amount of fundamental research is going on in universities and engineering schools that is inspired by and partly or wholly paid for by industry. Usually this begins as private research by some member of the teaching staff, to whom industry turns as his reputation becomes established.[536]

Among the industrial research laboratories started by Davis was a "Human Engineering Laboratory" run by the new humanities instructor in psychology, Johnson O'Connor. An industrial psychologist who had worked for General Electric, O'Connor gave aptitude and vocational guidance tests to Stevens students and irritated the faculty by effecting a change in the grading system from a precise mathematical one to simple letter grades. His laboratory was one of the first of its kind in the New York metropolitan area and was so successful in testing personnel of local companies that O'Connor resigned from Stevens and moved his testing and consulting laboratory to New York City in the early forties.[537] Another Davis research effort, in what today would be considered environmental engineering, was conducted in "smoke abatement." Davis hired Colonel Elliot Whitlock, a retired Army officer and member of the class of 1890, as research professor of mechanical engineering. Whitlock conducted research with students, for example making thousands of observations of smoke from locomotives in the railroad yards in Jersey City and from stacks of local businesses. He and Davis went on the radio to make anti-pollution addresses and were instrumental in fostering a Hudson County law which lessened smoke generation.[538]

In 1930, Harold Burris-Meyer joined the Humanities faculty to help present the ASME's fiftieth anniversary play, *Control: A Pageant of Engineering Progress*, in the Stevens auditorium where the founding meeting of the ASME had taken place. This play was directed by G. P. Baker, head of the Yale Drama School, and is said to have been the first multi-media theatrical presentation, having used sound, still projections, 16mm silent

---

[536] H. N. Davis and C. E. Davies, "Industrial Research by Mechanical Engineers." *National Resources Planning Board.* (1943), VI-8, 328.

[537] Newell Mason, "Harvey N. Davis," in Potter, ed., Op.Cit., I-C, 51.

[538] Ibid., 51; Wm. G. Cristy, "The Story of the Fight on Smoke," *Stevens Indicator*, 48 (1931), 144, Elliot H. Whitlock, "Smoke Abatement Work," and Harvey N. Davis, "How the Problem of Smoke Abatement Has Been Attacked," *Ibid.*, 49 (1932), 68-72.

film, 16mm sound film, 33mm silent film and a wide variety of lighting techniques. A drama teacher and specialist in acoustics, Burris-Meyer became a humanities professor and did applied acoustical research for nearby Broadway theaters. Carrying on work in acoustics started by A. M. Mayer at Stevens, he developed a "Stevens Sound Control System," which was used at the New York Metropolitan Opera, and conducted research in psychoacoustics supported by the Rockefeller Foundation and government agencies during World War II.[539]

As it turned out, the most successful of the laboratories was that of Kenneth S. M. Davidson (1898-1958). Davidson created a premier testing laboratory for America's Cup yachts, both defenders and challengers. Davidson's Experimental Towing Tank Laboratory started with tests of yacht models in the sixty-foot swimming pool in Walker Gymnasium on the Stevens campus. Davidson, a professor of mechanical engineering who came to the institute in 1929, was a pioneer in testing small boat models as opposed to the larger and more costly ten- to twenty-foot models previously used in tests. Davidson's hypothesis about racing yachts was that, contrary to the prevailing opinion in the early 1930s, the hydrodynamic performance of the hull was as important as design of the rig. Davidson's use of small models, initiated in 1931, was cost-effective and made model testing a routine design tool by the late 1930s. Davidson's pioneering role was that he made experimental analysis as prominent in ship design as it was in the field of aerodynamics.

Early tests identified problems with using small models, which were later overcome. For example, small models were towed at reduced speeds, making measurement of resistance difficult. Davidson employed a combination of precise speed control, lightweight materials, and unique measuring tools to solve the problems. In 1932, Davidson visited Olin J. Stephens II to obtain a yacht model and to explain the nature of his research to this prominent Sparkman and Stephens yacht designer. As a result of this visit and the tests of a model which Stephens provided, the two became friends for life and associates in the development of America's Cup defenders. They shared a passion for yachts and sailing; for example, Davidson was a crew member on *Stormy Weather* in a race to Norway in 1935 captained by Rod Stephens and on the Stephens-designed *Ranger* during the 1937 America's Cup de-

---

[539] Sinclair, *A Centennial History, Op.Cit.*, 6-7, and L. S. Goodfriend, "Theater Acoustics - 1930," in unpublished Potter, ed., Op.Cit., VI-c.

fense. The early support and encouragement from Olin J. Stephens was crucial for the success of Davidson Laboratory.[540]

With the assistance of two undergraduates Allan B. Murray 1933 and
Anthony Suarez 1932, Davidson made a breakthrough in research in 1933
by comparing the performance of a full-scale yacht to its model. The result
was the first successful prediction of resistance on a full-sized hull on the
basis of tests on a small model -- in this case a replica of an actual yacht,
the *Gimcrack*. The demonstrated success of this breakthrough resulted in a
joint effort by Olin Stephens and other yachting enthusiasts, like Seward
Johnson, with Davidson in seeking funds for a proper towing tank facility.
This effort resulted in funding of five thousand dollars from the Research
Corporation and individuals to build the first Stevens towing tank in the
Navy Building by June 1935, a tank made of steel, one hundred and one feet
long, nine feet wide and four and one-half feet deep, with the foundation
isolated from building vibrations.[541] Davidson's testing apparatus was
designed for heeled as well as upright positions of the model, and it also
tested the aerodynamic lift/drag ratio of the rig. Later in 1935, Davidson for
the first time was able to predict the windward performance of a yacht from
tests performed using a replica of the yacht in the form of a small model.
This second breakthrough resulted in Olin Stephens's intention to utilize
the procedures in Davidson Laboratory in design of hulls. But further confirmation of reliability of the laboratory was needed. In 1936, Stephens and
W. Starling Burgess, both of the company of Sparkman and Stephens, made
a further confirmation by using the Stevens laboratory to test the previous
challenger and defender of the America's Cup in 1934, namely *Rainbow* and
Endeavor. The results gave the designers additional confidence to rely on
Davidson for partnership in the design process.

Consequently, later in 1936 the designers returned with four models of
hulls for the yacht *Ranger*. Davidson found the third model to be the best
performer, and *Ranger* was built from it. *Ranger* defended the cup in 1937
and brought fame to the designers and to the model-testing methods of
Davidson. Due to this wide recognition, Davidson's Towing Tank Laboratory was able to branch into a wide assortment of projects by 1939, when it
entered military-related research on vessels such as planing craft, flying
boats, and naval vessels. America's Cup races were suspended during
World War II and for over a decade afterwards, but they resumed in 1958

---

[540]See Michael S. Bruno, "Davidson Laboratory and the Experimental Towing Tank: The History
of Towing Tank Research at Stevens", unpublished paper dated April 13, 1993, and Obituary of
Davidson, *Stevens Indicator*, 74 (1958), no. 2, 14.

[541] "The America's Cup Races," *Ibid.*, 82 (1965), no. 1, 10.

with the twelve-meter class. Because of its pre-war reputation, Davidson's Towing Tank Laboratory tested both challengers and defenders in the 12 meter class from 1958 to 1967: Defenders tested included *Columbia* (1958), *Weatherly* (1962), and *Constellation* (1964), and the challengers included *Sceptre* (1958, after the race), *Gretel* (1962), and *Sovereign* (1964). As a result of the tests on *Sovereign*, the laboratory developed the ability to evaluate a yacht in oblique waves. *Intrepid*, the 1967 and 1970 winner -- with a revolutionary Stephens design of a shorter keel separated from the rudder -- and *Courageous*, the winner in 1974 and 1977, were both a result of the Olin Stephens-Davidson partnership in design of America's Cup sailing yachts.

A model is tested in rough wave conditions in Davidson's Towing Tank Laboratory.

Meanwhile, trustee chairman Kidde was able to bring aboard Robert C. Stanley, the "Nickel King," in 1934. Kidde handed off the reins of the chairmanship to the prestigious president of International Nickel in 1936, and Stanley made decided contributions until the end of Harvey Davis's presidency in 1951. He was able to bring onto the board the "Zinc King," Edgar Palmer, who built the second Stevens dormitory, Palmer Hall, the largest dormitory on campus at the time, housing seventy-six students. President of New Jersey Zinc from 1912 and an old yachting friend of Robert C. Stanley, Palmer also gave lavishly to Princeton University and dreamed of someday uniting Princeton's school of engineering with that of Stevens.[542]

As America's employment picture brightened in 1938, undergraduate enrollments improved by about one hundred to reach 605. Evening students were admitted to the graduate masters program in 1938, and graduate enrollments jumped from forty-eight in 1938-09 to 307 in 1939-40. Another trustee brought to Stevens by Post and Kidde was John Reynard Todd. Post knew Todd from the Rockefeller Center project: Todd managed the building and the business of the completed center. Walter Kidde knew Todd through his friendship with John D. Rockefeller, Jr. A lawyer and building contractor, Todd was a Republican activist who raised a record sum of $734,000 as financial chairman of the New Jersey Republican Committee in 1928. He was the father of Webster B. Todd who later rebuilt Williamsburg, Virginia, as a historic village for Rockefeller.[543] Webster B. Todd became a trustee in 1946 to replace his father on the board. Kidde also brought on another unrelated Todd, namely, J. Herbert Todd 1918, heir to the Todd Shipyards Corporation started by William H. Todd in the bay between Weehawken and Hoboken. J. Herbert Todd's formal education at Stevens was interrupted by World War I, when he dropped out to enlist in the Navy, but he was later commissioned as a naval engineer and assisted in the construction of the *Tennessee*. In the 1920s, he studied naval architecture and the construction and repair of ships in his father's firm. During World War II, the Todd family had five shipyards on the Atlantic, Pacific and Gulf coasts engaged in construction or conversion of ships for the government. J. Herbert Todd started at the bottom of the industry in ship repair as a riveter while on college vacation in 1915. During the time he was on the trustees, J. Herbert Todd was a recognized authority on design and construction of vessels, as well as marine-fuel oil equipment.[544]

In the years 1940-41, America was gearing up to produce Lend Lease arms for Britain and for its own possible entry into the war. Federal funds became available for all kinds of military-related research projects and for crash industrial training programs, and thus the Depression was definitely over. Moreover, by 1942, the giving to the Annual Fund had reached a record level of $185,000 and fully two-thirds of the alumni participated. Besides the gifts by the trustees, annual giving had been of vital assistance

---

[542] *Ibid.*, 60 (1943), 2, 9.

[543] "In Memoriam; John R. Todd," *Ibid.*, 62 (1945), 4, 42, and "Commencement Citations," *Ibid.*, 95 (1978), 21.

[544] *Ibid.*, 64 (1947), 1, 18, and 60 (1943), 4, 6.

to assure the survival of Stevens during the Great Depression when Stevens had eleven deficit budgets in a row.[545]

Around the end of World War II, Stanley contributed a good deal of the $51,400 raised for the creation of a Stevens Research Foundation which had its own board of directors led by Davis as its president.[546] This non-profit corporation was formed to carry out research to develop new products and manufacturing processes after the war. Grants were made to support current research in powder metallurgy, towing tank projects, and sound research.[547] In 1947, the Mott Field House was built through a $110,000 gift by the General Motors millionaire, Charles Stewart Mott 1897, who had been brought onto the board in 1939. This field house contained a new basketball court to supplement the older one in Walker Gymnasium.[548]

Walter Kidde's nephew, professor Alfred Bornemann 1927, carried on the tradition of the Stevens faculty in the study of metals. Bornemann did post-graduate work in Germany to earn a D.Ing. in chemistry, and he returned to Stevens in the early 1930s to teach chemistry with a specialty in metals.[549] Bornemann credits Robert C. Stanley with saying, "We are determined that more metallurgy shall be taught at Stevens," and, along with Harvey Davis, with helping to create a vision for a department of metallurgy which Bornemann was to head. In 1938, William H. Peirce, Stevens's Edison-era "Copper King" who was then seventy-three, was brought to the campus and gave money for a Peirce Metals Laboratory in the top floor of the Navy Building. In that year, Bornemann taught his first graduate course in metallurgy.

Also in 1938 when Davis was president of the ASME, Gregory J. Comstock, a powder metallurgy pioneer, delivered an ASME paper which so impressed Davis that he hired Comstock as associate professor of powder metallurgy and as director of a powder metallurgy laboratory at Stevens. Stanley's International Nickel Company subsidized Comstock's research and outfitted an old building next to the tennis courts at the northern end of the campus as a powder metallurgy laboratory. Westinghouse Electric, Western Electric, and other major companies also gave contracts to Comstock's Powder Metallurgy Laboratory during and after World War II. The technology involved sintering metal powder held in molds in ovens to

---

[545] Harvey N. Davis, "An Open Letter to Stevens Alumni," *Ibid.*, March 1942, 6.

[546] *Ibid.*, 61 (1944), 2, 11.

[547] *Ibid.*, 61 (1944), 3, 11-12.

[548] "Charles Stewart Mott Field House," *Ibid.*, 62 (1945), no. 5, 5-6.

[549] "Who Are the Faculty; Dr. Alfred Bornemann '27," *Ibid.*, 75 (1958), no. 4, 12. Bornemann attended Stevens at the same time as his two cousins, John Kidde '28 and Fred Gilman '29.

create special metal shapes, porous metal shapes, or metal-carborundum shapes. The laboratory produced cutting tools, high-heat-resistant turbine nozzle blades and afterburner linings for jet aircraft, radioactive-gas filters of porous nickel, and solid, nuclear-fuel elements.[550]

Meanwhile, Peirce set up a trust in his will for Bornemann's Peirce Metals Laboratory. After Peirce's death in 1944, funds from alumni were added to the Peirce bequest, and, in 1947, the Peirce Memorial Laboratory of Metallurgy building was constructed adjacent to the Morton Memorial building to house the newly created department of metallurgy with Bornemann as its head. Meanwhile, Walter Kidde had died in 1943, and his fellow trustees, along with the other alumni through the SAA, made contributions for the Kidde Memorial Building.[551]

This architect's sketch shows the Morton building to the left and the new Peirce (partly hidden) and Kidde buildings. The architect of both the Peirce and Kidde buildings was Robert F. Jacobus, 1904, the son of David S. Jacobus. The builder was the son of Walter Kidde, John F. Kidde, 1928, and later a trustee -- Kidde Construction Company put up both buildings at cost.

---

[550] H. Guendel, "Powder Metallurgy-1938," in Potter, ed., Op.Cit., VI-d, and Bornemann, *Ibid.*, 18-23.

[551] "The Stevens Fund -- An Interim Report," *Stevens Indicator*, 63 (1946), no. 5, 12; "The Stevens Fund -- An Interim Report," and "Ground Broken For Buildings," *Ibid.*, 64 (1947), no. 5, 6 and 10; "The Stevens Fund," *Ibid.*, (1948), no. 5, 6; and Alfred Bornemann, *Stevens Institute in the Field of Metallurgy, Op.Cit.*, 11.

CHAPTER 18

Stevens During World War II

One year before the Japanese surprise attack on Pearl Harbor on December 7, 1941, volunteer military drill started on the Stevens campus. Mathematics professor Charles O. Gunther signed up more than three hundred Stevens students to practice two hours of military drill under Lieutenant A. Northup, U.S. Army (ret.) and to take non-credit mini-courses on such subjects as organization of the ordnance department, defense against chemical warfare, and military discipline. A lieutenant-colonel in the Army's ordnance department reserve, Gunther was looking forward to the day when Stevens could have an ROTC unit, preferably in ordnance. Gunther stated at the start of the program that Stevens "has always done its part in every national emergency and has contributed much to both arms of the Service -- Army and Navy. Of this record, Stevens Institute of Technology is justly proud and naturally desires to do her part in carrying out the present program of national defense."[552] Gunther's voluntary program didn't last long, because Stevens, as in World War I, was picked for the site of an official Navy program which replaced the volunteer effort when war came.

Also, President Harvey N. Davis had other priorities and introduced a new program to train technical personnel in defense industries a year before Pearl Harbor. He said, "Production is more important to defense than combat training." There was, he said, a severe shortage of technical personnel, especially because Congress had instituted a draft for preparedness in September 1940 which temporarily allowed such personnel as well as engineers to be drafted.[553] Davis became nationally known at the time for his speeches and radio talks about industrial preparedness. In one speech he said,

Production is even more important than the training of soldiers. I therefore believe it to be the patriotic duty of every young engineer who is subject to the draft and is not already in a defense industry to get himself a job in such industry at once.[554]

In January 1941, Davis obtained a $140,000 grant from the U.S. Office of Education to establish a Defense Industries Training School at Stevens as

---

[552] "Volunteer Military Drill," *Stevens Indicator*, December 1940, 1.

[553] Quoted in *Ibid.*

[554] Quoted in N. O. Mason, *Op.Cit.*, 69.

part of a nine-million dollar federal program to give intensive three-month courses to train technical personnel on the sub-professional level. The grant paid for Stevens faculty to give non-credit and tuition-free courses to 650 adult students working in defense industries or to high-school graduates needing training to enter such industries.

After the attack on Pearl Harbor, American entry into the war did not have immediate beneficial effects for the Allies. In fact, in the first part of 1942, the Japanese continued to score victories in Southeast Asia and the Germans were consolidating their position in the Balkans as well as driving ever deeper into the USSR. At Stevens and several other engineering colleges, the reaction was to initiate an accelerated cooperative plan for the regular undergraduate engineering students. This wartime program combined study at an increased pace with work in war-related industries, and Stevens was one of the first colleges to undertake this effort by instituting a trimester format in the spring of 1942. Davis took the lead in this nation-wide effort with speeches on the duty of engineering colleges to increase production and to supply engineering manpower quickly. He estimated that there were only 300,000 engineering graduates in the United States, and there should be at least twice as many. He thought that Stevens had a unique responsibility given that "Stevens is in an area in which there is a great volume of war industry, much of it still rapidly expanding."[555] Thus, by May 1942, with faculty approval, Stevens went on a twelve-month trimester schedule of sixteen weeks each instead of the semesters of eighteen weeks. Students were required to spend two terms on campus and one term in a war industry. The war-industry jobs were always held by Stevens students who rotated into vacated positions. Throughout the war, Stevens made war work mandatory for all "civilian" students who were not in naval officers training programs. The faculty passed a patriotic regulation that required no less than thirty weeks of work in war industries as a pre-requisite for graduation. As a result, the number of hours doubled in which students studied and worked, but the program was a success -- portions of the sophomore and junior classes were participating in the war effort as engineers' assistants by the summer of 1942. Moreover, of the graduating class of 1942, 113 received commissions as naval officers, and Davis reported to the trustees that "Our graduates who did not enter the naval service went into defense industries. That is where they belong. That is where they are needed."[556] In addition, he arranged for pre-freshmen in 1942 to spend twelve weeks in July and August in a new orientation term at

---

[555] Harvey N. Davis, "The War Program of Stevens Institute," *Stevens Indicator*, May 1942, 3.

[556] "The College in Defense Service," *Ibid.*, December 1941, 7.

the Johnsonburg Camp to do surveying, leveling, and road and bridge layouts. Prior to this, students had taken this work at a leisurely pace over the course of the summer and one midwinter session. Davis said that the new orientation was to include a rigorous calisthenics and athletics program to "condition the group for the grind that lies ahead."[557]

Harvey N. Davis was president of Stevens Institute during World War II. Davis made the senior class "sprint" to graduate several weeks early in the spring of 1942 so that they could aid the war effort.

In early 1942, the Defense Industries Training School became the War Industries Training School and admitted more students. In a speech to the alumni association on the topic of "The Duty of Engineering Colleges," Davis said,

This War is going to be won -- or lost -- in the factories of America. . . . We used to talk about the man behind the gun. Now we must talk about the seventeen men behind the man behind the gun . . . . What the engineering schools must do, if they are to play their full part in helping to win this war, is to increase to the utmost the number of technically trained men available to the war production industries. We must somehow contrive to tap considerable new sources of human material capable of receiving technical training on each of the various levels from the lowest sub-professional engineering skills, to the highest professional activities that graduate students in engineering can fit themselves to perform.[558]

---

[557] *Ibid.*

[558] Harvey N. Davis, "Duty of the Engineering Colleges," *Stevens Indicator,* March 1942, 3.

He told the alumni that the faculty was straining to the utmost to perform double duty, not only increasing the training of regular engineers, but also of the sub-professionals. By mid-1942, the sub-professional trainees had increased to five hundred full-time students, a number nearly equivalent to all the regular undergraduates. Teaching loads for faculty went up forty percent.[559]

In all, some five thousand sub-professional technical personnel were trained in the Stevens War Industries Training School and its predecessor, the Defense Industries Training School. Each three-month term accommodated three hundred students in day and evening courses in twenty-nine different topics of engineering and engineering management. As much as possible, courses were lifted from the regular curriculum and modified to fit the needs of technical personnel. Certificates were awarded for mini-programs in drafting and machine design, electricity, metallurgy, and industrial engineering. The records of the program include aptitude tests by the Laboratory of Psychological Studies, as well as employment and placement records. Many of the younger trainees were of college-level caliber in aptitudes, and fully twenty-two percent found employment with Wright Aeronautical Corporation during the war, with lesser percentages being hired by Western Electric, Bendix, Bethlehem Steel, and Bell Labs. The women enrollees were known locally as WITS after the initials of the War Industries Training School, WAVES and WACS being the nicknames of women in the services at the time. The WITS were the first undergraduate female students on the Stevens campus, and during the war, they composed nearly fifty percent of the students in the program. At the end of the war, it was reported that the performance of several WITS at Bell Labs, Western Electric, and Worthington Pump and Machinery Corporation was highly praised.[560]

As a result of his reputation for promoting production, in November 1942, Davis was appointed head of the newly created Office of Production Research and Development (OPRD) "to insure rapid appraisal and prompt and effective use of new processes, materials, mechanisms, and inventions in the production of war goods." With the trustees' approval, Davis was given a leave of absence but retained his title as president of Stevens as he

---

[559] *Ibid.*

[560] Robert H. Baker, "The Stevens War Industries Training School," *Stevens Indicator*, vol. 62, no. 1 (1945), 3-5 and 20. After the war, Stevens retained its industries training program under another name, The Industries Training School. With funds from the federal government cut off in 1945, the new training school collected tuition often provided by corporate employers or by the GI Bill of Rights in the case of the many veterans who entered the program.

moved to Washington D.C. and returned to Hoboken on weekends. The idea of the OPRD was to complement the Office of Scientific Research and Development (OSRD) under Vannevar Bush. Bush's OSRD was the focal point for research and development on new weapons, and the OPRD was the focal point for research and development on increasing production of war-related goods and materials in the civilian sphere.[561] As it turned out, Vannevar Bush's operation, particularly in the Manhattan Project for atomic weapons development and in projects for radar development, became heavily involved in mobilizing civilian companies for weapons systems, and OSRD's activities and monetary resources were enormous compared to Davis's OPRD.

However, from 1942 to 1944 under Davis, OPRD reviewed and promoted inventions and improvements in production processes, and it centralized production problems from the half-dozen bureaus which previously dealt with them. It authorized research and development contracts with academic, industrial, and private laboratories to solve problems.[562] After pilot projects and prototypes showed an improvement could work, it disseminated information and in some cases subsidized with federal money the initiation of solutions in industries.[563] In Washington, Davis created subgroups from among the hundreds of expert consultants to OPRD. These included a War Metallurgy Board and a Chemical Referee Board. Through "know how" bulletins sent to corporations, these subgroups disseminated information on standard improvements in production methods.

Successful OPRD projects to increase production were the development of a new synthetic rubber for tires, lightweight magnesium-aluminum alloys for aircraft, processes for increased steel production and higher-speed milling of metal, and the use of powder metallurgy for small machine parts. Among the products which OPRD investigated and developed was penicillin, which was first used during the war for military personnel before it came into use for civilians. OPRD researchers identified strains of penicillin, seeing if they could be multiplied; discovered what nutrient solutions were best for them; and worked out the production processes. Davis said in 1944 that OPRD's work led to production of penicillin in "amounts that would have seemed utterly fabulous a year ago."[564] He also created an

---

[561] Donald M. Nelson's testimony before the House Appropriations Committee, quoted in *Stevens Indicator*, Oct. 1943, 3.

[562] *New York Times*, November 11, 1942.

[563] "President Davis Goes to Washington," *Stevens Indicator*, December 1942, 3.

[564] Harvey N. Davis, "Third Commencement in 1944," *Ibid.*, Dec. 1944, 5. At the end of his tenure in Washington in 1944, Davis supported a new organization which became known as the

OPRD-directed Technical Deferment Committee which worked to prevent technical personnel from being inducted into the armed services by local draft boards. This committee is credited with saving some ten thousand young technical experts for defense industries. In addition, in 1943 he headed the Davis-Keyes Mission to England to obtain closer transfer of technical information and inventions useful for increasing the Allies' wartime production.[565]

In 1943, Stevens was chosen by the Navy as one of 131 of the nation's 1,700 colleges and universities for a V-12 program. Previously, the United States Naval Academy and NROTC programs like the V-7 program of 1940 and V-10 program of 1942 had ensured the presence of enough graduates with sufficient mathematics and science subjects needed to become naval officers. However, in the summer of 1942, the Army draft age was lowered from twenty to eighteen, and the Navy concluded that its NROTC pool would therefore be squeezed just at the time its fleets were expanding dramatically. Consequently, the Navy initiated V-12 which was approved by the Roosevelt administration in December 1942. In place by May 1943, it was an accelerated year-round officer training program which required students to take an increased number of credits in a trimester format so that they could graduate and be on active duty in two years. Participating institutions had to admit at least two hundred men of superior ability enlisted or inducted into service by the Navy through nationwide academic testing and physical examinations. Since the trainees were exempt from the draft and obtained a free college degree, the program was immensely popular with students and their parents.

The silver lining for colleges was recognized by the government when it set up the program, i.e., since drafting all able-bodied eighteen year olds would dramatically lower the number of students, the V-12 students would help to keep colleges open during the war. In fact, during the selection of the 131 colleges, one thousand interested institutions scrambled to be included. Stevens was one of nine purely engineering colleges selected. Besides a steady flow of students, colleges chosen for the V-12 program received other benefits, namely, that colleges would be paid four percent of the pre-war value of buildings, and tuition, board, and lodging, as well as operating and administrative costs. Academic instruction and teaching

---

Technical Industrial Intelligence Committee under the Joint Chiefs of Staff. After victory in Europe in 1945, this committee sent over 600 experts to write reports on German industry and was a crucial player in the efforts to obtain German technology and expert scientific and engineering personnel.

[565] Donald B. Keyes, "Dr. Davis and War Production, 1942-44," *Stevens Indicator*, January 1948, 7.

personnel were chosen by the colleges. Curriculum requirements of the Navy included one hour per week in naval organization and also rigorous physical training and military drill. Officially, V-12 students were in the Navy, therefore they were assigned to colleges by the Navy and wore uniforms on campus; and the naval part of their instruction was given by naval officers. Since Stevens had already instituted a trimester format by the summer of 1942, few scheduling difficulties appeared. [566]

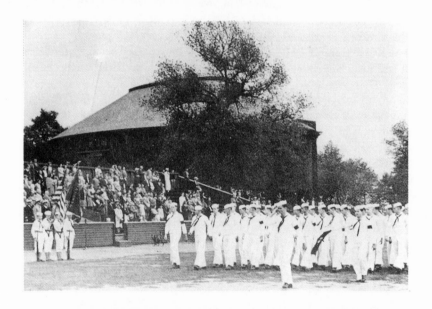

When the Stevens V-12 program began in July 1943, the institute looked like a military training school with a class of 510 uniformed students, as seen here in a Navy review with the William Hall Walker Gymnasium in the background.

The Navy's V-12 program allowed students to transfer to other units, and replacements were added to keep up the school's muster roll of about five hundred students until late in 1944 when the figure dropped to three hundred. At its height in 1944, the vast majority of students in undergraduate classes were in uniform. Among the outstanding Stevens students in this accelerated two-year degree program were several future professors including Robert F. Cotellessa, professor of electrical engineering and provost of Stevens; Richard A. Easterlin, an economics professor at the University

---

[566] James G. Schneider, *The Navy V-12 Program; Leadership for a Lifetime*(1987), 1-20.

of Pennsylvania; and Robin B. Gray, Regents' Professor and director of aerospace engineering at Georgia Tech. Industrial leaders included Joseph H. Anderer, president of Revlon; Oscar M. Gossett; chairman of Saatchi and Saatchi Compton Worldwide; Earl W. Mallick, a vice president with U.S. Steel; and Wallace Markert, Jr., a vice president with Babcock and Wilcox. Thomas J. Allshouse became a rear admiral in the Navy.[567] Under the wartime conditions there was a complete reversal of the Depression-era deficit budgets and lack of students -- Stevens had more students during World War II than at any time in its previous history.

Money also came in from war-related research grants in Davidson's Towing Tank Laboratory. Davidson received contracts as early as 1939. when the lab personnel grew to twelve, to test the performance of planing craft, flying-boat hulls, and some naval ships. At entry of America into the war, Professor Davidson was testing the Navy's warship designs in Stevens's towing tank and at the Navy's own towing tank at Carderock in Maryland. But in 1941, the Stevens facility was doing defense work exclusively, testing cruisers, destroyers, and high speed-naval craft such as PT boats. The projects investigated the steering, turning, and directional stability of hulls in conditions of pitching and rolling. In that year, Davidson was a member of the National Defense Research Committee and the National Advising Committee for Aeronautics, the predecessor of NASA.[568]

By 1942, Davidson Towing Tank Laboratory was heavily subsidized by the Navy and its staff grew to twenty-five early in the year, partly as a result of a new facility, Towing Tank No. 2, built on Hudson Street by Hegeman and Harris with funds supplied by Vannevar Bush's OSRD.[569] This tank was a very wide seventy-five feet and designed for study of surface and underwater ships' turning ability. It was bigger than any Navy or Allied test tank and equipped with a rotating arm -- the fact that the Navy did not build its own tank for such purposes showed extraordinary confidence in Davidson's work. During the war, it was in operation sixteen hours a day. In 1943, the Navy funded yet a third tank three hundred feet long for testing flying-boat hulls and high-speed craft. The building, again built by Hegeman, extended nearly a block down Hudson Street between 6th and 8th Streets adjacent to the building that housed the second tank. The personnel expanded to sixty by January 1944 when work was being conducted on amphibious LVT landing vehicles used in island invasions in the Pacific as

---

[567] *Ibid.*, 388.

[568] "Experimental Towing Tank. 1941 Annual Report," Davidson Laboratory Archives.

[569] K. Davidson and J.B. Drisco, "Technical Memorandum No. 64, Nov. 6, 1942, OSRD Section no. C7-sr458-440," Davidson Laboratory Archives.

well as on D-Day in Normandy; the DUKW, an amphibious two-and-a-half-ton army truck; and army pontoon bridges which were used over the Marne, Rhine, and other European rivers after D-day.[570] Davidson's work was crucially important for the Navy, owing to early release of new ships to the fleet -- many warships going into active service without adequate operational trials. His facility tested models which produced data on rudder angles when turning circles correlated with degrees of heel or yaw, data that full scale-trials would have produced in peacetime. In all, during World War II, the laboratory tested models of twenty-one military landing craft, 121 flying boats, eighty-one destroyers, eleven cruisers, and twenty-nine other types of Navy vessels as well as thirty-one cargo vessels and twenty-eight tankers.[571]

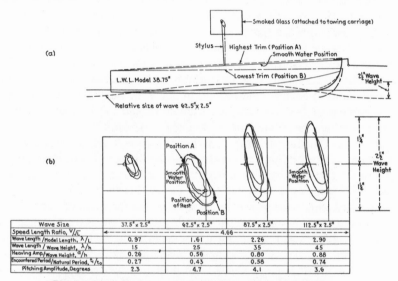

Wave Size	37.5"x 2.5"	62.5"x 2.5"	87.5"x 2.5"	112.5"x 2.5"
Speed Length Ratio, $V/\sqrt{L}$		4.66		
Wave Length/Model Length, λ/L	0.97	1.61	2.26	2.90
Wave Length/Wave Height, λ/h	15	25	35	45
Heaving Amp/Wave Height, a/h	0.26	0.56	0.80	0.88
Encountered Period/Natural Period, t_e/t_0	0.27	0.43	0.58	0.74
Pitching Amplitude, Degrees	2.3	4.7	4.1	3.6

Diagram (a) shows the arrangement of the model and apparatus to obtain a graphical record of pitching in waves at Professor Davidson's Towing Tank Laboratory. Diagram (b) shows graphical records obtained for a model of a v-bottom boat in waves of four different sizes.

Among other research work by faculty and alumni was a top-secret project in sound systems for psychological warfare that was carried out by Professor Burris-Meyer's acoustics laboratory. During this work in 1942, Burris-

---

[570] "1943 Annual Report. Experimental Towing Tank," dated January 1944, and "The Experimental Towing Tank. Ten Year Report," SIT, 1946, 14-15, Davidson Laboratory Archives.
[571] *Ibid.*, 10 and 14.

Meyer said that the research was developing new techniques in sound which would revolutionize the motion picture industry after the war, and that, "Almost anything can be done with sound as the sense of hearing is more effective as a path to the emotions than is vision."[572] One of Burris-Meyer's students, Lewis S. Goodfriend 1944, became editor of *Noise Control,* the journal of the Acoustical Society of America. Goodfriend attacked the problem caused by mechanical vibration and shock phenomena in airborne noise.[573] He was also a founding member of the Audio Engineering Society in 1948.[574]

Among alumni, H.V.R. Scheel 1905, worked to improve supplies for the production of uniforms on the Textile Clothing and Leather Section of the War Production Board, and Otto S. Beyer 1907 was appointed director of the Division of Transport Personnel of the Office of Defense Transportation starting in 1942.[575] Under August G. Pratt 1903 who had become its president, Babcock and Wilcox designed all the boilers for the hundreds of Liberty Ships, the emergency merchant fleet built to supply England.[576] As Chrysler's executive engineer, H. T. Woolson 1897 designed the engines for that company's tanks used in the war.[577] As chief civilian engineer for the United States Army Air Force, Frederick J. Wierk 1923, a plant-design engineer before the war, designed and constructed air bases at Quonset, Rhode Island; Gander, Newfoundland; Nova Scotia; Greenland; Iceland; Ireland; and Scotland. This chain of bases, which became known as the "Bridge of Invasion," was necessary for the tremendous buildup in preparation for the Normandy invasion. While working at Quonset, Wierk conceived of and designed a round, metal-plate hut which for a while bore his name but was later changed to designate the place of manufacture -- the Quonset Hut.[578]

The most noteworthy military-related projects of World War II were the development of radar by the MIT Radiation Laboratory and Bell Labs, and the Manhattan Project to develop the A-bomb. On the former project there were contributions by Stevens faculty and alumni: Physics professor Edwin J. Schneider was on leave from 1941 to 1945 to work at the MIT "Rad Lab" as a systems engineer and to lead a group in the development of ground radar, particularly the SCR-615 system. He was also a liaison with the

---

[572] *Stevens Indicator,* December 1942, 6.

[573] *Ibid.,* 74 (1957), no. 6, 22.

[574] *Ibid.,* 65 (1948), 3, 15.

[575] "Stevens Men in the Press," *Stevens Indicator,* July 1942, 8.

[576] "Maritime M Award," *Stevens Indicator,* December 1942, 10.

[577] *Stevens Indicator,* March, 1947, 21.

[578] *Ibid.,* 75 (1958), no. 4, 44-5.

British branch of the laboratory and a consultant to the secretary of war on radar.[579] Meanwhile, Robert E. Poole 1921 was developing key radars for Bell Labs, which in its work with the Rad Lab developed over seventy different radar models for different uses. Poole's work at the Whippany, New Jersey, Bell Labs facility included secret radio-object detection devices for the Navy's firing control systems as early as 1937. Later, he had key roles in the design and development of radar for use by the Navy's carrier-based planes and of the Army's automatic-tracking radar, the SCR-545, for anti-aircraft batteries. The output of his work included detailed manufacturing specifications and blueprints of the SCR-545, and then visits to Western Electric factories to work out the problems during early manufacture of these radar units, which became standard Army equipment.[580] Professor John Hawkes of the physics department took a leave to join the Naval Ordnance Laboratory in Washington to work on radar for sighting distances for naval guns.[581]

The origin of the Manhattan Project was in the 1939 letter of Albert Einstein to President Roosevelt asserting that vast amounts of power could be developed by a nuclear chain reaction; and, although he was uncertain that a bomb could be built, he warned of German physicists' work to that end. The first government research into the possibility of an A-Bomb started in 1940, but a crash program was not started until after the United States entered the war. In December 1941, research and development for an atomic bomb was overseen by Vannevar Bush's OSRD, and the Army's General L.R. Groves, backed by billions of dollars, was brought in during the summer of 1942. The early history of the project belongs to physicists drawn from Princeton, Chicago, Columbia, and Berkeley, but, soon after the most likely production possibilities were worked out, Groves and the physicists turned to America's engineering companies to help in the actual production of fissionable material and the components of the bomb itself. This top secret work involved scores of companies and thousands of engineers, many of whom were kept in the dark about the ultimate aim of their projects.[582]

Physicists discovered basically three possible ways to obtain enough fissionable material for a bomb: namely, Enrico Fermi's chemical pile method of producing plutonium, centered at the University of Chicago; Ernest O. Lawrence's isotope separation method using a huge cyclotron, centered at Berkeley; and the gaseous separation method of John R. Dunning and his

[579] *Stevens Indicator*, 63 (1946), 5, 11.

[580] Robert E. J. Poole, "Early Military Radar Design Experiences," *Ibid.*, 3.

[581] *Stevens Indicator*, May 1942, 8.

[582] Henry DeWolf Smyth, *Atomic Energy for Military Purposes* (Princeton, 1948), chapters 1-4.

colleagues at Columbia in New York City. Since it was undetermined which method would succeed, all three were pursued in a crash effort to beat the Germans in producing a bomb. Stevens alumni were heavily involved in all three efforts, but particularly in the gaseous diffusion effort. In gaseous diffusion, physicists determined that fissionable U-235 could be produced by filtering it out from a gaseous form of mostly U-238 in an electromagnetic separation process in which the gas would be repeatedly guided through banks of filters until the lighter U-235 was collected higher up in the banks. They were appalled but not daunted by the many technical operations of great difficulty which faced them.

A major engineering problem was that uranium gas was corrosive and ate into not only organic materials but also all man-made materials, as well as most metals -- except for nickel. Since the gas had to go through microscopic holes in thousands of "diffusion barriers," it would eat into such filters and the connecting piping if such equipment was not made of nickel or at least coated with nickel. Engineers determined that the barrier material had to be made of extremely purified nickel. All the piping, valves, pumps, and barrier chambers had to be absolutely airtight for the process to work. Also the gases and residues were highly radioactive, necessitating extremely careful design and utmost care in engineering. The technology developed during the Manhattan Project was totally revolutionary and untried, and many physicists doubted the project's success even while working on it with engineers.[583]

One immediate need was for a site to build the enormous factories that would house the equipment for the electromagnetic gaseous separation of U-235 from U-238, as well as the operations of the other projects attempting to produce the critical mass needed for a few bombs. Physicists calculated that the factories would be the world's biggest ever. Groves and his advisors chose Boston-based Stone and Webster Incorporated, the premier builder of electrical-generating and gas-works plants in the United States. The company specialized in containment structures, and was already building three TNT plants for the war effort. Contacts were made between the Army and Stone and Webster through Edward S. Steinbach 1908, who was sworn to secrecy before being briefed at a meeting in the Standard Oil Building in New York City. Subsequently, the company was retained for the largest government contract ever awarded to a private corporation. Chosen by a deputy of Groves with the help of Steinbach and M.J. Whitson of Stone and Webster, the site for the project was a deserted stretch of land in Tennessee

---

[583] *The Manhattan Project; Making of the Atomic Bomb.* U. S. Department of Energy, History Division(1999), 1-39.

which became known as Oak Ridge after the name of a local geographical rise. The project at its height required up to one-seventh of the electrical power in the entire United States, and the site had the advantage of being close to the enormous electrical generating power of the Tennessee Valley Authority. The Army's contract with Stone and Webster not only called for construction of the $400 million uranium separation plants at the Clinton Engineer Works at Oak Ridge, but also the factories for other methods there, as well as construction of villages and a city to hold 75,000 people, complete with schools and a hospital for the families of scientists, engineers, and technical personnel working on the bomb projects.[584]

Russell T. Branch (1889-1973) 1912 had been construction manager of Stone and Webster since 1930 and in 1942 was the executive vice president for construction. He was put in charge of all construction at Oak Ridge. Branch gathered eight hundred engineers and draftsmen in a special Stone and Webster unit in Boston which was under constant guard and working in secrecy on "Project X." One day a Stone and Webster engineer would be tapped for the unit and subsequently "disappear" into it. The project necessitated interaction with physicists, and Stone and Webster did pioneering work in communication with them: Company specialists became part physicist and were able to develop some physicists into part engineers in order to move the project forward. As a result of the success of Oak Ridge, Branch became president of Stone and Webster in 1944, and, under his direction, the company in 1954 pioneered the design of the first full-scale American nuclear power plant for the generation of electricity.[585] August C. Klein (1887-1948) 1908, who had joined Stone and Webster in 1920, was Branch's project engineer at Oak Ridge in charge of the actual construction of the electromagnetic diffusion factory as well as the design and on-site construction of the town of Oak Ridge. Under Branch, Klein also supervised the engineering design of the first atomic pile for plutonium production at Fermi's Argonne Forest Laboratory of the University of Chicago, and he later became Stone and Webster's vice president on atomic energy and supervised the company's role in the A-bomb tests in 1946 at the Bikini and Enewitok atolls in the Pacific.[586]

---

[584] David Neal Keller, *Stone and Webster, 1889-1989*(1989), 180-187.

[585] "Branch, Russell Taynton," *National Cyclopedia of American Biography,* 58 (1979), 126.

[586] *Stevens Indicator,* 65 (1948), no. 1, 22, and obituary of Klein, *Ibid.,* 65 (1948), no. 2, 47. A later graduate of Stevens, Louis R. Weissert of the class of 1951, was Manager of the Fuel Laboratory of Babcock and Wilcox's Nuclear Development Center in charge of research and development of the company's pressure vessel components for nuclear reactors. He was loaned to Oak Ridge in 1954 where he was engineering consultant on heavy equipment fabrication, nuclear

At the same time Oak Ridge was being built, the Jersey City laboratories of the M. W. Kellogg Company were doing secret research into the problem of gaseous diffusion. Morris W. Kellogg had been chosen as the specialist in chemical engineering because his company was judged to be the best at designing and building oil refineries, and during the early stages of the war his company was building a large percentage of the high-octane aviation gasoline plants.[587] Kellogg chose C. Keith to form a top-secret unit, Kellex, to work out the chemical and metallurgical engineering problems of gaseous diffusion -- "Kell" stood for Kellogg and "ex" for secret. The company's orders from General Groves were to design a plant for gaseous diffusion and do it fast. Kellex gathered Kellogg engineers and assembled other top talent on three floors of the Woolworth Building in New York City, its personnel totaling over three thousand at the height of activity. Kellex worked with Columbia University physicist Harold C. Urey and Princeton's Hugh Taylor among others to solve the barrier and containment problems. After agonizing trial and error, Kellex developed a suitable barrier tube made from powdered nickel sintered together in ovens -- a process used by Stevens's Professor Comstock in the powder metallurgy laboratory on campus before the war.[588]

The powdered nickel barrier was only found suitable after very high quality nickel was obtained from Robert C. Stanley's International Nickel Company. In fact, Stanley's company, which then produced eighty-five percent of the world's supply of nickel, was approached in 1943 and asked to supply tons of powdered and highly purified nickel for the Manhattan Project. Groves financed expensive special equipment in an International Nickel factory to produce it, and by 1944 the company had produced eighty tons of such powder. In a closely guarded Nash garage in upper Manhattan, Kellex engineers and Columbia University physicists tested sintered nickel barriers with uranium gas and sent the test results to Professor Taylor at Princeton for analysis. For months he kept reporting back that the barriers were not efficient enough. Then International Nickel refined its powder until its purity was such that it passed the test.[589]

The next problem was how to mass-produce barrier tubes from powdered nickel which hitherto had been made in small experimental units in a

---

fuel element manufacturing, nuclear metallurgy, reactor system chemistry and quality control. *Ibid.*, 81 (1964) no 1, 27.

[587] "Stevens Holds Spring Commencement," *Stevens Indicator*, July 1945, 5.

[588] Stephane Groueff, *Manhattan Project; The Untold Story of the Making of the Atomic Bomb*(1967), 22, 105.

[589] *Ibid.*, 161, 274.

Columbia University laboratory. The Oak Ridge plant needed thousands of barriers, and Kellex brought in Union Carbide to design and develop mass production techniques. Lyman A. Bliss 1922, president of Union Carbide Nuclear Company by 1956, participated in the development of mass production of the nickel filters through a research team at Union Carbide.[590] Next, International Nickel's laboratories in Huntington, West Virginia, developed for Kellex the first successful large-scale production of the barrier tubes. This process was based on a batch method -- assembly line manufacture being considered unfeasible -- devised by the Bakelite Company's laboratory.[591] According to this scheme, laminating machines were needed in the manufacture of the tubes. Kellex chose a company specializing in design and construction of machines to label and package small arms for the military, the New Jersey Machine (NJM) Corporation of Hoboken located at Willow Avenue and 16th Street. Its president was George W. Von Hofe 1921. The company was already involved in top-secret research projects. NJM's Walter Fried, Stevens M.E. 1931, had designed, constructed, and installed the instruments and apparatus, including the rotating arm, for Towing Tank Nos. 2 and 3 at Davidson's Towing Tank Laboratory on the Stevens campus. The company also had contracts with the Frankfort Arsenal and the Naval Gun Factory to design and construct optical production machines for gunnery sighting. Other projects included designing and developing machines to automatically load fabric machine-gun belts, machines for the manufacture of sighting devices for tanks, as well as subcontracting for other war-related contracts with Picatinny Arsenal. On the Manhattan Project, NJM's Edwin K. Wolff 1937 supervised design of the special production machinery for "diffuser barrier tubes," and Richard F. Dede 1936 was in charge of setting up and operating a pilot plant to test production.[592]

All this took place in 1944, and it was not until after the defeat of Germany in the spring of 1945 that Oak Ridge's gaseous diffusion and isotope separation plants had produced enough U-235 for a bomb, the second and third bombs being made from plutonium. The world's first A-bomb test took place at the earliest possible date, on July 16, 1945, at a desert site in Los Alamos, New Mexico. In attendance were all the luminaries of the

---

[590] *Stevens Indicator*, 77 (1960), no. 1, 7.

[591] Groueff, *Op.Cit.*, 274-8.

[592] Unpublished post-1948 company document entitled "History and Background of the Personnel of the New Jersey Machine Corporation, Hoboken, New Jersey. Design Engineers, Developers, and Producers of Special Machines and Equipment," in Stevens Special Collections. Arthur R. Schaefer '41 later became President and Chairman of the Board of NJM.

project, with J. Robert Oppenheimer, General Groves, and Vannevar Bush leading the group. Also in attendance was a young physicist who had graduated from Stevens with an M.E. in 1939, and who had also earned an M.S. in physics from there in 1941: Frederick Reines, who was a teaching fellow at Stevens in 1940-1941.[593] Like Wolff and Dede, Reines had been a student of David D. Jacobus, another son of David S. Jacobus, who, after graduating from Stevens as an M.E. in 1921, had obtained a Ph.D. in physics from Harvard and taught mathematics and physics at Stevens from 1930 to 1937. He worked at the MIT Rad Lab from 1942 to 1946 in the mechanical section of the ground division before returning to Stevens.[594] Later, Jacobus was to direct the mechanical engineering division of the Brookhaven Laboratories before returning to Harvard in 1957 as a research fellow where he supervised the construction of Harvard's first Electron Accelerator.[595]

Reines obtained his Ph.D. in physics from NYU in 1944, and in 1956, with Clyde Cowen of the Los Alamos Scientific Laboratory, discovered the neutrino for which he was later awarded a Nobel Prize. Enrico Fermi, a physicist whose work helped to harness the atom for the first atomic bomb, and another physicist, Wolfgang Pauli, had theorized about the existence of the neutrino to account for disappearance of energy from the decay of radioactive material in which electrons are emitted. Reines, in 1956, built an apparatus to actually detect the existence of the neutrino, a particle without electrical charge and with a vanishingly small mass, but theoretically part of the "glue" which holds atomic nuclei together. The apparatus was a subterranean tank holding one hundred gallons of water which served as the target for neutrinos emitted by a reactor. The neutrinos were sensed by a scintillation system containing more than one thousand gallons of sensitive liquid and 330 photoelectric eyes.[596]

Somebody had recognized early the brilliance of the young man, because he wound up near the Trinity test site's ground zero on July 15, 1945, adjusting measuring instruments only hours before the countdown to the world's first atomic blast. In October 1945 after the end of the war, when it was permissible to reveal non-secret aspects of the atomic bomb project, Reines wrote from Los Alamos, New Mexico, in the *Stevens Indicator* for his classmates:

---

[593] *71st Annual Catalog. Stevens Institute of Technology, 1941,* 67.

[594] *Ibid.,* 16.

[595] See "Men in the News," *Stevens Indicator,* 88 (1971), 3, 26.

[596] "Reines Helps Trap Nuclear Ghost," *Ibid.,* 73 (1956), 5, 17.

The night of the test we had occasion to go out to the near vicinity of the tower now complete with bomb. With normal weather this action would call for no comment but this was not normal weather. Lightning storms were in evidence at all points of the compass. We were more than concerned that a lightning stroke on the tower might set off the bomb and blast us into oblivion. From what we saw early the next morning, we realized that "blast" was the wrong term -- at the distance we were working, the proper word was "vaporized."

Finishing his work at 2 a.m., Reines and his colleagues retreated to the base camp 9½ miles away, showered, and proceeded to wait for the blast. The test time approached, but the weather caused a delay for an hour and a half. At 5:20, just before dawn, Reines was informed over the public address system that the firing would

. . . occur in ten minutes and another voice instructed us to lie on the ground, facing away from the bomb. The instructions continued, not to look at the bomb even through our welder's glass (.5% transmission of normal sunlight) until the mountains to the south lit up. Minute by minute Dr. Allison calmly informed us of the passage of time, "5 minutes," "4 minutes." The unbearable agony of waiting mounted and people started muttering nervous remarks. Then it was one minute, then 45 seconds. The automatic mechanism took over and a blinding flash lit up the mountains to the south with an apparent intensity many times that of the noon-day sun, delineating all the features of the mountains, and giving a definite feeling of warmth. . . . We rolled over and looked at the explosion through our welder's glass. I saw an extremely bright ball which rose rapidly into the air, cooling as it went. Removing the glass, a beautiful purple ball could be seen. It rose to about 40,000 feet and then mushroomed out forming a huge gray cloud. At about 45 seconds after the first flash the blast wave arrived. It lasted about a second. There was a sort of rumble and the silence followed by a feeling of increased pressure on the ears, of the kind you get when descending a steep hill in a car. By that time the gray cloud drifted along and we at the base camp began to realize that the era of nuclear explosives had begun. A short period of awed silence followed and then suddenly everyone started cheering, shaking hands, and exchanging comments of amazement at the "miracle" they had just witnessed.[597]

Later, as the head of the testing division of the Los Alamos Scientific Laboratory, Reines directed the technical phase of the explosion of the first hydrogen bomb at the Enewitok Atoll in the Pacific.[598]

---

[597] Frederick Reines, "Atomic Bomb Experiment," *Stevens Indicator*, October 1945, 15-16.
[598] "Reines Helps Trap Nuclear Ghost," *Op. Cit.*, 18.

CHAPTER 19

Funded Research During the Height of the Cold War

S tevens Institute of Technology participated in the wave of expansion in funded research during the Cold War which dramatically increased sections of its faculty. According to Jess Davis, the fourth president of Stevens, who served from 1951 to 1971 during the height of the Cold War, out of some 1,500 institutions of higher learning in the United States in 1960, Stevens was twenty-sixth in the dollar volume of its funded research.[599] This ranking was astounding for such a small institution, essentially an undergraduate engineering college with a tiny graduate program before World War II. Moreover, federal grants provide money for overhead beyond the costs of the specific research project for the support of research facilities, such as the towing tanks in Davidson's laboratory. The Department of the Navy, because it funded more research than any other federal agency at the institute, determined the overhead rate for all federal research grants obtained by Stevens during the height of the Cold War -- at a whopping 150 percent. For every federal dollar in research money awarded to Stevens by any federal agency, say the National Science Foundation (NSF) for medicine-related research, another $1.50 was added automatically for overhead.

During the Cold War, the Department of Defense (DOD) spending for research and development rose from $2,63 billion in 1955 to $8,16 billion in 1968. Similarly, research sponsored by NASA rose from $74 million to a high of $5,93 billion in 1966, and the AEC from $385 million to a high of $1,65 billion in 1969. In total, the federal government's R&D expenditures went from $3,31 billion in 1955 to $16,21 billion in 1969.[600] As a result, from the end of World War II to approximately the end of the Vietnam War, the science and engineering community had little need to fight for government funds for fundamental and applied research because they were readily forthcoming.

Leading the way at Stevens Institute in the dollar level of funded research during the Cold War was Davidson's Towing Tank Laboratory (later called Davidson Laboratories). It built upon its world-leading reputation established during World War II, and, during the Cold War, it became a recognized national resource for military research. As a result of its reputation

---

[599] "At the Alumni Banquet, Dr. Davis Reflects on the 60s at Stevens," *Stevens Indicator*, March, 1960, 8-10.
[600] Daniel S. Greenberg, *The Politics of Pure Science* (1971), 311.

and close ties with military personnel, research contracts were often brought to the laboratory instead of the laboratory seeking out such contracts. Its top-secret contracts with the DOD, particularly the Department of the Navy, consistently accounted for over half the total sum of funded research at Stevens during the 1950s and 1960s, some $1.5 million to $2 million a year.[601]

In 1946, Professor Kenneth Davidson and L. Schiff published a landmark paper on the procedures for testing models of displacement vessels for the prediction of vessel maneuverability, procedures developed during World War II. In the late 1940s, staff which included Boris V. Korvin-Kroukovsky and Daniel Savitsky began research on the spray and porpoising characteristics of various hulls of seaplanes and naval planing vessels.[602] To accurately and rapidly process the wealth of data obtained from these investigations, Davidson's laboratory bought the campus's first computer in 1951 with the help of Office of Naval Research (ONR) funding, a machine designed by Northrup dubbed "Mad Ida" because of its name: Magnetic Drum Digital Analyzer. This machine had hundreds of vacuum tubes which gave off enormous heat and required the "blockhouse" which housed it in the Shippen Building to be thoroughly air conditioned. Especially important

---

[601] A typical example of the level of funding of Davidson Laboratory compared to other departments is shown in a memo from the director of research to department heads dated October 5, 1966, Stevens Special Collections:

	FY 1964-5	FY 1965-6
Computer Center	$ 98,894	$ 122,877
Physics	566,510	686,455
Chemistry	235,183	270,898
Metallurgy	81,891	107,112
Mech. Eng.	44,150	77,404
Elect. Eng.	40,313	39,071
Mathematics	21,070	8,315
Mngmnt. Sci.	---	5,048
total of acad. dept.	$1,089,016	$1,317,178
Interdisciplinary	$ 14,525	$ 7,353
Psych. Studies	211,848	236,534
Davidson Labs.	1,457,351	1,534,640
Stevens total	$2,772,740	$3,095,705

For a more complete comparison of volume of research by departments for the years 1964 to 1973, see K.C. Rogers, *A Report from the President: Traditions and Tomorrow*, SIT printed pamphlet, June 1974, in Rogers's file in Stevens Special Collections, 12, which shows well over fifty percent of the total research revenues of the institute came in through Davidson Laboratories in the period.

[602] Bruno, *Op.Cit.*, 14.

was that the use of computers allowed Davidson Laboratories to lead the way in defining the behavior of surface ships in confused irregular seas. This breakthrough development was then adapted by hydrodynamic research laboratories throughout the world. Some of Davidson Laboratories' software was purchased by the U.S. Navy to analyze the seakeeping behavior of high speed naval vessels.[603]

In the stability of submerged vessels, the lab tested design characteristics of a model of the submarine USS *Albacore,* a pioneering experimental torpedo-shaped vessel that was the forerunner of the nuclear submarine fleet.[604] Then it tested a model of the USS *George Washington,* the world's first standard nuclear-powered, missile-firing submarine. In these and other tests of naval and commercial ship designs, the lab studied factors such as ability to maintain a straight course, to change course without overshoot, to turn in small radii, to stop in a prescribed distance, to hover at a certain depth, and to maneuver while backing. This work involved measuring the stabilities and instabilities caused by relationships between hull design and tail fins, the size of the fins and rudders, steering control systems, propeller design, and vibration, among other factors. Such design variables were used in investigations of models of Navy torpedoes, the Mark 13, Mark 16 and Mark 40. In addition, the finless Polaris missile's instabilities were predicted correctly by the lab.[605]

In 1948, C. Nuttal and M. Bekker started the Transportation Research Group which would lead to some of the laboratories' most historically significant work decades later. This group adapted the techniques of testing scale models of sea-going vessels to testing land vehicles in a soil-tank which was built in the laboratories in 1950. Later, an endless rubber belt was constructed to test Army tracked-and-wheeled model vehicles for stability and resistances. Bekker left in 1952 to become founding director of the U.S. Army's Land Locomotion Laboratory.[606]

After the death of Davidson in 1958, the new director of Davidson Laboratories, Professor John P. Breslin, obtained an Elecom vacuum tube computer with so many vacuum tubes that one technician was employed

---

[603] Phone conversation with Daniel Savitsky, professor emeritus of ocean engineering and past director of Davidson Laboratories, Oct. 22, 1999.

[604] Bruno, *Op.Cit.,* 14.

[605] Lukasik, "Ocean Waves," *Op.Cit.*; "The Davidson Laboratory," *Research Report 1961,* 36-37; Stevens Special Collections, and Albert Strumpf, "Design Factors That Presently Limit the Maneuverability of Controlled Hydrodynamic Vessels," *Research on the Campus: Its Meaning for Industry and Society; Transcript of Proceedings at the Third Research Conference, Nov. 17, 1965,* 53-57, Stevens Special Collections, and Bruno, *Op.Cit.,* 14.

[606] Bruno, *Op.Cit.,* 15.

almost full-time changing them. Under Breslin, Stephen J. Lukasik also worked on studies for the Ballistics Research Laboratories of the U.S. Army, such as investigations of explosives emitting extremely high-temperature condensed plasmas enclosed in electromagnetic fields.[607] Davidson Laboratories continued the study of the fluid dynamics of helicopters, seaplanes, hydrofoils, and landing craft, as well as ship propeller dynamics and acoustics -- the latter being a specialty of Breslin and S. Tsakonas. Daniel Savitsky created a design methodology for planing hulls which has been used throughout the twentieth century. Other research involved assisting the Navy plan fleet movements by determining, for given sea conditions, the most efficient route ships could take to achieve maximum speed. This work led to the lab calculating the point of impact of the Apollo Command Module on the basis of the immediate sea and weather conditions.[608] Effects of the ocean on drilling rigs, sea walls, bridges, and shorelines were studied by placing sensitive pressure indicators, fluid velocity indicators, and shear stress indicators on the ocean floor. For these studies, analogous records were used to create computer models of the frequencies of ocean phenomena which then could be replicated as much as possible in the lab.

Other government sponsors of projects for the Davidson Laboratories in the early years of the Cold War were the U.S. Coast Guard, the Maritime Administration of the Department of Commerce, the U.S. Bureau of Public Roads, the U.S. Tank Automotive Center, and the Limited Warfare Laboratory. Among the corporate sponsors were Westinghouse Electric Corporation, North American Aviation, Continental Aviation and Engineering Corporation, Chrysler Corporation, and General Dynamics. But, the largest contracts came from the Navy Department, whose sponsors for studies done at the lab were its Bureau of Ships, David Taylor Model Basin, U.S. Naval Training Devices Center, Bureau of Naval Weapons, and ONR.[609] As a result of contracts in the period 1946-1965, the testing facilities and research staff of Davidson Laboratories grew rapidly from eighteen in 1946 to 120 at the peak of the Cold War.[610]

In 1962, I. Robert Ehrlich, a graduate of West Point and a former tank commander, became head of the Land Transportation Division after serving as Bekker's deputy in the Army Land Locomotive Laboratory. He and his

[607] Lukasik, *Op.Cit.*, and "Studies in Ballistics," *Research at Stevens. Report for 1966, Op.Cit.*, 72.

[608] J. P. Breslin, "The Davidson Laboratory," in Potter, *Op.Cit.*, II, vi-b, 13; Bruno, *Op.Cit.*, 18; and "Motion Response Characteristics of the Apollo Command Module in Rough Water," *Research at Stevens; Report for 1966, Op.Cit.*, 54.

[609] *Research at Stevens. Report for 1966. Op.Cit.*, 51-72.

[610] J. P. Breslin, *Op.Cit.*, II, section vi-b, 12.

staff obtained a five year DOD THEMIS grant in 1965 to create an academic center of excellence in vehicle mobility. In the late 1960s and early 1970s, Erlich, Irmin Kamm, the son of the German engineer who developed the aerodynamic form for automobiles called the K-body, and M. Peter Jurkat did research on such transportation topics as highway center-barrier effectiveness, characteristics of tire-usage on different terrains, and driver behavior in varying degrees of stability, as well as investigations of the stability of various military vehicles. This research led to the design of the reinforced concrete New Jersey barrier used to divide lanes on the nation's highways, as well as an early model of a computerized driving simulator.[611]

M. Peter Jurkat, a 1957 Swarthmore graduate, held an M.A. from North Carolina in mathematics and statistics earned in 1960. As a statistician and engineer for Marketer's Research Service between 1959 and 1961, Jurkat had established his reputation in the field of computer applications to transportation planning by creating demographic and economic models of metropolitan areas to determine the investment capacities of rail and road systems. This led to his participation in laying out the plan for the Interstate Highway system around Philadelphia. Then, while working for the ITT Corporation as a senior programmer analyst from 1962-1965, Jurkat in his late twenties helped to design and develop computer-based communications and control systems for the USAF Strategic Air Command (SAC) to secure high-speed message and data communications among all SAC bases worldwide, Washington D.C. and the SAC Headquarters in Omaha -- the first secret military computer network using multiple IBM 7030 (Stretch) mainframes, ITT proprietary communications, switching processors, and terminals. With this background, Jurkat was hired in 1965 by Ehrlich and Breslin to head the transportation analysis group of the Davidson Laboratories' transportation research division.

Beginning with funding under the THEMIS grant and continuing at the rate of some $250,000 a year for the next ten years, Jurkat's group continued research in off-road mobility of various Army vehicles, including jeeps, trucks, armored personnel carriers, amphibious vehicles, and tanks

---

[611] M. Peter Jurkat and James A. Starrett, "Automobile-Barrier Impact Studies Using Scale Model Vehicles," *Highway Research Record,* 1967, no. 174; I. Robert Ehrlich and M. Peter Jurkat, "Characteristics of Tire Usage in the Eastern United States," Davidson Laboratory Report No. SIT-DL-68-7-798, August 1968; F. D. Hales and M. Peter Jurkat, "Driver Behavior in Controlling a Driving Simulator with Varying Stability," *Proceedings of a Symposium on Handling of Vehicles Under Emergency Conditions,* Institute of Mechanical Engineers, 1969, M. Peter Jurkat, "A Theoretical Investigation of the Stability of the M151 1/4-ton Military Truck," Davidson Laboratory Report, No. SIT-DL-69-1420, September 1969, and M. Peter Jurkat, "The Davidson Laboratory Driving Simulator," Davidson Laboratory Technical Note No. SIT-DL-69-7-812, December 1969.

like the M60-A1 and the Abrams. This project synthesized the work of a generation of research into a computer model that predicted the speed with which a vehicle could travel over any terrain, taking into account soil characteristics, slope, surface roughness, visibility, driver capability and time on and off obstacles and crossing rivers. Jurkat, along with C. Nuttall who had left Stevens to join the Corps of Engineers' Waterways Experiment Station in Vicksburg, and Peter Haley of the Tank and Automotive Research and Development Command in Warren, Michigan, published this model along with its computer code in 1979. Subsequently, the use of this model was mandated by the DOD in the procurement of all military vehicles.[612] With further modifications done by Jurkat and Peter M. Brady, Jr., B.S. 1961, another researcher in Davidson Laboratory who later became an associate dean, the model became the NATO Reference Mobility Model for movement of military vehicles to counter a Soviet attack through such terrain as the Fulda Gap in Germany.[613] It was also used as a guide for the design of new military vehicles like the Bradley Fighting Vehicle and NASA's Lunar Rover.[614] After the Army added realistic graphics to the simulation model, it was used for battlefield training at West Point and for planning and executing actual attacks such as in the Gulf War and the operations in Serbia.

Funded research in academic departments was also helped by the attitude of the military during the era of the Cold War. In 1957, Vice Admiral Howard E. Orem, USN (Ret.) was made assistant to Jess Davis for devel-

---

[612] M. Peter Jurkat, "Mathematical Formulation of Wheeled Vehicle Dynamics for Hybrid Computer Simulation," Davidson Laboratory Report, No. SIT-DL-70-9-1452, February 1970, M. Peter Jurkat, "Background Notes in Vehicle Dynamics," Davidson Laboratory Report No. SIT-DL-70-9-1466, June 1970, M. Peter Jurkat, "Data and Program Considerations for Path Selection in the AMC Mobility Model," Davidson Laboratory Report No. SIT-DL-71-9-1564, October 1971, Awni N. Bkoutros and M. Peter Jurkat, "Effect of Variations of the Terrain Digitizing Interval of the AMC '71 Mobility Model," Davidson Laboratory Report No. SIT-DL-73-9-1682, October 1973, and M. Peter Jurkat, Clifford J. Nuttall and Peter Haley, "AMC '74 Mobility Model," Davidson Laboratory Report No. SIT-DL-74-9-1769, August 1974. The latter report was published by the U.S. Army Tank Automotive Command (TACOM) as Technical Report No. 11921 (LL-149) in August 1974.

[613] M. Peter Jurkat and Peter M. Brady, Jr., "Terrain-Vehicle Interrelationships (The Underground Guide to the NATO Mobility Model), Volume 1: Operational Modules; Volume 2: Obstacle Module," Davidson Laboratory Report No. SIT-DL-79-0-2058, September 1979; Peter W. Haley, M. Peter Jurkat, and Peter M. Brady, Jr., "NATO Reference Mobility Model," Edition I, U.S. Tank-Automotive Research and Development Command Technical Report No. 12503 for the North Atlantic Treaty Organization, October 1979; and Peter M. Brady, Jr. and M. Peter Jurkat, "Analysis of Vehicles Grossing Gaps, a Fording Model," Davidson Laboratory Report SIT-DL-83-9-2370, September 1983.

[614] I. Robert Ehrlich, "Vehicle Research," *Research at Stevens. Report for 1966. Op.Cit.*, and Bruno, *Op Cit.*, 20-22.

opment of research and was soon made director of research in charge of organizing and developing the entire Stevens funded-research program, a position he held until 1969. He was a 1922 Annapolis graduate who received a Navy-sponsored engineering degree from Columbia in 1929. During World War II he had been chief of naval operations, and his last appointment before retirement was as the Navy representative to the three-member Joint Strategic Survey Committee which advised the Joint Chiefs of Staff on political-military policy and strategy.[615] In spite of his statement that, "Under the present world conditions, I believe the West should have at its disposal all the military strength it can muster," Orem followed the ONR's enlightened policy on fundamental research.[616] The ONR's policy, influenced by the physicist Alan T. Waterman as its chief scientist and future founding director of the NSF, was that the Navy could benefit from a general advancement in science instead of science simply applied to naval advancement. During the late forties and early fifties, Waterman and en-lightened naval officers, known as "bird dogs" for their persistence, funded many projects which had little immediate utility for the Navy, including experiments in high-energy physics. Orem followed this policy at Stevens, stating in 1966 that

Fundamental research is an integral part of Stevens's existence. The scale and in-tensity of research performed on the campus add significantly to the vitality of the college. In turn, the spirit of free inquiry which has traditionally been a part of academic life is the driving force for the pursuit of new knowledge by research scientists and engineers. One of the principal aims of the science and engineering college is to contribute to man's basic fund of knowledge and to sharpen the intellectual tools of investigation and experimentation. By fostering an active research program, Stevens is fulfilling its obligation in this area and is, at the same time, training new researchers to make significant contributions in the future.[617]

As I. I. Rabi, the Nobel Laureate at Columbia University, said, "The Navy saved the bacon for American Science" during the early Cold War period. That is not to say the Army was lacking such an attitude. As Dwight D. Eisenhower said, "Scientists and industrialists must be given the greatest possible freedom to carry out their research. . . . Scientists and industrialists are more likely to make new and unsuspected contributions to the devel-opment of the Army if detailed instructions are held to a minimum."[618]

---

[615] "Research Program," *Stevens Indicator*, October 1957, 17.

[616] *Stevens Indicator*, April 1962, 9.

[617] *Research at Stevens. Report for 1966, Op.Cit.*, 1-2.

[618] Quoted in Greenberg, *Op.Cit.*, 133.

During the late 1950s and 1960s, the most successful academic department in funded research was the physics department with levels of funding approaching one million dollars a year. In part, this success came because physicists in general had attained an unprecedented position of influence with the federal government through their leading roles in the two most important projects of the second world war, the Manhattan Project to develop the A-bomb and the Radiation Laboratory work at MIT to develop radar. These successful crash programs had mobilized thousands of the best scientists and engineers in the nation, thus setting up a model for post-war research activity led by physicists. Leaders of the wartime projects -- Rabi at Columbia, Lawrence at Berkeley, and Waterman with the ONR and NSF -- were able to convince the government to sponsor enormous increases in funding for scientific research in general, and physics in particular. In 1956, it was revealed that Russian physicists were building a high-energy center at Dubna near Moscow. Recognizing an "accelerator gap," a panel of distinguished physicists recommended that federal spending for research in physics be expanded dramatically. After the panic created by the 1957 Soviet launching of Sputnik, the same panel recommended even more spending on physics research.[619] In this context, sizable grants totaling millions of dollars came to Stevens's physics department, particularly in plasma research, but also in other areas.

Grants for research in physics took off at Stevens after the arrival in 1956 of Winston H. Bostick (1916-1993) as the physics department's head. Bostick had the connections necessary to obtain grants. He had earned his Ph.D. from the University of Chicago in 1941 just before the United States entered World War II. In 1941, his first job was with the top-secret Radiation Laboratory at MIT, the spawning ground for the Cold War younger generation of physicists who had been protégés of Waterman, Rabi, Bethe, and others. There, he became a section chief from 1945 to 1946 and wrote four chapters on pulse transformers for MIT's technical series volume, *Pulse Generators*. Bostick remained at MIT after the war, when the name of the Radiation Laboratory was changed to the Research Laboratory for Electronics. During his research in this lab from 1946 to 1949, he invented a "fizz chamber," an early bubble chamber to observe atomic particle behavior, and he participated in the design and construction of MIT's microwave linear accelerator. As a professor at nearby Tufts College from 1948 to 1954, Bostick commenced research on plasmas, which became his specialty, namely, on how to control these gaseous ions and electrons by magnetic forces as well as how to study their diffusion patterns. At that

---

[619] *Ibid.,* 214-228.

time, some of the first of Bostick's ninety-plus articles on plasmas appeared. From 1954 to 1956 he returned to full-time research at the Livermore Laboratory at Berkeley where he photographed what he called "plasmoids" or well-defined vortex-shaped rings or spirals of plasma gases. In 1956, he was considered an old hand in the plasma field and was conducting research for containment of H-bomb emissions for the AEC when he was hired as department head at Stevens.[620]

Two leading research professors during the height of the Cold War were Kenneth S. M. Davidson and Winston H. Bostick.

Bostick received considerable funding to continue his work developing plasma "guns" and plasma "motors." Bostick's plasma "gun" consisted of two tiny wires of titanium with deuterium occluded in the metal, the wires held in a ceramic button-like base the size of a pencil eraser. Currents of up to ten thousand amperes were forced through the wires in a fraction of a second to vaporize the wires, thus creating a jet of titanium and deuterium ions and electrons traveling at a speed of 450,000 miles per hour -- in 1956, the highest speed attained with plasma. Using multiple guns fired across a magnetic field, these bursts of plasma created "plasmoids," which, when

---

[620] *World Who's Who in Science. A Biographical Dictionary of Notable Scientists from Antiquity to the Present.* (R. R. Bowker, 1968), 216, biographical sketch of Bostick in *International Journal of Fusion Energy,* I, no. 1 (March 1977), 55, and "Atomic Physicist to Head Department," *Stevens Indicator,* July 1956, 10.

photographed, resembled various shapes of galaxies during formation and aging. He returned to his work on plasmoids with David Finkelstein and later with V. Nardi and W. Prior.[621] Using his technique, Bostick created miniature "barred" spiral galaxies, many-armed spiraled galaxies, and "S" shapes. Known for his interest in astrophysics, Bostick then came up with some heady theories. He thought galaxies acted like his plasmoids, their spiraling arms folding in towards the center due to magnetic forces. Bostick theorized that his laboratory experiments were replicating the formation and youth of galaxies, and, further, that the gravitational energy generated in the process was transformed into magnetic energy that created an ever-growing magnetic field around each galaxy. As the strength of the field increased, the galaxies repelled each other. As a result, he suggested, "It may be that these magnetic fields repel the magnetic fields surrounding other galaxies which are in the process of formation. Thus, for the first time, we can begin to understand the mechanism that brings on the expansion of the well-documented expanding universe."[622] In addition, Bostick received contracts from the AEC, the United States Air Force, Republic Aviation, and Grumman Aircraft for research in the fields of thermonuclear fusion and thrust from plasma.[623] In the ten years from 1946 to 1955, Stevens's physics department averaged seven full-time regular faculty, but, after the arrival of Bostick, the number rose to fourteen members in 1959 and doubled again to twenty-nine full-time regular faculty by 1969. These figures do not include visiting and full-time research professors who were hired as a consequence of funded research. Thus, the physics department became Stevens's largest and most prestigious academic department.

Grants totaling millions of dollars were obtained for a multi-year MEGA-TRON project of physics Professor Kenneth C. Rogers. A Columbia Ph.D. of 1956, Rogers had been a post-doctorate research associate at Cornell's Laboratory of Nuclear Studies from 1955 to 1957 when he rapidly learned the technology of particle-accelerator design and constraints. At Stevens, David Finkelstein involved Rogers with an idea for a megatron or a million gauss betatron which Rogers subsequently built in the late 1950s and early 1960s. Rogers obtained funding for a string of grants totaling millions of dollars from the DOD's Advanced Research Projects Agency (ARPA) to do

[621] Prof. George Schmit was the theoretician of the plasma group who wrote his pioneering book, *Physics of High Temperature Plasmas* in 1966.

[622] Winston H. Bostick, "The Pinch Effect Revisited," *International Journal of Fusion Energy*, I (1977), no. 1, 20-27, "Galaxy Matter," *Stevens Indicator*, January 1957, 13-14, and "Smallest Rocket Motor Developed at Stevens," *Ibid.*, 77 (1960), no. 1, 11-12.

[623] "Who Are the Faculty?" *Ibid.*, 75 (1958), 1, 9.

fundamental research on intense relativistic electron beams which might be used in another type of generator to disable ICBMs.[624] In this MEGATRON project, Rogers and his Ph.D. student Lawrence A. Ferrari designed and built a betatron to accelerate electrons into a circular orbit within a toriodal vacuum chamber filled with plasma. Next, they designed and used a very rapid discharge capacitor bank to drive a magnetic field which squeezed the electrons down to a thin thread. In contrast to conventional betatrons where magnetic fields reach their peak values in the order of milliseconds, the fields in the Stevens Megatron reached their peak values in microseconds. The project overcame severe technical difficulties in construction of the apparatus by invention of components. These included a new design and construction of plasma switches in a vacuum using "Bostick Guns" to withstand the high currents involved -- these switches were an advancement in plasma-switch design and were developed by Rogers and Professor George Yevick through another grant.[625] The research, which went on for nearly ten years, was ultimately successful although the beam had a modest intensity of 1,000-amp and one million-volt electron energy, not up to the expected level and not enough for a weapon, but much stronger than energies created in traditional betatrons. The funding from this project supported twenty researchers in various capacities including Stephen J. Lukasik as a research professor of physics.

Based on Rogers's accomplishment with the megatron and on his managerial skills in obtaining large grants, Rogers replaced Bostick as department head in 1967. As head, Rogers restructured the physics department and successfully competed nationally for a one-million-dollar NSF Department Development Grant which resulted in the hiring of promising new faculty and the acquisition of improved research equipment. In turn, this accomplishment factored in his being chosen in 1972 as the fifth president of Stevens.[626]

Another well-funded physics department research project using plasma was called CHALICE (Compression Heating and Long Injection Cusp

---

[624] Only a few of Rogers' grants are in Special Collections, for example $172,257 listed in K.C. Rogers, "QUARTERLY LETTER REPORT NO. 5 on Megatron Accelerator," 12 September 1962; no figure is attached to K. C. Rogers, D. Finkelstein, L. Ferrari, and I. Mansfield, "A High Efficiency Capacitor Bank Study" AT(30-1)1921 supported by the AEC, U.S. Army Signal Supply Agency, and Republic Aircraft Corporation, but in a phone call of Oct. 25, 1999, Rogers recalled that the MEGATRON project brought in around $500,000 a year at its peak.

[625] George J. Yevick and K. C. Rogers, "The Development of High Energy, Low Inductance Switches," Proposal to the AEC, March 9, 1962.

[626] See the historical and then-current overview of research teams in the physics department in Kenneth C. Rogers, "An Outline of the First Three Years of a Ten Year Development Plan in Physics," Oct. 15, 1968, Stevens Special Collections.

Experiment), an early attempt to control plasma in magnetic fields through concentration in a "cusp." The head of project CHALICE, Professor George Yevick, an MIT Ph.D. in 1947, had credentials as a Rad Lab staff member from 1944 to 1946. The basic idea was to use powerful electromagnets to "pinch" the plasma gases into concentrated threads and then to use piston-like magnetic pumping action to force the threads together into a central cavity where the superheated, concentrated plasma would be held in the shape of two inverted cups of a chalice by sustained electromagnetic action.[627]

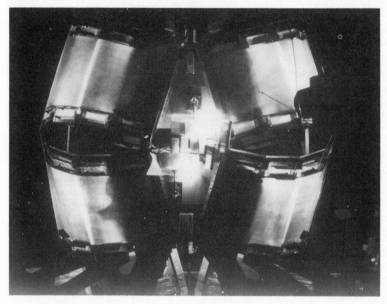

This shows the firing of Professor George J. Yevick's Project CHALICE apparatus.

Yevick's group of researchers included seven Stevens full-time faculty, six visiting scientists, twelve graduate students, nineteen undergraduates, seven technical staff, and four supporting personnel. This project also continued for nearly a decade and overcame similar types of problems as the MEGATRON project -- chambers broke down in the literally shuddering, fifteen- to twenty-kilovolt impulsed, thousands of amperes of electrical currents. According to Yevick, the engineering achievements of CHALICE included the fast dialectric, high-current plasma switches developed with

[627] George J. Yevick, "Historical Survey of Project CHALICE." Report to the AEC, 1967, 2.

Rogers, high-voltage (50kv) low-inductance transmission lines and connectors, use of copper sheets for connections to the magnetic coils, and novel design of copper coils encased in steel. In this multi-year project funded by the AEC with millions of dollars, the researchers contained dense plasma for some thirty nanoseconds before dissipation, an extremely modest accomplishment.[628] According to Yevick, the project stopped once it was realized that it was like "trying to shoot an elephant with a BB gun," something no one knew ten years earlier when the project started.

Under Bostick and Rogers, the physics department also obtained large grants for its low-temperature team led by Professor John Daunt in his Cryogenics Laboratory. The Army Materials and Mechanics Research Center and the NSF in the period from 1967 to 1972 funded multifaceted research. One THEMIS grant obtained by Daunt investigated the mechanical and thermal effects of metals, plastics, and liquid and solid gases at temperatures ranging from -50 to -250 degrees centigrade. Professor Hans Meissner investigated superconductivity of thin films at such temperatures.[629] Meanwhile, a group of high-energy physicists obtained grants for analysis of behavior of subatomic particles, pions and mesons, in bubble chambers. The department also published scores of articles and important books during this "publish or perish" era.[630]

Other science departments at Stevens benefited from the leading example of the physicists. Under department head, Luigi Z. Pollara (1914-1994), the chemistry and chemical engineering department obtained large numbers of grants totaling around $250,000 per year. Pollara was a strong, earthy, and engaging personality, whose gaze and gestures captivated his students and

---

[628] *Ibid.*, 12-24.

[629] John Daunt, "Cryogenics Center, Annual Progress Report," August 31, 1968; John Daunt, "Cryogenics Center Publications, 1967-1972;" and Rogers, *Op.Cit.*, 3-4.

[630] There was a small group of physicists interested in relativity whose colloquia at Stevens in the late 1950s and early 1960s drew participants from Princeton and Syracuse regularly and also on occasion from the whole east coast and Europe. One of this group, J. L. Anderson published his important scholarly book *Principles of Relativity Physics* in 1967. Another physicist, Jeremy Bernstein, was a popular scientific author: His essays on Einstein were originally published in the *New Yorker*, and in book form, *Einstein*(1973), went through eight editions under various titles. Other early titles of Bernstein's books were *The Analytical Machine; The Computer-- Past Present and Future*(1964, 1965), *Elementary Particles and Their Currents*(1968), and *The Elusive Neutrino*(1969). Later he wrote books on Hitler's physicists, Bell Labs, and cosmology, perhaps a dozen more in all on science-related subjects. In addition, Bernstein traveled in the Himalayas and wrote four books on mountain climbing, including the classic, *Ascent: Of the Invention of Mountain Climbing and Its Practice*(1965) which went through many editions spanning decades.

made him a great teacher.[631] Moreover, he had breadth and depth of inter-disciplinary vision, having taught mathematics, physical chemistry, and thermodynamics. Pollara filled a crucial role as the dynamic faculty god-father who promoted ideas for research among professors -- not only in his own department but in many others as well. He was a firm believer in the benefits of interdisciplinary research and curricula and in merit raises and larger salaries for exceptional research. He teamed up with Bostick and Professor Nicholas Rose of the mathematics department, and, as the wistful stories went later, "took over the school" in promoting more science faculty, higher salaries, and better research facilities. President Jess Davis agreed and liberally hired and promoted research faculty, who were given merit raises, rapid promotion, and tenure for obtaining research contracts and overhead moneys. Pollara was a driving force behind a new chemistry-chemical engineering building because his faculty increased so rapidly that they no longer fit into the Morton Memorial Laboratory of Chemistry and therefore spilled over into the Peirce and Kidde buildings.[632] The chemistry and chemical engineering department nearly quadrupled in size from six professors before Pollara took over in 1955 to twenty-three in 1969.

In Pollara's department, a main specialty was polymers, both natural, as in proteins and living life forms, and synthetic, as in plastics and man-made fibers. His colleague, Professor Salvatore S. Stivala, who had come to Ste-vens in 1952, was a polymer researcher and held degrees in both chemistry and chemical engineering. Noting that one-third of the chemists in the United States were being hired in polymer-related fields and foreseeing a revolutionary boom in both chemical biology and plastics in the late 1950s, Pollara and Stivala, as they built the department, actively recruited chemists and engineers in the polymer fields.[633] In the area of chemical biology, Stivala obtained grants from the National Heart Institute, among others, to study the physical and biological properties of heparin, a compound found in body tissues that worked as a blood anti-coagulant. These studies held out the prospect of discovering the common physical parameters of blood anti-coagulants, then either synthesizing them or isolating them to create drugs of enhanced anti-coagulant activity. Professors Ajay K. Bose and Magyar Manhas were recruited in 1959 and 1962 respectively to pursue such work on heparin and other natural products with pharmaceutical uses. Their work

---

[631] Pollara's gestures and gait are graphically described in "Great Teachers of Castle Point II," *Stevens Indicator*, June 1962, 4-5.

[632] *Ibid.*

[633] *Research Report, 1961. Op.Cit.*, 4-5, and S. Stivala, "Polymer and Plastics Research," *Research at Stevens, 1963. Op.Cit.*, 1-2.

on steroids and beta-lactams was funded by the National Institute of Health and Hoffman-La Roche, among others.

Fundamental pioneering research into beta-lactams, the chemical foundations of penicillins, was led by Bose starting in the early 1960s. Scores of Bose's 200-plus technical papers were concerned with investigations of the properties and chemical activity of beta-lactams, and he and Manhas and their students made a breakthrough in 1968. The original penicillins were obtained by natural processes of fermentation, and, since their introduction in 1940, they had saved millions of lives. New penicillins were constantly and urgently needed, however, because of development of allergies in patients and resistances in bacteria to the original forms of the wonder drugs. Pharmaceutical companies had developed semisynthetic penicillins through processes created by John C. Sheehan of MIT, but the problem was that the Sheehan method was considered commercially unfeasible, as one company head put it, "unless it yields entirely new types of penicillin." By 1968, in a London meeting of the Fifth International Symposium on the Chemistry of Natural Products, Bose outlined a method of using common commercial chemicals to synthesize new penicillin structures.[634] The problem with this breakthrough was that it used the highly explosive azido acetyl chloride, and this made manufacture of the new penicillin unfeasible -- in fact there were powerful explosions both in Bose's laboratory on campus and in the research laboratory of a pharmaceutical company investigating his new synthesis. Thus, the breakthrough was only suitable for careful experimentation in laboratories and became known as the "Bose Reaction." Bose and Manhas continued with this work until they discovered an alternative preparation of beta-lactams, namely, using the cheap and safe amino acid glycine. This new technique was subsequently used by pharmaceutical companies to create new synthetic penicillins.[635]

In the chemical engineering wing of the department, Pollara and Stivala invited the Plastics Institute of America (PIA) to house its headquarters on the campus in 1963. This non-profit autonomous organization contracted with industry to support graduate research and education programs in plastics in order to supply member corporations with specialists in the increasingly important field of polymer research and engineering. In 1967, the joint efforts of PIA and the Stevens polymer engineers resulted in an

---

[634] "Synthesis Yields New Penicillins," *Chemical Engineering News,* July 15, 1968, 15-16.

[635] "Lactam Synthesis Routes to Better Antibiotics," *Science,* Oct. 1, 1979, and unpublished typescript by A. Bose and M. Manhas, "Significance of the New Method for the Synthesis of Beta Lactam Antibiotics," 1-3, Stevens Special Collections.

ONR-sponsored project THEMIS grant for $500,000.[636] Professor Rodney Andrews, editor of the journal *Reology,* was the principal investigator, and participating faculty included Stivala, Angelo Volpe, Costas Gogos, and Joseph Biesenberger. This grant was to study non-linear properties of polymers and their synthesis, basic research which was necessary to develop plastics later used in the aircraft, automobile, and other industries. Grants were obtained from the U.S. Army Natick Laboratories to study crystalline polymers, from Picatinny Arsenal for thermal oxidative studies of azulene polymers, and from the NSF for investigation of the velocity field in capillary flow of high polymers as well as for studies of polycrystalline polymers.[637] Also, Pollara created and was first president of the Polymer Processing Institute (PPI) in 1982, another autonomous not-for-profit organization funded by $100,000 of Stevens money, which focused on obtaining funds for academic research from member companies interested in advancing knowledge in polymer engineering.[638] These organizations located at Stevens added to the reputation of Stevens scholarship in polymers.[639]

Another quasi-independent facility was the Laboratory of Psychological Studies. It too had some hundreds of thousands of dollars a year in funded research during the Cold War. Professor Frederick J. Gaudet, a Ph.D. in psychology from Columbia who specialized in personnel relations for industrial clients, was the creator of this facility. In 1945, the Veterans Administration spawned regional guidance centers to help young veterans cope with entry into the civilian work force and avail themselves of educational benefits under the GI Bill of Rights. Gaudet ran one of these centers in which veterans were interviewed, given a battery of tests to determine mental and manual skills, and appraised for occupations or educational programs for which they were best fitted. Gaudet's veterans work also included widows and children of veterans and continued through the Korean and Vietnamese conflicts. By the time the program ended in 1971, an estimated 54,000 to 55,000 veterans and their relations had been served.[640]

---

[636] A. W. Meyer, "Plastics Institute of America," in Potter, *Op.Cit.,* II, VI-h, 38.

[637] *Research at Stevens, 1966. Op.Cit.,* 6-13.

[638] The incorporators of PPI were Pollara and Biesenberger, along with President Rogers, Provost Cotellessa, and the Chairman of the Board of Trustees, Frederick L. Bissinger, "Minutes of the Board of Trustees," April 28, 1982.

[639] The department produced a stream of technical articles rivaling the production of the physics department as well as books like L. Reich and Stivala's *Autooxidation of Hydrocarbons Mechanisms* in 1969 and C. Gogos and Z. Tadmor's *Principles of Polymer Processing* in 1979.

[640] H. Karl Springob, "A History of the Laboratory of Psychological Studies, Stevens Institute of Technology, 1945-1995," unpublished paper dated Sept. 1994, Stevens Special Collections.

In 1945, Gaudet also established the Laboratory of Psychological Studies (1945-1995). The core of this facility was an offshoot of the work for veterans, namely, counseling and testing of individuals, including teenagers, college students, housewives returning to the work force, and adults seeking career changes, who paid for advice about career problems. Starting in 1947, "Psych Studies" obtained income by administering high school equivalency tests to almost thirty thousand individuals. It also offered college entrance exams, English as a second language exams, and other more specialized tests. In 1948, the laboratory's counseling service was accredited by the American Board on Counseling Services and later by the International Association of Counseling Services. By 1970, Psych Studies had acquired a nationwide reputation for its work in career counseling, and over seventy thousand individuals had come to Stevens from every state of the union and from foreign countries to seek such personalized assistance -- even "the son of a baron, a woman who became a member of high royalty, and the children of a renowned author as well as those of high-level international representatives to the United Nations."[641]

A second activity of the laboratory was a continuation of Gaudet's previous work with corporations on "selecting the right person for the right job," but including the insights of industrial psychologists on training and retraining programs, obsolescence of personnel, motivation to perform effectively, and adaptability of corporate management. By the mid-1960s, Psych Studies' contractual arrangements with an array of clients were over the $200,000-a-year level.[642] Among corporate clients were International Business Machines, P.S.E.&G., and Blue Cross/Blue Shield. Many of the psychology faculty had research professor status at Stevens, and their salaries and benefits were supported half by the laboratory and half by teaching activity. Among their clients were municipalities that took advantage of the facility's expertise in screening applicants for employment, e.g., for fire and police departments. [643]

---

[641] *Ibid.*, 8, and Johnson and Springob, *Op.Cit.*, 31-32.

[642] Orem, "Memo," *Op.Cit.*

[643] This work for industrial and municipal clients declined in the 1980s and 1990s as a result of the reactions of employers to the Equal Opportunity Commission Guidelines as well as cutbacks in faculty in the area of psychology. In the later years of the facility there was a demographic decline in high-school and college-aged clients, corporate downsizing, and a tighter job market, all of which had the effect of reducing the number of outside clients-- they were not willing to pay for the service without a greater probability of obtaining preferred employment. Thus, there was more stress on serving Stevens students with counseling through such programs as Academic Effectiveness Training, informal sessions which focused on goal setting, time management, and scheduling besides basics like note-taking and reading techniques. Also, through the Stevens Health Service, students could obtain counseling for stresses of an individual nature. Under its last director, H. Karl

The work of Comstock and Bornemann had already put Stevens on the map in metallurgy which accounts for the level of funded research received by the metallurgy department. The reputation of the Powder Metallurgy Laboratory attracted researchers like Professor Rolf Weil in 1956. A graduate of Carnegie-Mellon and Penn State Universities, Weil had been a full-time researcher from 1951 to 1954 at the Argonne Metallurgical Laboratory of the University of Chicago, the premier metallurgical laboratory in the United States.[644] After arriving at Stevens, Weil obtained sizable grants as the principal investigator on a project funded by Picatinny Arsenal for improving the fragmentation of artillery shells, a multi-year, $100,000 project involving many other members of the small department. Professor Theodore Gela, for two years a senior scientist on anti-tank weapons systems at nearby Picatinny Arsenal, also received several military-funded grants and conducted x-ray studies of metal crystals at Stevens and at the Picatinny laboratories.[645] In more fundamental research, Weil received a series of grants funded mostly by the NSF, but also by IBM, to use an electron microscope to study the properties of electroplated or chemically deposited thin metal films, for example cobalt-phosphorus and nickel. These 1960s studies investigated different chemical constituents in electroplating baths to produce the smoothest and most shiny metal film surfaces possible, and they investigated the surface structural faults of metal crystals as they grew through chemical deposit methods. [646]

In mechanical engineering, sizable grants were obtained by Professor Robert F. McAlevy III 1954, a Princeton Ph.D. holder, and others in the field of rocket fuel combustion. Early grants obtained by McAlevy included one funded jointly by the ONR and NASA on rocket propulsion, specifically the flame zone structure caused by burning various liquid propellant combinations as well as solid propellants of the Polaris missile type. The combustion laboratory produced an exact experimental analog of actual firings of such rockets. Another $130,000 grant funded by ARPA was "Hydrogen as a Fuel" used on the Saturn rockets which took astronauts to the moon. This project led by McAlevy included professors Richard B. Cole

---

Springob in the late 1980s, the facility changed its name to Psychological Studies and Student Counseling Services, and the laboratory went out of existence with Springob's retirement in 1995. Springob, *Op.Cit.*, 5-6 and 20-21.

[644] ECPD Questionnaire for the Review of Engineering Curricula, 1973, Stevens Institute of Technology, II.

[645] *Research at Stevens, 1966. Op.Cit.*, 31, and "ECPD Questionnaire, 1973," *Op.Cit.*, II.

[646] Rolf Weil, "Some Examples of the Purpose of Performing Research in Materials," *Research on the Campus, 1965. Op.Cit.*, 47-52. Among other later projects, the work of Prof. M. Ohring's NSF grants for research into thin metal films resulted in his book, *The Materials of Thin Films*(1991); see C. V. Thomson, "Thinly Spread," *Nature*, vol. 357, May 28, 1992.

and Richard S. Magee 1963, doctoral students of McAlevy; and also professors Lubomir Kurylko and Kurt H. Weil. It investigated different methods of hydrogen production, namely electrolysis, coal gasification, and thermochemical decomposition of water. It investigated techniques of hydrogen pipeline transmission in terms of feasibility. It also considered the thermodynamic parameters of hydrogen-fueled engines, as well as the results of operating experience using hydrogen/air engines, hydrogen/oxygen engines, and mixed-fuel hydrogen engines.[647]

In electrical engineering, grants were received for research in solid state electronics and control systems. In 1966, Professor Gerald Herskowitz, a staff researcher at Bell Labs between 1963 and 1965, developed for the Picatinny Arsenal mathematical models for miniature electronic circuits adaptable for use in space vehicle guidance and control systems.[648] After the arrival of Professor Preston R. Clement as department head of the electrical engineering department in 1964 and as dean of the faculty in 1966, there was an infusion of not less than ten affiliate professors, all full-time researchers at Bell Labs and RCA Laboratories who taught at Stevens part-time, and these faculty, particularly Francis T. Boesch, who was brought in as department head in 1979, stimulated funded research into advanced telecommunications at Stevens.[649]

As already indicated, funded research was obtained from private companies as well as from government during the Cold War. In 1956, Admiral Orem initiated a program which had been pioneered by MIT earlier in the century and which had been taken up by other technical schools such as Case and RPI. The model was MIT's "Technology Plan" of 1920 in which private companies and corporations could take advantage of MIT's research expertise in exchange for a standard contractual fee.[650] The program at Stevens was called "The Stevens Associates" and offered "use of its resources including faculty" to private industry for a set fee of $2,000 per year. Companies were offered easy access to academic and research departments prepared to do the companies' sponsored research. "Honor projects" or senior research experiments could be proposed by companies, and, if accepted by faculty, the results were made available to company sponsors.

---

[647] "Hydrogen as a Fuel," August 1974, Semi-Annual Technical Report, Stevens Special Collections.

[648] *Research at Stevens, 1966. Op.Cit.,* 18. Prof. Paul M. Chirlian turned out many textbooks including *Integrated and Active Network Analysis and Synthesis* in 1967 and *Basic Network Theory* in 1969.

[649] ECPD Questionnaire, 1973, II. Boesch was co-founder of the journal *Networks* and later its co-editor with Stevens' Prof. Charles Suffel.

[650] Noble, *Op.Cit.,* 136-143.

The placement office would help to find graduating students whom companies needed, and placement interviews could be scheduled at the companies' convenience. Faculty could be contracted as researchers and consultants, and their research results, if not restricted by sponsorship or security, could be made available to companies before publication in academic journals. Representatives of companies were invited to annual meetings to meet professors and hear directly of their expertise in on-going research projects.[651] The Stevens Associates started modestly with eight participating companies in 1956 but increased to twenty-five in 1962 when Jess Davis calculated their unrestricted contributions were the equivalent of the benefits of $1,250,000 in endowment.[652] By 1966, sixty-six private companies sponsoring research at Stevens.[653]

During the early Cold War, Stevens's funded research on rockets and space vehicles was complemented by faculty who taught in the field and by the success of graduates who rose to top positions in management of space programs. Faculty included the head of the mechanical engineering department, Professor Kurt Weil, who, as a German engineer, had designed the Junkers JU-52 transport plane, the three-engine corrugated metal craft used extensively by the Luftwaffe during World War II. Others included Professor Sidney Borg who had started his career at Annapolis teaching aeronautical engineering before working for Grumman Aircraft which he left in 1952 to teach at Stevens.

Earlier graduates of Stevens became successful professors in aeronautics or its associated fields elsewhere: Howard W. Emmons 1933, an instructor at Stevens in the 1930s while earning a master's degree, obtained a Ph.D. at Harvard where he became Gordon McKay Professor of Mechanical Engineering and an authority on supersonic flow of gases and properties of hydrogen at high temperatures. In 1940, he built America's first supersonic wind tunnel at Harvard, and later built the largest one in the country at the Aberdeen Proving Grounds.[654] When he retired, his replacement at Harvard was R. E. Kronauer 1945, a retired Navy engineer specializing in guided missiles. Another Harvard Ph.D., Kronauer was an authority in fluid dynamics and control systems, and he designed an apparatus to measure thrust in large, solid-propellant rocket engines and invented a precise three-component wind velocity meter. For the Navy, he measured ocean currents and investigated the dynamics of control systems when confronted with

---

[651] "The Stevens Associates," *Stevens Indicator*, March 1957, 11-13.
[652] *Stevens Indicator*, July 1962, 10.
[653] "Research at Stevens. Report for 1966," 83-84, Stevens Special Collections.
[654] "Commencement, 1963," *Ibid.*, 80 (1963), no. 3, 7.

external ocean noise, eddies, and vortices.[655] Another graduate was Professor Stephen H. Crandall 1942 who, as an MIT professor of mechanical engineering, became the world's leading authority on vibrations in aircraft and rockets by 1958 when he was a consultant to the Air Force and author of *Random Vibrations*. McGraw-Hill published a whole series, the *McGraw Hill Series in Engineering Sciences* under Crandall's consulting editorship.[656]

Other graduates, such as Alfred Africano 1929 who was a founder of the American Rocket Society, were successful in aerospace or associated fields as NASA prepared for its trip to the moon in 1969. Africano worked for North American Rockwell from 1962 to 1971 on exhaust-plume impingement effects and on investigations of the impact sensitivity of liquid- oxygen fuels for the company's rockets, missiles and spacecraft, including those for the Apollo flights that landing on the moon on July 18, 1969 -- an event which was the culmination of Africano's dream as a young man.[657] In the field of rocketry, Walter Kidde Company developed a chemically fueled power supply unit to provide electrical energy for missile control systems. Manufactured by Kidde in several different sizes, these small units provided a great amount of power. For example, a one-hundred-horsepower unit only four inches in diameter contained a turbine which rotated eighty thousand times per minute.[658]

Robert F. Garbarini 1940 studied under mechanical engineering professor Richard E. Deimel (1878-1955), a nationally know authority on the gyro compass with his book *Mechanics of the Gyroscope* and a consultant to Sperry Gyroscope Company and the General Time Corporation. Garbarini then earned a Stevens master's degree in 1945 before working for Sperry Gyroscope for twenty-two years. There he was inventor or co-inventor on eleven patents including the "K Series" navigation and bombing systems used in the B-36, B-47, B-52 and B-58 aircraft. Unlike World War II systems that required the aircraft to stay on the heading of the bombing run, the K Series system used an electromechanical computing machine to determine the run to target ahead of time so that evasive action could be taken up to the time of the release of the bombs. Garbarini's job was to take the variables involved and to design the actual apparatus. He also directed the development of the inertial flight reference system for the X-15, the experimental super-high-altitude plane.

---

[655] *Ibid.*, 81 (1964), no. 3, 21.

[656] *Ibid.*, 74 (1958), no. 5, 18.

[657] Letter of Africano in "Log of the Class Secretaries, '29," *Stevens Indicator*, 88 (1971), 1, 46.

[658] "Missile Meeting," *Ibid.*, 74 (1958), 2, 18.

After Sputnik prodded America into a crash competition with the USSR in the "Space Race," Garbarini moved to NASA in 1963 where he had oversight responsibility of all unmanned, science-oriented, space-flight programs including Ranger, Mariner, Pioneer, Surveyor, Lunar Orbiter, Relay, Syncom, Tiros, and Nimbus. He received NASA Exceptional Service medals for his role in the success of Tiros and the Surveyor I landing on the moon. Several of these projects were important for the later manned Apollo mission to the moon, because they investigated the environment the astronauts were going to encounter. At the time, the terrain of the moon was not known. Ranger took pictures as it crashed on the moon, Lunar Orbiter took pictures as it circled the moon, and Surveyor I took pictures after a soft landing on the moon. On the Surveyor I project, Garbarini was sent by NASA to the factory of the joint Hughes Aircraft-Jet Propulsion Laboratory site to oversee the troubled project which was behind schedule and beset with satellite control system malfunctions in flight tests. He was part of an approval board which reviewed what went wrong, took corrective actions, and oversaw flight retests. He says he was lucky because the next major tests and the Surveyor landing on the moon went without a hitch. Among other duties in the same period, he was chairman of the Unmanned Spacecraft Panel of the joint NASA-DOD Aeronautics and Astronautics Coordination Board.

In 1967, Garbarini moved to Western Union Telegraph Company where he planned and implemented the first U.S. synchronous domestic satellite communications system using the Hughes HS 333 satellite and a complex of five earth stations. This satellite was the first commercial system after the FAA established its "open skies" policy.[659]

Caleb B. Hurtt 1953 was a Stevens AFROTC graduate.[660] In the Air Force from 1953-1955, he was a project officer on the Matador and Falcon Missile programs. Starting in 1956, he rose through the ranks of Martin Marietta Aerospace Corporation to become its president and chief operating officer in 1987. On the way up, Hurtt was project director for airborne design and test for the Titan I missile, project director for test of Titan III, program director of the Apollo Applications Program/Manned Spacecraft Center, and executive vice president of Manned Space Systems, which included Martin Marietta's participation in the NASA Skylab and the Space Shuttle programs. Stationed at Cape Kennedy, he received a NASA Public Service

---

[659] R. F. Garbarini to Geoffrey Clark, June 6, 1999.

[660] In 1949 an AFROTC unit was established at Stevens and provided students with scholarships and Air Science and Aerospace studies for three decades.

Award for his role in the Skylab program.[661] In addition, John D. Movius 1953 managed Air Force and NASA programs for the Aeronutronic Division of Ford Motor Company, and in 1964 he was the senior eastern region representative for Northrop Space Laboratories headquartered in Washington, D.C.[662]

William R. Cuming received first prize of $50 for a speech entitled "The Engineer as Executive" at the end of a contest held in 1939. The judges rated students on communicative contact with the audience, organization and ideas, articulation and pronunciation, fluency of delivery and platform manner.

William R. Cuming 1942 was a graduate with an interest in chemistry and electronics. He was a Navy radar officer in World War II when his ship

[661] See Stevens Alumni Office file.

[662] *Stevens Indicator*, 81 (1964), no. 1, 28.

was sunk in the Pacific. The Navy then sent him for advanced training in radar at MIT's Radiation Laboratory, where he stayed on as an instructor in the late 1940s. Based on the knowledge thus obtained, he started his first company, Emerson and Cuming, which specialized in the design and manufacture of dielectric materials to reflect or absorb microwaves, particularly radar. After this company was sold, he started the Cuming Corporation and its subsidiary the Cuming Microwave Corporation, which advanced his pioneering work on radar absorbent and reflecting products, and the latter company became a world-class supplier of such materials. His products were built into the most modern stealth bomber and fighter aircraft.[663]

Lastly, one of Cuming's fellow 1942 classmates, Homer Lowenberg, worked on a project to develop a nuclear powered plane. From 1948 to 1966, he worked for Kellex Corporation and its successor, Vitro Engineering Co. to develop the production of plutonium at the Hanford site in Washington state for General Electric. Rising to the position of manager of operations for Vitro, Lowenberg had varied responsibilities at the Hanford facility: for approval of flow sheets and flow diagrams; for developing detailed designs for buildings; for procuring remotely operated equipment; for installing equipment; and for developing remote maintenance procedures. Other specialized projects while working for Kellex and Vitro included: construction of NASA's Saturn Structural Test Facility in Huntsville, Alabama; studies of Saturn D Nuclear Facilities for General Dynamics; and construction of a High Radiation Level Examination Laboratory for the AEC at Brookhaven National Laboratory. Perhaps Lowenberg's most interesting work was in trying to apply nuclear power to missiles and planes: For Boeing Aircraft Company he worked on development of nuclear-powered rockets, and, for Lockheed Aircraft Corporation's Nuclear Aircraft Development Center, he worked on a project to develop a nuclear-powered aircraft -- pioneering projects abandoned only because of reasons of safety. Lowenberg was also a charter member of the American Nuclear Society, and, after retirement, was a consultant in studies on containment of radiation, its cleanup, and its environmental effects at the Hanford site.[664]

---

[663] See two manuals of products of the Cuming Microwave Corporation in Stevens Special Collections.

[664] Letters of Homer Lowenberg to Harold J. Raveché et al, Jan. 4, 12, and 25, 2000, and "Information for Alumni Files" data sheet dated 6/30/70, Alumni Association files. Also, in a project for the U.S. Army, Lowenberg was program manager of Vitro's design and construction of the first three-step nerve gas plant for the production of hydroflouric acid methylphosphonic dicloride (diclor, one of three chemicals for nerve gas) in Mussel Shoals, Alabama.

CHAPTER 20

Early Cold War Expansion in Programs and Facilities

S tevens participated in a nationwide trend in higher education in the 1950s and early 1960s by dramatically expanding its educational programs and campus facilities. During the Jess Davis administration (1951-1972), Stevens changed from a small undergraduate, engineering college with a smaller graduate school only awarding master's degrees to a larger university with a new undergraduate science degree program and with a greatly enlarged graduate school awarding doctorates in engineering fields, the sciences, and management. New laboratories, classrooms, administration buildings and especially many dormitories sprang up on campus, the latter changing the students from a largely tri-state commuting population to a much broader geographical representation of the United States and foreign countries.

Funding for higher-education programs and expansion of campuses nationwide was provided by governments, foundations, and private industry and individual gifts at a rate never before seen, especially after the 1957 launching of Sputnik. During the early Cold War, funding for academe was generated by the belief that education on all levels created a democratic citizenry which would strengthen western institutions. For example, Stevens trustee Charles G. Mortimer 1922, the chairman and chief executive officer of General Foods, stated before a Stevens Associates gathering in 1963,

. . . both business and education, as indispensable elements of our free society, share an increasingly heavy responsibility for helping to strengthen our democracy. Our teamed ability to do just that will be successful in direct proportion to our ability to provide America's young people with the sound, all around knowledge-ability which produces the kind of good citizenship on which enduring democracy is completely dependent.[665]

While private companies and foundations participated in funding research, most of the money for the rapid expansion of public higher education as well as for providing scholarships, fellowships, and matching funds for private colleges and universities came from federal and state governments. By 1960, a record 3.5 million young Americans were matriculated in 2,026 American institutions of higher learning.

---

[665] "Industry's Stake in Education," *Ibid.*, 80 (1963), no. 2, 9.

At the same time, national studies called for an expansion of programs to produce more scientists and engineers because of a "gap" with the USSR. In 1956, President Jess Davis pointed out that the USSR graduated fifty-three thousand engineers per year compared to 22,500 in the United States.[666] In 1963, American undergraduate and graduate programs in the sciences had a boost when President Kennedy's Science Advisory Committee called for a rise in the number of science and engineering students on all levels and for federal programs to subsidize tuition. In particular, the committee called for an increase in doctoral students from the then current 2,900 per year to 7,500 per year by 1970.

The biggest innovation at Stevens on the undergraduate level during this era was the creation of a new Unified Science Curriculum by the heads of the expanding science faculty: Luigi Z. Pollara, Winston Bostick, and Nicholas Rose. Created in 1958, the science curriculum was based on the same broad-based philosophy which underlay the engineering curriculum. Its concentrations were in chemical biology, physics, and applied mathematics, areas in which science faculty had expertise and conducted active funded research. In its heyday in the 1960s, the science program leading to a B.S. degree had some twenty-five percent of the undergraduate enrollments.[667]

In the science program, the major in chemical biology, created in 1965, was particularly successful. By that time, the science curriculum only had one biology course but the major included three undergraduate biology courses as well as biochemistry and a lot of chemistry courses. This intensive program was designed by Professor Francis T. Jones and others to prepare students for medical or dental schools as well as biochemical engineering and pharmaceutical careers. It successfully prepared students for MCAT tests and entry to medical schools. At the time medicine was becoming more science-based and dependent on research and there was need for an increased number of doctors because of the passage of Medicare.

Professor Ajay Bose encouraged chemical biology majors to volunteer their time for participating in funded research activity in his laboratory and was surprised at the high quality of their contributions. After five years of observing undergraduates do research, he decided to apply for money made available by the bequest of the family of Edward L. Lempke of the class of 1948 to create a summer research program for undergraduates. Thus, in

---

[666] "President Davis' Timely Address," *Stevens Indicator*, 73 (1956), 2, 10.

[667] This initiative actually reestablished a science curriculum at Stevens leading to a B.S. degree, a program which had been dropped in the 1880s. For enrollments see *ECPD Questionnaire for the Review of the Engineering Curriculum*, I (1973), 16.

1971, he started his award winning program, Undergraduate Projects in Technology and Medicine (UPTAM). This program has continued for twenty-eight years and has been funded mainly by foundations and pharmaceutical corporations with an interest in chemical biology and biosciences. By 1974, UPTAM students developed a portable iron lung, an oxygen-measuring device for newborn infants, and an operating table for infants that maintains body temperature during surgery.[668] In addition, By 1987, Jones negotiated an accelerated medical and dental dual-degree program that allowed qualifying Stevens students entry into a medical and a dental school after three years at Stevens, a B.S. degree being earned after one successful year at the University of Medicine and Dentistry of New Jersey.

A Stevens graduate from the class of 1931 and holder of a Stevens M.S. degree earned in 1953, Wesley J. Howe, had joined the firm of Becton Dickinson in 1949 and had become first president of the health products company's manufacturing division by 1965. As president of the whole company by 1972, Howe lead the "disposable revolution" as the company became the leading manufacturer of syringes and gloves which could be thrown out after one use. He was deeply interested in education and was a founding member and chairman of the Board of Trustees of the University of Medicine and Dentistry of New Jersey. In addition, Howe had a deep historical interest in Stevens curricula and his dedication to the college later led him to contribute funds for the renovation of the Stevens Center, now named after him, and to found the Wesley J. Howe School of Management at Stevens.

Another notable graduate in the field of medicine was the inventor of the eye bank, Dr. John M. McLean of the class of 1930. After obtaining an M.D. at Cornell, McLean taught at both Johns Hopkins and Cornell medical schools and specialized in ophthalmology. He perfected the corneal transplant operation, organized the original eye bank at New York Hospital, and helped to develop techniques for glaucoma, cataracts, and ocular muscle surgeries. When questioned about his engineering background, he said,

I am an engineer and I am still practicing engineering. I just happen to work with somewhat different materials . . . The engineer is not, as so many people think, primarily a technically trained man whose strong point is specialized factual information. He is rather a broadly educated man who has learned to think clearly, to analyze problems, to make decisions, and to act on them.[669]

---

[668] Kenneth C. Rogers, *Traditions & Tomorrow*(SIT, 1974), 4.

[669] *Stevens Indicator*, 82 (1965), 3, 19.

If the creation of the science degree program enhanced undergraduate programs, the expansion of the graduate school was even more important for Stevens. Again, Pollara led the way. Before coming to Stevens he had created and become director of a graduate school at Siena College, and he came to Stevens with a vision of an expanded graduate school. In 1951, his vision was given a boost by endowment of the Robert Crooks Stanley Fellowships provided for by Robert C. Stanley's will, such fellowships allowing graduate students to study in a variety of fields.[670] At the time, the board of trustees approved of only one doctoral program in applied mechanics, but the Stanley fellowships could be held for doctoral study in chemistry, physics, and mathematics as well. By the late 1960s, the doctoral programs had been expanded to include a D.Eng. in such areas as chemical and electrical engineering and a Ph.D. in metallurgy. By 1956, the graduate school's number of full-time and part-time students had grown so rapidly that its total of 1,035 surpassed the 976 undergraduates for the first time in Stevens history.[671]

Subsequently, the scientists persuaded Jess Davis to hire a first rate dean of the graduate school, Ralph A. Morgan. He was a Berkeley Ph.D. in chemistry who had been a National Science Foundation director of engineering sciences and an ex-president of Rose Polytechnic Institute. Like Pollara, in whose department he held a professorship, Morgan believed in expansion of the faculty engaged in funded research and doctoral programs. In 1963 Morgan said that if Stevens was to "do its share to meet the needs of the country," the proportion of faculty devoted to research and teaching on the graduate level had to increase dramatically. He cited an NSF study showing that the 140,500 full time faculty in the United States spent fifty-six percent of their time on teaching and forty-four percent on research, but at Stevens faculty spent sixty-five percent of their time on teaching and only thirty-five percent on research.

As a result of availability of government grants and fellowships, the number of graduate-level students working as research and teaching assistants increased, and the graduate school as a whole expanded by 260 percent. By 1965, Stevens student enrollments totaled 2,500, including 1,150 undergraduates and 1,350 graduate students. Among the latter were two hundred doctoral candidates, more than many universities and an astounding number for such a small faculty and campus. Ten years earlier in 1955, the trustees had envisioned 1,200 undergraduates which at that

---

[670] "The Robert Crooks Stanley Fellowships," *Ibid.*, 73 (1956), 3, 24-25.
[671] "Report of the Admissions and Records Department, 1956-7," 3.

time was considered the maximum number trustees were willing to authorize in order to preserve the concept of a small college.[672] But by 1963, the Jess Davis administration was planning for expansion of facilities for 3,750, students including 1,450 undergraduates.

The first priority for facilities was an expansion in dormitory space to hold the increased number of students. An initial $150,000 grant from the Charles Hayden Foundation provided for opening of construction on Hayden Hall, the campus's third dormitory built along the cliff of Castle Point and the first dormitory of the Jess Davis administration. This dormitory, holding 135 students, was sorely needed by 1955-56 when it was built.[673] Charles Hayden was a magazine-publishing magnate responsible for the funding of the Hayden Planetarium, part of the New York Museum of Natural History in nearby Manhattan. The Hayden Foundation wound up contributing $290,000 of the total $575,000 cost of the sixty-seven room dormitory with its spacious lounge and windows which give a view of the New York skyline across the Hudson river.

To obtain dormitory space for graduate students and additional faculty offices, in 1955, the administration sold the Johnsonburg Camp which had been used for civil engineering and surveying courses for freshmen since 1930. The 340-acre camp and its facilities were expensive to maintain, and surveying could be conducted on campus without taking four weeks out of the freshman class's summer session.[674] The camp was exchanged for Hoboken property, owned by the First Presbyterian Church, adjacent to the campus: a block of brownstone and brick buildings north of 6th Street between Hudson and River Streets. Part of the property, on the corner of 6th and Hudson Streets across from the Lieb building, was cleared to provide much-needed additional parking for commuting students. The Church also gave Stevens forty thousand dollars in the deal.[675]

Also in 1955, Recitation Hall, which was originally built in 1888 to house the Stevens School, was demolished to make space for the Burchard Memorial Science and Engineering Building erected by 1958. Major funding for what is still the largest teaching and faculty office building on campus was provided by the estate of the widow of Anson Wood Burchard 1885.[676] Lawrence Schacht 1927 and his Schacht Steel Corporation erected the steel

[672] "President Davis' Talk At the Banquet," *Ibid.*, 80 (1963), no. 4, 7, and "600,000 More For Library," *Stevens Indicator*, 82 (1965), no. 3, 28. "President Davis Foretells the Future," *Ibid.*, 58 (1958), no. 1, 10.

[673] "President Davis' Kindly Address," *Ibid.*, 73 (1956), 2, 9.

[674] "Johnsonburg Camp No Longer To Be Used," *Stevens Indicator*, 72 (1955), 6, 9.

[675] John Spano, "The Johnsonburg Camp," *Op.Cit.*, 26.

[676] *Stevens Indicator*, 76 (1959), 4, 6.

framework for the building, Schacht later funding the Schacht Laboratory of Management at Stevens. This major seven-story, 84,000-square foot building housed the expanded physics, electrical engineering, and metallurgy faculty and their laboratories as well as a 250-seat auditorium.[677] According to Donald Sullivan, Stevens's director of plant and operations, the need for the Burchard building came from increased research activity and from lack of laboratories and faculty offices for those who had been displaced by the increase in Pollara's chemistry and chemical engineering faculty who had spread from the Morton Building into the Peirce and Kidde buildings.[678]

Anson W. Burchard,
who has the largest academic building
on campus named after him,
was the chairman of the board
of General Electric
and married to a
countess.

In order to accommodate the increase in students on all levels, Jess Davis's administration developed a master plan by 1958 for new buildings which would meet Stevens's present and future needs. To raise capital funds for this ambitious plan, Jess Davis established a development and public relations office staffed by expert fund-raisers and copy writers. This office created the *Alumniletter* to bring positive news about the institute to the alumni, to the press, and to sources of funding. The development office contacted foundations, successful alumni and friends of the institute for capital gifts for building projects. It helped alumni establish bequests in their wills which allowed for a portion of an estate to be left in trust for dependents while they lived, and after their deaths the principle could be given to the college, a method which provided lifelong protection for

[677] "The New Science Engineering Building," *Ibid.*, 74 (1958), no. 6, 3.
[678] Donald A. Sullivan, "The Changing Face of Stevens," *Ibid.*, 77 (1960), no. 5, 7-8.

dependents as well as substantial tax savings. It alerted alumni to matching gift programs by companies, and it asked alumni to introduce Stevens development personnel to company executives to generate corporate support.[679] This effort resulted in record giving of more than one million dollars a year in gifts and bequests by the late 1950s.[680] In addition, in 1957 the SAA's Stevens Fund had raised a record $85,000 with 3,182 of some 5,900 living alumni participating or 53.9 percent compared to 35.4 percent at Caltech, 31.4 percent at MIT and 17.3 percent at RPI in that year.[681] By 1958, the Stevens Fund raised over $89,000 and brought in a record over $111,000 in 1959 and over $121,000 in 1960.[682] The master plan for the development of the campus announced in 1958 included two new undergraduate dormitories, a student-faculty center with new dining room facilities, a new library, a new graduate dormitory and additional research laboratories including a large digital computer.[683] A notable bequest was a nine-hundred-thousand-dollar mansion on twenty acres in Norwalk, Connecticut, the estate of Edward B. Gallaher 1894, the auto pioneer, who had left it to his widow until her death in 1958, when it devolved to Stevens.[684]

A lot of alumni were shocked and some outraged when the Jess Davis administration announced its intention of replacing the Stevens Castle with a modern administration-student activities building. The announcement came with no warning in the fall of 1958, the building slated to be demolished early in 1959. The Castle, purchased from Edwin A. Stevens II in 1911 was the most beloved building on campus for Stevens alumni. Its stately, high-ceilinged rooms had been the center of activities on campus: student "proms," official dinners, initiations into student societies, had taken place. Generations of students had been impressed with the imposing graceful structure situated on the highest elevation of Castle Point. Many students had resided in the Castle, the first campus dormitory. The alumni were aghast because a group of them had defeated a previous attempt to replace the Castle in 1954, and they had erected a plaque on the entrance to the Castle commemorating the battle to save it. Later, Arthur R. "Pete" Schaefer of the class of 1941 and others had led a fundraising campaign to refurbish the Castle, such improvements having only just been completed by

---

[679] Marshall Sewell, Jr., "Can Stevens Survive the Crisis in Education?" *Stevens Indicator,* 82 (1965), no. 1, 12-13.

[680] "At the Alumni Banquet Dr. Davis Reflects on the 60s at Stevens," *Ibid.,* 77 (1960), 2, 9.

[681] "1957 Stevens Fund-Class Achievements," *Stevens Indicator,* 74 91958), 2, 26-27.

[682] "1960 Fund Tops All," *Ibid.,* 78 (1961), 2, 18.

[683] *Ibid.*

[684] *Ibid.,* 74 (1958), no. 65, 13, and "The Gallaher Estate-- Gift to Stevens," *Ibid.,* 74 (1958), no. 6, 6.

1958. A flurry of opposition among alumni followed the announcement, and the slogan was "Save the Castle." Some alumni talked to the press and fought the demolition in newspaper articles. When the demolition started in early 1959, some alumni and students were incredulous. The demolition of the Castle was an emotional issue for many alumni. The SAA President William Nordling wrote as the Castle came down,

Some alumni feel that sufficient opportunity has not been given to opponents of the plan as they apply to the replacement of the Castle . . . Opportunity was available and expressions of dissatisfaction were given at the Executive Committee Meetings of September 9th, October 7th and November 4th, also at the Council Meeting of November 17th and at a special meeting with some members of the college Board at the Stevens Metropolitan Club on September 30th.

Nordling explained that an "unauthorized poll" showing alumni disapproval was ignored because it was "based on sentiment only."[685]

The trustees had been considering alternative modern buildings on the site of the Stevens Castle since the 1930s when they held a contest among architects for the best design of a modern campus -- the rendering by T. Matsumoto won first prize.

The administration and trustees explained their reasons for the Castle's replacement. It was old and hard to maintain. Architects had presented plans for the administration-student activities center several times in 1957, and, each time the site of the Castle was chosen, the trustees rejected the

---

[685] William G. Nordling, "Progress: Per Aspera ad Astra," *Ibid.*, 76 (1959), no. 6, 4.

plans. Finally, after considering all other alternatives, they relented in 1958. One major argument used was that the Castle was situated on the most prime land on Castle Point, land which would have little utility if the fourteen-story center building was built elsewhere. It was decided to use the most imposing land for the new building around which all campus life would revolve. The planned fourteen-story, 65,000-square foot center building was designed to have 30,000 square feet on the first two floors including a dining hall to hold 750 students at a sitting, a post office, snack bars, campus store, and student activities rooms. According to the architect John J. McNamara, who was also the architect of the Burchard building, the center was designed to be "neither so extreme as to be quickly out of style, or so traditional as to be uninteresting."[686] To mollify the alumni, McNamara created a remembrance of a feature of the Castle by including a hanging staircase in the lobby of the new building. Later in 1964, with a gift from Henry Torrence of the class of 1890, a Stevens Memorial Castle Room was created to house Stevens family furniture and busts of Colonel John Stevens donated by Mary Stevens Baird and Mrs. Basil M. Stevens.

The center building was scheduled to cost $1.75 million and to be completed by 1961, mostly with funds provided by the Kotzebue estate.[687] However, even though the whole master plan was only going to cost five million dollars when conceived in 1958, it turned out that rising inflation necessitated more funding before the center was completed in 1962. Additional funds to pay for most of the construction of the center were provided by Eugene McDermott, the president of Texas Instruments, who came to the rescue. In 1960, McDermott gave to both MIT and SIT one thousand shares of Texas Instruments stock, and in 1965 the *Stevens Indicator* reported that "he has given many other gifts since then."[688] The 1960 gift of stock was worth $1,430,500 and turned out to be the pace-setting gift in the building-fund campaign for the center building.[689] A daughter of James B. Pierce 1877 -- not to be confused with William H. Peirce the copper king who gave money for the Peirce building -- donated $400,000 for the dining hall named after her father.

Another major contributor to the building fund with an undisclosed amount of money in the early 1960s was Edmund F. Martin of the class of 1922. He had visited a steel mill at fourteen and was so impressed that he

---

[686] "Stevens Center Plans Announced," *Ibid.*, 77 (1960), no. 1, 15.

[687] William G. Nordling, "Report on the Current Status of the Stevens Development Plan," *Ibid.*, 76 (1959), no. 5, 3-4, and "Requiem for a Castle," *Ibid.*, 5.

[688] *Ibid.*, 77 (1960), no. 4, 26.

[689] "Alumni Participate in Building Fund," *Ibid.*, 78 (1961), no. 3, 21.

decided he wanted to go into steel making. As a young boy he used a hammer and saw in the basement of his Chicago house, and he regarded arithmetic and even higher mathematics as a form of recreation. At Stevens, he was near the top of his class and a member of Tau Beta Pi. Upon graduation he was one of the first to take the Bethlehem Steel Loop Course, a newly created elite training for Bethlehem's future management. Thereafter, he worked his way up as a repairman's helper in the roll shop, a tool grinder, a roll shop draftsman, a supervisor of a mill by 1924, and superintendent of four mills by the age of twenty-six. He helped to develop new steels during World War II, and during the same period increased the Lackawanna plant's steel-making capacity from 3.6 million to 6 million tons. As a result, he became chairman and chief executive officer of Bethlehem Steel by 1964.[690]

John McNamara, the center architect, also designed the two new dormitories, Humphreys and Davis Halls, which were being constructed at the same time as the center. In 1960, the upper campus was so full of construction that the only grass not covered with equipment and supplies was a plot in front of Palmer Hall. The new dormitories were needed to complete the change from a mainly commuting college in the metropolitan area to a residential college enrolling students from across the country. Before the Jess Davis era, there was room for 130 undergraduates in dormitories, but by 1961 out of a total undergraduate student body of 1,065, six hundred undergraduates lived in dormitories in addition to another two hundred in fraternity mansions.[691] An added reason for new dormitories was that middle-class and upper middle class students used to come from the cities around Hoboken, but during the 1950s their families had moved to the outlying suburbs which made commuting more difficult. The center building with its recreational areas was needed for these residential students as well as for administrative offices.[692] A contributor to Humphreys Hall was Sherman Loud 1921, the grandson of Alexander C. Humphreys. He and his sister presented a plaque in 1963 which is affixed to the dormitory in memory of Humphreys. As Stevens enrollments continued to climb during the early stages of the Vietnam War, in 1965 the docks just below Castle Point were purchased from the city of Hoboken in order to provide space for further expansion and to berth a ship, the SS *Stevens,* which was used as a dormitory until the rising cost of heating and lower enrollments of the mid-1970s necessitated its removal.

[690] "Stevens Men of Prominence," *Ibid.,* 81 (1964), no. 2, 10-11.

[691] Donald A. Sullivan, "The Changing Face of Stevens," *Ibid.,* 77 (1960), 5, 7-9.

[692] Sullivan, *Op.Cit.,* 8.

By the mid-1960s, the Berkeley Free Speech movement against the war in Vietnam was in full swing, and the 1968 college riots brought on by the undeclared war soured segments of the American public about the potential benefits of higher education. Also by the mid-1960s, public institutions with lower tuition rates were seriously challenging the smaller private institutions for the supply of students on the one hand and investment in higher education on the other. State colleges and community colleges were throwing up buildings with public money with apparent ease. Thus, the need for private colleges to present a prestigious image and to obtain tuition fees became a prime activity as the market became intensely competitive. This need generated expanded admissions personnel and a public relations departments at Stevens. Of course, these new administrative personnel added to operating costs in the same way they did elsewhere during the era.[693]

Thus in 1965, the Stevens director of development and public relations, Marshall Sewell, Jr., wrote a frank and forthright article for the *Stevens Indicator* entitled "Can Stevens Survive the Crisis in Education?" The problem outlined in the article was the need to stay competitive with "more and larger colleges and universities" by attracting the necessary funds for crucial cutting-edge research facilities, rising faculty salaries, and operating costs. By that time, only sixty percent of Stevens's yearly spending was paid by tuition fees -- tuition fees already being much higher than at state institutions. In addition, although Stevens had been successful in obtaining government funding and overhead to support facilities, it still needed to raise more private funds. Crucial to this effort were the alumni who could help with not only direct support but also with obtaining corporate support. In Sewell's words, this meant "moral backing of your college. . . . By talking about Stevens to your friends and associates, you help spread the good name of your college to an ever widening circle of people who are important to our existence."[694] This message had added urgency because it was coming through just at the time that funding for Cold-War research was leveling off and becoming more competitive to obtain. Thus, Stevens struggled to expand and build in the last years of Davis's administration.

Davis's master plan called for a complex of buildings that stretched from the lower campus onto the docks, and elaborate brochures were printed showing architects' renderings of how it would appear. According to Sewell, "Part of this property would be used to expand our educational and research facilities, and part would probably be made available to industry

---

[693] Rudolph, *Op.Cit.*, 486-7.
[694] Marshall Sewell, Jr., "Can Stevens Survive the Crisis in Education?" *Stevens Indicator*, 82 (1965), no. 1, 121-15.

for private research facilities which would bring needed tax revenue to the city."[695] Another part of the master plan called for a new gymnasium to supplement the William Hall Walker Gymnasium, which was too small to accommodate the increased enrollments. The dock complex and gymnasium were put on the back burner, however, because other more immediate parts of the plan had to be met. One was for a married graduate students' apartment building to house the graduate teaching and research assistants, and it was finished in 1965 through a self-liquidating loan from the federal government's Housing and Home Finance Agency. In the period from 1955 to 1965, the institute received $17,800,000 in gifts and bequests and about $11,500,000 was spent on six building projects.[696]

Another pressing need was for a new library and computer center to replace the antiquated facilities in the Lieb building. By the mid-sixties, the old library created by Barstow in the 1930s was too small and too old. The "information explosion" had created an urgent need for more space and better facilities. The Lieb library had only 175 seats, and, although it had been accredited by the Middle Atlantic States Association and the ECPD, it did not meet the standards of the American Library Association.[697] The campaign to raise money for a library and computer center started in 1964. By 1965, Davis and Sewell had raised $769,000 -- $383,000 from alumni and trustee gifts, $207,000 from corporations and $151,000 from private foundations -- but much more was needed.[698] Later that year, a $600,000 grant was obtained from the U.S. Department of Education and with smaller grants of $40,000 from Edmund Martin's U.S. Steel and $25,000 from Kresge Foundation to make the total $1.5 million of the estimated $2.5 million, ground was broken for the combined library-computer center building in 1966. Given inflation and increased costs incurred during construction, the trustees had to withdraw several millions of dollars from the endowment to complete the project.[699]

The Samuel C. Williams Library and Computer Center was the last building constructed during the Jess Davis era, although another building, a chemistry and chemical engineering building, was planned by Jess Davis and completed in 1973. In all, Jess Davis and the trustees used over $6.8 million from the endowment for expenditures for mainly the library and

---

[695] *Ibid.*, 12.

[696] "Expansion Continues," *Ibid.*, 81 (1964), no. 2, 4.

[697] Francis I. Duck, "The Stevens Library, Past, Present, and Future," *Stevens Indicator*, 81 (1964), no. 2, 8.

[698] "Fund for New Library Continues to Grow- Architects' Plans Revised," *Stevens Indicator*, 82 (1965), no. 2, 27.

[699] "$600,000 More For Library," *Stevens Indicator*, 82 (1965), no. 3, 29.

chemistry buildings at the end of the administration, and, although the endowment grew during Davis's tenure as president, funds from which income could be derived were only around the thirty-million-dollar mark by 1971-72.[700] Nonetheless, the Davis administration planned and constructed the bulk of the buildings on the modern Stevens campus -- one of the lasting and most important accomplishments of the booming early Cold War years.

Professor Samuel C. Williams of the class of 1915 had led an alumni fund drive for a new library before his death in the mid-1960s, and the new library built by 1969, seen here in an architect's rendering, was named after him.

The last Davis years were also witness to two notable events: a program to expand access to engineering and science for minorities and the inclusion of women in Stevens's undergraduate programs. The former came after the devastating urban riots of the early 1960s led to federal funding for programs to help disadvantaged minority students attain college educations. Although Stevens had a record of admitting minority students from its inception, Jess Davis was not enthusiastic about the government rules and regulations which came with the federal funds and the state's Equal Opportunity Fund, so he decided to raise private funds for Stevens's own program in 1967 through an administrative assistant, Charlie Redden.[701] He encouraged Dean of Student Affairs "Colonel" William L. Bingham to organize the Stevens Technical Enrichment Program (STEP) with volunteer teachers from the undergraduate student body, the idea being to teach and

---

[700] Kenneth C. Rogers, *A Report from the President: Traditions and Tomorrow*(SIT, 1974), 23.

[701] A Japanese student, Yokicki Yamada, and a student of Spanish-American heritage, Hector Fezandie, graduated in the first full class of Stevens in 1875. This trend continued with Jews and African-American students being admitted in the 19th century and early 20th century respectively.

tutor minority students from local high schools and prepare them for entry into college. Thus, in the winter of 1967-68, Bingham asked a junior, Philip J. Prijma 1970, to coordinate the project. Prijma was a skilled organizer who had run a students' festival, "Stevens Night," two years in a row and who had wide tutoring experience as a dormitory resident assistant and as a volunteer tutor for Tau Beta Pi honorary fraternity. Consequently, Prijma recruited motivated and idealistic undergraduate volunteers who would be paid minimal wages to help minority students learn science and mathematics for six weeks in the summer of 1968. After the recruitment of sixteen undergraduates, Prijma was taken aback when told by Bingham that the STEP program's expected level of funding from Redden would not be forthcoming, and there was only money for the summer salaries of the undergraduates. Moreover, classes had to be held in unfurnished apartments in a building under repair adjacent to the Stevens campus, and the STEP volunteers had to raise funds to pay for the space. Also, no money was available for supplies or for staff to recruit the minority students. In short, the undergraduate volunteers were thenceforth on their own.[702]

Undeterred and dedicated like a lot of other young people in the 1960s to the idea of helping minorities and the disadvantaged, Prijma and his committed activist volunteers, including Norby Machado, Ted Szauski, Joe Garvey and Al Stein among others, raised more funds by phoning private companies.[703] In addition, they phoned counselors and teachers they knew from Hoboken, Jersey City, Newark, New York City, and metropolitan-area high schools to find minority students who were good in mathematics. Thus, no sophisticated screening occurred in the first year of the program, and the volunteers took anyone recommended to them, including two junior-high students. When the summer came, Prijma and Machado even had to "borrow" the necessary bunks, desks, and chairs from vacant campus dormitories to set up quarters for the twenty-two pre-college students. As it turned out, their students had such a wide variety of ability that the teaching was done on a nearly one-to-one basis. The undergraduates believed that all their students could succeed and taught them accordingly. After the six-week course, the instructors and high school students turned out a pamphlet with photographs to commemorate their effort. In it, Prijma wrote the following:

---

[702] Phone conversation with Philip J. Prijma, Sept. 17, 1999 and with Snowden Taylor, Sept. 23, 1999.

[703] Other STEP volunteers in 1968 were Al Chernak, Jim Schneider, Gordon Quinones, Clive Dawson, Chris Wool, Gary Caine, Bert Davis, Tom Feneran, Bob Barker, Cardinal Warde, Don Liao, and Steve Howard, as listed in "STEP 1968," a pamphlet with photos of instructors and students in typeset written by the same in the summer of 1968, courtesy of the Stevens STEP office.

. . . speaking for the instructors, we have personally received a great deal in return. We have learned to work with people whose ideas and preferences were at times different from ours. We have realized the patience necessary to be a teacher and the understanding needed to be a friend. We have performed our jobs to the best of our ability. Now the burden of a search for more knowledge rests on your shoulders. We have been proud of your performance here at Stevens, and we expect to be equally proud of your performance in the coming year.

This program was not designed to increase only your skills in various subjects, but it was structured so that you would also recognize the value of each individual in the program, seeing the true person within, and at times overlooking his faults. It is our hope to have imparted to you a spark, at least, of the enthusiasm we instructors have had for this program, and that you are leaving with the desire to strive hard for all your ambitions which we hope will not only serve yourself but mankind as well.[704]

Thus, Prijma, later a medical doctor specializing in psychiatry, and other volunteer Stevens undergraduates were the pioneers of Stevens's successful STEP effort to expand the participation of minorities and the economically disadvantaged in careers in engineering and science, fields from which African-Americans in particular were mostly excluded until the late 1960s when they were helped by federal funding programs like the Equal Opportunity Fund (EOF).

With the help of its most dedicated faculty advisor and champion supporter for over twenty years, physics Professor Snowden Taylor 1950, STEP obtained a professional appointed director in the third year of its operation and proceeded to avail itself of federal, state, corporate, and foundation funding -- even though the majority of funds came from federal and state governments, the Exxon Corporation was a leading donor from private industry to STEP. By the 1970s, the new Rogers administration's dean of the college, Edward A. Friedman, appointed Debora Minor as director, which gave the program capable leadership for its success. Since 1968, through its various programs, STEP has helped over ninety percent of 2,800 minority high-school and junior-high-school students obtain a college education not only at Stevens but also at other colleges. STEP has also provided the model for campus-wide five-year retention program which allows any student in academic trouble to take a reduced load and graduate in five years, the fifth year being free of tuition if the student is advised and opts to take it late in the firs semester of the freshman year. Lastly, millions

---

[704] Ibid., 4. Trevor G. Williams, one of the 1968 minority students in the STEP program and now a Dean of Student Affairs at Stevens had only good words to describe his 1968 experience, telling the author, "Prijma changed my life."

of dollars in tuition fees for talented disadvantaged students who would not have been financially able to attend Stevens have been provided by STEP.

Just after Jess Davis announced his intention to retire because of brain cancer, there was a decision to admit women as undergraduates. Stevens had been more conservative than most engineering institutions and had retained the pre-Cold War attitude that engineering was a man's occupation. Nationally, that attitude changed in the revolutionary 1960s when women were admitted to most engineering institutions, and by 1971, in a Stevens conducted poll, only Caltech, Rose Polytechnic Institute, and Stevens were on a list of ten competing engineering colleges still turning women away. Moreover, Lehigh had just gone co-ed. Up to 1971, the Stevens admissions office used to send what was called a "No Tomato" letter to female applicants which politely said "no." However, since the Jess Davis administration sought to increase enrollments to 1,600 undergraduates by 1975 as part of its master plan, and the poll showed that four institutions had one hundred or more women enrolled, Director of Admissions Robert Seavy thought the institute should not hold out any longer. In a presentation to the faculty, Seavy reported that if women were admitted, there would be more quality applicants as well as more total applicants. MIT and RPI reported that the female students "more than hold their own academically." In his inimitable way, Seavy persuaded both the administration and the faculty with his argument which included the following:

We could not expect a truly co-ed atmosphere at Stevens nor could we expect to increase the low ratio of women to men without major additions to the curricula offerings. However, many girls have expressed an interest in Stevens through phone calls and contacts at their high schools with our admissions counselors. . . . there is little open resentment (at MIT and RPI), and after a while the girls fit into the program. It is interesting to note that a complaint from the girls is that they are ignored by a good number of students.[705]

At Stevens, the first nineteen women were admitted in the fall of 1971 as Stevens initiated a search for a new president, and, without any changes to the curriculum but with considerable changes in plumbing to add a suitable number of women's bathrooms, the enrollment of women grew at a modest rate, to 108 women in 1975 or eight percent of undergraduates and then to 207 or fourteen percent of undergraduates by 1979.[706]

---

[705] "No More Tomatoes," *Stevens Indicator,* winter 1971, 16-17.
[706] *ECPD Questionaire for Review of the Engineering Curriculum,* 1973, I, 16 and President's Report to the Board of Trustees, Nov. 24, 1982, 10.

CHAPTER 21

Legacies of the Cold War and Governance

S tarting in the 1970s, Stevens Institute suffered from budget deficits as a result of the legacy of the first half of the Cold War -- an expanded, overly tenured faculty. At the same time, the issues of rules for tenure, "governance" or the role of faculty in decision making, and faculty unionization arose. The result was a resounding defeat of collective bargaining at Stevens during the administration of President Kenneth C. Rogers. An unsuccessful strike by a weak union resulted in a strengthening of the principle of merit raises for faculty and bolstered the Stevens tradition of strong central decision-making by the president and trustees of the institute.

From the time of Henry Morton who served thirty-two years in office, the presidents of Stevens tended to have considerable power and lengthy terms. Humphreys served for twenty-four years and was both president of the institute and of the board of trustees which gave him the nickname the "Czar." Harvey N. Davis ceded power over the trustees to powerful alumni during the Great Depression but created new programs and hired new faculty as soon as he arrived for his twenty-three years at the helm. Under these first three presidents, the faculty typically not only taught and conducted research but also served as deans, registrars, admissions directors, and even treasurers, due to the small size of the institute. The only administrative position not filled by faculty members was the librarian, and even presidents taught. During the years before and during World War II, faculty were often gentlemen with an outside income like Hazeltine, or they supplemented their meager income as professors with consulting. Either way, they identified with and were loyal to the institute and there were few turnovers in faculty as many spent their whole careers at Stevens.

During these earlier decades, tenure was not an issue with the Stevens faculty. Faculty wages and benefits were so low that continued willingness to remain at Stevens was appreciated as an expression of loyalty and dedication. Governance was not an issue during these years when faculty were administrators. In 1915, the newly formed American Association of University Professors (AAUP) turned out its *General Report on Academic Freedom and Tenure* enumerating the first principles on tenure and legitimate grounds for dismissal of faculty. Later, in 1940, the AAUP and the American Association of Colleges formulated a new *Statement of Principles; Academic Freedom and Tenure*, a document which specified probationary periods before the award of tenure and due-process procedures for revoking tenure. At Stevens there was no discernible pro-or-con reaction to these statements.

The zenith of presidential power was held by Jess Davis in his administration of twenty years (1951-1971) during the heyday of the Cold War -- never before had a president of Stevens commanded such enormous balanced budgets, carried out such ambitious expansions in programs and buildings, and generally run the institute virtually as a president of a profitable corporation. Following trends elsewhere in America, during the Cold War Stevens increased the division of labor between an enlarging administration and faculty. A new range of administrative activities required professionals: in accounting; in the computer center; in the dean of research's office; in human resources; in the management of federal rules and regulations; in federal scholarships and loans; and in the array of expanded facilities and buildings which were often constructed or supported in part by overhead on research contracts. Under Jess Davis, the administration grew and became more professional.

At the same time, the expanded faculty followed a national trend of identification with specific disciplines, with the need to publish in one's field, and with an increased concern for academic professionalism. At Stevens, this trend first manifested itself among the newer research-oriented science faculty instead of the older engineering faculty who focused on teaching and found their professional identity in entrepreneurial activity and consulting. The expanded science faculty were conscious of their movement out of secondary service department status to become the most highly paid and tenured faculty group on the campus. During the late 1950s and early 1960s when employment boomed in academe and industry, tenure and merit raises were awarded by the Jess Davis administration with liberality.

During the Davis years, the profile of the faculty changed dramatically. The institute's modest thirty-five faculty of professorial rank after World War II expanded to 129 academics of professorial rank by 1973: First, those academic departments which obtained the most grant money grew the most in numbers. Comparing the academic years 1946-47 to 1972-73, physicists grew from five professors to twenty-six, and chemists from four professors to twelve. On the other end of the spectrum, those departments which obtained smaller grants did not share in the overall expansion of faculty, for example, the nine humanities professors the start of the cold war rose only to 12 by the early 1970s -- moreover, humanities professors as a percentage of the total faculty fell from twenty-five percent to ten percent. Second, the faculty dramatically improved in quality based on highest degree earned as was common elsewhere in the publish or perish era. At the start of the Cold War only thirteen of thirty-five professors held doctorates, but, by 1972-73, one hundred and eighteen of 129 professors held Ph.D.s or other doctorates. Also, in 1946 the thirty-five faculty of professorial rank were supplemented by twenty-nine faculty of instructor rank -- rarely holding doctorates -- or forty-five percent of the total faculty. By 1973, a score of teaching assistants from the ranks of full-time Ph.D. students had displaced the instructors to assist professors in grading, laboratory instruction, and recitation classes. [707]

During the period there was a nearly four hundred percent increase in full-time regular faculty of professorial rank which exceeded increases in the student body, the result being fewer contact hours teaching so that faculty would have more time to devote to research and Ph.D. students.[708] Before World War II, undergraduate enrollments rarely exceeded five hundred and only reached 803 during the wartime V-12 program of the Navy. In 1946, the figure is atypical because veterans programs swelled undergraduate enrollments to over one thousand temporarily, the figure of around 800 being more typical in the late 1940s and beginning of the 1950s. This figure compares with 1,407 undergraduate students at the height of enrollments during the Vietnam War in 1970 and gives a maximum undergraduate increase of 146 percent. Graduate enrollments grew from 346 masters-degree students in 1946 to 897 masters and doctoral students in 1973. The burden of teaching graduate students was offset for regular full-time faculty by an increase of part-time faculty, many of whom were full-time employees in technical corporations. Such adjunct, visiting, and research professors grew from twelve in 1946 to sixty by 1973. Typically, teaching loads of professors in physics and chemistry who were engaged in funded research were reduced during the Cold War from four to two or fewer courses. Under Jess Davis, funded research which provided overhead led to promotion, tenure, and merit raises at Stevens, and such activity justified Jess Davis awarding an average increase in compensation of more than eighty percent to all faculty during the late 1950s and 1960s, albeit a widening gap in salaries existed between the successful funded research faculty and those who taught and consulted.

---

[707] Comparisons of faculty are based on lists in yearly catalogues as well as *ECPD Questionnaire, 1973, Op.Cit.*

[708] The percentage increase in professorial ranks omits physical education faculty who were full-time faculty with the ranks of "Director," "Assoc. Director," and "Assistant Director" in 1946 but of professorial rank in 1973.

In 1966, the AAUP turned out its *Statement on Governance in Colleges and Universities* which laid out roles that trustees, administrators, and faculties should play in the new more-complicated institutions of higher learning. It expressed the concern of the more professional faculty that they had to have a share in decision-making and that governance structures should be written down. At the time such concerns of faculty were made stronger because of the rising opposition to the Vietnam War and involvement of professors in environmental concerns nationwide. The AAUP statement said that faculty should have primary authority over curriculum, research, and faculty participation in tenure and promotion procedures. In these areas, faculty should only be overruled in exceptional circumstances. [709]

Even before the AAUP statement was published, the Stevens Faculty Council, an elected body of tenured full professors created to advise the president on faculty concerns, had been aware of the issue and had asked Jess Davis for a written clarification on tenure and promotion procedures. At Stevens, such procedures had never been written down, and Jess Davis had not been wholly consistent -- in some cases, he had not sent a letter confirming tenure after a faculty member had been approved by a committee of peers and approved by a dean. Thus, in 1966, at the faculty council's urging, Jess Davis introduced the first written statement of a Stevens Promotions and Tenure (P&T) policy, "formulated with advice and suggestions of the Faculty Council."[710] This first policy written by the administration was vague and unsatisfactory to many of the Stevens faculty: For example, it specified that associate professors who passed through the peer review and were approved by the dean would not necessarily receive tenure if they were under thirty-five years of age. Moreover, Davis coupled the tenure policy with a statement that salary adjustments would be made based on twelve duties of faculty members -- this was the first written statement on what was later called "merit raises." He also included a "dismissal with cause" procedure which was unfavorable to faculty: A committee of faculty chosen by the president after consultation with the faculty council would hear both sides and forward their recommendation to the president, who, in turn, would add his recommendation and submit it to

---

[709] Courtney Leatherman, "Shared Governance Under Siege: Is It Time to Revive It or Get Rid of It?" *Chronicle of Higher Education*, Jan. 30, 1988.
[710] Letter of Jess Davis, January 24, 1966, to "All members of the Faculty," covering the 1966 P&T Policy.

the trustees for final action.[711] Faculty considered this procedure to be a wholly one-sided process.

By the late sixties, Davis was beginning to hedge on tenure and put the brakes on expansion of faculty. The reason was that money was starting to become tight. By 1967, Jess Davis had his first sizable budgetary deficit which was only covered by appropriations from the endowment. This deficit of over a quarter of a million dollars in a budget of over eleven million dollars was followed by another deficit in 1970. By that time it was already discernible that the federal government's Cold War policy of sponsoring academic research and development was in recession relative to the high point earlier.[712] With the advent of the Nixon administration and the Mansfield Amendment which specified that the DOD's research had to have immediate application to defense systems, there began an era with an increased stress on practical research as opposed to pure scientific research. For example, the NSF was told to stress the practical results coming from grants. In addition, the scientific community lost influence in Washington.[713]

The background to this change in attitude included the dismay of the nation with academe's revolt against the Vietnam War. Even on the Stevens campus which had few protests, the Vietnam War almost wrecked the Honor System as students did not want to turn in their fellow students in the fear that if they were thrown out of school they would be drafted. Moreover, physics faculty, led by George Yevick, Winston Bostick, and I. Richard Lapidus, spoke out against the war and decried the use of research to support weapons systems. Yevick called spending so many billions yearly for military purposes a "heinous crime." His reasoning was that "since the preponderance of hunger and poverty in the underdeveloped nations is the main threat to world peace, this money could be used for the positive purpose of helping these people."[714]

If Jess Davis was lucky in riding the crest of the wave of funding which only started to break by the time he retired and died in 1971, the next president was unlucky in having to lead the institute as the wave crashed. As federal grants started to become more competitive in the mid-1960s, they did so at an even more rapid rate in the early 1970s when double digit inflation caused severe budgetary problems to surface at Stevens. Thus, much of the efforts of the presidency of Kenneth C. Rogers was taken up

---

[711] Paragraphs 2.2 and 2.4 of the 1966 P&T Policy.

[712] Greenberg, *Op.Cit.*, xvi.

[713] *Ibid.*, xviii.

[714] "Physics Department Concerned over the Use of Its Research," *The Stute*, Mar. 7, 1969, 1.

with managing budgetary crises. The legacy of the Cold War expansion under Jess Davis was an aging, highly tenured and costly faculty who were not as able in obtaining funded research grants in a much more competitive era. Rogers' budgetary troubles had their origins in the previous administration, in the nationwide economic trends as well as in federal policy on research funds.[715]:

A budget deficit of 2.7 percent occurred during the interim year of 1971 while the institute found a new president. Kenneth C. Rogers had headed the physics department and obtained sizable grants in the last years of the Davis administration, and this achievement was a significant factor in his selection. Rogers immediately faced a budget crisis of major proportions. First, Rogers reduced the untenured faculty by ten percent in the second year of his administration, but he could not reduce the tenured physics and chemistry-chemical engineering faculty, whose numbers were to remain at a high level for another generation or more. It should be noted that Davidson Laboratories and the Laboratory of Psychological Studies, although they had large increases in staff during the peak years of the Cold War, were not generally teaching facilities and therefore the staff increases were not in professorial, tenure-track ranks. Thus, during the downturn in federal research money in the 1970s, such non-tenured staff were reduced comparatively easily and quickly.

Deficits were compounded by a reduction of enrollments after the end of the Vietnam War: Graduate enrollments declined from a high of 1,382 in 1968 to 875 in 1974, and undergraduate enrollments declined from a high of 1,402 in 1970 to 1,173 in 1974. In 1971, Stevens suffered a sixteeen percent decline of applications for undergraduate enrollment following the national trend: for example, Harvard had twelve percent fewer applications and Yale eighteen percent.[716] At Stevens, these declines would have been easier to withstand if the endowment had been large enough, but Stevens's small endowment did not allow for much withdrawal from its largely restricted funds. The endowment was approximately forty million dollars in 1967-68, but, by the end of the Davis administration, it had declined by ten million dollars. During Rogers's early deficits, the trustees authorized some further drawing down from the endowment which had bounced back in a rising stock market to $45 million by 1972, but then declined by five million dollars by 1975-76. Meanwhile, costs were soaring because of

---

[715] Frederick Rudolph, *The American College and University; a History*(1990), 489-96.
[716] "The Well's Run Dry," *Stevens Indicator*, 88 (1971), 16, cited the *Wall Street Journal*, Sept. 2, 1971 for these statistics.

inflation, particularly in fuel oil and electricity as a result of the OPEC oil cartel.

One pressing problem that faced the new administration was the poor result of the Centennial Drive established by Jess Davis to implement part of his ambitious plan: the construction of a new Chemistry-Chemical Engineering building to accommodate Pollara's expanded department. It was found that the regular yearly alumni "Stevens Fund" drive conducted by the Stevens Alumni Association (SAA) suffered as a result of giving to the Centennial Drive, which in turn fell short of expectations.[717] This led to negotiations between the independent corporate entity of the SAA and the president and board of trustees to increase coordination between the institute's and the alumni's fundraising efforts. From the administration's point of view, few alumni associations in the country still acted independently in fundraising. From the SAA's perspective, loss of its traditional fundraising role was seen as a threat to its independent status. Nonetheless, given the "deepening financial situation of the Institute" as well as pressure from the trustees over "the reduced income of the Institute," the SAA agreed in 1973 to amend its by-laws so that contributions to the Stevens Fund would be "under the direction of the Institute" and the funds would "flow into the treasury of Stevens." The autonomy of the SAA was retained, but its budget, however, would be provided by the institute. Under the previous procedure, the SAA paid for its own budget first and then gave the remainder of the funds it raised to the institute. It was clear from the reportage of this agreement that many alumni still felt some reservations about the new arrangement.[718]

In 1972, Rogers organized an institute-wide conference on governance because faculty were vocally not satisfied with governance as it had been conducted under Davis. A president from the faculty ranks, Rogers took these faculty concerns seriously and appointed a special President's Committee on Governance later in 1972 to make recommendations "to enhance the relationships between all members of the community and allow for a fuller enfranchisement of faculty and students vis a vis their dealings with the staff and administration." Chaired by Professor Alfred Bornemann and influenced by the new vice president for academic affairs, Henry Burlage, the committee recommended the replacement of faculty committees with a complicated system of boards and creation of a senate representing all

---

[717] Frank Cashin, "Letter from the Alumni Association President," *Stevens Indicator*, Oct. 1971, 2, and Robert C. Sturken, "Letter from the Alumni Association President," *Ibid.*, Sept. 1972, 2.
[718] "Association Moves Closer to Institute; By-Law Changes Approved-- A Unified Fund Raising Approach," *Stevens Indicator*, 91 (1974), 2, 4.

constituencies in order to alleviate the "current crisis" and "dissatisfaction and discontent." The committee found a "lack of clear-cut statement of the role of the faculty in the governance of the Institute" and a "lack of a set of faculty rules and procedures." The report concluded that

The government of industries, universities and colleges as well as many other of our institutions contains autocratic elements (probably handed down from feudal times) modified and tempered throughout the last one or two hundred years by democratic principles. Furthermore, limits on the exercise of absolute and arbitrary power by an individual are pragmatic realities as there is a well recognized axiom that one cannot govern long without the consent of the governed.[719]

Ironically, it was not Rogers who objected to the solutions presented by the document but rather the faculty itself. On the one hand, it was thought by a majority of faculty to be too complicated and too time-consuming to man the boards and senate, and, on the other hand, a minority of faculty talked of a simpler and more direct solution, unionization of the faculty. The structure was dubbed "Burlage's Boards" and denigrated as an administrative solution which would involve faculty in too many administrative, mundane, day-to-day decisions and tasks.[720]

At the same time, Rogers and the faculty council worked on revising the unsatisfactory P&T policy of 1966 with more fruitful results. Faculty council members, professors Larry Levine, Snowden Taylor, Angelo Volpe, Preston Clement, and Richard Magee, and the president conducted ongoing discussions "for several hours each week" during the spring and fall of 1973 to turn out a new P&T policy by 1974.[721] The result was a much-improved policy which, for the first time, had the approval of elected faculty representatives. Terms of appointment by ranks were established, and the procedure of peer review by the P&T committee and the president were laid out in writing. Showing his willingness to share power at the time, Rogers approved a 1974 revision which created a review panel consisting of three members, one chosen by the president and one chosen by the faculty council and the third chosen by both of these parties. The panel would review

---

[719] A. Bornemann, et al, "Report of the President's Committee on Governance," February, 1974.

[720] In a letter from Kenneth C. Rogers to the author dated December 5, 1999, the ex-president commented, "The rising faculty disaffection for Henry Burlage was also an important factor in the move to unionization. At one point, prior to the AAUP decision to request NLRB to oversee the definition of a potential bargaining unit which would then vote on whether to unionize or not, I asked Professor Lapidus what I could do to halt the movement towards unionization. His response was immediate and simple, 'Get rid of Henry Burlage.' "

[721] Testimony of K. Rogers, *United States of America Before the National Labor Relations Board Division of Judges Branch Office, New York, N. Y.* JD-(NY)-108-82, 36.

decisions of the president when he could not concur with the P&T committee. If the review panel unanimously disagreed with the president's decision, then the decision was automatically overturned and the faculty member's name was forwarded to the trustees for the award of tenure.

One problem facing the drafters of the 1974 P&T policy involved those faculty of associate professor rank who had either been retained past any reasonable time to dismiss them or who had earlier been recommended by peer review but had not been recommended for tenure to the board of trustees by Jess Davis because he considered them too young. These faculty were to be brought to the P&T Committee immediately, and, if found suitable for tenure, their names were to be recommended to the trustees for award of tenure in 1974. Having been fair to the faculty in limbo, the 1974 P&T policy nevertheless continued the Davis policy of postponing tenure for some faculty who had passed through peer review. The president and faculty council created a special appointment status, namely, faculty who could be given "special appointments with tenure decision deferred." This status was to be granted when "the president finds that the continued service of the individual would be of great value to Stevens, but finds that the financial position of Stevens will not permit the award of tenure." The context of this special appointment was an overly-tenured faculty, the budgetary problems, as well as Davis's precedents.[722] From the faculty's point of view, the 1974 P&T policy's clause on "dismissal with cause" was a great improvement on the 1966 version because it had redundant peer-review checks and balances which assured due process. In addition, the policy also introduced a "grievance" procedure for the first time.[723]

Almost immediately, members of the Stevens chapter of the AAUP criticized the faculty council and Rogers for the 1974 P&T policy, because it included the decision-on-tenure-deferred rank and failed to meet AAUP guidelines for grievance procedures. The AAUP, led by the outspoken physics professor I. Richard Lapidus, also criticized the plan of Rogers and the trustees to balance the budget. Called the "Three Year Recovery Plan" (1975-1978), it froze salaries institute-wide in its first year, and then provided for merit raises for faculty at five percent of total faculty salaries in the second year. Under this plan, by 1975 the actual deficit was reduced

---

[722] "1974 Policy on Faculty Promotions and Tenure," para IV-10 and VII-1(c). The appointment in this status was limited and not to exceed three years, during which time the faculty member remained eligible for tenure on a list of faculty approved for tenure by the committee unless it specifically removed the member; the faculty member with decision on tenure deferred status had to be notified one year before the end of the appointment if the appointment was terminal.

[723] See G. Clark, "Review of SIT Grievance/Dismissal with Cause Procedures With Recommendations," Report to Faculty Council, Dec. 20, 1996, 4-7.

$1.5 million or a whopping ten percent of the budget, to $773,000 in the second year, and then a projected $327,000 in the third year. Successful as it was in reducing the budget deficits, it nevertheless was unpopular with faculty caught in the double-digit inflation of the early 1970s. Thus, the three-year recovery plan was the chief reason why a segment of the faculty decided to form a union under the auspices of the AAUP to try to obtain raises through collective bargaining. Improvement of P&T policy, the grievance procedures, and faculty participation in governance were important secondary reasons for forming the union. This union movement occurred even though Rogers held meetings with all faculty to explain in detail the reasons for the recovery plan, and even though many faculty reluctantly supported the plan. The problem for the AAUP was that the faculty was almost evenly split on the issue of unionization -- the faculty vote in January 1976 for NLRB certification of the AAUP as agent for Stevens's union carrying only by a single ballot, fifty-one to fifty. Many faculty did not even take the time to vote, which Rogers afterwards said was shocking, given the vote's importance.

During the subsequent negotiations, the AAUP leadership led by management professor Frederick W. Cleveland and physics professor I. Richard Lapidus followed the agenda of unions in trying to include as many faculty as possible in the bargaining unit, and thus challenged the administration's traditional management practice of appointing department heads and special faculty. They proposed that department heads be elected and therefore be included in the bargaining unit. They also proposed that full-time research and affiliate professorships be eradicated, that faculty in the status of "decision on tenure deferred" be given tenure, and that raises be based partly on an index of inflation instead of wholly on merit -- most importantly, they proposed immediate raises based on an inflation index.[724] The administration and trustees consequently hardened their attitudes by rejecting these proposals and responded with a tough management rights clause, a provision for raises solely on merit, and a reiteration, even up to the eleventh hour, that there could be no movement on deviation from the salary pool as it was laid out the recovery plan.[725] After months of deadlock, the Stevens chapter of the AAUP voted to walk out on December 15, 1976. Knowing the weakness of the union by its own poll of reliable faculty conducted by Pollara, provost at the time, the administration decided to bargain only on the peripheral issues that it was required to do by law. One

---

[724] See AAUP negotiation proposals dated April 28, 1976, attached to the Minutes of the Stevens Board of Trustees, January 17, 1977.
[725] Ibid., 4.

week before the strike during a meeting of the board of trustees, the minutes record the attitude of Rogers and the trustees:

The President emphasized that the Administration would not depart from its position with respect to the proposal presented to the AAUP, representing a merit salary increase averaging 5%, even if a strike should be called, and the Trustees expressed firm agreement with this position. The President stated further that the Institute's negotiations would continue to make every effort to resolve the many outstanding contract issues in an equitable basis while also attempting to preserve the fundamental concepts of collegiality in so far as attainable under unionization, and the principle of basing all adjustments in faculty compensation on merit.[726]

In the last week of negotiations, held at the neutral setting of a Jersey City motel, the union negotiators, sensing their weakness, gave in on issues of governance. Since the administration held firm on the size of the salary pool, which was the main issue for most of the rank and file, the AAUP commenced a strike at the start of the semester in January 1977 in frigid weather conditions in one of the coldest winters on record. Not surprisingly, the first day only half of the regular full-time faculty appeared on the picket lines. Generally, the strikers turned out to be lesser-paid management, humanities, mathematics, and engineering faculty. The other half of the full-time regular faculty, mostly higher-paid physicists, chemists, and engineers, along with department heads, administrators, and part-time adjunct faculty, kept Stevens open for three weeks in what turned out to be the longest-running strike in AAUP history. During the strike, the pickets attempted to win over the non-striking faculty whom they knew personally, and this effort, as well as an effort to win over the student body by having them boycott classes, gave the strike a rather genteel quality of knots of people engaged in conversations between classes. The non-striking faculty and students, evidently more influenced by an open and sobering letter by the chairman of the board of trustees, Frederick L. Bissinger, than by the leaflets of the strikers, listened politely or reasoned with the pickets to give up their effort. Bissinger's letter reiterated the rationale for the recovery plan and noted its success thus far in dollar figures. He noted also the decline in enrollments, as the cause of the budgetary crisis. Finally, the letter stated the trustees' opposition to the union's challenge to the institute's management prerogatives, particularly to the election of department heads, and finished by saying the "union is philosophically at odds with the concept of collegiality."[727]

---

[726] Ibid., page C.
[727] See copy of Bissinger's letter attached to January 18, 1977 Minutes of the Board of Trustees.

In spite of the intervention of an NLRB mediator at the request of the union, negotiations went nowhere, given the lack of numbers of strikers and their inability to close down classes. At the end of the second week of the strike, Provost Pollara had two willing department heads replace two tenured, striking professors, a legal act, according to the rules of the NLRB, if such replacements kept the institute open and running during a strike.[728] Even though union spokesmen branded this action as intimidation and an attempt to bust the union, it was obvious that the ill-fated strike was not succeeding in its aims. After another desultory week of no movement in negotiations, the union leadership called for a vote to end the strike without obtaining a contract.

Striking professors and some supportive students react to bad news in the Union Club, the headquarters of the union during the cold winter of 1977.

Subsequently, because the strike was so long and resulted in such a resounding defeat, Stevens came to national attention through an article in the respected journal *Science*. Through extended interviews, the reporter provided a picture of the faculty division which underlay the strike at Stevens: Although the fundamental issue was the freeze on salaries and the recovery

---

[728] See undated "Memorandum regarding strikes" from the law firm of Apruzzi and McDermott which listed the rights of management during strikes attached to Ibid.

plan in a period of inflation, the article outlined antagonisms among the faculty. Referring to the physics department, the reporter said that during the 1950s and 1960s,

Energetic new people were brought in and the department took off, particularly in plasma physics and the related areas of solid-state and low-temperature physics. The young turks were successful in bringing in federal grants, they pushed through curriculum changes . . . . There was a clash between old and new. The physicists were seen by their critics as without loyalty to Stevens's traditions, and as rather self-seeking careerists looking for personal recognition in the national competition for publication and research grants. The chemists followed the same path as the physicists, forming a combined department of chemistry and chemical engineering and allying with the physicists in their expansionary ways. . . . But a more than symbolic event occurred with the naming of Kenneth C. Rogers to the Stevens presidency in 1972. Rogers was chairman of the physics department at Stevens when he was appointed president. His accession and the later appointment of Pollara as provost was seen as capping the rise of the "scientists" to the top posts which had traditionally been held by engineers. The legacy of the transition period was a coolness between the science and engineering faculty . . . . It is clear that the engineers as a group feel that they carry an unfair burden of teaching and regard the scientists as generally being better paid and having more time for research. Unquestionably, the engineers felt they were slighted in the 1960s. . . . As for relations between scientists and engineers, the comment by one engineer that "the two groups are not close at all," seems fair.[729]

After the fruitless strike, the AAUP negotiating team, led by Cleveland, prodded a reluctant administration for more negotiations, its idea being to sign the best possible contract for the union's mere survival. Meanwhile, the administration felt pressure to rehire the two "replaced" tenured faculty who were suing the institute, a development which subsequently led to their reinstatement. With the administration standing firm on its last contract proposal, union leadership chose to sign the contract which the administration had been forced by NLRB rules to put on the table as its last offer, a contract written by the administration and its lawyer which Rogers said was

. . . wholly consistent with our Financial Recovery Plan requirements. It does not jeopardize the Institute's future as a quality institution because individual accountability and merit are explicitly recognized. Moreover, the contract defines faculty responsibilities and the management rights of the Board of Trustees in much clearer terms than ever before at Stevens. Given the legal necessity of a faculty union con-

---

[729] John Walsh, "Stevens Institute of Technology: After the Strike, Still Unsettled," *Science*, 195 (1977), April 15, 282.

tract, we feel this agreement (which incorporates the Institute's final offer as approved by the Board of Trustees last spring) is very satisfactory from Stevens' point of view.[730]

For the rank and file of the AAUP chapter, the contract was a bitter pill to swallow after picketing in the freezing temperatures in the January-February 1977 strike which resulted in them being docked in salary for the three weeks they withheld their services. In the years after the strike, the dispirited membership dwindled, but the leadership of the chapter and chief negotiator Cleveland doggedly continued to go through the motions of negotiation of two-year contracts with the administration. The union, claiming unfair labor practices, supported suits against the institute, and the AAUP censored Stevens.

President Kenneth C. Rogers and Chairman of the Board of Trustees of Stevens Institute of Technology Frederick L. Bissinger are shown here around the time of their triumph over the faculty union in the late 1970s.

In spite of these developments, the policy of Rogers was to seek no reprisal against the strikers, and many of them were promoted in rank and given raises -- even made administrators and department heads later -- in the years that followed. Rogers told his deans and the provost to ignore the past and base raises and promotions solely on merit. He sympathized with faculty whose income was squeezed by the recovery plan which had been

---

[730] "So, Where Is the Strike Now?" *Stevens Indicator,* Spring 1977, 6.

brought on by factors beyond the control of either the current administration or current faculty. This conciliatory attitude on the part of the president was based on his desire to bring the faculty together after the ordeal, something he later said was his greatest accomplishment at Stevens.[731] Thus, apart from a few individuals, surprisingly little bitterness emerged from the strike episode on either side, certainly not from the administration which had won hands-down, nor from most of the faculty.

Then came the *Yeshiva* decision which led to the end of the union on the Stevens campus: In 1980, a judge decertified a faculty union at Yeshiva University based on the finding that faculty members were actually administrators. Subsequently, the Rogers administration, following trends elsewhere, ceased to bargain with the AAUP by using the same claim. The beleaguered union rump, unable to even ask for support for another strike, fought a rear-guard action by suing the institute for withdrawing recognition of a collective-bargaining representative certified by the NLRB. The institute won the case by essentially replicating the argument of Yeshiva University that the faculty were not mere employees but were also part of management, given their participation in such activities as hiring and promotions and tenure decisions.[732] According to Rogers, one important factor in identification of the Stevens faculty as managers was their participation in committees:

I insisted, sometimes over the objections of some hard-line members of the Board of Trustees, that the traditional pre-union faculty governance role in the academic life of the Institute not be lost under collective bargaining. It is my recollection that Faculty meetings chaired by the President continued with debates and votes on curriculum and other matters, and the Faculty Council continued to exist to advise the President although somewhat constrained since it could not "bargain" on behalf of the faculty, and that most of the pre-union Faculty Committees continued to function. When the Institute decided to no longer recognize the Faculty Union and was obligated to defend its actions in NLRB hearings, the continuation of those faculty responsibilities as well as the pre-union contract faculty responsibilities led to an NLRB decision to sustain the Institute's actions in breaking off with the Faculty Union.[733]

---

[731] Phone conversation with Kenneth C. Rogers, Oct. 25, 1999.

[732] See decision of November 8, 1982 rendered by Winifred. D. Morio, Administrative Law Judge, in the case of *The Trustees of Stevens Institute of Technology and The Stevens Chapter of the American Association of University Professors. United States of America Before the National Labor Relations Board. Division of Judges, Branch Office, New York, New York.*

[733] Notes addended to the latter of K. C. Rogers to the author dated Dec. 5, 1999.

After this judicial rendering in 1982, the Stevens AAUP chapter ceased to operate as a union and became insignificant as a force on campus. Thereafter, Rogers used the last union contract as a reference point for promotions and tenure and other practices like merit raises. Thus, there was a resignation by faculty to issues of governance, and the attention of faculty was turned to other initiatives such as the curriculum -- the administration appointed a large number of union activists to a curriculum committee in 1978.

Returning to the relations between the institute and the SAA, there seemed to be distrust on each side. In 1981, the leadership of the SAA decided to apply for trademarks for the alumni association logo, for the Stevens Fund and for the *Stevens Indicator,* the alumni magazine. Rogers and the trustees responded with a strong resolution to block the applications in the November 1981 board meeting. At that meeting, the board of trustees reaffirmed Rogers's authority over all fundraising activity, including the Stevens Fund and stripped the SAA of its traditional function of job placement for graduates. The board demanded that the SAA abandon its trademark applications and indicated the institute would undertake to make such applications. The SAA's executive committee conceded to the wishes of the board of trustees, but stated it had "serious reservations regarding and does not agree with the actions of the board of trustees of the institute taken on November 18, 1981, with respect to the alumni association."[734]

Meanwhile, the old Jess Davis era's master plan calling for a new gymnasium and buildings on the docks was put off in favor of Rogers's plan to refurbish current buildings and raise funds for a new dormitory, Technology Hall. The dormitory was subsequently built partly with a bond issue because a major fundraising drive, Technology for Tomorrow, did not meet expectations. In addition, although Rogers was able to enhance some departments, particularly the metallurgy department, he was hampered by the over-tenured faculty in being able to recruit a critical mass of new and younger faculty in many departments.[735] This inability resulted in critics

---

[734] *Stevens Indicator,* 99 (1982), 2, 14, and "Minutes of Board of Trustees," Nov. 18, 1981, 3, and April 27, 1982.

[735] Rogers recalls, "The Metallurgy Department was a focus of my interest, because it joined science and engineering very naturally, and because it offered promise of considerable opportunities for expansion and distinction. I put Gerry Rothberg in as Department Head, despite his position as Professor of Physics, because he had good working relations with the faculty in the department and could lead them into modern materials work. I made considerable personal effort to negotiate the acquisition of sophisticated surface studies equipment by getting a donation of and low purchase of equipment from an industrial lab in Tuxedo Park that was shutting down and moving to the Research Triangle. I traveled by myself to the lab to inspect the equipment, made them an offer of $100,000 for all the equipment in the lab on the spot. The total had a book value of probably ten

who claimed the administration was allowing the reputation of the institute to flounder.

Rogers continued to show he was a strong president but not without a counter-reaction: He replaced several department heads because of opposition to the policies of his vice president of academic affairs, and one of them brought suit. The suit was settled out of court but not until after it became a celebrated cause in the student newspaper and among some alumni circles. As a result, some disgruntled alumni and faculty led a "Time for A Change" movement which spread to a segment of the trustees and student body. In particular, in the fall of 1986 the *Stute* called for a change in administration. Also, in the spring of 1987 the institute tried to do away with the autonomy of the SAA which resulted in a suit and a counter-suit which were later dropped.[736] Clearly, the situation had grown completely out of hand for Rogers. At the end of the year, he decided to leave Stevens to accept President Reagan's offer of a prestigious seat on the Nuclear Regulatory Commission, having been appointed by President George Bush, where he served two five-year terms.

Looked at with the perspective of time, one important historical result of the Rogers years (1972-1987) was the preservation, if not the strengthening, of the power of the institute's president and trustees -- an ironic legacy for Rogers, who had been intent on expanding the power of faculty in governance at the start of his administration. In the end, it was the financial situation of the institute which Rogers inherited that necessitated a strong hand with both the SAA and the union. In the case of the former, its traditional independent procedures at the end of a period of increasing nationwide professionalization of fundraising in higher education resulted in concessions to the institute, and, in the case of the latter, the choice of striking with barely half of the faculty sealed the fate of shared governance based on the model of collective bargaining.

By the 1990s, the pendulum of opinion on governance had swung in a direction against the AAUP guidelines on shared governance. Boards of

---

times that even though I didn't know where the money was going to come from, and it was a large enough purchase to require Board of Trustees approval (which I didn't have at that point). However, a nearby commercial research company was very anxious to buy the equipment, and was willing to pay more than $100,000 just for the two major pieces, not the entire suite of equipment. By using the leverage of some Stevens Alumni and a Stevens Trustee, I got the laboratory director to accept my offer, even though, to improve his bottom line, he would have liked to sell to the commercial lab. That equipment made it possible for the Department to begin competing for important new grants and contracts and ultimately to qualify for significant State of NJ assistance." President Rogers also hired the future Department Head, Bernard Gallois, who later became Dean of the Schaefer School of Engineering at Stevens. Letter of Rogers to the author, Dec. 5, 1999.

[736] Bill Campbell, "Alumni Fighting Stevens' Takeover," *The Jersey Journal*, May 2, 1987.

trustees and regents nationwide were attacking the concept. Moreover, they were abrogating AAUP guidelines on governance on such issues as appointment of increasing numbers of special faculty which was seen as an alternative to tenure by boards of trustees. Collective bargaining agreements or governance schemes loaded down with complicated faculty by-laws were said to hamper the kind of quick and effective decision making needed by presidents in the new post-Cold War era. As institutions of higher learning competed with each other over new programs to attract students, over obtaining earmarked congressional funds, and even over potential markets for distance learning, restrictions on quick decision-making were said to make institutions dysfunctional. During the reform of education at all levels and its corresponding antagonism to faculty unions, the Association of Governing Boards of Universities and Colleges turned out a controversial statement on institutional governance which cited greater accountability of faculty, the changing demands of technology, and the shifting faculty job market for justifying a more flexible and stronger role in decision-making for presidents.[737]

At the beginning of the twenty-first century, the president and trustees at Stevens enjoy a good deal of that power and flexibility of action. However, the collegial work started by Rogers and the faculty council in 1974 to have clear-cut written procedures of promotion and tenure, as well as grievance, dismissal with cause, and other procedures, was nearly completed with the publication of a lengthy faculty manual. This was accomplished in 1999 through the urgings of the faculty council and through consultations with a dean's council led by Dean Bernard Gallois under the sixth president of Stevens, Harold J. Raveché.

---

[737] See John Walker Scott, "Defending the Tradition of A Shared Governance," *Chronicle of Higher Education,* Aug. 9, 1996, 131, Courtney Leatherman, "Colleges Failure to Tackle Academic Problems in 1980s Led to Lack of Collaboration," *Ibid.,* Jan. 23, 1991, A13, Courtney Leatherman, "Commission Recommends Strengthening College Presidents' Power," *Ibid.,* Sept. 13,1996, and James T. Richardson, "Centralizing Governance Isn't Simply Wrong; It's Bad Business Too," *Ibid.,* Feb. 12, 1999,

CHAPTER 22

Computer Education and Wiring the Campus

S tevens was the first college in the nation to require all its students to own a computer. In addition, Stevens was one of the first colleges to completely network its campus, not only linking work-stations, laboratories, the computer center, administration and faculty offices but also all dormitory rooms. This effort at Stevens was remarkable given the limited resources of the institute -- it meant that the expensive hardware and software had to be obtained through agreements with industrial suppliers and through grants. Being first to require that all students own computers helped in obtaining favorable deals and grants, an effort led by Stevens administrators and science faculty.

As early as 1946, Stevens's mathematicians introduced undergraduates to computer theory using mechanical calculators to simulate ideas because the campus did not have a computer. By the 1954-55 academic year, a group of undergraduates, working with professor Frederick C. Strong III in his chemistry laboratory in the Morton building, actually built a simple computer in a senior design project. The project had been proposed to the students by Strong and a previous undergraduate, William J. Ambs 1954. The project was to automate a procedure in chemical laboratory work, gravimetric analysis. In this procedure, a sample is weighed, solution added, and the solution and sample heated and agitated. An insoluble compound precipitates out, the precipitant is washed, dried, and then weighed again to determine the amount of the compound in the original sample. The team of students was David Farber, Melvyn Nutkis, Charles Staloff and Thomas Velky of the class of 1956. Using chemistry and a lot of mechanical and electrical, the students designed and constructed a robot which eliminated human labor except for the weighing and insertion of a punched card which programmed their computerized robot. The robot operated motors, including a motor to drag the card over fingers which read it and tripped relay switches, a motor which turned a turntable full of flasks, a motor to suck up a solution, and another to open and close valves. Electrical circuits employed on-off switches which were convenient to set up with binary logic, and the logic of the whole computational circuitry was worked out prior to construction. Since some operations of the apparatus occurred more than once or were interlocked, some recursion was built into the circuitry. To make the apparatus more flexible, only the interlocking operations were built in, and the rest of the logic was programmed on punch cards to assure flexibility in use of the robot for analysis of different chemical compounds.[738]

This project directly helped the career of David Farber. It helped him land a job during the summer of 1955 between his junior and senior year with a U.S. Navy laboratory helping to develop the world's first transistorized analog computer, a machine used to check the designs of the first nuclear submarines. Farber found himself on the cutting edge of computer engineering because the use of transistors in computers was being developed at the same time by Bell Telephone Laboratories in New Jersey. After receiving his M.E. degree in 1956, Farber was recruited by Bell Labs where he helped design the first electric switching system (ESS) -- every current telephone is switched by descendants of this system. Of course, Bell Labs was the place to be in the development of software as well as networks. At Bell Labs, Farber and his colleagues designed the programming language SNOBOL used in manipulation of texts.[739] At an early point in his career at Bell Labs, Farber was going to return to academe for a Ph.D., but was dissuaded by a colleague with the argument that the Stevens graduate was already at the cutting edge of computer technology and didn't need a doctorate. He supplemented his M.E. degree by returning to nearby Stevens to improve his foundation in mathematics, in which he earned an M.S. in 1961.

In 1955, an M.S. degree was established in computers and taught by an interdepartmental team with the assistance of part-time professors from Bell Labs which also sent many of its staff to earn the degree at Stevens.[740] Computers were taking off after transistors were used in their construction in 1956, the first powerful computers being developed for atomic scientists. Under the leadership of mathematics professor Nicholas J. Rose 1945, the first academic computer center was established on campus on the first floor of the Navy Building in 1962 under the direction of Professor Anthony Ralston, another mathematician who later became editor of the *Encyclopedia of Computer Science and Engineering* and who wrote a well-received text on numerical analysis. In that year, Stevens acquired its first computer for teaching and academic research, a used three-million-dollar Sperry Rand UNIVAC 1105, which was soon joined by a smaller yet useful IBM

---

[738] Farber, Nutkis, Staloff, Velky and Zaorski, "The Gravimeter Robot," *Senior Report*, 1956. Stevens Special Collections.

[739] SNOBOL was developed initially by David Farber, Ralph Griswold and Ivan Polonsky at Bell Labs in the mid-1960s. Anthony Ralston, ed., *Encyclopedia of Computer Science and Engineering*. 2nd edition, 1354.

[740] The program and its history are described briefly in *Stevens Institute of Technology Annual Catalog, 1957*, 51.

1620.[741] A year afterward, a computer course to teach the FORTRAN programming language was added to the undergraduate engineering and science programs. After the modern computer center was built in 1969, Stevens purchased its first time-sharing mainframe computer, a Digital Equipment Corporation PDP-10. This type of new state of the art mainframe computer initially supported access via punch card technology and soon evolved to support terminal access via teletype machines.

Meanwhile, the first national computer network designed for the protection of military communication, in case of nuclear attack was built and demonstrated in 1972. ARPANET, built by the Advanced Research Projects Agency (ARPA), was a distributed communication system which would work even if central nodes were knocked out. In 1969, Bell Labs' Francis T. Boesch was part of a White House Division of Emergency Preparedness task force to test the reliability of the design of the ARPANET, particularly the needed redundancy of line capacity. The question was how much redundancy should be built into the ARPANET, and the answers came from Bell Labs, where redundancy in telephone networks was an expertise. As a result of this work, Boesch along with two other participants, Ivan Frisch and Daniel Kleitman, founded the journal *Networks* in 1971. This journal, which covered mathematical analysis of network performance and reliability, the first such journal covering the new field at the time, had Boesch as co-editor from 1971 to 1999. In 1971, Boesch began teaching at Stevens while continuing to work at Bell Labs, and he later became head of the electrical engineering and computer science department in 1979 and Dean of the Faculty in 1987.

Another Stevens professor who had worked in Davidson Laboratories for nine years was instrumental in establishing the ARPANET. Research Professor of Physics Stephen J. Lukasik had been chief of the fluid physics division of Davidson Laboratories from 1957-1966. His work at Davidson Laboratories was the springboard to his job at ARPA from 1966 to 1974, and he became director of ARPA from 1971 to 1974 when the ARPANET became operational. Lukasik's leadership was enlightened but politically aware. Thus, while he fostered research which had little to do with military applications, he knew that such research should not have ARPA's name on it because Congress would criticize such projects.[742] Lukasik's testimony before Congress about the cost-savings of using the ARPANET for military

---

[741] "Great Teachers at Castle Point," *Stevens Indicator*, 79 (1962), no. 1, 14.

[742] Katie Hafner and Matthew Lyon, *Where Wizards Stay Up Late: The Origins of the Internet*(1996), 192-3.

data transmission was crucial in obtaining more funding for the ARPANET. He pointed out that

Before the network we were in many cases forced to select research groups at institutions with large computing resources or which were large enough to justify their own dedicated computer system. Now it is feasible to contract with small talented groups anywhere in the country and supply them, rapidly and economically, with the computer resources they require via the network.[743]

Also, after David Farber had participated in the formation of electronic communications on the ARPANET by being coordinator of the Message Services Group which developed early e-mail addresses, Lukasik became the chief promoter of e-mail over this first national network when he became director of ARPA. He is recognized as having created an organizational need for e-mail when it was a new phenomenon by requiring all ARPA personnel to communicate with him via the medium, thus making it a crucial communications link.[744] During his career at ARPA, Lukasik also tried to protect federal funding for the computer science community when its field was taking off.[745] Later, Lukasik, who earlier had worked with Rogers in the physics department, accepted his invitation to become a Stevens trustee.

On campus, the computer center manager and technical hardware expert for subsequent developments was Leslie Maltz. She arrived on campus in December 1970, one year before Stevens admitted women undergraduates for the first time.[746] She was twenty-four years old and one of the first women to obtain a master's degree in computer science from Rutgers University. Computer science programs were in their infancy at the time -- the first one being established at Carnegie-Mellon University in 1965. Maltz was the only member of the new computer center staff with a degree in computer science, and as a result, she was made manager of the programming staff and led teams of undergraduates on software projects. At the time, Digital Equipment Corporation's "Tops Ten" software was an incomplete operating system, and the problem of developing an operating system for academic purposes was solved by Maltz. Her teams of typically

---

[743] Lukasik's statement before Congress in 1972 quoted in Janet Ellen Abbate, "From ARPANET to Internet: A History of ARPA-sponsored computer networks, 1966-1988," University of Michigan Ph.D. dissertation, 81.

[744] R. R. Bowker, *American Men and Women of Science, 1998-99*, 1105-6, Abbate, *Op.Cit.*, 71, and Hafner and Lyon, *Op.Cit.*, 201.

[745] Hafner and Lyon, *Op.Cit.*, 182.

[746] Enrollment of women started in 1971 with under twenty and grew steadily to 170 by 1978, "Women in Engineering; A Milestone in Ruth Adelman's Life," *Stevens Indicator*, 95 (1978), 11.

six students developed missing parts of the operating system software for the PDP-10, as well as a FORTRAN compiler which allowed faculty and students to use that language on the computer. Her FORTRAN software was copyrighted by Stevens and sold to Digital. As manager of programming, she presented many papers about the development of Stevens's software for the PDP-10, not only at Digital but also at conferences. As a result, in 1976, Stevens appointed Maltz director of the computer center, perhaps the first female director of an academic computer center at thirty years of age.

Two new educational programs arose at Stevens indirectly or directly as a result of the new tool. One was a B.S. degree program which used the computer in management systems, the Systems Planning and Management (SP&M) curriculum of 1977, a program designed by a management faculty team led by Professor M. Peter Jurkat. Even more importantly, in 1977, Provost Robert Cotellessa appointed a three-man committee consisting of Boesch, Jurkat, and professor of mathematics Ralph Tindell to create a curriculum for a B.S. in computer science. Some of the course work in the SP&M curriculum was applicable for the courses in the computer science curriculum, and the two curricula overlapped to some degree. After the creation of the U.S. Computer Science Accreditation Board in 1986, the Stevens computer science degree program was one of only some twenty accredited computer science programs in the United States that year.

Another early user of computers on campus was the librarian, Richard P. Widdicombe. As early as 1966 when he was an assistant librarian, Widdicombe used the techniques created at the University of Illinois to create a database for periodicals.[747] In 1975, after becoming the librarian, Widdicombe used techniques already in use at the University of California at Berkeley to utilize on-line searching of academic literature using a Hazeltine 2000 cathode-ray-tube dumb terminal -- the first such use on the East Coast.[748] In 1980, he and a student, Gregory Gianforte 1983, set up an Apple microcomputer laboratory in the basement of the Samuel C. Williams Library where they developed software for an automated circulation system in 1981-- at the time larger libraries were using dumb terminals, not microcomputers. In addition, Widdicombe and an alumnus, Richard Trueswell 1952, conducted a computer analysis of borrowers' use of holdings and found that forty-one percent of the books never circulated, twenty-one percent circulated only once, twelve percent circulated twice, and only

---

[747] See original periodical typelist dated Sept. 1966 in "The Library: Stevens Institute of Technology: Master List of all Journals and Periodicals and Serials Currently Received Formally Received and Held and Stored," Mar. 12, 1968. Stevens Special Collections.

[748] See Widdicombe's report to President K. C. Rogers, "Computer-Based Information Services; Samuel C. Williams Library," April 1975.

twenty-four percent circulated three times or more. This study analyzed the circulation of both Stevens and Rice University, the only other library with completely computerized holdings in 1975.[749] The study later led Widdicombe in the direction of relying on search engines to identify articles and books at other institutions, then using interlibrary loans to obtain books, and fax machines to obtain articles, a general technique among smaller libraries by the 1990s.[750]

The pioneering decision to have students buy their own computers came in stages:[751] In the 1978 report of the recommendations of an Ad Hoc Committee to Review the Engineering Curriculum (Ad Hoc CREC), the chairman of the committee and dean of the college, Edward A. Friedman, a physicist, wrote,

That more emphasis should be placed on the computer. Every course beyond the Introduction to Computer programming course should contain, where appropriate, computer applications. A list of computer applications problems should be developed for each course and be filed with the Undergraduate Curriculums Committee.[752]

This recommendation came at the insistence of committee members like professors Sidney F. Borg, Richard S. Magee, Stanley H. Smith, Ralph Tindell, and particularly the physicist Ralph Schiller. Friedman from that time on became the promoter of this educational goal of including computers in every appropriate course at Stevens as well as of other initiatives involving computers in education.

Dean Friedman obtained a crucially important grant from the Alfred P. Sloan Foundation to carry out a survey of the application of the computer to engineering curricula around the country. Out of the some three hundred engineering programs, the most promising eighty-five were identified. Of

---

[749] See "First Listing of Rice University Circulation, 1976-7," and Widdicombe's report on analysis of data dated 9 Nov. 1976, Stevens Special Collections.

[750] By 1993, Widdicombe made the radical suggestion that some libraries could dispense with journals altogether, see his report in R. Widdicombe, "Stevens Institute of Technology: Electronic Access, Not Subscriptions," *Innovative Use of Information Technology by Colleges.* Council on Library and Information Resources. Washington, D.C., August 1999, 64-69.

[751] "Developing a Computer Intensive Environment at Stevens Institute of Technology," an internal Stevens document dated fall 1984, Stevens Special Collections, and Joseph J. Moeller, Jr., "Stevens Institute of Technology: Integrating Information Technology into the Curriculum," in William H. Graves, ed., *Computing Across the Curriculum: Academic Perspectives*(EDUCOM Strategies Series on Information Technology, 1989), 331-336.

[752] Edward A. Friedman, et al, "Recommendations Regarding Educational Procedures and Curriculum Revisions Submitted to the Faculty by the Ad Hoc Committee for the Revision of the Engineering Curriculum," Dec. 19, 1978, 3.

those, forty-nine responded. Dean Friedman and professors Jurkat and Joseph J. Moeller conducted telephone interviews and visited many colleges throughout the 1979-80 academic year. They found that the three institutions applying the computer in the most rigorous and promising ways were the military service academies, which were consciously building a computer thread throughout their engineering curricula. Unlike MIT and Carnegie-Mellon, which were concentrating on electrical engineering and computer science applications of the computer, the Naval, Air Force, and Army academies were trying to integrate the computer into all engineering courses. Apart from the service academies, the general picture supplied by the rest of the colleges showed that they had a great deal in common: Almost every institution had an introductory programming course based on FORTRAN or PASCAL, but beyond this there were only computer-related activities based on individual efforts of some faculty, instead of a computer thread. Most of these individual efforts were in computer simulation of physical phenomena in laboratories, advanced courses, or senior design. A limiting factor was the cost and limited availability of software packages, as well as the cost of hardware. The focus at the time was on computer graphics, which were either in place or planned for the immediate future, but some institutions also had large databases in chemical and civil engineering, as well as management and social science. The most significant finding of the survey was that fewer than a dozen colleges had computer literacy as an educational goal. Thus, when the results of the Stevens survey were presented at the IEEE Frontiers in Education Conference at Houston, Texas, in 1980, Friedman and his colleagues stated,

At the vast majority of engineering colleges a laissez-faire attitude prevails. "Computnik" faculty and students indulge their proclivities while the mainstream faculty and students make only occasional utilization of computers. This is true even at institutions that are leaders in computer science research. The institutions seem to have a "filter down" philosophy which assumes that the advanced research activities will eventually have an impact on undergraduate education through individual interaction between students and faculty. Such an approach leaves some students out of the computer culture. Those students who do participate in independent study assume a substantial burden. While the most capable students can cope with this approach, the typical engineering student in the United States must be guided through a systematic development program.[753]

---

[753] E. A. Friedman, M. P. Jurkat, and J. Moeller, "Comprehensive Utilization of Computers in Undergraduate Engineering Education," *1980 Frontiers in Education Conference Proceedings* (IEEE, 1980), 478. Later in 1983, an in-depth study of selected schools was John W. McCredie, ed., *Campus Computing Strategies*(EDUCOM/Digital Equipment Corp., 1983).

The Sloan-financed Stevens survey also indicated the problems with implementation of such a thorough program at most colleges, with the exception of the service academies, namely, lack of funds. The universal picture was lack of computing facilities, both hardware and software because of cost, and lack of funds to have faculty overcome computer illiteracy by developing new curriculum materials, as well as lack of technical staff. Even though the NSF was funding grants for the development of Computer Aided Design (CAD), Computer Aided Manufacturing (CAM), and Computer Graphics (CAG) at a rate of two million dollars per year, Friedman and his colleagues cited a study by the University of Kansas Center for Research, Inc. that estimated a minimum cost of thirty million dollars to develop a microcomputer laboratory in every American engineering school. This survey and its dissemination in a national forum established Stevens's reputation not only as one of the most knowledgeable sources on application of computers to engineering education but also as having established an institutional goal of attaining a computer-intensive environment. This reputation helped enable Stevens to obtain the grants necessary for the attainment of that goal.

The immediate problem for Stevens, however, was that it was not as wealthy as many other colleges and universities. While the costs of introducing computers and networking waylaid other engineering colleges, they proved even more difficult to bear at Stevens. For example, on the Stevens campus, faculty-administration committees had investigated the prices of the newest mainframes and found them almost prohibitive. When microcomputers were first coming onto the market in the late 1970s, the administration investigated the option of the institute buying microcomputers and setting them up in labs and hallways as was being done at Carnegie-Mellon, MIT, and other schools. Again, these solutions were costly. The first such microcomputer laboratories were for computer graphics, a type of utilization which could not be done effectively on mainframes. In fact, Professor Jurkat had obtained an NSF grant to set up an Undergraduate Computer Graphics Facility in 1978, but the purchasing maintenance, and development of software packages for this first Stevens computer laboratory had already proved to be expensive, as had the need to update the hardware. According to Jurkat and professor Bernard Rosen, it was thought at the time that Stevens could not remain competitive if it simply added costs to students' tuition fees to cover the costs of institutionally-owned computers, and, since millions of dollars were needed up front, such a solution was not feasible. Thus, the problem was where to find the resources to implement the visionary plan of creating a computer intensive environment at Stevens.

Dean of the College Edward A. Friedman and Professor Bernard Rosen, both physicists, led the effort to have a mandatory computer requirement for all Stevens students -- a pioneering first in the country.

The idea of having the students buy computers was that of physics Professor Bernard Rosen. In the spring of 1980, Rosen was comparing the price tags of microcomputers in newspaper ads and realized that such a solution to the "computer power bottleneck" was workable. At the same time, his personal motivation came from his own class, i.e., if students in his class on computational physics had their own computers, they could solve numerical homework problems much more quickly than if they used calculators or queued up for the mainframe. The students would find their errors right away. With a computer in their dorm rooms, the students could quickly redo a problem with an error. When he shared this idea with other faculty, he stressed the academic benefit to students of using a-state-of-the-art tool. He stressed that it was better to have the students, instead of the institute, own the computers so that each entering freshman class could buy the latest hardware. Even though there would be the added cost of purchasing a computer for each entering student, this cost was more palatable for parents and students than a tuition hike because it was for personal ownership. A lot of faculty Rosen talked to were not enthusiastic about the idea, and even Friedman was skeptical at first, given the proposed gamble that an increased cost, even if peripheral, might reduce enrollments. Rosen's department head, Ralph Schiller, convinced Friedman of the educational and revolutionary nature of the proposal, and Friedman subsequently became the project's foremost champion.

Friedman brought the issue to President Kenneth C. Rogers who, along with the trustees, had to make the ultimate decision whether to go ahead with the plan or not. Rogers thought that the pros outweighed the cons: He thought that a mandatory computer requirement was a bold step which would ultimately strengthen the unique broad-based engineering and science curricula at Stevens by providing a common integrating tool. The challenge was to assure that the computer did not turn out to be merely a costly toy. Even though he had just led Stevens out of serious budgetary problems, Rogers nevertheless thought that educational needs necessitated an investment in the costs of support and maintenance of a mandatory computer initiative.[754] As a result, Rogers provided Friedman with assistance by appointing Joseph J. Moeller, a Stevens 1967 B.E. and 1975 Ph.D., as Associate Dean for Educational Development and Personal Computer Program Manager.

Director of the Computer Center Leslie Maltz and Vice President Joseph J. Moeller were the key technical and management personnel in the successful funding of the mandatory computer requirement and networking of the campus.

Moeller provided the effort with an expert manager and grantsman. Earlier, as assistant dean of educational development, Moeller had obtained

---

[754] Phone conversation with Kenneth C. Rogers, Oct. 25, 1999.

grants to integrate the computer into courses and curricula. These included $250,000 from the NSF to develop computer graphics with Jurkat and other faculty in 1978 and, in that same year, grants of $13,763, $24,000, and $40,000 from the New Jersey Department of Higher Education to develop special programs. In 1980, Moeller obtained $20,000 from the Sloan Foundation to develop computers in engineering education with professors DeLancey, Sirkar, and Suffel, as well as $36,000 and $46,000 grants, both from the New Jersey Department of Higher Education, to develop laboratories in chemistry. Other grants included one from Hewlett-Packard Company in 1981 to develop an instrumentation laboratory.[755] Thus Moeller, who later shared his expertise in obtaining grants by giving a paper, "Grantsmanship: A Manager's Perspective," at a New Jersey Department of Higher Education workshop, was considered the best choice to oversee and raise funds for the Stevens mandatory computer program. Moeller then chaired an ad hoc faculty-administration committee to consider all aspects of the idea of requiring students to buy a computer. This committee consisted of the main faculty champions of the idea, Jurkat of the management, Schiller and Rosen of physics, and Roger Pinkham of the mathematics department. They and Maltz devised a plan for partial implementation for the fall semester of 1982.

Professors M. Peter Jurkat and Roger Pinkham led some of the early efforts in using the computer in teaching, the former in computer graphics and the latter teaching freshmen during the first year of mandatory computers.

---

[755] On grants received by Stevens, see résumé of J. J. Moeller, in "Jobs, Science and Technology Bond Act Projects, The Create Project," Dec. 12, 1985, section 4, 3.

The Moeller-led committee decided to require only the relatively small freshman student populations of the SP&M and science curricula to buy a microcomputer -- a total of only eighty students. This solution avoided the drawn-out process of having to obtain support of the entire faculty for implementation for the majority of students in the engineering curriculum, the major program at Stevens. The committee surveyed the available hardware and chose an Atari 800 machine for the first year. Professor of mathematics Roger Pinkham volunteered to teach courses common to the two curricula. A crucial test of the plan came when Dean Friedman personally wrote to the parents of each of the entering freshmen in these programs to explain why Stevens was requiring them to add some eight hundred dollars to their fees. His argument was that they had chosen Stevens because it was poised to take advantage of technical change, and this new requirement was an example of Stevens doing it now. There were no complaints by parents and a number applauded the initiative.

When the freshmen arrived in the fall of 1982, Pinkham taught a freshman course in each semester to all students in the science and SP&M curricula with the assistance of Dean Friedman, who acted literally as Pinkham's graduate assistant by teaching sections and grading homework. Friedman volunteered for this difficult duty in order to become computer literate and to learn the problems of teaching applications personally -- an experience which later led to his subsequent leading role in applications of the computer to science and mathematics K-12 curricula nationwide. One course was an introduction to computers and the other was linear algebra, both courses being revolutionary and innovative in the depth of their computer problem-solving. In this first year, Pinkham used BASIC and had the students write their own software. Since each student wrote individual programs, the course was time-consuming and difficult to grade. Pinkham's philosophy was for students to create models so they could understand basic applications in an exploratory way, each student's program or model being creative and different -- a piece of poetry. He contrasted this approach with typical engineering uses of the computer in industry, where the machine was used for more practical design. He used the language BASIC because immediate results could be obtained by students in linear algebra, and students were encouraged to develop their own software in a "toolbox" for applications in later courses. His idea was to make the computer just as much a part of the students' tools as a calculator or pencil and paper. They would use it without even thinking about it. When the *New York Times* reported on the first-ever experiment of Stevens requiring college freshmen to buy a computer, the reporter interviewed Pinkham at length and came to the conclusion that the eighty students in the two programs were "pioneers."[756]

Based on this successful first use of the student-owned minicomputers in these two curricula as well as the favorable publicity which resulted, the Moeller-led faculty committee decided to push for implementation of the requirement for all freshmen by September 1983. This mandatory computer requirement and the purchase plan had to be approved by the trustees, and when Rogers and the executive committee of the board of trustees outlined a Personal Computer Purchasing Plan in April 1983, "several of the Trustees expressed enthusiasm about the development and implementation of the plan."[757] At that point, the Stevens faculty and administration were aware of the hard work ahead to obtain development grants to assure success in integrating the computer into undergraduate courses. The engineering faculty insisted that the choice of hardware be able to accommodate the FORTRAN language, the language of choice for engineers and software packages in industry at the time.

After much time spent on investigating different models of personal computers, which were replacing microcomputers on the market, the committee made its choice of the Digital Equipment Corporation's Pro325 -- in part because of the on-going association with Digital through the campus mainframe. According to President Rogers,

Although Maltz and her staff had excellent and close working relations with Digital Equipment Corporation (DEC) staff, to be able to carry out its ambitious plan Stevens had to develop a partnership arrangement with the computer supplier which allowed for an extremely favorable purchase price for the student and faculty personal computers. If the DEC Professional Computer was to be adopted, such an arrangement could only be obtained with approval at the highest management level of DEC, which was Kenneth Olsen the founder, President and Chief Executive Officer. Olsen was a creative maverick engineer who founded DEC and guided it into a very profitable niche position in the computer industry that IBM had overlooked in its zeal to dominate the mainframe market. Olsen saw the need and market for mini-computers and developed a highly successful line of minicomputers particularly attractive for research and development users who did not require or want IBM's full service, a more expensive approach. Olsen was skeptical about the practicality of a personal computer in every home, but he appreciated their value as personal tools for engineers. To get his approval of a DEC-Stevens partnership, Maltz, Moeller and I met with Olsen in his office in Maynard, Massachusetts. Olsen, a no-nonsense engineer, opened the meeting by subjecting the Stevens team, particularly me, to a pop-quiz on engineering fundamentals,

---

[756] *The New York Times,* Sept. 5, 1982, XI, 18:5.
[757] Minutes of the Board of Trustees of Stevens Institute of Technology, April 21, 1983, 6.

because he wanted to be sure that the Stevens team knew what it was doing; that the project would have the strong backing of the Stevens President and Trustees and that it would be a benefit and not an embarrassment to DEC. He satisfied himself that we passed his test and agreed to a Stevens-DEC joint effort with the details to be worked out by his and Stevens senior staff. This meeting was crucial because it later turned out that, to satisfy the original partnership objectives, DEC would ultimately have to go well beyond the agreement as originally envisioned. Every Stevens student obtained a new computer and software, a more than $5,000 package, for $1,800.[758]

For DEC, the arrangement meant more software could be developed for its newly created personal computer at Stevens, and insights into the utility of the PC could be a spinoff of its use by Stevens's faculty and students. Moreover, more sales for DEC's computers would be forthcoming once students moved into industry.

Subsequently, Moeller negotiated the details of a favorable contract with DEC for the Pro325, which was thought to be able to accommodate FORTRAN. According to Maltz, the main problem from a technical point of view was "getting to see the machine," the DEC Pro325 personal computer then being in the final development stage. Maltz, Moeller, and others had to fly to Massachusetts to see it and obtain a prototype before it was released for sale by the company. The DEC Pro325 lacked a hard drive, and Maltz found it unacceptable for the FORTRAN language. Subsequently, citing the contract DEC had negotiated with Stevens, which required that the computer had to accommodate FORTRAN, Moeller and Maltz obtained the DEC Pro350, an upgraded and more costly model of the machine with a hard drive at no cost to Stevens. The Pro350 was one of the first PC's to have a hard drive and could accommodate ten megabytes, a record at the time.

Thus, Stevens was the nation's first college to require that all freshmen buy a personal computer, and the announcement was made and the computers delivered to Stevens in the summer of 1983. During that summer, President Rogers came up with a half million dollars in funding to expeditiously change the freshman students' dormitory accommodations. New desks in dormitory rooms had to be built because the old ones were too small to hold the computers and books. The new desks required so much space that the twin beds had to be replaced with stacked bunk beds. Circuit breakers and surge protectors had to be added to electrical wiring to protect the computers from appliances such as hair dryers and hot plates. Since

---

[758] Attached notes to letter of K. C. Rogers to the author, Dec. 5, 1999.

Stevens already had the idea of networking the computers, extra cable was installed when the rooms were rewired. Lastly, stronger locks were put on the doors for security.[759] That same year, Drexel and Clarkson followed Stevens and also required some of their freshmen to buy the Macintosh computer, and the Zenith with 8088 processor, respectively, but without hard drives. The *New York Times* reported on the pioneering developments at Stevens:

. . . this year's entering class at the Stevens Institute of Technology here are breaking new ground: They are the first students in the country required to own personal computers . . . . Last fall, Stevens became the first school to require some freshmen in certain fields to buy their own microcomputers. This year it is requiring personal computers for all 500 entering freshmen.[760]

In conjunction with this effort in March 1983, Moeller, Friedman and the Stevens provost, Robert Cotellessa, obtained a $270,000 educational grant from DEC for personal computer plan development." Also, Exxon Corporation funded a grant obtained by Professor Donald Sebastian for the use of computers in chemical engineering to model and simulate chemical processing design. In addition, although Digital subscribed to the lower cost of the computer, Exxon also contributed to fund part of the cost of the Pro350 so that the cut-rate price for computers in bulk from Digital was lowered even further. Students that year paid only $1,800 instead of the $4,400 commercial price tag.[761] In addition, the Stevens faculty worked hard to make adjustments in course requirements to apply the computer to common homework problems, to writing of reports and humanities papers, and to CAD projects.[762] By 1984, a plan for a computer-intensive environment was presented to the trustees and became a goal of the institute.[763] Moeller described the accomplishments on campus by 1985 in these words:

In the computer intensive environment at Stevens, sequences of undergraduate courses are being addressed such that activities in earlier courses will provide effec-

---

[759] John Hogan, "A Resourceful Look at Micros on Campus," *Popular Computing,* Oct. 1984, 116.

[760] George Stolz, "Stevens Class of '87: Computers for All," *The New York Times,* Sept. 4, 1983, XI, 21:1.

[761] Minutes of the Board of Trustees of Stevens Institute of Technology, April 21, 1983, 6 and Attachment C on the Personal Computer Plan, and "Microcomputers Invade Tech," *The Stute,* April 15, 1983, 1.

[762] Elizabeth M. Finley, "Stevens Focuses on Computers," *The New York Times,* Oct. 31, 1984, IV, 23:1.

[763] "Developing a Computer Intensive Environment at Stevens Institute of Technology. August, 1984," Minutes of the Executive and Joint Committees of the Board of Trustees, Sept. 12, 1984.

tive basic computing skills and support specific computer experiences in later courses. This is leading to a variety of continuous "computer threads" which establish an efficient integration of computer methods into the curricula structure, and which serve to supplement and strengthen both the delivery of instruction and the learning processes in engineering, science, mathematics, management and humanities. . . . The activities at Stevens comprise much more than isolated courseware/software development projects. Rather, the full impact of this initiative is resulting in restructuring of the curriculum. With the personal desktop computer as a focal point, faculty members at Stevens have already identified and produced courseware and computer applications in every academic discipline offered at the Institute. These materials range from computer-assisted instruction and tutorial modules and simulations for core courses, to sophisticated analysis and design programs for engineering practice in upper-level technical electives.[764]

In 1983, at the same time that all students were required to buy a personal computer, Stevens envisioned a thorough networking of the campus, including dormitories, where the undergraduates would house their computers. When, in July 1983, Moeller gave a presentation to the executive committee of the trustees which included "future networking of the entire campus," his report was received "with enthusiasm," according to minutes.[765] Even before the mandatory computer requirement, Leslie Maltz had begun to work on a campus network by experimenting with twisted pairs of wires to link Stevens's computers together. Then, between 1978 and 1981, Digital, the Xerox Corporation, and the Intel Corporation created ethernet technology.[766] In 1981, Maltz installed a local ethernet to link fifty-five personal computers of faculty in seven of the ten academic buildings on campus. This network was a "fully distributed computing environment," namely, there was wired communication between any of the computers connected to the network of minicomputer workstations and the mainframe. This achievement was no easy task. Maltz had few contacts to ask about how to design the system, and it was a process of experimentation with no guarantees of success. A major problem was that there were no packages for supporting multiple protocols on the ethernet, that is, Stevens's DECNet software did not support all of the machines, some of which came from other companies. She was faced with a kind of jigsaw puzzle as she purchased pieces of hardware and software and fit them together by trial and error to achieve a multiprotocol environment. The main problem was

---

[764] J. J. Moeller in "Jobs, Science and Technology Bond Act," *Op. Cit.*, 3-5.

[765] Minutes of the Executive and Joint Committees of the Board of Trustees, July 21, 1983, 5.

[766] *Ibid.*, 3-9 gives the date of 1982 for the first Stevens Ethernet. Maureen Nevin Duffy, "Stevens Signs Agreement to Widen Its Use of Computers," *The New York Times*, May 12, 1985, XI, 2:1 outlines the extent of the Stevens Ethernet in 1985.

that no industry standards existed for networking with the result that equipment bought from one company didn't work with equipment from another one. At the time, the ethernet technology was being used experimentally in corporate and research institutions, and Maltz was unaware of any other institution of higher learning intent on creating a campus-wide network in 1981 -- Stevens was one of the first, and perhaps even the first, to deploy the technology in academe. As a result of Stevens's unique accomplishment, Maltz was invited to give a paper describing the effort for the Association for Computing Machinery's subgroup, the Special Interest Group for University Computer Center Services (SIGUCCS) in 1983.[767]

At the same time, Friedman established a Computer Planning Committee (CPC) to complement Moeller's Computer Operations Committee (COM-OP), and both committees wanted to make the students' computers in the dormitories interactive with each other and with faculty offices. This vision resulted in a project called Computing for Research and Education in an Advanced Technology Environment (CREATE) whose aim was to raise funds for the creation of a computer intensive environment through a complete networking of the campus.

On May 10, 1984, the two committees had a joint meeting with David Farber who had become an authority on networking. He had joined the electrical engineering and computer science department of the University of Delaware after eleven years at Bell Labs, a stint at the Rand Corporation, and a professorship at the University of California at Irvine. Farber had helped to develop ethernet technology by working on a token ring, an accessing method by which connected machines took turns sending packet messages.[768] By 1984, he had also helped to lay the foundation for the future internet. He had helped to conceive and organize CSNet and NSFNet. CSNet was a five-million-dollar, NSF-sponsored project to network the computer science departments in the nation. The idea was to give computer scientists the access to computational resources and e-mail similar to ARPANET. Since ARPANET was supposed to be restricted to its contractors, CSNet, which used ARPANET protocols and became tied to it, was the first national network open to academic, commercial, or government

---

[767] Leslie Maltz, "Micros Through Mainframes: A Successful Implementation," *Association for Computing Machinery*, 1983. After the network was extended to tie in personal computers in faculty offices and one dormitory by 1985, Maltz delivered other invited papers on that accomplishment, "Micros, Minis, and Mainframes: An Integrated Computer Environment," *HICSS-10 Proceedings*, 1985; "Micros, Minis, and Mainframes, An Integrated Computing Environment," *DECUS Refereed Paper Journal*, 1985; and "Integrating DECsystem-10s and 20s and VAX Systems," *Large Systems News*, 1985.

[768] Peter H. Salus, *Casting the Net: From ARPANET to Internet and Beyond*(1995), 77.

computer science institutions for a fee in 1982. The NSF then established NSFNet in 1984 to make supercomputers accessible to researchers via the combined networks.[769] Farber's role designing these networks made him one of the "fathers of the internet," and he later earned recognition as one of the twenty-five most powerful visionary minds in the field of networking. The meeting's agenda with Farber was to include his advice on networking the campus and on Stevens's CREATE plan.[770] Participating faculty recall that he both encouraged them in their efforts to network the whole campus and inspired them with a talk on the potential of a wired campus linked to the then-emerging NSFNet combined with the existing CSNet.[771]

In the same year, Friedman conducted another national survey, this time on networking at engineering colleges. Published in the *IEEE Spectrum* in 1984, Friedman's article stated that the next step was to thoroughly network campuses. His survey of the ten most-advanced colleges and universities with a computer environment which were in some stage of networking their campuses showed that two institutions, namely, Carnegie-Mellon and the University of Michigan, had achieved extensive networking with ethernets or other fiber-optic systems by 1984. The other eight, including Stevens, were in some lesser stage of networking, but all ten were intent on extending their networks campus-wide, particularly Dartmouth, which in 1984 became perhaps the first institution of higher learning to network its dormitories. Most institutions, including Carnegie-Mellon and Michigan, had taken the route of networking workstations at first, instead of networking student-owned computers in dormitories.[772] Friedman presented the daunting costs of networking efforts: "At current prices, for example, it would cost over $10 billion to equip each of the 460,000 full-time engineering students in the U.S. with a high-powered personal workstation and appropriate networking facilities."[773] He warned that unless legislatures were willing to fund networks in private institutions as well as public ones, "then private universities and colleges will face significant financial burdens to match them, or their students will have to pay even more for a private education."[774]

[769] Abbate, *Op.Cit.*, 93-94, and Hafner and Lyon, *Op.Cit.*, 242.

[770] Memorandum from Prof. W. C. Ermler, Chairman of Computer Planning Committee, to members of the two committees, May 7, 1984.

[771] Phone conversation with David Farber and paricipating faculty, Oct. 12, 1999.

[772] Edward A. Friedman, "The Wired University," *IEEE Spectrum*, Nov. 1984, 119.

[773] *Ibid.*, 115.

[774] *Ibid.*, and see the later more comprehensive book-length overview by Caroline Arms, ed., *Campus Networking Strategies*(EDUCOM Strategies Series on Information Technology, 1988).

The way that Stevens met the enormous costs of full networking of the campus was partly through private and partly through public funding. A further agreement with Digital Equipment Corporation signed in May 1985 provided for Digital donating a whopping $22 million in equipment and services to Stevens over a three year period to help to complete a thorough networking of the campus.[775] Stevens was one of five colleges nationwide to receive Digital's "Campus Wide Investment Program." In addition, Moeller and the faculty obtained funding for applications of the computer to teaching and networking special laboratories from a string of companies and foundations: the Alden Trust, AT&T, Allied-Bendix, Bell Communications Research, Bell Telephone Laboratories, the Dreyfus Foundation, E. I. DuPont, Exxon Corporation, the Exxon Education Foundation, the General Electric Foundation, Hewlett Packard Company, Intel Corporation, L. K. Comstock Company, New Jersey Bell, Northrop, Western Electric, and the Westinghouse Educational Foundation.[776] Maltz's plan, to be completed by 1988, was to replace the older mainframe with a 8600 series mainframe, to add 350 VAX workstations and at least six more 780/785 super minicomputers, as well as to increase the number of Pro350s for laboratories and workstations beyond the then-current 1,400 owned by undergraduates and faculty. The plan called for linking every office in academic departments, every desk in each dormitory room, and every office in the administration building and the library.[777] By 1985, however, the level of funding did not meet the costs of completely networking the campus which was estimated by Moeller to be $29,350,000. Thus, seven months after Digital's commitment in December 1985, another CREATE grant application was sent out by Moeller for a further $5,600,000 in state funds, specifically for the costs of equipment for undergraduates, i.e., for networking academic buildings and dormitories as well as computing laboratories for undergraduate education.[778] The application was sent to the Jobs, Science and Technology Bond Act Projects program created by the New Jersey legislature and supported by Governor Thomas Kean.

In 1986, the State Board of Higher Education approved $3.4 million of the $5.6 million application, but it also had to be approved by the New Jersey legislature which delayed the apportionment of the money until 1987.[779] The $3.4 million was by far the largest competitive award made

---

[775] Duffy, *Op.Cit.*

[776] Moeller, "Jobs, Science and Technology Bond Act," *Op.Cit.*, 3-48.

[777] Duffy, *Op.Cit.*

[778] Moeller, "Jobs, Science and Technology Bond Act," *Op.Cit.*, 3-49.

[779] Christopher P. Horan, "Create Update: A Network Yet to Come," *The Stute,* Oct. 10, 1986, 1.

under the bond act and was at the time the largest single grant ever received by Stevens. Meanwhile, another grant from AT&T in January 1987 for $1.1 million helped make up the difference, and it was used for the funding of a Computer Aided Manufacturing (CAM) laboratory, a UNIX development laboratory, as well as microprocessor and robotics laboratories.[780] After these awards, the CREATE project rapidly moved towards completion. By April 1987, the new mainframe arrived and was tied to VAX clusters. DEC and Stevens personnel started to find suitable pathways to "rod and rope" the campus, and bids to build "wiring closets" and wire the dormitories and academic buildings were accepted. The main work of digging up the campus and punching through walls was to be done in the summer when most students were absent.[781] Finally, according to the scheduled agreement with Digital, the campus was completely networked with bundles of fiber-optic cables going to buildings and with coaxial cable installed throughout all dormitories, academic, and administrative buildings by February 26, 1988.[782]

By the late 1990s, the comparative position of Stevens as a computer intensive environment was indicated by Kenneth C. Green's survey of desktop computing and information technology in higher education. In his latest survey in 1998, Green received 571 responses from 1,623 institutions contacted. Overall, less than five percent of responding institutions required all students to buy a computer, and less than ten percent of all institutions required students in some specific discipline to buy a computer. Mandatory computer purchases were highest in universities (as opposed to four-year colleges), presumably because universities had engineering and computer science programs. Only slightly over thirty percent of public universities and slightly under twenty percent of private universities were mandating purchase of a computer for students in specific programs in 1998.[783]

In fact, a mandatory computer requirement is still a controversial issue. In the mid- to-late 1990s, the *Chronicle of Higher Education* has reported the various arguments pro and con. Fundamentally, the arguments against a computer requirement have to do with costs and students' freedom to choose a computer rather than doubting the necessity of use of the tool and its application to education. Few doubt that American students should have

[780] "Recent Grants to Stevens from AT&T Exceed 1.1 Million," *The Stute*, Jan. 30, 1987, 1.

[781] "CREATE Happenings," *The Stute*, March 13, 1987, 1; "New Computer Announced," *The Stute*, April 10, 1987, 1; and "Networking the Campus-- The Final Countdown," *The Stute*, April 20, 1987, 1.

[782] "Stevens Network Finally a Reality," *The Stute*, February 26, 1988, 1.

[783] Kenneth C. Green, *Campus Computing 1998: The Ninth National Survey of Desktop Computing and Information Technology in Higher Education*(1998), 6.

a basic competence in computer literacy or that all students should have access to a computer in college. It is recognized that for graduates to be competitive in the modern world such competence is a necessity. One major argument for mandating computers and folding the cost of the computers into tuition is that all students would then have them, thus assuring a "democracy of access."[784] Thus, mandatory computers help solve the current social question of a "digital divide" between the haves and have-nots -- computers become available to poorer families instead of only to the students whose families can afford them. Moreover, the Department of Education was intent on spreading computer access to all students, and it ruled in 1989-90 that colleges could not consider computer costs in financial-aid calculations unless students were required to own the equipment. This ruling led to Dartmouth's mandatory computer requirement in 1991.[785] Major universities like the University of Florida and North Carolina are now in the process of instituting mandatory computers as a "baseline" requirement for competition in the modern world.[786] In addition, colleges argue that mandatory computer requirements save universities and students money because negotiated contracts with suppliers lower the costs of computers bought in bulk and the standardization of equipment cuts down on support costs -- arguments which mirror the concerns on the Stevens campus when it pioneered mandatory ownership of computers in the first place. At Stevens in the last fifteen years, however, students were not required to purchase the same model PC. Rather, Stevens defined a standard configuration which students had to meet or exceed. Thus, most students bought their computer through Stevens, but a minority bought other brands and models outside or brought the PCs they already owned. Having all freshman students in all programs buy computers with the same capabilities (even though the model may change every year) assured economy and effectiveness in instruction. Stevens's experience shows that computer-center personnel can give common workshops, and professors can teach a common course introducing the computer, as well as count on the common capacities of the machines for applications of the computer in upper level courses. Elsewhere the arguments against a mandatory requirement -- which usually involves standard equipment at first -- are that it limits student choices of machines and raises costs of tuition for all students, argu-

---

[784] Thomas J. DeLoughry, "Mandatory Computers," *The Chronicle of Higher Education*, May 5, 1995.

[785] David L. Wilson, "Dartmouth Requires All Freshmen to Own Computers," *The Chronicle of Higher Education*, June 19, 1991.

[786] Kelly McCollum, "University of Florida's President Plans on Staying Ahead of the Technology Curve," *The Chronicle of Higher Education*, March 20, 1998.

ments which were put forth in 1998 by a small group of staff and students at the University of North Carolina who were opposed to implementation of a mandatory computer plan to go into effect in 2000.[787]

As the movement for mandatory computers continues and is taken up by larger universities, for example 42,000 computers will be needed at the University of Florida, the problems of coordination of services and faculty involvement seem more complicated. Initially, the mandatory requirement was taken up in smaller institutions: Stevens in 1982, Clarkson and Drexel in 1983, Drew University in 1984, and Bentley and NJIT in 1985. Students at the military academies are paid a small salary, and the costs of the computer requirement are deducted from this salary; thus, the USNA at Annapolis instituted an ownership requirement in 1986, and both the USAF academy and West Point followed its example in 1988. Thereafter, it was Indiana Institute of Technology and Nichols College in 1987, Dartmouth College and George Fox College in 1991, and the University of Minnesota at Crookstown in 1993.[788] The perennial concern of administrations, as it was at Stevens in the early years, continued to be utilization of the computer by faculty in their teaching. Utilization has been growing steadily according to Green's surveys, even in institutions which do not have a computer requirement. For example, e-mail was used in a third of college courses and a web site was used in a quarter of college courses by 1997.[789] Lastly, the creation of the laptop computer seems to have given a boost to a mandatory computer requirement because of the laptop's utility in classrooms rigged for interactive teaching. Stevens has followed the example of Wake Forest University, which mandated laptops in 1995. At Wake Forest, an institution sharing the Stevens goal of achieving a computer intensive environment, the mantra was "Computers for all."[790]

On the issue of networking campuses, Green's 1998 survey showed that slightly over half of responding institutions had networked their campus to accommodate student-owned computers of different varieties. Some 50.4% of all campuses had installed a network connection for each bed in dormitories, the highest figure being 90.8% for private universities.[791] Thus, full

---

[787] Jeffrey R. Young, "University of North Carolina Criticized for Plan to Require Students to Own PCs," *The Chronicle of Higher Education*, May 22, 1998.

[788] DeLoughry, *Op. Cit.*

[789] Lisa Guernsey, "E-Mail Now Used in a Third of College Courses, Survey Finds," *The Chronicle of Higher Education*, Oct. 17, 1997.

[790] Jeffrey R. Young, "Invasion of the Laptop: More Colleges Adopt Mandatory Computing Program; Officials at Wake Forest Say Making the Machine Ubiquitous is Worth the Trouble and Expense," *The Chronicle of Higher Education*, Dec. 5, 1997.

[791] Green, *Op.Cit.*, 19.

campus networking is less controversial and is held up by the matter of its cost.

At Stevens, the mandatory computer requirement for every student and a fully networked campus has created a computer intensive environment as originally envisioned by the faculty in 1982-83, and currently Stevens claims its curricula and programs are "Computer-Integrated."[792] Faculty in the engineering curriculum have developed extensive use of the computer in freshman-sophomore courses on the engineering sciences such as statics, strength of materials, and circuits and systems. In upper-level courses, extensive use of computers appears in such areas as computer-based simulation methods in chemical engineering, computer aided design and manufacturing (CAD-CAM) in mechanical engineering, as well as structural and fluid modeling in civil engineering. In the science courses and programs, the computer is used in such courses as electricity and magnetism, computer science, principles of biology, and introduction to experimentation and mathematics. In management and the liberal arts programs, there are specific computer laboratories for different uses. In fact, every academic department has a computer laboratory for instruction and research. Moreover, there are computer laboratories in Stevens's array of research laboratories which involve graduates and undergraduates in funded research, so the computer is indeed ubiquitous.

Moeller went on to become vice president for Information Services and later vice president for the Graduate School and Research Services. In these positions, he organized a college-wide distance learning committee, and is promoting the use of interactive video-based and web-based distance learning for delivery of graduate programs. Outside the campus, Moeller organized and served as first president of the New Jersey Intercomputer Network (NJIN), a consortium of forty-five New Jersey colleges focused on information tools and networking and the creation of a state-wide network for faculty and staff.

Upon completion of the work of creating the computer intensive environment at Stevens, Edward A. Friedman returned to teaching and started a program to introduce computers into pre-college education. He obtained grants to start his nationally recognized pioneering program to conduct research and disseminate information on the best ways to use the computer to teach mathematics and other science subjects on the K-12 level of education. Established in 1988, his Center for Improved Engineering and Science Education (CIESE) provides teacher training in classroom and video-conference formats to science and mathematics teachers. Jurkat and Pink-

---

[792] *The Undergraduate Catalog: Academic Year 1998-9*, 2.

ham taught the first courses in the CIESE program, and Jurkat helped develop the web-based courses after developing Stevens's first web-based courses on the graduate level. Also, Friedman, Jurkat and Pinkham documented the effectiveness of computers in K-12 education with several statistical studies.[793] By early 1994, CIESE had spread new K-12 computer-aided technology to over five hundred teachers from fifteen states, and by 1995 it was offering training sessions over the internet.

This initiative partly came from an NSF report calling for integration of engineering education with K-12 education. Also, the initiative partly came from a desire to foster the competitiveness of American education, i.e., improvements had to be made in K-12 education -- particularly in the application of computers to the teaching of mathematics and science -- to keep up with developments in Japan and Europe. Friedman thought that colleges had to help in this effort and also adjust to the new type of computer-literate students, who would be pervasive in the future. Under Friedman, co-founder and co-editor of the journal *Machine Mediated Learning*, CIESE has received over $9.4 million, since its inception, to work with school systems and other colleges in applying several computer technologies, including Lego/Logo, microcomputer-based laboratories, internet, and data analysis software to enhance mathematics and science instruction in K-12. Instead of being a publishing house for textbooks or a software business, CIESE works directly with teachers and school administrators to learn about and implement actual programs.[794]

---

[793] For example, E. Friedman, P. Jurkat and R. Pinkham, "Computer Integration in Secondary School Mathematics," paper presented at SALT Interactive Instruction Delivery Conference, Orlando, FL, 1990, *Conference Proceedings*, 29-31 and E. Friedman, P. Jurkat and R. Pinkham, "Enhancing School Mathematics Education Through Computer Integration," *T.H.E. Journal*, Sept. 1991.

[794] E. Friedman, "The Effective Integration of Technology in Education: A Management Perspective, Top Ten Questions for School Administrators," *T.H.E. Journal*, Nov. 1994, E. Friedman, "Web Adventures in K-12 Science," *TECHNOS*, Winter, 1997, and E. Friedman and B. McGrath, "The Internet Isn't a Threat to Students . . . It's a Tool for Teachers," *Education Week*, Sept. 30, 1998.

CHAPTER 23
Alexander Calder and Creative Alumni in Liberal Arts

Alexander Calder (1898-1976) was Stevens Institute's most widely known graduate by the 1960s and 1970s. His kinetic and metallic mobiles and grand, dynamic stabiles were uniquely American in the century which America came to dominate with its machines of peace and war. And if his background and perhaps his genes reeked of art, he was nonetheless demonstrably influenced by his engineering education at Stevens. In the words of the art critic Robert Osborn,

At heart Calder has always been an engineer. He has clothed the forces of his engineering with his joyful imagination and his lithe sense of beauty, but the wellspring of his art remains the thrusts, the tensions, the stress loads, the balances, the forces of gravity, which he, the engineer, proceeds to adjust and join.[795]

And, in the words of Calder himself when he was talking of the mobile, "I don't know whether it was the moving toys in the circus which got me interested in the idea of motion as an art form or whether it was my training in engineering at Stevens."[796] Although Calder was making toy figures as a boy, his education at Stevens predated his toy circus, an early performance-art form which he created in the 1920s to entertain fellow artists.

Calder was not the first well-known artist who received an education at Stevens. The earliest was Eugene Lawrence Vail (1857-1934) of the class of 1876. His father and grandfather were painters, but his father insisted Vail attend Stevens, even though the boy showed early promise as an artist. Like Calder later, Vail took an immense interest in college life: He drew caricatures for the early student humor magazine, the *Eccentric*; established Theta Xi fraternity; was a crew member on the rowing club; organized theatricals; and presided over the first Glee Club. Described as a vivid personality, he drew caricatures of professors on the blackboard before classes, and, when professor of physics Alfred M. Mayer caught him in the act, he was forgiven because the professor acknowledged his obvious talent. Subsequent to graduation, he studied at the Art Student's League in New York City and then at the École des Beaux Arts in Paris.

---

[795] Robert Osborn, "Calder's International Monuments," *Art in America* 57 (1969), no. 2, 32-49.
[796] Quoted in Jean Lipman, *Calder's Universe*(1976), 263.

Eugene L. Vail was Stevens's first graduate to become a well-known artist.
While at Stevens, Vail created its school colors of crimson and light gray adjusted in
shades so they were chromatically complementary.
At right is a detail from his painting "Reflections."

Born and educated in Paris, Vail was recognized almost immediately by French critics for his early paintings, which resembled those of Whistler and Sargeant, and his painting of Brittany, *Seulette,* won a prize in the first exhibition that he entered. Subsequently, his paintings obtained scores of medals including a gold of the first class at the Exposition Universelle of 1889 for his seascape *Ready About.* Medals were won at exhibitions in St. Louis, Munich, Liège, and Antwerp. In Berlin in 1891, he won a Grand Diploma of Honor. His later paintings, particularly impressionistic oils of Venice but also works in watercolors, gouache, and pastel, successfully found their way into private collections and major museums, including the Corcoran in Washington.[797] In 1939, his widow, Gertrude Vail, presented to Stevens a large impressionistic canvas portraying Venice, *Reflections,* which for years hung in Jacobus Lounge.[798]

---

[797] *Memorial Exhibition of Paintings by Eugene Vail; American Fine Arts Society Galleries* (1939); Louise Gebhard Cann, *Eugene Lawrence Vail, 1857-1934*(1937), 1-3, and *New York Herald,* May 3, 1935.
[798] "Gene Vail, Well-Known Artist, Class of '76, Honors Stevens," *The Stute,* 35, Feb. 23, 1939, 1.

Another even better-known artist was John Marin (1870-1953), the abstract watercolorist. He was a student in the Edwin A. Stevens Building for nearly six years, four years in the Stevens High School from 1882-86 and nearly two years in the institute proper from 1886-88. The Stevens School curriculum included a full classical course besides mechanical drawing and other subjects. As a student, he excelled in mechanical drawing, and he left in his sophomore year to use this talent as an architectural draftsman in four firms before establishing his own architectural firm in 1892. After designing six residences in Union, New Jersey, his savings allowed him, at the age of twenty-seven, to study at the Pennsylvania Academy of Fine Arts and at the Art Students' League in New York City. He moved to France and studied briefly at the Delecluse and Julien academies in Paris where he met Alfred Stieglitz. Starting in 1909, Stieglitz's gallery in New York City was the principle outlet for Marin's avant-garde work.

Living in New Jersey, Marin painted scenes of the metropolitan area. His early paintings depicted the new skyscrapers of New York City in dynamic, bustling, almost abstract forms with vivid colors. In his own words, "I see great forces at work; great movements; the large buildings and the small buildings; the warring of the great and the small, the influence of one mass on another greater or smaller mass."[799] He participated in the famous Armory Show of 1913, and his abstracts *Woolworth Building* and *Brooklyn Bridge*, showing the beat of the city, were acclaimed by critics. He used "ray lines" to convey the energy of a site, and later he used integrated interlocking planes as his style grew increasingly more abstract. By the 1920s, when he started to paint scenes in Maine, Marin was considered the preeminent American watercolorist as he explored the whole visual field for its potential abstraction and used such design elements as flat geometric shapes and wave-like patterns to portray heat, movement, and even sounds. One biographer wrote, "The urban landscape seems to erupt; buildings and streets break apart, heaving under the pressure of the frenetic pace and congestion of city life."[800] He did not stop painting the metropolitan area, and one of his graphite and black-chalk drawings of 1925 was *Stevens Institute*.[801] A painting which is said to show his background in architecture was his *Mid-Manhattan* of 1932, portraying the new skyline created by the Chrysler, Empire State, and Rockefeller Center buildings.[802] By 1948,

---

[799] Quoted in Carol Salus, "Marin, John," *American National Biography*(1999), 507.

[800] Ilene Susan Fort, "Marin, John," in Jane Turner, ed., *Dictionary of Art*(1996), vol. 16, 421.

[801] Ruth E. Fine, *John Marin*(1990), 22.

[802] Salus, *Op.Cit.*, 508. Of course, Stevens Institute turned out scores of architects including Ackerman and Litchfield as previously mentioned. William O. Ludlow of the class of 1892 who

Marin's expressionist realism earned him the rating of the number one painter in the nation in a *Look* magazine survey of museum directors, curators, and art critics, but his popularity waned thereafter as abstract expressionism led to pop and minimalist styles.[803]

As for Calder, he came from a family of classical sculptors: Calder's grandfather was Alexander Milne Calder (1846-1923), an immigrant Scot from a family of stonecutters. Arriving in Philadelphia in 1868, the grandfather obtained commissions for marble statues, namely *General Meade* in Philadelphia's Fairmount Park, and, most importantly, the four eagles and four figure groups on the Philadelphia City Hall tower whose top is capped with his thirty-seven-foot-high high statue *William Penn*. Calder's father was Alexander Stirling Calder (1870-1945) who studied art at the Pennsylvania Academy in the 1880s and subsequently in the Académie Julien and the École des Beaux Arts in Paris. He pursued a life dedicated to classical sculpture, his most well-known works being the figure of *George Washington* on the triumphal arch in Washington Square Park at the foot of Fifth Avenue in Manhattan's Greenwich Village and *Swan Fountain* in Logan Square near the city hall work of his father in Philadelphia. Calder's mother was Nanette Lederer (1866-1960) who met his father at the Pennsylvania Academy and became a professional portrait painter. The family moved frequently to work on the massive sculptural projects of the father, so spent his early school days in places like the politically left-of-center Croton-on-Hudson, Pasadena, and later Berkeley in California.

Although discouraging their boy from entering art as a profession, given its vicissitudes, his parents nonetheless encouraged his early propensity to make toys, jewelry and gadgets with household materials. They told him that homemade toys were better than ones bought in a store, thus encouraging his imagination, his innovative ability, and his habit of working with his hands. His upbringing was unconventional in other ways: His mother made his early clothes which were of odd design, his father's often erotic statues were created from nude models in studios which were often located in the house, and friends of the family were often bohemian artists. At age five, Calder recalled, he was already making wood-and-wire figures, and his mother or his sister Peggy gave him a pair of pliers for his work with wire. Many toys, especially of animals, were made for play with his sister, and by

---

designed the classic William Hall Walker gymnasium was a New York City architect of the New York Times and the Johns-Manfille buildings. Also a painter, he was perhaps Stevens's most prolific amateur artist, having many paintings, including *Four O'Clock* and *The Storm is Over*, chosen by the Newark Art Club for its annual exhibit in 1948, as well as having other of his paintings exhibited in New York metropolitan area museums.

[803] William Gordon, "Strokes of Genius," *The Star Ledger*, Feb. 22, 1990, 61, 70.

his early school days he had a Noah's Ark filled with homemade animal toys. Before he was in the fourth grade, he had his first workshop in a tent with a wooden floor in the back yard, and subsequently his workshops were usually in the cellars of the houses his parents rented. At Spuyten Duyvil in the Bronx, the son had a well-equipped workshop in the cellar while his father used the attic with a skylight for his studio.[804]

However, young Calder was an excellent academic student, having been placed by school authorities in San Francisco's Lowell High School which was reserved for students of high ability.[805] According to his sister's memoirs, Calder had a high-school chum who wanted to be an engineer, and the idea was appealing to her young brother. Besides, it was a time when engineering was bringing progress, and engineers were more popular than at any other time in American history. His father inquired about engineering colleges and was advised that Stevens was one of the best, and it was accessible to New York City where the father desired to live at the time. Thus, just before Calder entered Stevens Institute in 1915, the family moved to New York City and stayed with friends.

Entrance requirements to Stevens were rigorous. Calder visited the campus with his mother as soon as possible, and he passed entrance examinations in algebra, geometry, trigonometry, physics, and chemistry, as well as English and one foreign language besides two other topics of his choice.[806] He registered by giving his old Berkeley address although the family soon found an apartment at 29 Claremont Avenue next to Columbia University in Manhattan.[807] It was arranged that Calder could live on campus during the week in the only dormitory at the time, the limited rooms in the Stevens Castle. On the first day of class in 1915, Calder recalled moving into a "really wonderful room" with two other students in the tower of the Castle, it being Edwin A. Stevens's drafting room with windows on every side with a view up and down the Hudson and across to the Manhattan skyline. For Calder, the first day of classes at Stevens was like "racing cars starting from a standstill," and his first class was shop practice.[808]

Shop practice looms big in Calder's education at Stevens because it introduced Calder to all forms of metal working and hence his future medium. This course gave Calder what the critic Osborn called "full command of his materials."[809] The professor of shop practice was a self-made man, Alfred S.

---

[804] Lipman, *Op.Cit.*, 16.

[805] Margaret Calder Hayes, *Three Alexander Calders*(1977), 46.

[806] Hayes, *Op.Cit.*, 55, and *Annual Catalog of Stevens Institute of Technology, 1915-16.* 37-40.

[807] See addresses of students in *Ibid., 1916-17* and *1917-18,* 153, 162.

[808] Alexander Calder, *An Autobiography with Pictures*(1966), 39.

[809] Lipman, *Op.Cit.*, 307.

Kinsey (1871-1943), who started working at Stevens at fifteen years of age in 1886 as a machinist's helper. While thus employed at Stevens, Kinsey took courses at night and graduated from Cooper Union in 1890. Subsequently, he worked with Professor James E. Denton in the Department of Tests for eighteen years, participating in research work on boilers, pumps, lubrication, early Curtiss turbines, and the first diesel engines. At the same time, he also taught under Professor David S. Jacobus as an instructor in shop practice. In addition, he served as the first director of the department of buildings and grounds, a position which oversaw the campus store, purchasing, and the print shop. In 1908, he expanded and modernized the course on shop practice in the newly built Carnegie Mechanical Laboratory and wrote a textbook for engineering students taking shop practice. When Jacobus left to work for Babcock and Wilcox, Kinsey became professor of shop practice, a rank he held until he retired in 1941 after fifty-five years of service at Stevens.[810]

At left "Sandy Calder" as a Stevens student amuses a friend during the winter of 1918 on the Stevens campus. At right is Alfred S. Kinsey, Calder's shop professor.

Kinsey's textbook of over three hundred pages shows the content of the freshman course taken by Calder and several generations of Stevens fresh-

[810] "Professor Kinsey Retires," *Stevens Indicator*, 58 (1941), no. 5, 7.

men: It began with practical metallurgy, hands-on founding and casting of various metals, including cast iron, brass, and aluminum which were poured into molds by the student. As in the case of the apprenticeship of Frederick W. Taylor, the students were introduced to pattern-making of different-shaped metal objects. Then the freshmen ran machine tools which drilled, punched, and lathed samples of metals and of steel alloys. Kinsey taught the students which type of cutting tool to use, the right speeds and feeds, including the most efficient stopwatch times to accomplish the tasks. Different sections of the text were guides to hands-on cutting of cast iron, as well as alloy steels including tool steel. Also included were guides to cutting tin, nickel, monel, zinc, copper, brass, bronze, aluminum, and lead in their various forms, including bars, rods, pipes, and sheets. The students were introduced to different-shaped cutting tools, high-speed tungsten steel tools, and diamond-tipped tools and shown their uses in the shop's lathes, milling, and drilling machines. Coolants and lubricants were demonstrated systematically for different operations. Round holes in metals were drilled and reamed, but square, triangular, hexagonal or oval holes were punched. Templates and pilots were explained and used to make shapes in sheet metal. Millwrighting, i.e., the gears and pulleys and belts which drove the machine tools, was demonstrated.

Most important for Calder's art, the course proceeded to give a hands-on experience in joining of metals by brazing, soft soldering, hard soldering, riveting, fusion welding (which included butt welds, lap welds, scarf welds, and cleft welds), oxy-acetylene welding -- including the benefits of hammering and annealing to strengthen the bond -- and electric-arc welding. At every step Kinsey discussed the chemistry of the bonds and procedures to lessen corrosion. After a thorough study of metals, woodworking was taken up. It included a classification of the different characteristics of woods, wood screws, nails, chisels, rasps, augers, and saws. In sum, each subject was covered exhaustively and the text illustrated and named the different tools and their uses, including, for example eleven different auger bits.[811]

Kinsey was a director of the American Welding Society and, as his textbook indicates, highly organized and demanding; so demanding that his famous son, Alfred C. Kinsey (1894-1956), thought he was domineering. However, the son turned out to have similar intellectual and demanding qualities: He clashed with his father by leaving Stevens after two years of instruction to take up zoology at Bowdoin College. After a Harvard Ph.D. with a dissertation on the systematic categorization of species of gall wasps, the son became a professor of zoology at Indiana University where, in 1938,

---

[811] Alfred S. Kinsey, *Lecture Notes Prepared for Engineering Students*(1910).

he taught what he thought was a rigorously scientific course on marriage and the family. The son delivered candid lectures on the physiology of human erotic stimulation, the mechanics of sexual intercourse, techniques of contraception, and classifications of diverse sexual behavior. The course covered human sexuality as thoroughly as his father's covered shop practice. He then investigated sexual diversity through interviews which he carried out for years, some 5,300 case histories in all, before publishing his classic *Sexual Behavior of the Human Male* in 1948. This best-selling book claimed that about half the American male population had participated in homosexual behavior by adolescence, that ninety percent masturbated, that up to forty-five percent had committed adultery during marriage, that seventy percent had visited prostitutes, and that seventeen percent of farmer's boys had sex with animals. The book was followed up by his *Sexual Behavior of the Human Female* in 1953, which first highlighted the importance of the female orgasm. Stevens literature has never recognized the son as one of its own, perhaps because the professor and son were estranged. The elder Alfred Kinsey died in 1943, and, contrary to the opinions of his son, was cited in the *Stevens Indicator* as a professor recalled with affection for his amusing digressions in class and his colorful personality.[812]

Another course in which Calder excelled was descriptive geometry and mechanical drawing.[813] Professor Edwin R. Knapp taught the course to freshmen in 1915, and his technique included quick sketches including "shades and shadows," "perspective," as well as exact design on a drafting table. Included were

Solution of problems consisting of relations of points, lines, and planes to developable single-curved surfaces, and to double-curved surfaces of revolution. Intersections and developments. Practice in transferring to graphical diagrams, conceptions of determining representations on reference planes, of geometrical magnitudes and their relations in space.[814]

According to William B. F. Drew, another freshman and Calder's best friend in college and afterwards, "Prof. Knapp would advise the class to close their eyes so they could concentrate better because the subject was supposedly so difficult. Sandy would look at the sheet with the problem,

---

[812] Obituary of Kinsey, *Stevens Indicator,* 60 (1943), 3, 4-5.
[813] The "Stevens Institute of Technology Faculty Minutes," Vols. 4 (1909-1918) and 5 (1918-1923) give the names of the professors teaching the courses while Calder was at Stevens.
[814] *Annual Catalog, 1915-16,* 100.

sketch the answer on it and put it in his inside pocket and wonder why they had to bother teaching such a simple subject."[815]

A third course in which Calder excelled was applied kinetics taught by Professor Louis F. Martin, Jr. The course taught the mathematical principles of the motions of machine parts in dynamic action. The course was again exhaustive and covered "all" mechanical movements, including instantaneous motion, motion in a given time, acceleration, velocities, and the effects of friction and resistance. Applications to connecting rods, flywheels, governors, and gyroscopes were studied. The catalog in Calder's senior year continues the description of the Applied Kinetics course: "Discussion of the laws governing the plane motion of rigid bodies with applications to machines, compound and torsion pendulums, translating and rotational bodies, discussion of work and energy, with simple applications to machines."[816]

At Stevens, Calder displayed the qualities which kept his art fresh during his whole lifetime, a joyful innocent personality cherished by his pal, Billy Drew. A baseball and football player, Drew passed many a night with Calder being tutored on integral and differential calculus, another subject easy for "Sandy." In return, Drew introduced Calder to fraternity life in the Delta Tau Delta house. Later the best man at Calder's wedding in 1931 and lender of a down payment on Calder's farm at Roxbury in 1933, Drew recalled his friend as a delightful companion in college:

What struck me from the very start was a very quiet, warm person, physically solid and ready to roughhouse at any moment just for fun. He also played football and lacrosse just for sheer physical pleasure; and as for dancing, nobody whirled the girls more rapidly . . . His direct approach to problems was refreshing. If anyone lacked studs for a formal affair's stiff white shirt, Sandy suggested brass fasteners that we used to clip the lab reports together. If a visible hole appeared in a black sock for some formal affair, Sandy used black India ink to cover the flesh.[817]

The Stevens senior yearbook, the *Link,* portrayed Calder as a "blithe heart" who was "evidently always happy, or perhaps up to some joke," and "one of the best-natured fellows there is whose facial expressions were 'the laugh, the grin, and the smile.' " It went on to say, "Billy Drew has stepped in as self-appointed Professor of 'Ways and Means in Public' to Sandy-child,

---

[815] Quoted in Jean Lipman, *Calder's Universe*(1976), 19.

[816] Quoted in *Ibid.,* 18.

[817] Quoted in *Ibid.,* 19.

and the latter is, as a result, becoming quite sophisticated."[818] Calder's sister Peggy also commented on her brother's child-like personality:

Sandy, fortunately, never lost that confidence, that originality and wholeness which Erik Erikson, in his book *Toys and Reasons*, has recently reminded us is commonly found in the young child . . . and recovered only in creative moments in adult life. Sandy remained interested in the object for its form and was not troubled by any impropriety. Can the result be properly be called childlike? Yes, if by childlike one means to convey spontaneity, wholeness, cosmic gaiety.[819]

Another Stevens student who noted this charming character of Calder was Harold Fee 1920. He took Calder to his parents' home in Mt. Vernon, New York, on a weekend, and later described that Calder loved to climb up on an old water tank in the coal-and-fuel-oil yard of Fee's father and spend an afternoon sketching on the back of used pieces of paper or anything else at hand. Calder could also spur behavior which was uncharacteristic in his more conventional engineering friends, for example, in 1953, he had his old friend Fee, who was secretary of the Stevens Alumni Association and editor of the *Indicator* at the time, climb up onto the roof of the tower of the Stevens Castle and wave a red blanket when Sandy was leaving New York harbor by ship.[820]

Luckily, Calder failed to hold various engineering jobs in spite of three years of trying after graduation. He even grew a mustache and wore conventional suits to look more seriously like an engineer. By 1923, he gave up and joined the Art Student's League in New York City. He lived with his parents and found some pocket money doing illustrations for the *Police Gazette*. Other money came from designing toys with eccentric wheels for an Oshkosh toy company. In 1926, he worked his way to England on a steamship and stayed in London with a fraternity brother, Bob Trube, before meeting Trube's father who introduced him to Paris. There, his well-documented connections with other avant-garde artists began. [821]

That same year, Calder made his famous toy circus with animals made of wood and wire, the animation caused by wires worked by his hands. He entertained fellow artists and friends with performances in which he barked like a seal and used cymbals to introduce acts. His circus became so popular among the artistic and literary crowd that he later set up boxes and viewing

---

[818] *Ibid.*

[819] Hayes, *Op.Cit.,* 84.

[820] Calder, *Autobiography, Op.Cit.,* 213. Another Stevens classmate, James M. Horn, helped to design Calder's Roxbury farm studio-workshop, *Ibid.,* 170.

[821] *Ibid.,* 54 (1927), 1, 19.

stands and charged admission to support his art. Through the circus, he made lasting connections with architects and directors of galleries who later supported his mobiles and stabiles. Carrying it around in five suitcases, he continued to perform with his circus even after he became famous.

One of Calder's earliest mobiles was two wire metal fish which swam by the use of a hand crank attached to connecting rods and gears, and later by a small electric motor with a reducing gear to slow the speed.[822] In his own autobiography, he sounds like an engineer when describing some of his works, including one of his first mobiles moved by air, made in 1931:

There were two slightly articulated objects that swayed in the breeze. One was a more or less horizontal rod with a square sheet of tin on one end and an ebony counterweight on the other. The second object was an almost vertical rod, slightly inclined, about a yard long with at the top a little wire loop with a counterweight at its far end, and another little piece, with another counterweight – there were three elements.[823]

In other passages, he describes a later work with "a screw eye and a pulley," an "eccentric" wheel, a "cantilever" effect (achieved by suspending a heavy sphere from the apex of a wire), and "belting" (which supplied movement to a mobile with a motor).[824]

According to Calder's friend and promoter, the art critic James J. Sweeny, international interest in Calder had stemmed from his originality, which was considered as American as a Yankee whittling a figure out of hickory. As Fernand Leger wrote in 1931 on the occasion of the first exhibition of Calder's mobiles at the Galerie Percier in Paris, "Before these new works, transparent, objective, exact, I think of Satie, Mondrian, Marcel Duchamp, Brancusi, Arp: Those incontestable masters of reticent and silent beauty. Calder is of that line. He is American 100 percent. Satie and Duchamp are 100 percent French. Yet we meet."[825] Calder was discovered and appreciated by Europeans for his uniquely "American" art before he was appreciated in the United States. According to Sweeny who was editor of a book, *3 Young Rats and Other Rhymes* (1944) illustrated with 85 Calder drawings, "his fellow countrymen, in looking at incidentals and finding there

---

[822] William Shoudy, "Man of Mobiles," *Stevens Indicator,* 82 (1965), no. 2, 14.

[823] Calder, *An Autobiography, Op.Cit.,* 118.

[824] *Ibid.,* 106, 137, 148.

[825] Quoted in James J. Sweeny, "The Position of Alexander Calder," *Stevens Indicator,* 61 (1944), 5, 11.

nothing either exotic or jingoistically exaggerated, could see no interest in further investigating an unfamiliar structure."[826]

Calder's Stevens classmates took an early interest in Sandy's shows. In 1937, the *Stevens Indicator* took note that Calder's art was being displayed in New York's Museum of Modern Art in a show entitled "Exhibition of Fantastic Art."[827] At the show, Calder was wearing a lavender shirt and a mustard colored sweater and was described by a critic as a "mobilist." At the show, Calder explained his piece, multi-colored balls hanging from strings, to a reporter for the *New Yorker:* "The balls are suspended in space, so you must, plastically, ignore the strings." Subsequently, a *New Yorker* editor visited Pierre Matisse's Manhattan gallery where Calder had a show and left a note for Calder inquiring what his art was all about. Calder wrote back that "There is no 'meaning.' The things are merely *plastic*."[828]

Meanwhile Calder was being promoted by Billy Drew who supplied the *Stevens Indicator* and MIT's *Technology Review* with an article written by Calder on his *Mercury Fountain,* a project whose design and engineering solutions would have particular interest for engineers. The fountain was in the Spanish Republic's pavilion in the 1937 Paris Exposition, and, since Spain was in the midst of its civil war against the fascists, it was a partisan exhibit. The fountain was displayed in the center of the pavilion in front of Picasso's anti-Franco painting *Guernica* depicting the bombing of the Basque city by the Luftwaffe. Calder's friend Joan Miró also had paintings in the exhibit and was instrumental in having Calder featured even though he was not Spanish. The director of the pavilion wanted to have a fountain of mercury to promote sales from the Almaden mercury mines which were still in Republican hands. The problem for Calder was that the mercury was corrosive of other metals, except stainless steel, unless they were protected by glazing. Calder didn't like these solutions to the problem, and instead used a coating of pitch to protect hammered iron in his ingenious mercury fountain-mobile:

That was fine, for pitch with a flat black surface would give a color which is the greatest possible contrast to the shining metallic mercury, much more so than glass, or polished steel . . . . As the intent was to show mercury, in the basin, and in the air . . . I started at about a meter height and let it spew onto a plate, of irregular contour and warped surface, which in itself was a dynamic shape. After the mercury had trickled across this, it poured out of a weir onto a second plate of a different contour and surface. It flowed across this making a sort of lagoon on its way. The third plate

---

[826] *Ibid.*

[827] *New Yorker,* December 12, 1936.

[828] *Stevens Indicator,* 54 (1937), no. 3, 6.

was a chute, with a dam at the head end, making a basin into which the mercury could spill. . . I hung a rod vertically from a ring at its middle, whose lower end widened out into a plate of irregular form, at the center of the basin, so that the jet of mercury leaving the chute would strike the plate causing it and the rod to sway about. From the upper end of the rod I hung another, lighter rod, in similar fashion, at whose lower extremity was a circular disc painted red, and from whose upper end was flaunted the name of the mines, Almaden, in brass wire. [829]

In this *Mercury Fountain,* he used a pump hidden under a stairwell to draw up mercury into a cistern where it could fall by gravity and a siphon effect through pipes under the floor to the fountain. To make the pump work, he added a little water to the mercury to wet the pump.[830]

In spite of his art's "American" engineering quality, Calder was leftist in his politics, something uncharacteristic for most engineers: Besides supporting the republican side in the civil war in Spain, he absented himself from the United States during the McCarthy era after World War II. If Calder was playful and humorous, he became serious about politics, and he spoke out against nuclear war and wars he considered unjust. Thus, in 1965, as chairman of Artists for SANE, he led a group to Washington D.C. to protest the escalating war in Vietnam. In 1966, he and his wife took out a full-page ad in the *New York Times* wishing their countrymen a happy new year and urging them to dedicate themselves to peace. In 1972 before the Watergate scandal, he joined others in another *Times* ad for the removal of President Nixon for continuing to conduct an undeclared and therefore unconstitutional war.[831]

At this time, Calder was all the rage and at the height of his fame. The *Saturday Evening Post,* in its February 27, 1965, issue reported that "His mobiles have fascinated everybody from children to philosophers and scientists and it is reported Albert Einstein once spent forty minutes watching the complete cycle of a motorized Calder mobile called *A Universe* and said that he wished he had thought of it himself." The *Stevens Indicator* reported that Calder had told William Shoudy of the class of 1899 that he could not have built his mobiles without his engineering education and that engineering components of some mobiles included frictionless bearings. The article reported that Calder said that in 1955 his mobiles were selling "like hot cakes" at prices from $50 to $3,000, but by 1965 his small table-top mobiles were selling for $500 and he was obtaining $100,000 for larger

---

[829] Sandy Calder, "Mercury Fountain," *Stevens Indicator,* 55 (1938), no. 2, 3, and Lipman, *Op.Cit.,* 343
[830] *Ibid.,* 159.
[831] Lipman, *Op.Cit.,* 38.

stabiles.[832] His huge stabiles made Calder a wealthy man. They now adorn public places in Mexico City, Goteborg in Sweden, Spoleto in Italy, and many other cities including Los Angeles and Montreal, which boast the largest ones.[833]

Alexander Calder 1919

Calder also indirectly influenced the curriculum at Stevens. At commencement in 1969 on the fiftieth anniversary of his graduation from Stevens Institute, Calder was given an Honorary Doctor of Engineering degree. At the same time, Calder gave to Stevens one of his mobiles which today hangs in the Great Hall of the Samuel C. Williams Library on campus.

---

[832] *Ibid.*, 81 (1963), no. 2, 49, and Shoudy, *Op.Cit.*, 14.

[833] Richard Burdi, "Alexander Calder, 1898-1976: Mobiles Were His Business, But Not His Only Business," *Stevens Indicator*, 94 (1977), 34.

Immediately after these events, art instruction was added to the electives in the humanities department in the fall semester of 1969. Previously, in early 1931, an instructor in humanities, Harvey Stevenson, taught a lecture course on architecture and allied arts. He had helped organize an exhibit of student, faculty, and alumni art on campus, and Calder participated along with about a dozen other alumni.[834] But in 1969, Stevens hired Paul Miller as artist in residence. A student of Hans Hoffman, the abstract expressionist, Miller's specialty was, appropriately, metal geometric designs made of wire. At Stevens, he not only taught drawing and painting, but also fostered creativity and imagination by having students create art with whatever was at hand. The art included ingenious kinetic machines made with odds and ends from engineering labs, junk piles, or the local hardware store.

According to Miller, one of his best students was Steve M. Legensky 1977, who went on to earn an M.S. in 1979. Legensky was a pioneer artist in computer graphics, which were at the time in their infancy. In Miller's undergraduate course, Legensky recalls having had the opportunity to develop and explore his artistic creativity. His computer art started when he experimented with writing programs on a plotter in the computer center to create line drawings. With such hacking experience, in 1977-78 he teamed up with Professor M. Peter Jurkat to obtain an NSF grant to develop the Undergraduate Computer Graphics Facility at Stevens. Legensky learned about emerging computer graphics technology by doing background research and by supplying a good deal of the hardware and software plan for the grant application.

After graduation, his first full-time job was manager of the Stevens graphics lab. Legensky's big break was obtaining a seventy-thousand-dollar contract for the Stevens graphics lab from Advanced Technology Systems to work on development of hardware and software for one of the world's most powerful 3-D graphics for aircraft flight simulation, a project Advanced Technology Systems was conducting for Hughes Aircraft. Later he joined Advanced Technology Systems as a full-time employee, but in 1984 he founded his own company, Intelligent Light, Inc. By purchasing the rights to software, his company pioneered the computer graphics used in television commercials and colorful, moving TV network logos for companies like HBO. Today, Legensky's clients are worldwide and include NASA, Ford, Toyota, British Aerospace and GM. His product, called FIELDVIEW, is the

---

[834] "Work by Alumni, Faculty and Students Features Stevens Art Exhibit," *Stevens Indicator*, 48 (1931), 9.

recognized world-leader in the technology of engineering computer graphics.[835]

Besides artists, Stevens had its share of graduates talented in writing. Among Stevens's many authors of non-technical and non-academic articles and books, perhaps Richard Reeves 1960 stands out as the most well-known. He was known as Richie to his classmates at Stevens where he wrote a weekly humor column called "Have Pen Will Travel" for the *Stute*. In this column he wrote satiric articles like "Behind the Ivy Curtain," which exposed the vice and crime in the country's colleges. Another exposed "how love-starved faculty members are making the nation's campuses hell on earth." The name of the column was prophetic because Reeves has written eleven full-length books, thousands of articles as a reporter and a syndicated columnist, and made award-winning documentaries as he traveled the United States and the world doing investigative reporting, covering the presidential beat, and writing social and political commentary.

Reeves said later that the Stevens education "gave me a good background," and that there was nothing in the rules that said he had to be an engineer. At Stevens, he gained, "an enormously valuable intellectual discipline, a sense of logic and progression toward a conceptual endpoint; also, I learned to work like hell -- not many people take that away from college." His education did not simply prepare him for a job, money and status; it helped develop his intellectual faculties, adult sensibilities, and a world view. Later in life, speaking of the problems of cities, which he found not insurmountable, Reeves said,

I remember a humanities lecture that Doc Humphrey gave one day in the Kidde Building. He talked for an hour about the miserable lives of serfs in the Middle Ages and then at the end, he said something like 'but it was a time when the spring still came, and the people walked in the fields, and they fell in love.' That has really stuck with me and I suppose it's my basic view of the human condition.[836]

After graduating Reeves was hired by Ingersoll-Rand where he wound up writing advertising copy. Reeves then started to work part-time as a reporter for a local newspaper, the *Phillipsburg Free Press*, and he subsequently became one of its editors. He moved to the *Newark News* where his investigative reporting and exposés of New Jersey politics established his career as an exceptional journalist. In 1965, he moved to the *New York Herald Tribune* and in 1966 to the *New York Times* where he was named city hall

---

[835] Steve Legensky to Geoffrey W. Clark, July 14, 1999.
[836] Quoted in Geoffrey W. Clark, "Have Pen Will Travel: An Iconoclastic Paladin on the Trail of President Ford," *Stevens Indicator*, 93 (1976), 1, 10.

bureau chief and then chief political correspondent by 1971. In those positions, he wrote articles critical of the lack of social awareness of such Cold War, technically-oriented think tanks as the Rand Corporation. By his early thirties, he had acquired a national reputation for his articles covering presidential politics, particularly campaign of Robert Kennedy, as well as municipal politics during the administration of New York Mayor John Lindsay. His articles showed a social consciousness including a deep faith in democracy and fair play, but they also exhibit his special enjoyment in exposing ridiculous personal and political foibles -- a technique which touched a respondent chord in his readers.

While continuing his journalistic career as well as a stint teaching part-time as an adjunct professor of political writing at CCNY, in 1967 he started a long association with WNET, the Newark station of the Public Broadcasting System (PBS). Earlier at Stevens, Reeves had been president of the dramatic society and had created a popular program, "Showtime," on the campus radio station, and so he already had a liking for the more dramatic forms of news media. In 1968, during the height of opposition to the Vietnam War, he was a PBS national political commentator and served as chief correspondent on PBS's "Frontline" documentary series.

Always seeming to live by the words "will travel" in the name of his *Stute* column, he left the *Times* to become contributing editor for the independent weekly *New York Magazine* during the years 1971-77, a choice which gave him more room for editorial political and social commentary. Not just a career journalist, Reeves was interested in journalism as civic activism. Already he had shown his activism by serving on the Phillipsburg Citizens Advisory Commission in 1962-63, by winning the Citizens for Clean Air Award in 1965, and, in the seventies, by being nominated for Emmies for his program called "The Jersey Side," an independent, public-affairs TV series which ran on WOR-TV and covered problems confronting New Jersey's cities and towns. While an editor for *New York Magazine,* Reeves was a sought-after TV host on commercial channels, and from 1973 to 1975 he was co-host of NBC-TV's "Sunday" program. His television work was nationally recognized with an Emmy for the ABC network's exposé-documentary "Lights, Camera . . . Politics!" in 1980. Later he received awards for his PBS on-site "Struggle for Birmingham" and "Red Star Over Khyber" shown in 1984.[837]

While involved in the above activities, Reeves wrote eleven full-length books, among which were *A Ford, Not A Lincoln* (1975), an exposé of

---

[837] He became editor of *Esquire* in 1977 and found time to contribute articles to the *New York Times Magazine,* and *The New Yorker.*

President Gerald Ford's mediocre leadership; *Old Faces of 1976* (1976); and *Convention* (1977) on the banalities of democratic politics as described through interviews and diaries. The rest of his books include *The Reagan Detour* (1985); *President Kennedy: Profile of Power* (1994), which noted JFK's sexual liaisons even on the very day of his inauguration; *Running in Place: How Bill Clinton Disappointed America* (1996); and his more serious *Do the Media Govern? Politicians, Voters, and Reporters in America* (1997).

Perhaps the most unusual book was his *American Journey: Traveling with Tocqueville in Search of Democracy in America* (1982). It traced the nineteenth-century, 18,000-mile route of the French political commentator Alexis de Tocqueville, who interviewed Americans and commented on American politics and society in his book *Democracy in America*. Reeves had heard about Tocqueville's book when he was an A student in a Jersey City high school before reading it in a humanities class at Stevens, and then "really reading" it later. Like Tocqueville, Reeves was not a politician or political scientist, not even a professionally trained journalist, but rather someone who seemed to have always approached his work as an outsider, slightly detached and bemused, but always curious and interested in plumbing the meaning of American democratic processes with disarming honesty. For Reeves and Tocqueville, politicians were mostly mediocre and often ignorant, their main interests elections, prestige, polls and the "business of politics" rather than actual government or bold, enlightened leadership.

In the book, Reeves retraces Tocqueville's travels, visits the same cities and towns, asks similar questions of similar types of people. Apart from movements like those of civil rights, anti-war activists, environmentalists, conservative Christians, and coalitions against big government and taxes, he finds most voters apathetic and manipulated by one-liners or sound bites with which pols manipulate even journalists. And the press, even though it is one of the guarantors of the democratic system, is also a business which all too often does not rise to a higher level of investigative reporting and serious commentary. Reeves shows that politicians, voters, and journalists are often blunt and forthright in self-criticism, and they are more self-aware of these problems than in the days of Tocqueville -- along with the tradition of American individualism, therein lies the hope and greatness of American democracy for Reeves.

CHAPTER 24

Updating the Broad-Based Engineering Curriculum

The tradition of a broad-based and credit-rich engineering curriculum at Stevens has been maintained through the leading role of its trustees who are motivated by the accomplishments of alumni as inventors, innovators and entrepreneurs. In addition, since the mid-twentieth century, the recommendations of national studies of engineering education have further encouraged the institute to strengthen its unique tradition of including all the engineering sciences in the core for every student -- the most unusual and broadening part of the Stevens engineering curriculum for alumni because it gave them an overview of all major engineering disciplines and allowed them rapid advancement in management ranks.

To assure the continuation of this tradition, generations of dedicated faculty and deans spent an enormous amount of time and energy on curriculum committees reviewing components of courses, resequencing courses in the core, creating new design and laboratory components, and continually readjusting and reintegrating supporting mathematics and science content. Since technologies changed at an unprecedented rate after mid-century, the Stevens broad-based engineering curriculum had to be updated often to keep its content and teaching methods abreast of new advances. This task was not easy and sometimes involved disagreements about solutions, as this history shows.

On the one hand, an updated version of the engineering sciences had to be included, as well as a solid foundation in the sciences and humanities to assure the continuation of the philosophy based on fundamentals. These components of the curriculum were always the givens. On the other hand, exponential growth in technology in the specialized areas of engineering put pressure on engineers to somehow include new, specialized content in the curriculum. Curriculum committees were aware that it was much simpler in other institutions to include such "crucial" specialized content through technical electives, courses that were, at Stevens, limited in number because of the huge size of the common core. Moreover, another tricky problem was the sequencing of engineering sciences: would materials come before electronic circuits or after, and what was the effect on upper-level courses in particular departments? What course would pop out of the core if another course was added? At other institutions with specialized curricula, only the engineering professors of the specialty were usually involved in its formation. But at Stevens representatives of all engineering specialties were necessarily involved because changes affected them all. Moreover, at Stevens, the science, humanities, and management faculty also had a stake in the core of the engineering curriculum, and the tradition was to have changes approved by a vote of the whole faculty after revisions.

In 1955, the Stevens administrations and faculty were witnesses to a call from the American Society of Engineering Education (ASEE, the successor to the SPEE) for engineering curricula to move away from very specialized curricula back to a more general core resembling Stevens's to a greater degree. The call for a retreat from specialization initiated by the Carnegie Foundation's Mann and Wickenden Reports was made even more strongly in the Grinter Report of the ASEE in that year. The report called for an increase in liberal arts content to one-fifth of the engineering curriculum, an increase in sciences and mathematics to one-fourth, an increase in engineering sciences to one-fourth, a reduction of specialized sequences of engineering analysis and design to one-fourth, with an inclusion of management and electives at about one-tenth. There were considerable changes in these categories of curriculum content at other engineering colleges, but they nevertheless remained more specialized than at Stevens. In 1956, President Jess Davis praised the Stevens broad-based engineering curriculum with these words:

Instead of trying to educate specialists who are good only in a limited field of engineering, let's throw away the blinders and let American engineering students see more of all fields. Let us help them also to gain a better understanding of the relationship of each of the fields to the others. . . The engineering undergraduate of the years ahead will have to learn more of science, more of the engineering principles and, unfortunately, less of the practical applications of the principles. There will be fewer undergraduate classes in air conditioning and more in thermodynamics, fewer in hydraulic turbines and more in fluid dynamics. There will be less of design work of the empirical nature but a deeper study of mathematics and of the physical and engineering sciences where the principles of design of all kinds originate. If we are to keep ahead of the world, there must be fewer engineering vocational schools and more engineering academies. . . Only by this "know why" can we hit upon the new and startling inventions that will keep us ahead of the Soviets and their over-specialized technologists. . . The Committee on Evaluation of Engineering Education of the American Society for Engineering Education recently made recommendations to the engineering colleges that they move to strengthen their undergraduate programs in the basic engineering sciences and make them a common core for all their engineering curricula. . . What I wanted to do . . . as I approach the middle of my fifth year at Stevens, was to reaffirm my faith in the single, non-specialized curriculum with its heavy emphasis on science that for so many years has given the Institute an alumni body of whose achievements it is justly proud.[838]

Thus, at Stevens, there were almost no changes in the proportions of time allotted to the areas proposed by the Grinter Report because the overall proportions were already being met.

The Stevens core already included the humanities (eight courses) and engineering sciences (statics, dynamics, strength of materials, electronics, thermodynamics, transport phenomena, and fluid dynamics). In effect, Stevens Institute had skipped the nationwide trend to specialization that occurred from the 1880s through the 1920s by retaining a single broad M.E. program, and, when the Grinter Report's call came, it was unnecessary for Stevens to change its curriculum to meet the suggested proportions. In fact, Stevens exceeded the suggested proportions in engineering sciences and had only two electives for a concentration in a field, *many fewer* than recommended.

Nonetheless, even though the distribution met the new criteria, Stevens's core still had a residual bias towards mechanical engineering. Stevens's expanded faculty in the sciences added pressure to modernize the engineering curriculum and to include new science content suitable to the nuclear age. At the same time, alumni and the placement office pressured the institute to change the M.E. degree to a more general B.Eng. It was thought that the M.E. degree identified alumni as strictly mechanical engineers instead of the broadly-educated graduates that they were in reality.[839] Thus, in 1958, the degree was changed to a B.Eng. although there was a transitional period in which students could choose the old degree as an option. At the same time, outdated mechanical engineering core courses such as shop work and mechanical laboratory practice were dropped altogether, machine design was deleted from the core, and mechanical drawing was reduced to a minimum. By 1966, five technical electives were available so that other engineering areas besides mechanical engineering could pursue concentrations based on the common core.

A notable study of the engineering curriculum was undertaken by a Stevens faculty committee in 1964. Funded by a sizable grant of $62,000 from the Victoria Foundation, the report by Stevens's "Victoria Committee" strongly supported the broad-based engineering curriculum and stressed the benefits of including two sequences, one in design and one in the humanities and social sciences, both of which were to be integrated with the usual

[838] "President Davis' Timely Address," *Stevens Indicator*, 73 (1956), 2, 11.
[839] "Proposed Degree Change," *Ibid.*, 75 (1958), no. 1, 11.

engineering sciences, sciences, management and senior design content. The Victoria Committee was chaired by Luigi Z. Pollara, head of the chemistry-chemical engineering department and one of the young turks who had pushed through the science curriculum. Another influential member of the committee was Pollara's close friend Richard Dale Humphreys, head of the humanities department who wrote the text of the report of the committee. In describing the most important recommendations, the report said,

> The first of these sequences is in Engineering Design, beginning with a unique course in the Freshman Year that will introduce, with some conceptual and mathematical rigor, techniques of decision making, feasibility, iteration, and optimization. Succeeding courses will prepare the student for a major design project in the senior year where he will have an opportunity of drawing fully on the resources provided in his previous education.
>
> Closely related in many of its functions, and in some of its possible problems and assignments, is a second sequence in the Humanities and Social Sciences. It will begin with a rigorous writing project that will require the student to face the problems not only of communication but of observation, identification, definition, and meaning, as they arise in the process of verbalizing experience. Succeeding courses will provide an historical background as a necessary dimension to human understanding; an analysis of the customs, institutions and ideas that give form to human society and meaning to human action; and a series of elective courses in the Social Sciences and Humanities resting on the foundation provided by the previous core courses.[840]

The report of the Victoria Committee has been cited as far ahead of its time for its support of humanities and social sciences; for example, Z. Tadmor and his colleagues in the Technion report "Engineering Education 2001" of 1987 pointed out that the report argued that "politics, economics, social arrangement, and arts and letters can no longer be usefully conceived as isolated and distinct from the technology on which our society lives and grows."[841] The recommendations of the Victoria Committee, including a trimester format, were found too radical by both the faculty and the administration, but the idea of a design thread throughout the curriculum was to be used years later.

Also in 1964, Stevens continued to stress that the broad based engineering degree not only resulted in graduates' inventiveness but also their rise in

---

[840] Luigi Pollara et al, "Report to the President from the Stevens Committee on Engineering Education, March 26, 1964, 31.

[841] Analysis of the footnotes of the report of the Victoria Committee shows that the Grinter Report was frequently cited-- Grinter had laid much stress on integrating the humanities and social sciences and also a design thread into engineering curricula.

management ranks, an old argument used since the late nineteenth century. Professor Frederick Gaudet of Stevens's Laboratory of Psychological Studies proved that Stevens graduates moved up from engineering design in the early years of their careers into management in the later years. He analyzed 450 graduates of the classes of 1926-29, 1936-39, and 1946-49 and found that 37.5 percent of 1920s graduates, 32.3 percent of 1930s graduates and 3.6 percent of the 1940s graduates had attained management positions.[842]

Following a faculty vote necessitating a review every six years, President Kenneth C. Rogers appointed a committee in 1974 to review the engineering curriculum. This Engineering Review Committee, consisting wholly of engineering faculty and chaired by Paul Chirlian, a professor of electrical engineering, is notable because it presented the needs of engineering faculty within the context of the broad-based engineering curriculum.

Its report in 1976 recognized the engineering faculty's many valid "arguments favoring the adoption of specialized engineering curricula by Stevens Institute" which would necessitate a "small core of courses and many departmental electives." These arguments were characterized as "logical and numerous . . . . Not the least of them is the one which reminds us that it is better to be a master of one trade than be jack of all." Nevertheless, the committee took into account "our reputation for rigor and the demand for our graduates" because of the broad-based engineering curriculum, and it suggested continuing the Stevens tradition by adhering to a common core -- but in a trimester format which allowed more space for an increase in the number of technical electives to ten in order to strengthen the specialized concentrations in different engineering disciplines. The engineers' aim was to strengthen the professionalism of the specialized engineering areas which, during the last decades, had seen an increase in the amount of fundamental knowledge which was considered by each to be essential. Thus, more electives and design courses in addition to the broad-based core would be made available by the trimester format, with some eight more courses than were allowed in the semester format.[843]

Even though Stevens Institute had a trimester format under President Morton from 1871 to 1902 and some other engineering colleges like Worcester Polytechnic Institute had switched to the trimester calendar to achieve flexibility by 1976, the Chirlian committee's trimester calendar and its concomitant need to redesign all courses was considered too costly by the administration -- as was the case with the Victoria Committee recommenda-

[842] Frederick J. Gaudet, "Engineers as Managers; Good or No Good?" *Stevens Indicator*, 81 (1964), no. 1, 5-7.

[843] P. Chirlian *et al,* "Report of the Engineering Review Committee," July 1976.

tion for a trimester format. It was defeated in a vote of the faculty over the calendar issues but also over the issue of increased technical electives. Some faculty, mostly from the science departments, thought so many technical electives diluted the broad-based unified curriculum because they allowed for increased specialization. The debate indicated that many engineers wanted such electives to teach material considered crucial in their specialties, a contention which would resurface later. Engineers thought the engineering curriculum was too rigid, because of the large common core and heavy inclusion of sciences. At no time, however, did the engineering departments advocate specialized curricula as they existed at other colleges. During the debates, their contention was to increase the number of technical electives -- not to change the broad-based core. Additional "professionalism" was advocated in order to improve understanding of state-of-the-art knowledge in the major concentrations of chemical, electrical, mechanical and civil engineering, such modern knowledge having grown appreciably in each area in the Space Age and Cold War era.

Finally, some accommodation of the engineers' point of view was achieved in a curriculum revision in 1978. The new 1978 curriculum was a result of the work of another faculty curriculum review committee, the Ad Hoc Committee for the Revision of the Engineering Curriculum (Ad Hoc CREC) chaired by Dean Edward A. Friedman. Provost Pollara constructed a committee with representatives from every academic department and insisted on a thorough review of content of every course the institute offered before allowing the committee to consider revisions. Pollara's directive made the committee large in number of faculty and their task onerous, but, although the proceedings were sometimes contentious, the strategy succeeded in producing a curriculum based on subtle compromises under the chairmanship of Friedman. The Ad Hoc CREC of 1978 made space for an increase in technical electives to eight by a slight reduction in science content and by making some engineering science courses optional. Moreover, increased specialized content was achieved by a suggestion of the Victoria Committee, namely, bifurcating certain core courses like transport phenomena and thermodynamics so that they were more applicable to the different engineering specialties. Almost all the common core was kept in place by the chairman, who championed it as having unique appeal, there being only ten other engineering institutions in the country with a similar program. The only other small, private, top-rated competitor for such a generalized engineering education and accreditation in the general-engineering category was Harvey Mudd college on the West Coast -- in spite of the Grinter Report, most colleges retained highly specialized engineering curricula.[844] The Ad Hoc CREC's representation of all academic departments which fed information to the rest of the faculty, and its thoroughness and attention to detail to support its suggestions for pragmatic compromises led to satisfactory passage by a vote of the faculty.[845]

During the administration of President Kenneth C. Rogers, there was continued adherence to the broad-based curriculum despite serious concern about the competitiveness of the high number of credits in the traditional core. Rogers reviewed the historical tradition of the broad-based engineering curriculum in a speech called "Fundamentals First" delivered before the Newcomen Society of North America at the Pierre Hotel in New York City on June 21, 1979. He said,

From its inception, Stevens has stressed education of the "complete" person, the intellectually well rounded and physically fit individual who has a unified sense of how the world operates. Our philosophy has been to produce a graduate whose formal training has stressed common features among different branches of knowledge, and who will leave Stevens with a comprehensive view of a broad field and how its respective parts meld together. Our greatest emphasis has been on general concepts and a long-range perspective . . . . based on a core of required courses in mathematics, the sciences, fundamental engineering principles and the humanities. Unlike many other institutions providing undergraduate engineering education, Stevens has never fractionalized its curriculum into different specialties of engineering.[846]

Deficit budgets in the early 1980s effected the way the institute looked at the engineering curriculum, the bread-and-butter program in tuition fees. The end to the baby-boom generation of college entrants began in 1984 and caused concern about a drop in undergraduate enrollments over the following years. During the Reagan era, a further cutback in federal research reduced overhead revenues, which tended to make Stevens more reliant on tuition. Since the baby-boom generation was ending, these developments caused more budgetary trouble for Rogers. As a result, in 1983, a consulting firm was hired to do a strategic analysis of Stevens Institute's position vis à vis other engineering colleges in order to devise a strategy for competitive success.

---

[844] See E. A. Freidman, "Technology and Higher Education in America for the Next Decade," 1978, Stevens Special Collections.

[845] E. A. Friedman *et al,* "Summary of Review of the Engineering Curriculum Compiled by the Ad Hoc Committee for the Revision of the Engineering Curriculum," Dec. 6, 1978; E. A. Friedman *et al,* "Recommendations Regarding Educational Procedures and Curriculum Revisions Submitted by the Ad Hoc Committee for the Revision of the Engineering Curriculum," Dec. 19, 1978.

[846] Kenneth C. Rogers, *Fundamentals First: The Story of Stevens Institute of Technology*(Newcomen, 1979), 8-9.

Written by George Keller, the firm's report saw a lack of focus and a split among faculty between those who were interested in research and those who wanted more attention paid to undergraduate education. Keller suggested that "the faculty and administration consider building . . . chiefly upon Stevens's unusual general engineering curriculum . . . appropriate too for a small engineering college that does not permit large, separate departments and specialized majors. . . . There is one more element. General engineering curriculums may be the wave of the future . . . . By standing still with its curriculum, Stevens has serendipitously moved into the avant-garde." A "liberal arts and management grounded curriculum" could be practical training for engineering leadership; additionally,

The general engineering curriculum is not only traditional to Stevens, distinctive in the U.S.A, and especially appropriate for a small engineering college, but it is also suited for the coming widespread use of computers in engineering curriculums and geared to respond to the more integrated, less fragmented kind of engineering that will most likely be practiced in the future.[847]

The "Keller Report" recommended focus on a "tight little island" spirit in which small classes and friendliness would be stressed, as at Caltech, instead of the practice at larger, colder institutions. Keller also recommended focus on a few fields of applied engineering research in order to do a few things exceptionally well instead of focus on a spread of research efforts. He also promoted a strengthening of management and business education on both graduate and undergraduate levels, given the enrollment potential in the metropolitan area. Lastly, Keller called for modernization of operations, particularly in admissions, to attract students from a more widespread national base instead of mainly from the Northeast, and adding cooperative education to attract more students.

Subsequently, most of Keller's suggestions were later taken up by Stevens. For example, the new head of the management department, Professor Donald N. Merino 1960, who held a Stevens M.S. and Ph.D., created a B.S. program in management and business administration, and a concentration in engineering management in the engineering curriculum in 1987 -- the latter program was not only successful in enrollments but also won the American Society of Engineering Management's Academic Excellence Award for the best program of its kind in the country in 1992. Keller's suggestion for cooperative education was instituted in 1987, and the process

---

[847] G. Keller, "A Strategic Analysis for the Stevens Institute of Technology," Barton-Gillet Company, December 1983.

of focusing on a limited number of excellent research efforts was taken up in 1988-89 under Stevens's sixth president, Harold J. Raveché. However, Keller had warned against specialized accreditation because he thought it would weaken the core of the broad-based engineering curriculum.

Accreditation of engineering programs was not in existence when Stevens Institute of Technology opened its doors in 1871. The first accrediting institution was the Educational Committee for Professional Development (ECPD) founded in 1932 through efforts of engineering societies, particularly the ASME. The ECPD accredited Stevens Institute in its first list of accredited programs in 1936 under General Engineering, an accreditation which had been renewed since then.

In 1979 an umbrella organization, the Association of American Engineering Societies (AAES),was founded to speak for all engineers, and it created a new accrediting institution, the Accrediting Board for Engineering and Technology (ABET) which replaced the ECPD. The ECPD and the SPEE had been unable to resolve the competing interests -- of administration versus faculty, of deans versus teachers, of industry versus academia, and of research versus instruction -- which had been evident since the publish-or-perish era started in the 1960s.[848] With input in the 1980s from practicing engineers instead of academics, ABET put more emphasis on design in engineering education and on practice-oriented curricula. This new emphasis grew out of the perceived lack of American competitiveness in manufacturing and the nation's chronic trade deficits in the late 1970s. New ABET criteria for accreditation also prescribed specific engineering sciences for all the engineering specializations. It was in the context of this new criteria promoted by ABET that Stevens decided to seek specialized accreditation for its already existing "concentration" programs in addition to its accreditation in general engineering.

The idea to obtain specialized accreditation as well as general accreditation came from the vice president for academic affairs, Robert Cotellessa 1945, a Stevens professor of electrical engineering and computer science. Both Cotellessa and other engineering faculty had realized that the increase in the number of technical electives to eight, as a result of the 1978 revision of the engineering curriculum, would allow for enough specialized courses in the concentrations to allow Stevens to meet the ABET criteria for specialized accreditation in addition to general accreditation, and that specialized

---

[848] O. Allen Gianniny, Jr., "Educating Mechanical Engineers in America," *Mechanical Engineering*, Sept. 1982, 58-66; Terry S. Reynolds and Bruce Seely, "Striving for Balance: A Hundred Years of the American Society for Engineering Education," *Journal of Engineering Education*, July 1993, 136-149.

accreditation could be obtained by most engineering departments without changing the curriculum. In some departments, like civil engineering and electrical engineering, only some laboratory courses had to be added. An Ad Hoc Committee on Accreditation of Undergraduate Engineering Programs was established by the trustees, and this committee, chaired by trustee Lewis S. Goodfriend 1944, started its work in the summer of 1984 by hearing from Cotellessa and Rogers, and then proceeded to interview the engineering department heads who were generally supportive of specialized accreditation. Given yearly financial deficits in the Stevens budget in the later years of the Rogers administration, perhaps the crucial testimony came from the admissions and placement offices, both of which saw advantages in new enrollments and in easier placement if specialized accreditation was obtained.[849]

President Rogers presented the proposal for specialized accreditation to the trustees' committee on accreditation in an impartial and objective way, stressing the pros and cons of the issue. According to the minutes of the meeting of December 20, 1984, Rogers said,

It is doubtful that Stevens can maintain the present level of undergraduate engineering enrollment with only the attraction of the General Engineering Program, which would be very difficult to market aggressively even with major commitments of funds. Yet it might also prove difficult to preserve the integrity of a Core of the present type once specialized accreditation is added; specialized accreditation would have additional costs of its own; and it might lead to some loss of the Institute's distinction based on uniqueness.

On January 7, 1985, after several meetings and deliberations, the trustee committee approved resolutions allowing for specialized accreditation while making sure to preserve the broad-based core:

BE IT RESOLVED that the Faculty of the Stevens Institute of Technology reaffirms the basic Stevens educational philosophy embodied in a broad-based undergraduate curriculum which provides to every student enrolled therein an education including major elements of the classical fields of engineering, the basic sciences, the humanities and management, through a unified required core of courses that extends from the freshman year through the senior year and constitutes approximately three-quarters of the entire course requirement for the baccalaureate degree. BE IT FURTHER RESOLVED that the preservation of this educational philosophy will always

---

[849] D. Barus, "Minutes of the Meeting of the Ad Hoc Committee of the Board of Trustees on Accreditation of Undergraduate Engineering Programs," June 4, 1984, Nov. 20, 1984, and Jan. 7, 1985.

have a higher priority than any additional accreditation requirements beyond those for General Engineering.

Moreover, the trustees' minutes show they believed that the advantages of specialized accreditation seemed to outweigh the disadvantages, but then added the following resolution:

FURTHER RESOLVED that since the Board of Trustees continues to have the final authority for the Institute to approve each change in the curriculum, it shall exercise that authority in such a way as to assure the integrity of the Core Curriculum and the preservation of the Institute's ABET accreditation in General Engineering, and thus to resolve any situation of conflicting requirements for specialized accreditation that might arise in the future in favor of maintaining the Core and the accreditation in General Engineering.

Thus, the board of trustees firmly rededicated itself to the tradition of a broad-based engineering curriculum while permitting the faculty to vote on the issue of specialized accreditation.

Rogers then submitted the resolutions to the faculty, which split on the issue when it came to a vote in late January 1985. Arguments in favor claimed that disadvantages of not having specialized accreditation included discrimination against Stevens by recruiters, honor societies, professional societies, state licensing boards, publication lists, and prospective faculty. In addition, the argument that employers at that time were hiring more specialized graduates was presented. Pro-specialized accreditation faculty claimed there would be no change in the core, the degree, or the philosophy of broad-based education. However, anti-specialized accreditation faculty, including the department heads of materials, physics, mathematics, management science, and humanities (most representing non-engineering faculty), who signed a statement quoting the Keller report, argued that Stevens's size and resources did not permit large, separate departments and specialized majors; these heads stated that

We believe that choosing specialized accreditation will make that objective (an outstanding unified engineering curriculum) impossible to achieve, for it will undermine the common educational need in favor of parochial departmental interests driven in large measure by evaluators with experiences solely in conventional educational programs. Who can doubt that with specialized accreditation there will be ever-increasing individual departmental pressures against those core requirements providing breadth of educational experience and in favor of more specialized technical courses?

Other arguments used against specialized accreditation were possible proliferation of courses, increased competition for limited resources, and creation
of two types of departments (the haves and have-nots). They also argued
that it would ruin the unique quality of a Stevens education and weaken
Stevens's high ranking in generalized engineering education nationwide.[850]

Nonetheless, the faculty passed the resolution in favor of specialized accreditation in a relatively close vote which led to ABET accreditation of
chemical, mechanical, computer, electrical, materials and metallurgical,
and civil engineering along with engineering physics by ABET in 1986.
Other concentration programs, engineering management and environmental
engineering were accredited in 1992. At no time during these debates did
any engineering department suggest doing away with the broad-based core,
i.e., all departments supported the broad-based traditional, core curriculum,
even though there was disagreement over specialized accreditation. Core
curriculum and specialized accreditation were seen as distinctly separate
issues by most engineering faculty, and, as subsequent revisions of the
curriculum have shown, the broad-based curriculum has been retained in
spite of specialized accreditation.

This retention of the broad-based core necessitated retaining the
traditional large number of credits, usually twenty or so more than other
engineering colleges. Moreover, because ABET would not accredit specialized majors which had few students, and because, after specialized majors
were accredited and almost all engineering students entered them, ABET
ceased to accredit Stevens in the general engineering category by the early
1990s. Thus, the trustees' requirement that the broad-based core be retained
was upheld, but not their intention to retain generalized accreditation -- but
that was a result of lack of student interest.

Another curriculum revision occurred in the last year of the Rogers administration. At that point, Richard G. Griskey, a professor of chemistry
and chemical engineering and Rogers's last vice president for academic
affairs, took over direction of the institute during the search for a new
president. Griskey, a strong-willed and persuasive "let's-get-the-job-done
now" type of administrator, pushed through several new programs and
reforms. Griskey's energy and his sense that Stevens needed rapid reform to
correct its deficits was responsible for several startling changes which had
been suggested earlier by Keller or other administrators and faculty. He
instituted Stevens' Cooperative Education Plan, long resisted at Stevens, to
combine engineering education with on-the-job training in a five-year

---

[850] E. Neu, "Minutes of the Faculty Meeting, Stevens Institute of Technology," Jan. 23, 1985, and
attachments pro and con on accreditation.

program, and he initiated several programs in continuing education at off-campus sites -- both programs have turned out to be popular with students. Griskey sought and successfully obtained a revision of the undergraduate engineering curriculum which he judged was much too rigid and onerous to be competitive with other more specialized engineering programs.

Griskey asked a special faculty committee of three from engineering departments and the Undergraduate Curriculums Committee (UCC) to cooperate to devise a curriculum with fewer credits. Griskey put a priority on the curriculum revision and requested that it be done as rapidly as possible. Thus, the fundamental changes which resulted in the 1987 engineering curriculum were devised by three members of the engineering faculty, professors Paul Chirlian, Bernard Gallois, and Richard Magee, who worked intensively during the start of the 1986-87 academic year. The curriculum was designed to maintain both generalized and specialized accreditation, to adhere to the philosophy of a broad-based science and humanities core, and to keep a broad but nevertheless flexible engineering science core. In addition, it was devised to appeal to prospective student enrollees and also matriculated students by bringing the credit-total closer to the lower totals at most of the other engineering schools of the country which were admittedly more highly specialized. Chirlian was also chairman of the UCC, and he steered it through that committee and a faculty vote with minimal changes.

The 1987 curriculum revision lowered the number of credits from 153.5 to 143.5, strengthened the departmental concentrations by increasing the technical electives from eight to twelve, but the core lost common engineering science courses, namely, dynamics, energy conversion, and transport theory. In addition a second course in electrical circuits, a second course in materials, and modern physics and its alternative sophomore year offering CAD/CAG were also taken out of the core. However, all these courses were offered and often required through technical electives in the concentration programs. Engineering science courses were still some fifteen to twenty-one credits more in the Stevens curriculum than in specialized programs at other institutions.

Engineering faculty seemed genuinely enthusiastic about the new curriculum. Sample quotes from engineering faculty in a *Stevens Indicator* article were that it would "provide greater flexibility in meeting specific discipline requirements of students," and that it would provide easier entrance for transfer students who had been hampered by the "rigidity of the former curriculum." In short, it opened space for the engineering disciplines' "crucial material" which went beyond the classic engineering sciences.[851]

When the 1987 revision was announced and implementation began in 1988, junior and senior undergraduates immediately criticized it as "watered down" from the curriculum they had to take. The long-time chairman of the UCC, Paul Chirlian, was taken to task in the student press for his statement that, "Students don't make the curriculum," and the results of a student poll, taken later, stated,

The vast majority of upperclassmen are willing to take 160 credits. Many believe that the Stevens reputation is partially built on the large course load and feel it adds value to their diplomas . . . . Many students feel that, in accordance with the philosophy of a broad-based curriculum, courses such as Modern Physics, Strength of materials, Thermodynamics and Dynamics should be taken by ALL engineering students. All engineers should be at least partially versed in the basics of every engineering discipline in order to promote cross communication in the work place.[852]

In the midst of student criticism, alumni as well as some trustees objected to the "Griskey curriculum," because it deviated from Stevens's traditional broad-based core requiring all engineering sciences -- and it was considered not rigorous enough.

Harold J. Raveché , the new president installed by the trustees during commencement exercises in the spring of 1988, listened to both sides in the controversy. As he perceived it, the issue was also a question of whether the 1987 broad-based curriculum contained enough breadth to make the Stevens engineering program unique and competitive enough in the new engineering marketplace. After consultations with the trustees and key faculty, he decided to strengthen and uphold the Stevens tradition. At the time, Raveché's speeches and articles highlighted the need to arrest the decline in the American work ethic, and the new president agreed with the students and alumni who thought the lower-credit curriculum lacked sufficient breadth and rigor.[853]

Thus, in 1989, Raveché asked another three-man faculty team, again professors Chirlian and Gallois with the addition of Professor Erol Cesmebasi,

---

[851] H. G. Avery, "Updated Course Plan Maintains Stevens' Broad-Based Intense Tradition," *Stevens Indicator,* 1987, no. 3.

[852] Attachment to memorandum from Professor Donald Merino to President Raveché and Provost A. Shapiro dated Oct. 24, 1995.

[853] See Raveché memo to Chirlian *et al* entitled "Renaissance Engineer for the 21st Century" which delineated elements to be included in the curriculum, Stevens Special Collections, dossier on engineering curriculum.

to increase the number of credits to the level previous to the 1987 curriculum in order to reinforce rigor and breadth. Responding to Raveché's initiative, the Chirlian-Gallois-Cesmebasi group recommended to the UCC a proposed expansion of courses in the engineering curriculum in November 1989. Their report written by Chirlian, stated in its introduction stated that the previous revision had engendered much protest on the part of students and alumni because of the reduction in number of credits:

Up to 1963, the Stevens curriculum contained 160 credits . . . . We propose returning to that number. Although we find the current curriculum to be essentially sound in its technical emphasis, it is lacking in several areas. The Stevens' student has always been successful in part because of the work ethic instilled by a rigorous curriculum. The engineer's education must bring the realities of the marketplace closer to the realm of technical solutions. [854]

Their suggestions included an expansion in management courses, the concept of a free elective for interdisciplinary or humanities courses, and a much improved design sequence. Professor Gallois had a particular interest in creating design courses throughout the curriculum, as at Carnegie-Mellon University, courses which dealt with engineering methods like problem definition, analysis and synthasis, and evaluation..

Most of their suggestions were implement later by a UCC-appointed "Ad Hoc Committee to Review the Engineering Curriculum" chaired by Professor Harry Silla in 1990. The Silla committee had a uniquely happy experience for a Stevens engineering curriculum committee in that it had a mandate to add credits. The Silla committee constructed a curriculum which was instituted in two stages, A and B. Curriculum A was the part which could be implemented immediately, and curriculum B consisted of the laboratory-design courses which was put into place in subsequent implementation stages. Curriculum A was similar to the 1987 curriculum (amusingly called Z by Dean Peter Brady, chairman of the UCC, to quickly distinguish it from A and B) in science, engineering science, and humanities credits. There was no change in the core in these areas or in technical electives which remained twelve.

The main work of the Silla committee was curriculum B or the design thread. B was delayed because the new design courses were carefully planned and implemented. Silla, a specialist in senior design projects, obtained

---

[854] See memorandum from S. Tricamo to Mechanical Engineering Department dated Nov. 16, 1989 on the subject of "Proposed Engineering Curriculum Revision" with an attached document from the three man team led by Chirlian. Stevens Special Collections, dossier on engineering curriculum.

funding from AT&T to carefully and rationally plan and implement curriculum B, each new laboratory going through a pilot stage before final implementation. In a report to AT&T dated September 30, 1994, the design thread was described: namely, three design laboratories before senior design, a graphics course, and two engineering economic analysis courses with laboratories -- the concept of concurrent engineering being the educational aim for graduates to be able to help their "company in the developing competitive international economy." The report stated,

The value of the design laboratory is that the student gets a complete experience, realizing that he must consider all aspects of developing a successful product. Thus, he will recognize the importance of manufacturing and testing the product while it is in the design stage. Finally, by testing he gets valuable feedback on how the product can be improved and most importantly, how to avoid a failure . . . . In the design laboratories, each student team will design, construct and test at least one product in each laboratory. The project will increase in complexity as the student progresses through the curriculum. Any project will be interdisciplinary, having more or less mechanical, electrical, optical or chemical components.[855]

The new curriculum reaffirmed the Stevens traditon of more credits than most engineering schools -- the curriculum had 156.5 credits as opposed to 143.5 in the Griskey curriculum. The Silla committee did a comparative analysis of credit hours translated into a semester format in mechanical engineering curricula at American engineering colleges, and the statistics showed that Stevens Institute had far more: Stevens, 155 credits; NJIT, 137; PINY, 136; Rutgers, 134; Drexel, 131; Lehigh, 131; Purdue, 129; and Clarkson, 120.

In 1994, a major NSF-funded study by the ASEE, "Engineering Education for a Changing World," again came to conclusions similar to the Stevens philosophy of engineering education, Stevens's focus on a design thread and Raveché's theme of competitiveness. The study succinctly pointed out the changes in the world which challenged engineering educators, namely, that "the nation is making the difficult transition of refocusing a significant amount of its technology investment from national security to international economic competitiveness." It challenged engineering faculty to educate students with measurable outcomes -- namely, analytical, integrative and problem-solving abilities -- and with skills in team efforts. The report called for diverse approaches to curriculum reform so that colleges could find niches. As emphasis switched from national

---

[855] Harry Silla and Vijay Shroff, "Development of the Stevens Engineering Curriculum," Sept. 30, 1994.

security to "applications-oriented focus on economic growth and environmental preservation," some colleges might opt to focus on management, economics, and international relations. Collaborative research alliances were necessary to find new clients in the private sector, continuing education programs were necessary for working or unemployed engineers, and curricula should try to instill leadership, a systems perspective, an appreciation of diversity of cultures, business practices, a multidisciplinary approach, and understanding of the societal impact of engineering decisions.[856]

After study of these national developments by faculty task forces, Raveché encouraged another review of the engineering curriculum to include methods of measuring outcomes as well as further strengthening the design sequence. The idea of further highlighting design was addressed in 1995 by Raveché:

Design is the means by which principles and theories in engineering are transformed into useful artifacts such as devices, processes, machines, software and structures. . . . Thus, design is *the pedagogical tool* for teaching our students how to become creative problem solvers. . . A distinctive advantage of teaching design throughout the curriculum is that design has applications far beyond engineering. This is one of the reasons why we say that an engineering education (rooted in design) is the gateway to many different careers. For example, teachers design courses and curricula, economists design models of monetary flow, lawyers design rules and policies, physicians design treatments, scientists design experiments, and business people design processes for their businesses.[857]

Subsequently, Dean Bernard Gallois and his team of engineering faculty created an engineering curriculum in 1998 which was classic in its reaffirmation of the Stevens traditional broad-based engineering philosophy. The uniqueness of the Stevens 1998 engineering curriculum was based on a required core of all the major engineering sciences: statics, strength of materials, dynamics, thermodynamics, materials, circuits and electronics, transport phenomena, and materials science. In this latest engineering curriculum, there is only one option for students in different disciplinary versions of transport phenomena, but all students must take transport -- all engineering students must take all the engineering sciences. As in the past, this core is intended to provide the Stevens graduate with a fundamental competency in all the major fields of engineering and thus to provide an advantage in rising in management ranks.

---

[856] "Engineering Education for a Changing World," *ASEE* pamphlet dated Oct. 13, 1994.
[857] Harold J. Raveché to Geoffrey W. Clark, Nov. 1, 1995.

TERM I	
Chemistry I	2-3-3
Mathematics I	3-0-3
Physics I	2-0-2
Engineering Design I	0-3-1
Graphics	0-3-2
Computer & Inform Technology	2-3-3
Humanities/Social Science	3-0-3
Seminar	0-1-0
	12-13-17

TERM II	
Chemistry II	3-3-
Mathematics II	3-0-
Physics II	2-0-
Mechanics of Solids	4-0-
Engineering Design II	1-3-
Humanities/Social Science	3-0-
	16-6-

TERM III	
Mathematics III	4-0-4
Physics III	3-0-3
Thermodynamics & Energy Conv.	4-0-4
Circuits & Systems	3-0-3
Engineering Design III	1-3-2
Humanities/Social Science	3-0-3
	18-3-19

TERM IV	
Mathematics IV	3-0-
Physics IV	1-3-
Electronics & Instrumentation	2-3-
Dynamical Systems	4-0-
Engineering Design IV	1-3-
Technical Elective† or Probab & Stat.	3-0-
Humanities/Social Science	3-0-
	17-9

TERM V	
Transport/Fluid Mechanics†	3-3-4
Materials Processing	3-0-3
Engineering Design V	1-3-2
Probability & Statistics or Tech Elec†	3-0-3
Technical Elective†	3-0-3
Humanities/Social Science	3-0-3
	16-6-18

TERM VI	
Bio-Engineering	2-0-
Modeling & Simulation†	2-0-
Engineering Management	3-3-
Engineering Design VI (IPD/ Mnf)†	1-3-
Technical Elective†	3-0-
Technical Elective†	3-0-
Humanities/Social Science	3-0-
	17-6-

TERM VII	
Technical Elective†	3-0-3
Technical Elective†	3-0-3
Elective	3-0-3
Engineering Design VII†	2-6-4
Engineering Economic Design VIIb	1-3-2
Humanities/Social Science	3-0-3
	15-9-18

TERM VIII	
Technical Elective†	3-0-
Technical Elective†	3-0-
Elective	3-0-
Engineering Design VIII†	2-6-
Humanities/Social Science	3-0-
	14-6-

† Discipline specific courses that may include a laboratory component

INTEGRATED SCIENCE

DESIGN 1	DESIGN 3	DESIGN 5	
Intro to Graphics Early "hands on" Fit to Form	*Energy Conversion* *Circuits, Thermo.*	*Design with Materials* Structure/Properties/ Processing/Performance	SENIOR DESIGN Open-ended Multi-disciplinary teams Sponsored by Industry

DEVELOP COMPETENCIES THROUGHOUT THE DESIGN SPINE

Teaming	Project Management	Cost Analysis
Problem Solving	Ethics	Industrial Ecology
Communication	Computer Applications	Marketing

DESIGN 2	DESIGN 4	DESIGN 6
Mechanics of Solids Design, build and test structures	*Dynamical Systems* *Instrumentation Lab.* Mechanical and electrical systems	*Disciplinary Design in* *an IPPD environment*

INTEGRATED ENGINEERING SCIENCE	DISCIPLINARY ENGINEERING

HUMANITIES AND SOCIAL SCIENCES

Courses and schematic diagram of the 1998 engineering curriculum.

The core continues a strong emphasis on a required base in sciences, liberal arts and management, and most of the science and management topics are linked to the engineering sciences and design courses by a modular format. The curriculum's required courses in the humanities and social sciences are still eight, one for each semester, providing an emphasis on culture, language and liberal arts that few engineering curricula have today. In addition, computer and information technology, bio-engineering, engineering management, and modeling and simulation have been added to core course requirements for all students.

Even more importantly, the 1998 adjustment of the engineering curriculum stresses another new and unusual feature, a carefully conceived "design spine." It establishes eight hands-on design courses to build engineering competencies in all eight semesters of the student's four years. Dubbed the spine of the curriculum by faculty led by Dean Bernard Gallois, the sequence is integrated with material presented in the body of the core courses which are rationally sequenced. The design spine contains major threads: computer and information technology, modern instrumentation, engineering software, and industrial ecology. For example, in the first freshman semester, the design course is integrated with a computers and information technology and a computer graphics course in which the student learns to use software packages in computer-aided design and manufacturing (CAD-CAM). Thus, in Engineering Design I in the William Cuming Freshman Design Laboratories, the first semester freshmen learn to conceptualize physical devices and prepare engineering drawings using CAD-CAM packages, to perform preliminary design of physical devices, and to acquire preliminary knowledge of manufacturing tasks and their sequence.

Each following engineering design course aims to teach the students ever more sophisticated competencies: engineering analysis of simple devices, ability to select engineering materials for the task, engineering analysis of electrical circuits and energy conversion systems, ability to select and analyze performance of instruments, and ability to model dynamic systems and analyze performance in terms of efficiency as well as their economic and ecological effects. The Ruth and Warren Wells Design Laboratory, the Elsie Hattrick Design Laboratory, and the William Cuming Materials Laboratory are other investments supporting the design spine. According to Dean Gallois, "The design spine emphasizes developing the key competencies of teamwork, problem solving, effective communication, economic analysis, project management, ethics, and an awareness of industrial

377

ecology and sustainable growth."[858] The last three semesters of design are integrated with the student's concentration in an engineering field, the last two semesters being a capstone senior design project.

The senior design project is organized around contemporary engineering problems. To assure advanced research and design, senior design involves private industry or government sponsors as much as possible. The genesis of the idea for the project comes from varied sources: private enterprise, government, a professor, a professor and a student, or from a student or team of students. The student, or team of students, research, design, build, and test the apparatus or process with the participation of a professor and sponsor. Underlying the capstone course is the philosophy that a graduate's ability to create new technologies comes from not only the broad-based curriculum but also the experience of participating in research and development with faculty on cutting-edge research problems, a theme in the historical successes of generations of inventive Stevens alumni.

After the 1998 curriculum adjustment, the dean and vast majority of the engineering faculty believe the engineering curriculum is positioned for the continuation of Stevens's tradition of "technogenesis," a term for which Stevens applied for a trademark, into the twenty-first century.[859] This classical Stevens set of core requirements and innovative design spine totaling 152 credits, which included six credits of physical education, was larger than that of any other non-military engineering college in the United States. From the 1950s, has been around 150 credits, while other engineering curricula usually require some twenty credits less. Stevens's 1998 engineering curriculum has enough credits to assure the continuation of engineering graduates of having their unique overview of all major engineering disciplines, yet with enough technical electives, reduced to eight, to enable specialized accreditation in mechanical, electrical, computer, chemical, civil and environmental engineering as well as engineering management. Based on the pride that the institute's graduates feel about the rigor of the Stevens curriculum, a rigor which they identify with a work ethic and their success, Stevens's tradition of a credit-rich curriculum was reaffirmed. Stevens students were obtaining the most in-depth engineering education in the country, and the Stevens graduate obtained a bargain, namely, the equivalent of a double degree's worth of generalized and specialized engineering education while paying for one degree.

---

[858] Annual Report , Stevens Institute of Technology, 1998-1999, 9.

[859] B. Gallois et al., "Charles V. Schaefer, Jr. School of Engineering. The Engineering Curriculum. Final Report. February, 1998."

POSTSCRIPT
The Renaissance Engineer and Technogenesis

Harold J. Raveché, the sixth president of Stevens Institute of Technology, came to Stevens in 1988 from Rensselaer Polytechnic Institute where he was dean of science and headed their comprehensive science initiatives program, a high priority for Rensselaer's future. Before that, he worked for the National Institute for Standards and Technology in Washington where he was founding chief of the thermophysics division. In Washington and at RPI, Raveché, whose doctorate was in physical chemistry, had become focused on the need for educational initiatives to produce programs which would lead the United States out of the economic doldrums caused by decline in manufacturing capabilities and trade imbalances. Such focus was exhibited during his chairmanship of a federal commission whose report, "A National Computing Initiative: The Agenda for Leadership," became known as "The Raveché Report" and was in part responsible for his reputation as an energetic proponent of reviving U.S. competitiveness in world markets -- a revival to be accomplished through initiatives in technical education and research.

During his first two years at Stevens, President Raveché delivered scores of speeches and wrote articles about the need to revive U.S. competitiveness, and these articles often called for a new type of engineering education which would create a "Renaissance Engineer for the 21st Century."[860] This concept was intended to evoke a humanistic engineer in the tradition of Leonardo da Vinci, and to promote an engineering graduate with scientific and technical breadth in many fields, with creativity and foresight in design, with skill in hands-on applications, and with sensitivity to philosophical and aesthetic implications of scientific and engineering work. For Raveché, the concept of the renaissance engineer encompassed other areas of knowledge necessary for a "21st century engineer," namely awareness of diversity of world cultures, a knowledge of and appreciation for management techniques, and understanding of global finance and markets -- in short, he wanted Stevens graduates to be a modern version of the "universal man" of the Renaissance.

Thus, Raveché believed that engineers needed a broad university exposure in their education, an insight which made him supportive of Ste-

---

[860] For example, Harold J. Raveché, "A Blueprint for Revitalizing the Economy," *The Star Ledger*, Dec. 28, 1990.

vens's first Bachelor of Arts program in 1989.[861] After passage of the new curriculum which offered majors in history, literature, philosophy, and history of science and technology, Raveché told the press that, "This important new degree program will provide a much-needed bridge between the humanistic and the scientific-technological cultures."[862] In addition, he thought that the new B.A. gave engineering and science students the opportunity to earn a dual degree while gaining a more extensive understanding of the liberal arts.[863] An example of Raveché's ideas appeared in an opinion piece for the *Journal of Commerce*:

This new breed won't be narrowly focused in one field, but will have a broad technical education that places great emphasis on the humanities and engenders a deep appreciation for good management. The renaissance engineer will be able to deal effectively with ambiguity and complexity -- seeing the interrelatedness of design, quality, service and aesthetics. . . .The renaissance engineer can teach us to use high-tech methods to manufacture . . . products that are in demand worldwide. . . . The time has come for industry and government to cooperate and for academia to lead the way in ushering in an era of economic replenishment for the world's leading democracy.[864]

Another educational program which took off after the arrival of Raveché in 1988 was environmental engineering, a new successful concentration attractive to students. The origins of the environmental engineering concentration were in the work of Professor Richard Hires who obtained grants for study of the heavy-metal content of the waters of Newark Bay, the metals being mercury, lead, cadmium, and zinc. Stevens was one of seven schools in a New Jersey Marine Sciences Consortium doing research on the bay beginning in 1976. Funded by the U.S. Department of Commerce's Sea Grant program, the aim of the research was to provide data on the distribution of the metals and on the rate of water renewal through tidal change, pollutant transport patterns, and the effects on organisms. Undergraduates were involved in testing waters in the Kill Van Kull and Arthur Kill, two of the most polluted waters of the United States.[865]

---

[861] K. Dozier, "Harold Raveché: In Pursuit of the Renaissance Engineer," *New Technology Week*, Jun. 11, 1990.

[862] "Stevens Tech Plans to Offer Humanities Bachelors Degree," *The Jersey Journal*, Dec. 20, 1988, 17, and "Stevens Introduces New Degree," *Star Ledger*, Dec. 25, 1988.

[863] Harold J. Raveché to Geoffrey W. Clark, Nov. 1, 1995.

[864] Harold J. Raveché, "Dawn of Renaissance Economy-- Editorial/Opinion," *The Journal of Commerce*, Jan. 15, 1990.

[865] Eliza Cook, "The Plight of Newark Bay," *Stevens Indicator*, 96 (1979), 9-11.

In the area of research, Raveché led the faculty through a process in 1988 and 1989 to identify "steeples of excellence" at Stevens, i.e., the already existing research areas which, with additional funding and staffing, had the potential for national and world recognition in the more competitive post-Cold War environment. Like Keller, Raveché believed in focusing the energies of faculty and the institute's limited resources on a finite number of research initiatives, and then nurturing them in order to obtain for Stevens a recognition for excellence in research in several niches. Thus, the original steeples identified by faculty and administration were concurrent design and manufacturing, coastal and environmental engineering, and telecommunications. Other areas, such as highly filled materials, were added later.

Several of the steeples became associated with nationally and regionally known institutions and interdepartmental efforts on campus. The Center for Environmental Engineering conducted a variety of research and implementation projects in cooperative partnerships with industry and regional governments to solve environmental problems in such areas as coastal and waterway pollution, hazardous waste containment, soil and ground modeling, and remediation. In particular, a provisionally patented, easy-to-implement method of removing arsenic from water has been developed using co-precipitation and filtering to reduce arsenic levels below U.S. standards. Environmental research is conducted in a new campus building, the James C. Nichols, Jr., Environmental Laboratory dedicated in 1992, and also in Davidson Laboratories with its strong tradition in ocean engineering.

The Non-Linear Acoustics Group of Davidson Laboratories under Dimitri Donskoy has developed novel non-destructive methods for the evaluation of materials ranging from advanced composites to gas pipelines. This research has led to the development of an effective, low-cost method to detect landmines. The now-patented method discriminates between landmines made of plastic or metal and such natural objects in the soil as rocks or tree roots.

Under Raveché, the Carnegie Laboratory was completely rebuilt to house the Design and Manufacturing Institute (DMI) which was funded by several corporate grants and large federal contracts to enhance American competitiveness in manufacturing. The DMI specializes in concurrent design and manufacturing, the development of software for design alternatives, material selection, consideration of reliability and serviceability as a result of producing and testing, and the resulting design modification of the finished product. DMI has developed automated concurrent engineering software which evaluates the design of a product as it is created and provides instantaneous evaluations on performance and costs. For example, by 1998, DMI had completed a multi-year project for the U.S. Army to develop a knowledge-based software system for tank and vehicular components to be made by metal die-casting, forging and machining.

The Highly Filled Materials Institute (HFMI) has developed a new technology to determine particle size distributions in either wet or solid materials without having to separate the particles from the matrix. This technology is used for projects as diverse as the manufacture of chocolate or explosives. The HFMI has been funded by the U.S. Army to research the crystallization of the most potent non-nuclear explosive in existence, CL-20.

In 1993, President Raveché announced the goal of leading Stevens into the top five percent of engineering schools in national rankings, and this goal was used in fundraising. Raveché's initial fundraising was highly successful. Partly, success was due to the change in national conditions -- that is, the sustained stock market surge in the post-Cold War era -- but it was also due to a plan to dramatically improve and expand campus buildings and facilities which, in turn, fostered increased giving. The Raveché administration was particularly successful in obtaining federal and state funds for the large-scale reconstruction of both educational and research facilities as well as private industry efforts at generating new technologies and bringing them to the marketplace.

For example, in 1990 the Raveché administration obtained a sixty thousand dollar grant from the New Jersey Commission on Science and Technology to renovate a brownstone to house the Stevens Technology Ventures Incubator (TVI). According to Gina Boesch, the current director of TVI since 1992,

TVI's mission is to encourage and assist potential entrepreneurs with innovative ideas or commercially attractive technology to start their own companies *on campus* in a supportive environment. The goals are the creation of freestanding technology companies; high-value local jobs; tax revenues returned to the community; and new technology developed and retained in the state. TVI directs its effort toward meeting the special needs of technological entrepreneurs and facilitates the process from pre-enterprise development to product commercialization in a number of ways -- through the Incubator Advisory Board, mentoring help, Stevens' faculty, top-quality students, joint proposals, joint patents, etc.[866]

Based on the interest by start-up companies, TVI was able to obtain more state and private funding to expand into an adjacent building and support its operations. In its ten-year existence, TVI has nurtured 52 such start-up

---

[866] *The Technology Ventures Incubator at Stevens Institute of Technology,* May 2000.

companies. Its success was noted by Governor Christine Todd Whitman on January 12, 2000 after a tour of the Stevens facility where she met six representatives of TVI's start-up companies:

I don't think anyone on this tour today could come away anything but impressed by the fact that business incubators work, and anything but excited about the kind of breakthroughs that are being made here at Stevens whether they have to do with digital communications, technologies to take poisons out of water, helping to detect landmines, or cleaning the air.[867]

President Harold J. Raveché with Governor Christy Whitman
during the Governor's January, 2000 visit to Stevens.

More importantly for the Stevens campus, Raveché's administration raised money for new buildings like the Nichols Laboratory for civil, ocean, and environmental engineering. Then, a major gift from Wesley J. Howe resulted in renewal of the Center Building, now named after Howe, including a high-tech student service center on the first floor which puts the institute's financial aid, registrar, and student financial services offices all in one location. The most ambitious and architecturally opulent new building on campus was the Charles V. Schaefer, Jr., Athletic and Recreational Center, completed in 1994. Its exterior round end and its slate roofs complement the architecture of Walker Gymnasium, and the interior houses

---

[867] *Science and Technology News,* NJCST (Spring, 2000), vol. 1, no. 2, 1.

modern athletic facilities including an olympic-sized swimming pool. The college grounds and walkways, with victorian gas-light style lamps, were systematically improved with a view to make the campus beautiful. All campus buildings have been renovated, and the Edwin A. Stevens Building was completed, according to the original architect's plan, with a spire -- a structural deficit for nearly a century and a quarter.

According to the 1998-99 Annual Report of Stevens Institute, the vital statistical signs were never better: The improvement in the stock market and large gifts -- for example, ten million dollars from the estate of Frederick W. Taylor's heir -- resulted in an increase in the endowment from fifty-two million dollars in 1988 to $130.5 million in 1999, a more than doubling of the endowment since 1994. The Stevens Fund, a source of unrestricted gifts, reached $1.14 million by 1999, a ten percent increase since 1996, and of particular note is the thirty-four percent rate of undergraduate alumni participation which is above-average compared to peer institutions. Bequests and other deferred gifts totaled over seven million dollars for fiscal year 1999.

Meanwhile, growth in the undergraduate enrollment population to 1,533 students was a result of growth in applications. For the fall of 1999, applications were at the highest point in the history of Stevens (2,230) as were the average SAT scores (1300) and selectivity (less than sixty percent of students who applied were accepted). Moreover, with the growth of off-campus programs at industrial sites, the graduate enrollment, in terms of credit hours, has jumped from 18,356 total credits in 1994 to some 23,000 credits in 1998.

To help enhance the top ranking, Raveché encouraged the unique Stevens philosophy of education as a focused goal in a broader university setting. In 1997, the administration and trustees created three schools at Stevens, the Charles V. Schaefer, Jr., School of Engineering, the Wesley J. Howe School of Technology Management, and the School of Applied Sciences and Liberal Arts. The architects of the three schools wanted to focus planning and fundraising on Stevens's strength, engineering, but also on the two other areas, science and management. Long-time trustee Charles V. Schaefer, Jr., a man dedicated to "making a difference," endowed the school of engineering to further Stevens's broad-based engineering education and tradition of involving students in cutting-edge research. His long-time friend and fellow trustee, Wesley J. Howe, endowed the school of technology management to foster Stevens's pioneering record, dating to the nineteenth century, of teaching business and management in a technological context. The third school, whose current strength is in computer science, is still seeking a sponsor.

The plans of the new school of technology management have excited the campus. Primarily a graduate school which has traditionally attracted New York-metropolitan-area working professionals, it currently offers four master's degree programs: science in management, technology management, information management, and telecommunications management. The excitement, however, is about a new undergraduate bachelor's degree program to teach students -- many with corporate sponsors or mentors -- to prepare an entire business plan and "follow through from start to finish with marketing, manufacturing, economics, accounting, management, engineering, and design."[868] President Raveché had addressed the topic of marketing in technical education in a 1995 *New York Times* article:

> By marketing, I don't mean promotion, but those efforts that insure products carve a meaningful and competitive niche in the marketplace . . . . I'm reminded by study after study that information technology is failing in too many cases to live up to its promise of increasing productivity and profitability in financial services and manufacturing. That failure results largely from the disconnection between engineering and marketing. The problem is not the technology, but the gulf between delivering quality technology and including with it the means for users to understand it. Integrating marketing and technical education is . . . . a breakthrough . . . . Technology must come with a means for the business community and end-user customers to learn and apply it. Successful companies will require engineers who are comfortable with the idea that marketing defines the product and determines the elements needed to drive it into the marketplace.[869]

Thus, the Howe school has created a new undergraduate curriculum in Business and Technology slated to start in the fall of 2000. Several courses on e-business are in the curriculum and e-business techniques and methods also appear in courses like finance and marketing, thus reflecting current practice in the corporate world. In addition, the faculty, many with experience in technically-oriented corporations, has established a Center for Technology Management Research to develop new products through innovative teamwork, technology transfer, and project management. To lead these technology management programs and to create new programs in executive education and faculty research, Raveché recruited the Under Secretary of the Navy, Jerry Hultin, as dean of the Howe School of Tech-

---

[868] *Annual Report, 1998-1999,* 17.

[869] Harold J. Raveché, "Needed: Translators of Technology," *New York Times,* August 27, 1995, 3: 1.

nology Management early in 2000. As a new capital campaign began in the the year 2000, board of trustees chairman Lawrence T. Babbio made the lead gift for the construction of a state-of-the-art $25 million facility for the school of technology management.

As a result of his initiatives to make the U.S. more competitive and to further creation of new marketable technologies on campus, early in 1996 the Raveché administration, under Joseph J. Moeller, Jr., created an office of Technology Transfer and Corporate Development. The basic idea was to create partnerships with faculty to put their inventions into practical use through commercialization. New inventions or industrial know-how were patented or copyrighted by faculty and assigned to Stevens, and then licensed to Technology Holdings L.L.C. (TecHold), a separate commercial corporation, in return for Stevens-held shares in this private holding company. In turn, TecHold's general manager since 1998, Michael Epstein, also the head of the office of Technology Transfer and Corporate Development, assisted new start-up companies with market assessments, business planning, company formation, and linkages with venture capital. Often such venture capital was provided by interested trustees and alumni of Stevens as well as outsiders. In turn, TecHold licensed its patents to these new companies for an equity position in them. Typically, these new companies grew on-campus in the offices of the Stevens Technology Ventures Incubator.

By the year 2000, the faculty and students who created the new technologies were associated with these embryonic companies in some capacity. For example in the company Land Mine Detection Systems (LMDS), Professor Dimitri Donskoy of Davidson Laboratories held both an equity position and was chief technical advisor, and its president, Charles Cannon, had obtained over twenty private investors to develop a fully-working prototype of a landmine detector. Another example was the company PlasmaSol based on a Stevens patent of an invention of professors Erich Kunhardt and Kurt Becker creating plasma at atmospheric pressure. The company was formed by Kunhardt, professors George Korfiatis and Christos Chistodoulatos, and various others, including alumni. This company was sponsored by NASA and the state of New Jersey as well as by some Fortune 500 companies to develop a prototype in which the plasma treated emissions, for example from tailpipes, smokestacks, and boilers, by breaking down hydrocarbons. The plasma also had the potential of sterilizing surfaces, and therefore has environmental applications in surface cleaning. A separate company, Plasmion, whose president was Steven Kim, a former graduate student of Kunhardt's who helped in research on the technology, was developing the use of the plasma in flat panel displays to obtain high resolution images at lower costs than current technologies.

In 1999, Raveché used Stevens' newly created term, "technogenesis," now trademarked, to describe the university's supportive environment for generating technologies and bringing them to commercialization. For Raveché, these efforts in generation of technologies on campus and their transfer to companies which will market them are part of his goal of having educational programs "rooted in technogenesis" -- a new focus on Stevens's tradition of broad-based technical education which involved students in professors' funded research. To enhance Stevens's record of technogenesis in the twenty-first century, Raveché held retreats where faculty were encouraged to focus on using Stevens's non-compartmentalized programs and faculty-student research teams to create new technologies. He said of the institute's direction: "We are now communicating the message nationwide that we are committed to learning throughout the process of conception, design, and marketplace realization of new technologies. This distinctive educational process sets us apart from other models of higher education."[870]

---

[870] *Ibid.*, 4.

Bibliography

Primary sources:

AAUP-Stevens Institute union contracts.

Bruno, Michael S. "Davidson Laboratory and the Experimental Towing Tank: The History of Towing Tank Research at Stevens," unpublished paper. Davidson Laboratories.

Carnegie Foundation for the Advancement of Teaching Papers. Columbia University.

Correspondence and phone conversations with past alumni, faculty and administrators.

Davidson, K. and J. B. Drisco. "Technical Memorandum No 64, Nov. 6, 1942, OSRD Section no C7-sr458-440." Davidson Laboratory Archives.

Davidson Laboratory Archives. Various research reports both military and civilian.

Davis, Harvey N. Unpublished Notes to Trustees. Stevens Special Collections.

Edison Papers, Rutgers U. microfilm.

Faculty Council file on Promotion and Tenure issues.

Reports prepared by Stevens for ECPD and Middle States Reviews.

"Experimental Towing Tank. 1941 Annual Report." Davidson Laboratory Archives.

Faculty Funded Research Reports. In Administrative Room, Samuel C. Williams Library.

Furman, F. DeR. Unpublished Manuscript, Jan. 20, 1942, Box 36A, Stevens Special Collections.

"History and Background of the Personnel of the New Jersey Machine Corporation, Hoboken, NJ," Stevens Special Collections.

Humphreys, Alexander C. Unpublished Correspondence. Stevens Special Collections.

Minutes of the Faculty Meetings of the Stevens Institute of Technology.

Minutes of the Board of Trustees of the Stevens Institute of Technology. Samuel C. Williams Library, Stevens Institute of Technology. (Restricted entry by permission of the Secretary of the Board of Trustees.)

Monitor Drawings by C. W. MacCord and John Ericsson in Stevens Special Collections.

Morton, Henry. "Modern Education." Unpublished undated paper. Stevens Special Collections.

_____. Diaries. Stevens Special Collections.

"1943 Annual Report." Davidson Laboratory Archives.

Potter, J. H., ed. Unpublished typescript entitled "The Stevens Story," Stevens Special Collections.

Reports of Stevens Curriculum Committees. Stevens Special Collections.

Reports on Research at Stevens. Stevens Special Collections.

Ripley, S. Dillon. Unpublished "Talk for Stevens Institute of Technology," Stevens Special Collections.

Schwab, John and M. Peter Jurkat, "Center for Municipal Studies and Services; Hoboken Urban Observatory, Final Report." U.S. Department of Housing and

Urban Development, contract UO-T-R-08. Stevens Special Collections.
Senior Theses, Senior Reports, Masters Essays, Ph.D. Dissertations. Samuel C. Williams Library, Stevens Institute of Technology.
Stevens, Basil M. "The Stevens Family of Castle Point," unpublished manuscript in two volumes in Stevens Special Collections.
Stevensiana Archives. Samuel C. Williams Library, Stevens Institute of Technology.
Papers of Frederick W. Taylor, Stevens Special Collections.

Periodicals, journals, newspapers
Advanced Management.
American Gas Light Journal.
American Machinist.
American Physical Education Review.
American Scientist.
Annual Catalogs of the Stevens Institute of Technology.
Art in America.
Boyd's Jersey City and Hoboken Directory.
Bowker, R. R. *American Men and Women of Science.*
Canal History and Technology Proceedings.
Cassier's Magazine.
Census Reports of the U.S. Government.
Chronicle of Higher Education.
Dictionary of American Biography.
Dictionary of Scientific Biography.
Education Week.
Engineering Education.
ENR: Engineering News-Record.
Hoboken Advertiser.
Hudson Observer.
International Journal of Fusion Energy.
IEEE Spectrum.
Jersey Journal.
Johns Hopkins Alumni Magazine.
Journal of Commerce.
Journal of Commerce and Commercial Bulletin.
Journal of Engineering Education.
Journal of Physical Education, Recreation and Dance.
Mechanical Engineering.
National Cyclopaedia of American Biography.
Newark Eagle.
New Technology Week.
The New Yorker.
New York Evening Sun.
New York Times.

Philosophical Magazine.
Popular Computing.
Proc. of the American Society for Testing Materials.
Proc. of the Society for the Promotion of Engineering Education.
Science.
Scientific American.
The Star Ledger.
Stevens Indicator.
The Stute.
T.H.E. Journal.
TECHNOS
The Telegraph Journal and Electrical Revue..
Transactions of the American Institute of Electrical Engineers.
Transactions of the American Society of Civil Engineers..
Transactions of the American Society of Mechanical Engineers.
Transactions of the American Society of Mining Engineers.
Transactions of the Newcomen Society.
Transactions of the Society of Naval Architects and Marine Engineers.

Books, articles, dissertations:
Abbate, Janet Ellen. "From ARPANET to Internet; A History of ARPA-Sponsored Computer Networks, 1966-88" U. of Michigan Ph.D. dissertation.
Adams, R. Morton. "Our Association - How It Works," *Stevens Indicator,* 63, 1946, no. 4, 3.
Admiral Frederic R. Harris and His Legacy. 1988.
An Act to Incorporate the Stevens Institute of Technology. Hoboken, n.d.
Arms, Caroline, ed. *Campus Networking Strategies.* EDUCOM, 1988.
Aiken, Henry D. *The Age of Ideology.* 1956.
Alford, L. P. *Laurence Henry Gantt; Leader in Industry.* ASME, 1934.
Armytage, W. H. G. *A Social History of Engineering.* 1961.
Atkins, W. "Harvey N. Davis; Twenty Years of Achievement," *Stevens Indicator,* 1948 reprint.
Automotive Quarterly. *The American Car Since 1775.* 1971.
Avery, H. G. "Updated Course Plan Maintains Stevens' Broad-Based Intense Tradition," *Stevens Indicator,* 1987, no. 3.
Baker, Robert H. "The Stevens War Industries Training School," *Stevens Indicator,* 62, 1945, no. 1, 3-5.
Baritz, Loren. *The Servants of Power; A History of the Use of Social Science in American Industry.* 1960.
Barry, Joseph and John Derevlany, eds. *Yuppies Invade My House at Dinnertime; A Tale of Brunch, Bombs, and Gentrification in an American City.* 1987.
Beyer, Robert T. *Sounds of Our Times.* AIP, 1998.
Bobrick, Benson. *Parsons Brinkerhoff: The First 100 Years.* 1985.
Bond, George Meade. *Standards of Length and Their Subdivision.* 1887.

Bornemann, Alfred. *Stevens Institute in the Field of Metallurgy During Eight Decades.* 1949.

Bostick, Winston H. "Galaxy Matter," *Stevens Indicator,* Jan. 1957, 13-14.

_____. "The Pinch Effect Revisited," *International Journal of Fusion Energy, 1, 1977, no. 1, 20-27.*

Bourne, John. *A Treatise on the Screw Propeller, Screw Vessels, and Screw Engineers.* 1867.

Braverman, Harry. *Labor and Monopoly Capital; The Degradation of Work in the Twentieth Century.* 1974.

Buckley, R. J. *A History of Tramways from Iron Horse to Rapid Transit.* 1975.

Burdi, Richard. "Alexander Calder, 1898-1976: Mobiles Were His Business, But Not His Only Business," *Stevens Indicator,* 94, 1977, 34.

Burstall, Aubrey F. *A History of Mechanical Engineering.* 1965.

Calder, Alexander. *An Autobiography With Pictures.* 1966.

_____. "Mercury Fountain," *Stevens Indicator,* 55, 1938, no. 2, 3.

Cann, Louise Gebbhard. *Eugene Lawrence Vail, 1857-1934.* 1937.

Caldwell, Ann and Herb Shaffner. "Grand Alliances to Build a Better Tomorrow," *Stevens Indicator,* 112, 1995, no. 1, 8-15.

Calvert, Monte. *The Mechanical Engineer in America; 1830-1910.* Baltimore: Johns Hopkins Press, 1967.

Carnegie, Andrew. "Speech on 25th Anniversary of Founding of the Institute," *Stevens Indicator,* 14, 1897, 132.

Cashin, Frank. "Letter from the Alumni Association President," *Stevens Indicator,* Oct. 1971, 2.

Chesney, C. C. and Charles F. Scott. "Early History of the AC System in America," *AIEE Trans.,* 55, 1936, 228-30.

_____. "Some Contributions to the Electrical Industry," *Electrical Engineering, Fiftieth Anniversary, 1884-1934.* 1934, 727-8.

Clark, Geoffrey W. "A Footnote on Science and Graduate Programs in the 1870s and 1880s," *Stevens Indicator,* 1999, no. 2, 43.

_____. "Have Pen, Will Travel: An Iconoclastic Paladin on the Trail of President Ford," *Stevens Indicator,* 93, 1976, no. 1, 10.

_____. "Henry Gantt, 1884, Forgotten Luminary," *Stevens Indicator,* 1998, no. 4, 26-30.

_____. "An Interpretation of Hoboken's Population Trends," in Foster, Edward H. and Geoffrey W. Clark, eds., *Hoboken, A Collection of Essays.* 1976.

_____. "Machine-Shop Engineering Roots of Taylorism; The Efficiency of Machine-Tools and Machinists, 1865-1884" in Spender and Kijne, eds. *Scientific Management: Frederick W. Taylor's Gift to the World?* Kluwer, 1996.

_____. "130 Years of Technogenesis at Stevens," *Stevens Indicator,* 1999, no. 3, 19-42.

_____. "Origins and History of the Stevens Honor Board," *Stevens Indicator,* 1998, no. 1, 12-17.

_____. "The Progressives and the Political Machine in Hoboken, 1911-1915," in

Foster, Edward H. and Geoffrey W. Clark, eds. *Hoboken, A Collection of Essays.* 1976.

_____. "Stevens' Football Led to Its Unique Athletic Tradition," *Stevens Indicator,* 1998, no. 3, 32-35.

_____. "The Stevens Legacy," *Stevens Indicator,* 99, 1982.

_____. "Stevens' Pioneer in Electric Trains: George Gibbs, M.E. 1882, Hon. D.Eng. '30," *Stevens Indicator,* 1999, no. 1, 28-31.

_____. "Stevens President Was a Snook?" *Stevens Indicator,* 1998, no. 3, 14-15.

_____. "Thurston, A Learned Man of Science," *Stevens Indicator,* No. 4, 1981.

_____. "Whistleblowing: A Professional Responsibility of ASME," *Mechanical Engineering,* April 1982.

_____. "Whither ASME?" *Mechanical Engineering,* Oct. 1981.

_____. "Yachting at Stevens," *Stevens Indicator,* 1997, no. 1, 18-26.

Claudy, C. H. "Preparing the Navy Ashore; War Work of the Bureau of Docks and Yards," *Scientific American,* 117, 1917, 416-7.

Collins, William. *We Give You Walter Kidde.* 1940.

Cook, Eliza. "The Plight of Newark Bay," *Stevens Indicator,* 96, 1979, 9-11.

Coulson, Thomas. *Joseph Henry, His Life and Work.* Princeton, 1950.

Creeraft, E. W. *The Government of Hudson County, NJ.* 1915.

Cristy, William G. "The Story of the Fight on Smoke," *Stevens Indicator,* 48, 1931, 144.

Crocker, Malcolm J. "Direct Measurement of Sound Intensity and Practical Applicatons in Noise Control Engineering," *Inter-Noise,* 81, 1984.

Cross, Henry B. "The Establishment of the Honor System," *Stevens Indicator,* Oct. 1952, 5-6.

Davis, Harvey N. "Duty of the Engineering Colleges," *Stevens Indicator,* March 1942, 7.

_____. "How the Problem of Smoke Abatement Has Been Attacked," *Stevens Indicator,* 49, 1932, 68-72.

_____. *New Measure, New Man.* 1938.

_____. "Seventy-five Years of Engineering Education," *Stevens Indicator,* 58, 1940, no. 3, 1-3.

_____ and C. E. Davies, "Industrial Research by Mechanical Engineers," *National Resources Planning Board.* 1943.

_____. "The War Program of Stevens Institute," *Stevens Indicator,* May 1942, 3.

Davis, Henry B. O. *Electrical and Electronic Technologies: A Chronology of Events and Inventors from 1900 to 1940.* 1983.

De Forest, Lee. *Father of Radio; The Autobiography.* 1950.

DeLoughry, Thomas J. "Mandatory Computers," *The Chronicle of Higher Education,* May 5, 1995.

Duck, Frances I. "The Stevens Library, Past, Present, and Future," *Stevens Indicator,* 81, 1964, no. 2, 8.

Dozier, K. "Harold Raveché: In Pursuit of the Renaissance Engineer," *New Technology Week,* Jun. 11, 1990.

Duffy, Maureen Nevin. "Stevens Signs Agreement to Widen Its Use of Computers," *The New York Times,* May 12, 1985, XI, 2: 1.

Durand, William F. *Robert Henry Thurston: The Record of a Life Achievement as Engineer, Educator, and Author.* ASME, 1929.

Electrical Engineering, Fiftieth Anniversary AIEE, 1884-1934. AIEE, 1934.

Eliot, Charles W. "Changes in the Game of Football," in W. Carson Ryan, Jr., ed., *The Literature of American School and College Athletics.* 1929.

Filipetti, George. *Industrial Management in Transition.* 1953.

Finch, James Kip. *The Story of Engineering.* 1960.

Fine, Ruth E. *John Marin.* 1990.

Finley, Elizebeth. "Stevens Focuses on Computers," *The New York Times,* Oct. 31, 1984, IV, 23:1.

Foster, Edward H. and Geoffrey Clark, *Hoboken; A Collection of Essays.* 1976.

Framberger, David J. "Architectural Designs for New York's First Subway," *Interborough Rapid Transit Subway. Historic American Engineering Records.* 1979.

Friedman, Edward A. "The Wired University," *IEEE Spectrum,* Nov. 1984, 119.

_____ and M. P. Jurkat and J. Moeller. "Comprehensive Utilization of Computers in Undergraduate Engineering Education," *1980 Frontiers in Education Conference Proceedings.* IEEE, 1980.

_____. "The Effective Integration of Technology in Education: A Management Perspective, Top Ten Questions for School Administrators," *T.H.E. Journal,* Nov. 1994.

_____, P. Jurkat and R. Pinkham. "Enhancing School Mathematics; Education Through Computer Integration," *T.H.E. Journal,* Sept. 1991.

_____ and B. McGrath. "The Internet Isn't a Threat to Students . . . Its a Tool for Teachers," *Education Week,* Sept. 30, 1998.

_____. "Web Adventures in K-12 Science," *TECHNOS,* Winter 1997.

Furman, F. DeR. *Morton Memorial, A History of Stevens Institute of Technology.* SIT, 1904.

Gaudet, Frederick J. "Engineers as Managers: Good or No Good?" *Stevens Indicator,* 81, 1964, no. 1, 5-7.

Gantt, Henry L. "Training Workmen in the Habits of Industry," *ASME Trans.,* 30, 1908, 1061.

Georgano, G. N. *The Complete Encyclopedia of Motor Cars, 1885 to the Present.* 1973.

Gianniny, O. Allen, Jr. "Educating Mechanical Engineers in America," *Mechanical Engineering,* Sept. 1982, 58-66.

Gordon, William. "Strokes of Genius," *The Star Ledger,* Feb. 22, 1990, 61.

Graves, William H., ed. *Computing Across the Curriculum; Academic Perspectives.* EDUCOM, 1989.

Gray, Edwyn. *The Devil's Device; Robert Whitehead and the History of the Torpedo; A Century of Progress.* 1998.

Grayson, L. "A Brief History of Engineering Education in the United States,"

Engineering Education, 1977, 249.

Green, Kenneth C. *Campus Computing 1998; The Ninth National Survey of Desktop Computing and Information Technology in Higher Education.* 1998.

Greenberg, Daniel S. *The Politics of Pure Science.* 1971.

Gregg, Dorothy. "The Exploitation of the Steamboat; The Case of John Stevens." Ph.D dissertation, Columbia University, 1951.

Groueff, Stephane. *Manhattan Project; The Untold Story of the Making of the Atomic Bomb.* 1967.

Grundy, J. Owen. "Exclusive NYYC Had Its First Home in Hoboken," *Jersey Journal,* July 15, 1989.

Guernsey, Lisa. "E-Mail Now Used in a Third of College Courses, Survey Finds," *Chronicle of Higher Education,* Oct. 1997.

Hafner, Katie and Matthew Lyon. *Where Wizards Stay Up Late; The Origins of the Internet.* 1996.

Hammond, J. W. T. *Men and Volts; The Story of General Electric.* 1948.6/21/00

Hardenberg, Horst O. *The Middle Ages of the Internal Combustion Engine.* SAE International, 1999.

Hayes, Margaret Calder. *Three Alexander Calders.* 1977.

Hilgard, J.E. *Methods and Results, American Standards of Length.* U.S. Geodetic Survey, 1877.

Hirshfield, Fritz. "Linking the Nation by Water and Rail," *Mechanical Engineering,* Sept., 1976.

Hogan, John. "A Resourceful Look at Micros on Campus," *Popular Computing,* Oct. 1984, 116.

Holley, A. L. "The U.S. Testing Machine at the Watertown Arsenal," *Trans. AIME,* 7, 1878, 256..

Hoover, Edgar M. and Raymond Vernon. *Anatomy of a Metropolis; The Changing Distribution of People and Jobs within the New York Metropolitan Region.* 1962.

Hovgaard, William. *Modern History of Warships.* 1920.

Horan, Christopher P. "Create Update; A Network Yet To Come," *The Stute,* Oct. 10, 1986, 1.

Humphreys, Alexander C. "The Present Opportunities and Consequent Responsibilities of the Engineer," *Trans. ASME,* 34,1912, 19-21.

_____. "Address of Humphreys at the Annual Meeting of the Alumni Association," *Stevens Indicator,* 20, 1903, 326.

_____. "College Athletics, *"American Physical Education Review,* 26, 1921, 356.

_____. "Inaugural Address of Humphreys," *Stevens Indicator,* 20, 1903, 170-1.

Hurley, Edward N. "Bridging the Atlantic With Ships," *Scientific American,* 118, 1918, 304-5.

_____. *Bridge to Europe.* 1927.

Hutton, Frederick W. *A History of the American Society of Mechanical Engineers from 1880 to 1915.* ASME, 1915.

"International Exhibition of 1876; The Exhibit of Stevens Institute of Technology,"

Scientific American Supplement, 45, 1876, 704..

Jacobus, D. S. "Discussion: Original Research by Students," *Proc. Society for the Promotion of Engineering Education,* 1, 1993, 226-7

_____. "Education in Engineering," *Trans. ASME,* 38, 1916, 462.

_____. "Experimental Mechanics as Developed in Foreign Technical Schools," *Stevens Indicator,* 6, 1889, no. 4, 257-63.

_____. *Experimental Mechanics; Tests and Experiments Made by the Class of 1900 of the Stevens Institute of Technology.* 1899.

_____. "Laboratory Courses in Engineering Schools: Discussion," *Trans. ASME,* 26, 1905, 664-66.

_____. "New Apparatus for Instruction in Engine Testing," *Stevens Indicator,* 4, 1887, 24-27.

James, Theodore, Jr. *The Empire State Building.* 1975.

Jehl, Francis. *Menlo Park Reminiscences.* 1940.

Jones, Payson. *A Power History of the Consolidated Edison System, 1878-1900.* 1940.

Josephson, Matthew. *Edison; A Biography.* 1959.

Kanigal, Robert. *The One Best Way; Frederick W. Taylor and the Enigma of Efficiency.* Viking, 1997.

Keller, David Neal. *Stone and Webster, 1889-1989.* 1989.

Kelly, J.D. Jerold. *American Yachts; Their Clubs and Races.* 1884.

Kelsey, George W. "The Founding of Gear and Triangle," *Stevens Indicator,* 69, 1952, 7-8.

Kennelly, A.E. *Electrical Vibration Instruments.* 1923.

_____. "The Work of the Institute in Standardization," *Electrical Engineering, Fiftieth Anniversary AIEE, 1884-1934.* 1934, 676-80.

Kent, William. "An Autographic Transmitting Dynamometer," *Trans. AIME,* 8, 1879, 177-80.

_____. "Biographical Notice of Robert H. Thurston," *The Sibley Journal of Mechanical Engineering,* 18, 1903.

_____. "Dr. Thurston in Literature and Research," *Trans. ASME,* 32, 1910, 61-7..

Keyes, Donald B. "Dr. Davis and War Production, 1942-44," *Stevens Indicator,* Jan., 1948, 7.

Kimmelman, Barbara. "Design and Construction of the IRT: Electrical Engineering," *Interborough Rapid Transit Subway. Historic American Engineering Records.* 1979.

Kinsey, Alfred S. *Lecture Notes Prepared for Engineering Students.* 1910.

Kirby, Richard Shelton *et al. Engineering in History.* 1956.

Kyle, John M. "New Arterial Facilities for the Metropolitan Area," *Stevens Indicator,* 72, 1955, no. 1, 41.

Landes, David S. *The Unbound Prometheus; Technological Change and Industrial Development in Western Europe from 1750 to the Present.* 1969.

Langmuir, Irving. "The Relation Between Polarization and Corrosion and the Corrosion of Iron Pipes by Stray Currents," *Stevens Indicator,* 24, 1907, 348-63.

Lanza, G. "A Brief Review of the State of Testing in the U.S." *Proc. American Section of the International Assoc. for Testing Materials,* 4, 1904, 215.

_____. "Graduate Theses," *Proceedings of the Society for the Promotion of Engineering Education,* 1, 1893, 312.

Leatherman, Courtney. "Colleges Failure to Tackle Academic Problems in 1980s Led to Lack of Collaboration," *Chronicle of Higher Education,* Jan. 23, 1991, A13.

_____. "Commission Recommends Strengthening College Presidents' Power," *Chronicle of Higher Education,* Sept. 13, 1996.

_____. "Shared Governance Under Siege; Is It Time to Revive It or Get Rid of It?" *Chronicle of Higher Education,* Jan. 30, 1988.

Lee, W. S. "Water Power Development," *Electrical Engineering, Fiftieth Anniversary, 1884-1934.* 1934.

Lieb, John W. "An Historic Electric Central Station," *Cassier's Magazine,* 10, 1896, 57-62.

Lincoln, P. M. "Some Reminiscences of Niagara," *Electrical Engineering, Fiftieth Anniversary, 1884-1934.* 1934.

Lipman, Jean. *Calder's Universe.* 1976.

Llewellyn, F. T. "CB Rolled Steel Sections in the Empire State Building," *Stevens Indicator.* 48, 1931, no. 1, 6.

Lundberg, F. *America's 60 Families.* 1937.

Magruder, William T. "Mechanical Engineering Curriculums," *Engineering Education,* 16, 1909, 113-20.

Maltz, Leslie. "Integrating DECsystem 10s and 20s and VAX Systems," *Large Systems News,* 1985.

_____. "Micros, Minis, and Mainframes; An Integrated Computing Environment," *DECUS,* 1985.

_____. "Micros Through Mainframes, A Successful Implementation," *Association of Computing Machinery,* 1983.

Mann, Charles R. "Report of Joint Committee on Engineering Education," *Proc. Society for the Promotion of Engineering Education,* 25, 1917, 204-6.

_____. *A Study of Engineering Education Prepared for the Joint Committee on Engineering Education of the National Engineering Societies.* 1918.

Martin, T. C. *Forty Years of Edison Service, 1882-1922.* 1922.

Mayer, Alfred M. "An Experimental Proof of Ohm's Law," *American Journal of Science,* July, 1890.

_____. "A New Form of Lantern Galvanometer," *Journal of the Franklin Institute,* 1872.

_____. "Experiments with a Pendulum Electrometer," *American Journal of Science,* May, 1890.

_____. "On a Large Spring Balance Electrometer," *American Journal of Science,* June, 1890.

_____. "On the Experimental Determination of the Relative Intensities of Sounds," *Philosophical Magazine,* 1873.

McCollum, "University of Florida's President Plans on Staying Ahead of the Technology Curve," *The Chronicle of Higher Education*, March 20, 1998.

McCredie, W., ed. *Campus Computing Strategies*. EDUCOM/DEC, 1983.

McGivern, J. *First Hundred Years of Engineering Education in the United States, 1807-1907*. 1960.

Mechanical Engineers in America. A Biographical Dictionary. ASME, 1980.

Melville, George W. "The War's Teaching in Naval Engineering," *Stevens Indicator*, 16, 1899, 1-13.

Middleton, William D. *Manhattan Gateway; New York's Pennsylvania Station*. 1996.

Mitchell, Donald W. *History of the Modern Navy*. 1946.

Mitman, Carl. *Catalog of the Watercraft in the United States Museum*. 1923

_____. "Stevens' 'Porcupine' Boiler," *Transactions of the Newcomen Society*, 19, 1938.

Moller, G. L. *The Hoboken of Yesteryear*. 1964.

Morgan, Ralph A. "Graduate Studies Program at Stevens," *Stevens Indicator*, 81, 1963, no. 2, 14.

Morton, Henry. "Coleman Sellers, A Biographical Sketch," *Cassier's Magazine*, 24, 1903, 362.

_____. "Electricity in Lighting," in *Electricity in Everyday Life*. 1890.

_____. "Lecture Upon Electric Light," *American Gas Light Journal*, Jan., 1879.

_____, A. M. Mayer and B. F. Thomas. "Some Electrical Measurements of One of Mr. Edison's Horseshoe Lamps," *The Telegraph Journal and Electrical Revue*, 8, 1880, 50.

Nadworny, Milton J. *Scientific Management and the Unions*. 1955..

Nevins, Allan. *Abram S. Hewitt, with Some Account of Peter Cooper*. 1935.

Noble, David F. *America By Design*. Oxford, 1977.

Nordling, William G. "Progress: Per Aspera ad Astra," *Stevens Indicator*, 76, 1959, no. 6, 4.

_____. "Report on the Current Status of the Stevens Development Plan," *Stevens Indicator*, 76, 1959, no. 5, 3-4.

Orrok, "John William Lieb, An Apostle of Light and Power," *Stevens Indicator*, 47, 1930, 6-8.

Osborn, Robert. "Calder's International Monuments," *Art In America*, 57, 1969, no. 2, 32-49.

Oxendine, Joseph B. "100 Years of Basic Instruction," *Journal of Physical Education, Recreation and Dance*, Sept. 1985.

Passer, Harold C. *The Electrical Manufacturers: 1875-1900*. 1953.

Person, H. S. "Gantt, Henry Laurence," *Encyclopedia of the Social Sciences*, 6, 1931, 563.

Poole, Robert E. J. "Early Military Radar Design Experiences," *Stevens Indicator*, 63, 1946, 3.

Potter, James H. "The Honorary Fraternity of Sigma Xi," *Stevens Indicator*, 74, 1957, no. 5, 15-16.

Preble, George H. *A Chronological History of the Origin and Development of Steam Navigation, 1543-1882.* 1883.

"A Proposed Testing Laboratory," *Scientific American,* May 23, 1874.

Raveché, Harold J. "A Blueprint for Revitalizing the Economy," *The Star Ledger,* Dec. 28, 1990.

_____. "Dawn of Renaissance Economy," *The Journal of Commerce,* Jan. 15, 1990.

Read, David. *Nathan Read, His Invention of the Multitubular Boiler and Portable High Pressure Engine, and Discovery of the True Mode of Applying Steam Power and Railways.* 1870.

Reines, Frederick. "Atomic Bomb Experiment," *Stevens Indicator,* Oct. 1945, 15-16.

Renwick, James. *An Account of the Steam Boats Navigating the Hudson River in the State of New York.* 1928.

Report on a Preliminary Investigation of the Properties of Copper-tin-zinc in the Mechanical Laboratory of Stevens Institute of Technology Made Under the Direction of the Committee on Metal Alloys, U.S. Board to Test Iron and Steel and Other Metals. Washington, 1879.

Report of the U.S. Navy Liquid Fuel Board. 1904.

Reynolds, Terry S. and Bruce Seely. "Striving for Balance: A Hundred Years of the American Society for Engineering Education," *Journal of Engineering Education,* July 1993, 136-49.

Richardson, James T. "Centralizing Governance Isn't Simply Wrong: It's Bad Business Too," *Chronicle of Higher Education,* Feb. 12, 1999.

Rider, John D. and Donald G. Fink. *Engineers and Electrons.* 1984.

Robert L. Stevens Fund for Municipal Research. Survey on Health. 1913.

Rolt, Lionel. *A Short History of Machine Tools.* MIT, 1967.

Rogers, K. C. *Fundamentals First; The Story of Stevens Institute of Technology.* Newcomen, 1979.

_____. *A Report from the President: Traditions and Tomorrow.* 1974.

Rudolph, Frederick. *The American College and University; A History.* 1990.

Ryan, Harris J. "Developments in Electric Power Transmission," *Electrical Engineering, Fiftieth Anniversary AIEE, 1884-1934.* 1934.

Salus, Peter. *Casting the Net; From ARPANET to Internet and Beyond.* 1995.

Sansone, Gene. *Evolution of New York City Subways; An Illustrated History of New York City's Transit Cars, 1867-1997.* MTA, 1997.

Savage, Howard J. *Fruits of an Impulse; Forty-five Years of the Carnegie Foundation, 1905-1950.* 1953.

Schneider, James G. *The Navy V-12 Program; Leadership for a Lifetime.* 1987.

Scott, Charles F. "The Institute's First Half Century," in *Electrical Engineering, Fiftieth Anniversary AIEE, 1884-1934.* 1934.

Scott, John Walter. "Defending the Tradition of Shared Governance," *Chronicle of Higher Education,* August 9, 1996, 131.

Sellers, Coleman. "The Chair of Engineering Practice," *Stevens Indicator,* 5, 1888,

260-63.

_____. "President's Address," *Trans. ASME*, 8, 1887, 667.

_____. "Theory and Construction of the Self-Acting Slide Lathe," *Journal of the Franklin Institute*, 64, 1872, 106.

_____, and A. R. Leeds. *Biographical Notice of President Henry Morton.* 1892.

Sewell, Marshall, Jr. "Can Stevens Survive the Crisis in Education?" *Stevens Indicator*, 82, 1965, no. 1, 12-13.

Shaw, W. H. *History of Essex and Hudson Counties.* 1884.

Shenton, James P. *History of the United States from 1865 to the Present.* 1964.

Shoudy, W. A. "The Contributions of the Stevens Family to Steam Navigation," *Stevens Indicator*, 26, 1919.

_____. "Man of Mobiles," *Stevens Indicator*, 82, 1965, no. 2, 14.

Sinclair, Bruce. *Philadelphia's Philosopher Mechanics; A History of the Franklin Institute, 1821-65.* Baltimore: Johns Hopkins Press, 1974.

Sloan, David B. *George Gibbs, M.E., D.Eng. (1861-1940), L Rowland Hill, M.E., E.E. (1872-1948), Pioneers in Railroad Electrification.* Newcomen, 1957.

Smyth, Henry DeWolf. *Atomic Energy for Military Purposes.* 1948.

Sokol, Michael M. "Companions in Zealous Research, 1886-1986," *American Scientist*, 74 (1986), no. 5.

Spano, John. "The Johnsonburg Camp," *Stevens Indicator*, 115, 1998, no. 2. 24-26.

Spender, J.-C. and Hugo Kijne. *Scientific Management: Frederick W. Taylor's Gift to the World?* Kluwer, 1996.

Sprague, Frank J. "The History and Development of Electric Railroads," *Trans. International Elect. Conf.* 1904.

Stanley, Robert C. *Nickel Past and Present.* 1934.

Stephens, W. P. *American Yachting.* 1904.

Stevens, Edwin A. II. "Thoughts on the Design of New York Ferryboats," *Transactions of the Society of Naval Architects and Marine Engineers*, 1, 1896.

Stevens, Francis B. "The First Steam Screw Propeller Boats to Navigate the Waters of any Country, *Stevens Indicator*, 10, 1893.

"The Stevens Institute Mechanical Laboratory," *Journal of the Franklin Institute*, 98, 1874, 155.

"Stevens Institute of Technology," *Scientific American*, Oct. 28, 1874.

Stillwell, Lewis B. "Alternating Current Versus Direct Current," *Electrical Engineering, Fiftieth Anniversary, 1884-1934*, 1934, 709.

Stoltz, George. "Stevens Class of '87, Computers for All," *New York Times*, Sept. 4, 1983, XI, 21, 1.

Straub, Hans. *A History of Civil Engineering.* 1952.

Strickland, Carol. "On the Waterfront, the Filming of Hoboken," in Foster and Clark, eds. *Hoboken; A Collection of Essays.* 1976.

Sturken, Robert C. "Letter from the Alumni Association President," *Stevens Indicator*, Sept. 1972, 2.

Sullivan, Donald A. "The Changing Face of Stevens," *Stevens Indicator*, 77, 1960, no. 5, 7-8.

Sweeney, James J. "The Position of Alexander Calder," *Stevens Indicator*, 61, 1944, no. 5, 11.

Taylor, Frank A. *Catalogue of the Mechanical Collections of the Division of Engineering, U.S. National Museum.* 1923.

Taylor, Frederick W. "On the Art of Cutting Metals," *ASME Proc.*, 27, 1906.

_____. "Comparison of University and Industrial Discipline and Methods," *Stevens Indicator*, 24, 1907, 37-45.

_____. *The Principles of Scientific Management.* 1911.

_____. "Shop Management," *ASME Trans.*, 24, 1903.

Thurston, Robert H. *Abstract Statement of the Extent and Character of the Work of the United States Board Appointed to Test Iron, Steel and Other Metals.* 1878.

_____. "Annual Address as President," *Trans. ASME*, 2, 1881, 418

_____. "The Earliest Ironclad," *Cassier's Magazine*, 6, 1894.

_____. "The First Ten Years of Stevens Institute of Technology," *Stevens Indicator*, 2, 1885, 82.

_____. *A History of the Growth of the Steam Engine.* 1874.

_____. "The Improvement of the Steam Engine and the Education of Engineers," *Journal of the Franklin Institute*, 94, 1872.

_____. *The Mechanical Engineer, His Preparation and His Work.* 1875.

_____. "The Messrs. Stevens of Hoboken, as Engineers, Naval Architects, and Philanthropists," *Journal of the Franklin Institute*, Oct., 1874.

_____. "The Modern Mechanical Laboratory, Especially as in Process of Evolution in America," *Proceedings of the Society for the Promotion of Engineering Education*, 8, 1900, 337.

_____. "New Machine Shop at Stevens Institute," *American Machinist*, April 23, 1881, 8.

_____. "The New Shop Schedule," *Stevens Indicator*, 4, 1887, 45-6.

_____. "A Note on the Resistance of Materials," *Trans. ASCE*, 2, 1873.

_____. "The Stevens Ironclad Battery," *Journal of the Franklin Institute*, 68, 1874.

_____. "Our Progress in Mechanical Engineering," *ASME Trans.*, 1, 1880.

Turnbull, Archibald D. *John Stevens; An American Record.* 1928.

"The 25th Anniversary of the Founding of Stevens Institute of Technology," *Stevens Indicator*, 14, 1897.

Tyler, Charles C. "George Meade Bond," *ASCE Memoire no. 503*

U.S. Department of Energy, History Division. *The Manhattan Project, Making of the Atomic Bomb.* 1999.

Universities and Their Sons. 1899.

Urwick, L. "Management's Debt to Engineers," *Advanced Management*, Dec. 1952.

United States of America Before the National Labor Relations Board Division of Judges Branch Office, New York, N.Y. JD-(NY)-108-82.

Volk, A. J. and R. R. Eieser. "Three Centuries of Progress; The Story of Hoboken," *Stevens Indicator*, 63, 1941.

Wallace, Anthony F. C. *Rockdale; The Growth of an American Village in the Early*

Industrial Revolution. 1978.

Walsh. John. "Stevens Institute of Technology: After the Strike, Still Unsettled," *Science,*. April 15, 1977, 282.

Ward, Henry Baldwin. *Sigma Xi; Quarter Century Record and History, 1886-1911.* 1911.

Watkins, J. Elfreth. *Biographical Sketches of John Stevens, Robert L. Stevens, Edwin A. Stevens, John S. Darcy, John P. Jackson, Robert F. Stockton.* National Museum, Washington D.C., 1892.

Wheeler, Harold A. *Hazeltine the Professor.* 1978.

White, John H. "Col. John; Not Really a Great Inventor? A Reappraisal of the Work and Talent of John Stevens III," *Stevens Indicator,* 99, 1982.

_____. *The John Bull: One Hundred and Fifty Years of Locomotion.* Smithsonian, 1981.

Whitlock, Elliot H. "Smoke Abatement Work," *Stevens Indicator,* 49, 1932.

Widdicombe, Richard. "Stevens Institute of Technology; Electronic Access, Not Subscriptions," *Innovative Use of Information Technology by Colleges.* Council on Library and Information Resources, Washington D. C., Aug. 1999, 64-69.

Wiebe, Robert H. *The Search for Order, 1877-1920.* 1967.

Willits, Raymond S. "Colonel John Stevens," *Stevens Indicator,* 1940.

Wilson, David L. "Dartmouth Requires All Freshmen to Own Computers," *The Chronicle of Higher Education,* June 19,1991.

Wrege, C. D. and R. G. Greenwood. "The Early History of Midvale Steel and the Work of Frederick W. Taylor, 1865-1890," *Canal History and Technology Proceedings,* 11, 1992, 145-76.

Youmans, E. L. *Herbert Spencer on the Americans and the Americans on Herbert Spencer: Report on the Farewell Banquet of Nov. 11, 1882.* 1883.

Young, Clarence. *In Memorium, Charles Stewart Mott.* 1973.

Young, Jeffrey R. "Invasion of the Laptop: More Colleges Adopt Mandatory Computing Program: Officials at Wake Forest Say Making the Machine Ubiquitous is Worth the Trouble and Expense, " *Chronicle of Higher Education,* Dec. 5, 1997.

_____. "University of North Carolina Criticized for Plan to Require Students to Own PCs," *Chronicle of Higher Education,* May 22, 1998.

Zaret, Matthew Elias. "An Historical Study of the Development of the American Society for Engineering Education," Ph.D. Dissertation, NYU, 1967.

Ziel, R. and G. Foster. *Steel Rails Into the Sunset.* 1965.

Index

405

411

415

417